Cultivating Connections

Contemporary Chinese Studies

This series provides new scholarship and perspectives on modern and contemporary China, including China's contested borderlands and minority peoples; ongoing social, cultural, and political changes; and the varied histories that animate China today.

A list of titles in this series appears at the end of this book.

Cultivating Connections

The Making of Chinese Prairie Canada

By Alison R. Marshall

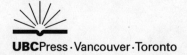

UBCPress · Vancouver · Toronto

22 21 20 19 18 17 16 15 14   5 4 3 2 1

Printed in Canada on FSC-certified ancient-forest-free paper
(100% post-consumer recycled) that is processed chlorine- and acid-free.

___

Library and Archives Canada Cataloguing in Publication

Marshall, Alison R., author
    Cultivating connections : the making of Chinese prairie Canada /
by Alison R. Marshall.

(Contemporary Chinese studies)
Includes bibliographical references and index.
Issued in print and electronic formats.
ISBN 978-0-7748-2800-0 (bound). – ISBN 978-0-7748-2801-7 (pbk.)
ISBN 978-0-7748-2802-4 (pdf). – ISBN 978-0-7748-2803-1 (epub)

    1. Chinese – Prairie Provinces – History – 20th century 2. Immigrants – Prairie Provinces – History – 20th century 3. Pioneers – Prairie Provinces – History – 20th century 4. Prairie Provinces – Emigration and immigration – History – 20th century I. Title II. Series: Contemporary Chinese studies

FC3250.C5C84 2014   971.2'004951   C2014-901912-2
                                                        C2014-901913-0

Canada

UBC Press gratefully acknowledges the financial support for our publishing program of the Government of Canada (through the Canada Book Fund), the Canada Council for the Arts, and the British Columbia Arts Council.

This book has been published with the help of a grant from the Canadian Federation for the Humanities and Social Sciences, through the Awards to Scholarly Publications Program, using funds provided by the Social Sciences and Humanities Research Council of Canada.

Printed and bound in Canada by Friesens
Set in Museo and Warnock by Artegraphica Design Co. Ltd.
Copy editor: Stephanie VanderMeulen
Proofreader: Deborah Kerr
Indexer: Noeline Bridge

UBC Press
The University of British Columbia
2029 West Mall
Vancouver, BC V6T 1Z2
www.ubcpress.ca

To Helen Wong

Contents

Illustrations

Acronyms

CBA	Chinese Benevolent Association
CCBA	Chinese Consolidated Benevolent Association
CCP	Chinese Communist Party
CDS	Chinese Dramatic Society: Wake Up the Soul Opera Troupe (Jinghun jushe)
CKT	Chee Kung Tong (Zhi Gongtang [Chinese Freemasons])
CNR	Canadian National Railway
CPL	Chinese Patriotic League (Jianada Wen[nipei] Diqun Huaqiao Kangri Jiuguo Hui Yong Jian)
CPR	Canadian Pacific Railway
KKK	Ku Klux Klan
KMT	Kuomintang (Guomindang, aka Chinese Nationalist League)
LAC	Library and Archives Canada
WCCCC	Winnipeg Chinese Cultural and Community Centre

Chinese Prairie Migration History Timeline

1850s	Migration of Chinese to Canada and the United States to mine for gold
1870s	Chinese migration to Canadian Prairies to open laundries and groceries
1880s	Beginning of a mostly male Chinese settlement of Canadian borderlands
1885	Completion of first phase of CPR, and Chinese Immigration Act (head tax of fifty dollars)
1895	Chinese begin to open cafes throughout the Prairies
1901	Chinese Immigration Act (head tax of a hundred dollars)
1903	Chinese Immigration Act (head tax of five hundred dollars)
1909	Stabilization of Chinese Canadian settlements
1911	Qing dynasty ends, men cut queues (pigtails), mass emigration of Chinese youths and men
1912	KMT/Chinese nationalist clubhouses open secretly throughout rural and urban Canada
1919	Second wave of largely male Chinese emigration to the Prairies
1921	Formation of Chinese Communist Party and tightening of KMT religious/social controls
1923	Beginning of exclusion era. Chinese Immigration Act revised to exclude most Chinese
1925	Sun Yat-sen, father of modern China, dies
1929	Great Depression begins
1931	Japanese invade northeast province of Manchuria in China. KMT fundraising intensifies. Return migration of Chinese Prairie families and bachelors to China, 1930 to 1935

1937   Marco Polo Bridge Incident in China. Second Sino-Japanese/ Pacific War (1937-45) begins. KMT fundraising intensifies. Creation of Chinese Patriotic League

1942   CCBA distributes, and Chinese wear, "Not Japanese" buttons throughout Canada

1947   Repeal of the Chinese Immigration Act. Families and wives migrate to Canada. End of exclusion era

Acknowledgments

I never imagined myself writing two books on Chinese Canadian history. As a graduate student and professor, I studied and wrote about religion, literature, and culture. I was an ethnographer who studied Chinese living elsewhere – in China, Taiwan, and Hong Kong. In many ways I have very little in common with the Chinese newcomers and Christians I write about in this book. I am not Chinese, and though I was raised as an Anglican, I have always admired Judaism and the customs and traditions observed by my cousins. My interest in the Chinese Canadian community came through family connections. My uncle owned an Asian import-export store in 1920s and 1930s Montreal, and I grew up surrounded by the things that once sat in his shop. Aunty Di introduced me to Cantonese opera and elderly performers in Toronto's Chinatown. Over time, I gravitated toward them, first as an English tutor and later as an ethnographer.

I am grateful to the board of the Winnipeg Chinese Cultural and Community Centre for inviting me into their group and treating me as part of the community. I am also grateful to the Manitoba KMT for allowing me to access its materials and participate in community events. Throughout the years I have had hundreds of conversations with Chinese Canadians. What these conversations have instilled in me is the importance of family. As one research participant reminded me on several occasions, "without family you are nothing." My partner, Brian Mayes, has patiently and lovingly supported me along the way. He read so many drafts that he committed many to memory. When I started to write another book even before the first one was completed, he didn't discourage me or complain, even though he knew that this would mean more personal sacrifice for him. He and our sons came to love the community and its street festivals, lion dances, and food, though they still don't quite appreciate Cantonese opera the way I do. Grandma Gerry, who filled in when I did research elsewhere, inspired me with her energy, warmth, and kindness. Alison Mayes was an invaluable copy editor, confidante, and trusted guide throughout it all. My mother, Heather, stepfather, Derek, sisters Ginny and Jane, good friends Sheila, Jim, Natalie, Elena, Geng Shanshan, Jennifer, Gerald, Lenny, Doug, and Kelly provided much-needed conversation and fun on the numerous ethnohistorical research trips, from British Columbia to Quebec.

Conducting ethnographic and historical research is expensive. I have been very fortunate to receive funding and assistance from the following organizations: the Federation for the Humanities and Social Sciences, through the Awards to Scholarly Publications Program; the Social Sciences and Humanities Research Council of Canada (SSHRC); the President and Vice-President Research and Dean of Arts, Brandon University; the Brandon University Research Council; the Chiang Ching-Kuo Foundation; and Heritage Canada. The Brandon University Research Ethics Committee reviewed and confirmed that my research met the appropriate standards. I also thank my SSHRC co-investigator Pauline Greenhill for her brilliant collaboration and kindness. Through the generosity of federal, university, and international granting agencies, I was able to hire several excellent research assistants, including Susannah Cameron, Marcie Fehr, Coco Kao, Lisa Kuly, Li Chunwei, Zabeen Khamisa, Morganna Malyon, Julie McNiece, Sarah Ramsden, and Caitlin Smith. I am also very grateful to Candice Bjur and Erwin Wodarczak of UBC Archives, and to Eileen Trott (Daly House Museum) and Diane Haglund (Conference of Manitoba and Northwestern Ontario United Church Archives) for their assistance over the years.

Dr. Joseph Du, Philip Lee, Tina Chen, Philip and Shirley Chang, Patrick Choy, Malinda Lee, and Ben Lee (and countless others) welcomed me as a researcher and Winnipeg Chinese Cultural and Community Centre board member. They became friends who embraced my family and involved me in their lives in ways I never expected but always enjoyed. I cannot express in words how much I missed these interactions after I left the board. Philip Chang's life was cut short before I was able to finish this book. This quiet, modest gentleman passed away too soon, but his sage comments were always near as I completed the final draft.

I am deeply indebted to those who repeatedly answered emails and phone calls, couriered documents and photographs, and assisted me throughout the years for longer than I expected. They defended and shepherded this work through its various stages and suggested sources, oral history interviews, and places where I might find information. These people include Helen Wong, Jacque Mar, Pamela Mar, Clarence Sihoe, Walker Wong, Mamie Wong, Katie Sihoe, Shi Peiyun, Sheldon Wu, Shirley Mar, Nancy McGovern, Kwan Yuen, Henry Yu, Sam Gee, Marcelle Gibson, Dan Yee, Lily Chan, Moon

Dong, William Yee, George and Faye Yee, Inky Mark, Lily Chow, Brian Wong, Allan Wong, Timothy Stanley, Bruce Strang, Scott Grills, Tom Mitchell, Paul Crowe, Jan Walls, Brigitte Baptandier, Isaac Farn, Kurt Noll, Steeven Lee, Terrence Russell, Barry Chan, Lorraine Chan, Edmond Lip, Irene Lea, Joan Harder, Lynne Marks, Maria Cheung, Adele Perry, Reg Bing Wo, Robert Yuen, Maria Lip, Charles Ho, Wade Yuen, Pak Choi, John Choi, Ruth Bond, Victor Chang, Daniel Wong, David Lim, Judy Lam Maxwell, Michael Puett, Roy Loewen, Charles Mathewes, Caroline Gee, Linda Hamilton, Lyn Wong, Stephen McIntyre, Bill Turner, David Lai, John Berry, Charles Wong, Kevin Fan, Raz Dong, Lisa Chilton, Vivienne Luk, Rhonda Hinther, Rita Johnson, Mallory Richard, Stephen Warner, Adam Chau, Imogen Lim, Alejandro Yoshikawa, Terry Kleeman, David Churchill, Phyllis Fraser, Naomi Wong, S. Chan, Gilbert Dong, Elizabeth Johnson, Esta Ungar, Ellen Judd, Emily Hill, James Miller, Mimi Lam, Mel Klassen, Paul Gilmore, Paul Bramadat, David Seljak, Vaughan Baird, Ray Berthelette, and Carol Steele. I sincerely apologize if I have forgotten anyone.

Finally, in an era when funding is being cut to archives, presses, and university research, I feel exceptionally fortunate to have worked with UBC Press. I thank the anonymous reviewers for their thoughtful, detailed, and constructive suggestions to edit and improve the book. I also express my gratitude to the entire team at UBC Press, from Megan Brand to the copy editor to the Publications Board. Most of all, however, I thank Emily Andrew, who from the beginning supported my project to understand the history of Chinese settlement on the Prairies. I am truly grateful for Emily's wisdom, grace, and expertise in helping bring these stories to light. I could never have hoped for a better editor.

A few sentences in the Introduction appeared in "Chinatown Steeped in 130 Years of History," *Winnipeg Free Press*, July 28, 2012. Portions of Chapters 2, 3, and 7 previously appeared in Alison R. Marshall, "Railways, Racism and Chineseness on the Prairies," in *Place and Replace*, ed. Leah Morton, Esyllt Jones, and Adele Perry (Winnipeg: University of Manitoba Press, 2013), Chapter 6. Portions of Chapter 5 previously appeared in "Interview with William Yee," in *Winnipeg Chinatown: Celebrating 100 Years, a Remarkable Achievement*, ed. Patrick Choy (Winnipeg: Winnipeg Chinese Cultural and Community Centre, 2011), 46-55.

Preface

The release of Alison Marshall's new book, *Cultivating Connections: The Making of Chinese Prairie Canada*, coincides with a rising level of interest among many Canadians of Chinese origin in discovering their family stories. It is a valuable resource for someone like me, a descendant of an immigrant, for it describes the various ways the early pioneers from China came together, in the face of many obstacles, to offer support, provide company, and build community in villages and towns across Western Canada.

My maternal grandparents, Yee Clun and Eng Shee Yee, arrived separately in Canada during the early part of the last century. Our search for even the most basic details of their experiences in this country began over ten years ago. As if we were on a good scavenger hunt – we moved about from family gatherings to small conversation, library to archive, special collection to family photograph, city directory to old newspaper, the story of their lives has slowly begun to emerge.

Grandfather Yee Clun arrived from the village in China in 1902 as a labourer and paid one hundred dollars to enter Canada. Following several years of travelling around rural Saskatchewan, he settled in Regina and eventually earned merchant status, enabling him to bring Grandmother into this country in late 1919, exempt from the head tax. He partnered with others to operate cafes, restaurants, and merchandise stores around the city, and together with Grandmother raised a family and established roots within this new land. They returned to China in 1932, reunited in Regina in 1941, and relocated to Vancouver in 1947 to spend their retirement years.

During the past few years, my mother Katie, Aunt Mamie, and late uncle Danny reminisced about their parents and recounted their own experiences of growing up in Regina during the late 1920s and into the 1940s. We were fortunate to hear of Alison's research on Chinese Canadian history in 2011, to meet with her that summer, and to be given the opportunity to contribute material toward the preparation of this book. Working together has been a rewarding experience, as a good portion of my mother's family's life was spent in the very places and during the years that Alison's book explores. The historical context that her work provides adds greater meaning to and understanding of our family's particular story. It is both a surprise and an honour to have it included in the book, and we are thankful to Alison for that, since in no way did my mother and her siblings consider their lives extraordinary or imagine that they would some day become the subject matter for academic study.

Clarence Sihoe

Cultivating Connections

Introduction

When I completed my book *The Way of the Bachelor* and was editing the final proofs, I saw I had built a considerable archive. I had so much material and many more stories that needed to be told. I had to tell people about Prairie networks, power brokers, and labourers, and most importantly about family and women. In this book, I try to include all the stories I have gathered since 2005, when I embarked on a research project to understand early Chinese Prairie settlement.[1] As I interviewed people in Quebec, Ontario, Manitoba, Saskatchewan, Alberta, and British Columbia, and collected materials in Chinese and English, I came to expect that many of the early settlers I was hearing about were connected. Almost all of them were. When I launched *The Way of the Bachelor* in April 2011, three families (now living in Vancouver or outside of it) of research participants attended, and the fathers and grandfathers knew each other. To them, the stories, photographs, and documents I had collected had personal significance. Research talks became reunions. Unlike my previous work on arcane aspects of Chinese religious literature and theory, this research endeavour actually meant something to people living today. Thus, it has been my pleasure to collect and share many (sadly not all) of the stories that were told to me.

The aim of this book is to document the processes of migration, settlement, and adaptation through the study of affect-sentiments, connections, and networks.[2] As I collected a large volume of material, I came to see that emotional experiences linking people to the past and to others were still dynamic and that they could be categorized. People wept when they sang the Chinese nationalist anthem. People spoke loudly and with enthusiasm when they talked about men for whom the Chinese community had "good feelings." I wasn't experiencing distinct disembodied moments in time. Having immersed myself in the Chinese Prairie community, I was experiencing moments along a temporal continuum. If I traced each moment back in time, I could understand positive and negative affect in various network channels. Narrative accounts, texts, and performances reinforced the idea that affect from the first five decades of twentieth-century Chinese Prairie Canada had lingering embers that I myself had seen and experienced. Although this book draws heavily on the influence of affect as Chinese na-tionalism between 1909 and 1949, I do not define affect as simply that which coalesced when people imagined and struggled to create a new modern China. Affect was ambiguous, but over time it came to mingle and swell with era-specific traits as I built a large collection of materials. Whereas I first noticed affect in old poems, songs, oral history accounts, and other archival materials, I tried to understand the basis for each emotional experience and tie through Chinese theory and *renqing* (human sentiment).[3]

This book also traces the relationships and political and/or religious af-filiations that enabled Chinese immigrants to have close ties and serve their friends. To this end, I examine the everyday lives of Chinese men and women that are documented in written archival, oral history, and other materials. I foreground the moments, encounters, and emotional situations that brought people together, knitting them into a specific kind of networked society. I pay attention to stories that simmer with meaning as homesick boys forged life-changing bonds.[4]

Poems, songs, and newspaper accounts teemed with patriotic language describing stoical, brave, loyal, respected male leaders with strong ties and alliances. By contrast, Chinese Canadian letters, diaries, biographies, and oral history accounts showed women's evolution from grief-stricken, selfish, lonely, dissatisfied, and grumpy young wives to similar kinds of affected elderly mothers.[5] Broader Christian society continued along these negative channels, emphasizing Chinese women's reputed involvement in prostitution and slavery. In the four chapters on women in this book, I challenge stereo-types and trace the arc of women's religious and family interactions that sutured lives of joy and contentment, despite racism and exclusion by Chinese and non-Chinese society. Those who were warmly regarded enjoyed stronger ties to Chinese and non-Chinese society. Those who were less warmly re-garded and formed weaker ties were more prone to exclusion in early Prairie life.[6] Prairie Chinese were linked to global networks and processes as well, and thus my discussion also draws on American literature.

In the summer of 1923, Arthur Mar (Cantonese: Mah Ping Chong) left Taishan, China, and sailed to Victoria, Canada. He paid five hundred dollars in head tax and then took the train to Winnipeg, Manitoba.[7] He was four-teen years old, alone and homesick. He didn't know a word of English. Arthur attended school for a few years, formed close friendships with teachers and students, and then went to work in Winnipeg Chinatown cafes. After thirteen years, he returned to China. He married Sue Fong Wong and then sailed back without her because Canadian law would not allow most Chinese wives as immigrants.

Arthur continued to live as a bachelor and laboured in Winnipeg's Chinatown, saving money, sending remittances to his wife and parents, and helping those in need. He waited eleven years in the hope that the restrictive Chinese Immigration Act would some day be repealed, permitting his loved ones to move to Canada. The act was finally repealed in 1947. Arthur returned to China and became a father. He sailed back to Canada alone, bought the Goodway Cafe in Lac du Bonnet, Manitoba, and made preparations for the family to join him. He was now a merchant and father, and life was good after Arthur's family arrived. He and his wife went on to have four more children in Lac du Bonnet and to form close ties to the community. Arthur loved politics and his friends. But most of all, he adored his family. While Arthur arrived at the end of the second wave of migration to the Prairies, he was like thousands of Chinese. He had found ways to persevere, flourish, and leave a legacy on the Canadian Prairies in spite of tremendous adversity.

Through goodwill, word of mouth, and advertisements in Chinese and English newspapers, Arthur and thousands of so-called bachelors between the 1870s and 1920 moved out of coastal British Columbia and the western United States.[8] They moved onto the Prairies and beyond, to Toronto, Ottawa, or Montreal.[9] They travelled east along new railway lines and old networks, and north through rancher pathways to Canada across the United States border.[10] They were attracted to the sparsely populated Prairies by opportunities to escape poverty, to open shops, and to become merchants.[11] With merchant status, men inched closer to "whiteness" and had economic, social, and cultural opportunities that labourers did not. They and their families could travel relatively freely between Canada and China. Most importantly, however, they were exempt from paying head tax until 1923. During the exclusion era between 1923 and 1947, most people of Chinese descent – but not merchants – were prohibited from entering Canada.[12] On the Prairies, valuable merchant status was more easily attained, and people were generally less hostile toward Chinese immigrants than were those who lived elsewhere in Canada.[13] Merchants dominated the realms of politics, religion, and business, brokering relations between Chinese and non-Chinese Canada. They opened the first laundry shops and groceries in dozens of small cities, towns, and villages.

Laundry work was the largest and earliest documented Chinese-run business on the Prairies. It was governed by early trade guild and clan territorial rules that determined where a man could operate a business. Laundries provided a Chinese location where men could gather, sleep, socialize, organize, recite poetry, and read Chinese newspapers. They provided the income and merchant status needed to bring wives and families to Canada before 1924, or to support wives met and married in Canada and children born there after that time. Laundry work required men to labour throughout the week and even on the Sabbath, when Christian society paused to worship at church. Thus, in many ways, laundry work placed Chinese men necessarily beyond the dominant frame of Canadian life until 1895, when cafes became more acceptable and positive enterprises.[14]

A global network of Chinese nationalism, or affective regimes, began to form in 1909 when Prairie settlements coalesced. Networks of affect strengthened as the last Chinese dynasty fell in 1911, and Chinese nationalist clubhouses opened a year later. Patriotism surged as Japan invaded and was at war with China in the 1930s. Nationalist ties became so valuable that over time they superseded familial ones. Affective regimes were experienced differently in 1920s Canada, depending on whether one lived on the Prairies or on the coast, and whether one was male or female. Experiences were also determined by merchant, nationalist, Confucian, Christian, Buddhist, or Daoist affiliation and practice. Ties and networks had momentum that moved people to act or not, to be racist or not. Affective regimes were developed by state elites, non-elites, and the populace in Canada and in China. At the same time, they were inhabited by men who came to take on, and then influence, favoured nationalist customs and ideas. They were the central but not the only network in early Prairie Canada.[15]

Prairie Chinese joined networks and organizations that were related to their clan, trade, and politics. In Canada and the United States, all Chinese were expected to be fee-paying members of the Chinese Benevolent Association (CBA).[16] The CBA, with its headquarters in Victoria, helped unite Chinese throughout Canada from 1884 to 1909.[17] Many Chinese who came to the Prairies initially lived in Victoria, where they competed with "whites" and other Chinese for work in mines, factories, canneries, wash shops, saloons, hotels, and stores.[18] Victoria's Chinatown had the infrastructure and activities one would expect in a community of southern Chinese migrants: clan, trade, and voluntary association buildings, schools, churches, missions, Chinese offering halls, temples, and sites where one could watch an opera or gamble.[19] By 1911, Vancouver's Chinatown had surpassed the

Figure 1 KMT Winnipeg picnic, 1918. *Source:* Manitoba KMT.

size of Victoria's and had become the main destination for Chinese new-comers.[20] The CBA led Chinese communities in Victoria, Vancouver, New York, and many other cities. But on the Prairies, the Kuomintang (KMT), otherwise known as the Chinese Nationalist League, held power; until 1950, Chinese were expected to belong to the association.[21]

In addition, Chinese political organizations with headquarters in New York and San Francisco reached into Canada, which meant that Prairie and American Chinese shared alliances, ties, and worldviews. Exclusionary racist legislation in the United States created the impetus for Chinese border crossings into Canada and the Prairies. However, Chinese who migrated to the Prairies shared experiences of racist legislation that privileged "white" British settlers. After transcontinental railways were built – the first phase of the United States railway was completed in 1869, and Canada's was done by 1885 – and Chinese labourers were no longer needed, both Canada and the United States enacted exclusionary legislation. The American 1882 Exclusion Act, in force until 1943, prohibited both citizenship and the entry of most Chinese.[22] North American institutionalized racism in the 1880s and 1890s inflamed racist ideologies and drove Chinese out of American settlements and into urban and rural Prairie Canada.[23]

Many Chinese immigrants came to Canada from the United States through ports and border checkpoints. These had guards and clerks who scrutinized arrivals and identities. Port and border agents collected head tax from 1885 to 1923 and monitored trans-border movement through land and water between more populous California and British Columbia, and Alberta and

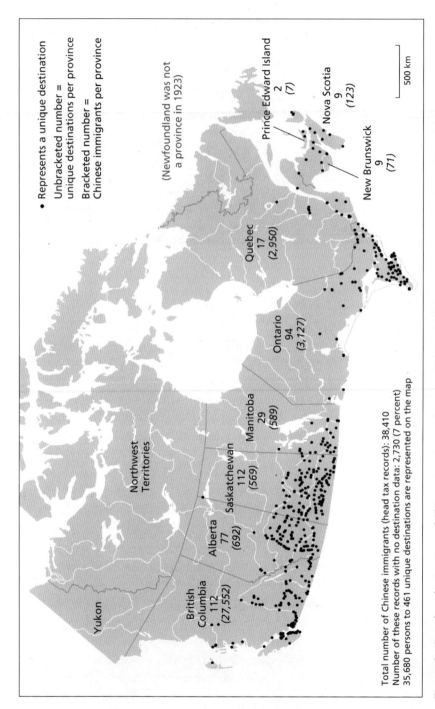

Represents a unique destination

Unbracketed number = unique destinations per province

Bracketed number = Chinese immigrants per province

(Newfoundland was not a province in 1923)

500 km

Yukon

Northwest Territories

British Columbia
112
(27,552)

Alberta
77
(692)

Saskatchewan
112
(569)

Manitoba
29
(589)

Ontario
94
(3,127)

Quebec
17
(2,950)

Prince Edward Island
2
(7)

Nova Scotia
9
(123)

New Brunswick
9
(71)

Total number of Chinese immigrants (head tax records): 38,410
Number of these records with no destination data: 2,730 (7 percent)
35,680 persons to 461 unique destinations are represented on the map

Figure 2 Canadian destinations of Chinese immigrants between 1910 and 1923. *Source:* Henry Yu, Canadian Chinese Head Tax database, redrawn by Eric Leinberger.

Montana.[24] Chinese communities throughout these borderlands shared networks, racism, cultures, and stereotypes.[25] The legal borders didn't seem to matter to the Chinese, who habitually moved across them. Sometimes they also used them to avoid deportation and paying head tax. Legal borders certainly mattered to most state agents, who wished to stem the perceived tide of illicit Chinese.[26] Traffic across eastern Prairie borders into Canada from North Dakota and Minnesota, however, was not well patrolled. Border officials may have turned a blind eye to Chinese illegal immigrants who served a purpose in border towns, offering laundry services and, after 1895, meals to non-Chinese bachelor communities.

Aside from shifting Chinese across borderlands within established networks, both Canadian and American exclusionary legislation severely limited the migration of women, which greatly altered Chinese society. The 1875 Page Law enacted in the United States drastically reduced the number of women who were able to immigrate.[27] Women who remained after the 1880s were mostly wealthy merchant-class wives or young women.[28] Chinese men in the United States who were desirous of family life and marriage found it nearly impossible to find Chinese wives, and Chinese and "white" mixed marriages were banned in fourteen states.[29] Institutionalized racism in the United States helped transform and then fix Chinese settlement as largely male.[30]

The dearth of women also contributed to overseas nationalist ideology and structures.[31] In traditional China, people identified with the empire (until 1911) or the state (after 1911) through the family and household unit. Overseas Chinese men identified with the state through friendship and nationalism. Nationalist networks provided new processes and structures to facilitate connections in bachelor society, which lacked family households or women.

Many Chinese who came from British Columbia or the United States in the 1880s and 1890s were drawn to Manitoba, where there was the possibility of becoming a merchant with enough money to marry either a Chinese or non-Chinese bride.[32] When Chinese moved into Manitoba, it was often to Mennonite and English-speaking towns and villages close to the United States border, such as Gretna. Most places that could be reached by railway lines in 1880s Manitoba had some kind of Chinese business. Chinese did not usually settle in Franco-Manitoban towns near the American border. Integrating into small English "white" Prairie towns was difficult enough.[33] Notably, in 1892, Gretna, located next to the American border, had a sizeable Chinese population. Reports of Chinese quarantined during the July 1892 smallpox outbreak contradict each other. One suggests that between fifteen and twenty males lived in and worked at Gretna's local laundry at the time of the outbreak.[34] A separate account of the smallpox epidemic targets Gretna's newly arrived Chinese residents as the source of contagion. In this account, the Chinese had come to Gretna from Winnipeg and were intending to migrate to the United States when they became sick. The summer of 1892 was a particularly severe time for smallpox, scarlet fever, and diphtheria outbreaks in immigration buildings. Infections spread through steamships and then railway cars.[35] Extensive research of the era's pattern of North American Chinese settlement and trans-border migration, however, indicate that the Gretna Chinese would probably not have wanted to return to the United States in 1892, when racism was particularly severe. Local histories and census data show settlements of varying sizes in Manitoba between the early 1880s and 1900s, including Brandon, Boissevain, Cartwright, Cypress River, Dominion City, Elgin, Emerson, Crystal City, Holland, Killarney, Lyleton, Miami, Souris, and Waskada.[36]

By the early 1900s, local histories and census data indicate similar settlements of varying sizes in Saskatchewan's Alameda, Arcola, Carnduff, Estevan, Gainsborough, Oxbow, Radville, and Lampman. (Saskatchewan did not join the Dominion of Canada as a province until 1905, and many towns had not yet been incorporated.)[37] Usually, these early settlements were located close to the American border. For instance, the 1901 census showed five Chinese men (from different clans) living in the border village of North Portal, Saskatchewan. The men, who were between thirty and fifty-five years old, self-identified as single and Christian. Unlike in other Chinese settlements of the era, only one of them worked in a laundry. The remainder were merchants, who probably facilitated the cross-border movement of goods. Archival research suggests that Chinese continued to enter Canada through North Portal into the 1910s.[38]

Manitoba's mature Chinese political and economic networks facilitated the connection of newcomers to powerful Chinese elders, useful information, and established associations. Newly arrived Chinese were visited by elders who drove to their small towns to fundraise for the dream of a new republic in China. Elders also invited newcomers to travel to Winnipeg for banquets or summer picnics. Networks, businesses, and affective ties developed as men helped their friends in Chinese and non-Chinese communities beyond Chinatown.

In Manitoba, people were modest and fairly accepting of newcomers who were different from themselves.[39] Chinese could reside in neighbourhoods beyond Manitoba Chinatowns, though they tended to stay on the margins of better districts.[40] Ma Seung (Ma Xiang, 1872-1951), a missionary and minister, brought his family to Manitoba because of the extreme racism in Cumberland, British Columbia. His youngest son, Jacque Mar (1912-2012), confirmed this, noting that the family went on to experience very little racism in Manitoba.[41] Winnipeg was a more tolerant place to live than many other cities in Western Canada.[42]

Around 1909, the population of Chinese settlers on the eastern Prairies began to stabilize. Chinese men, and sometimes women, were putting down roots in Manitoba, which became the geographical centre of Prairie Chinese Canada.[43] Many early Chinese settlers who left large coastal settlements were first drawn to Winnipeg's Chinatown. It was an enclave where Chinese political groups organized and dramatic troupes performed. It was also a haven where a Chinese newcomer who had just gotten off the train could get help from fellow countrymen. Around 1909, the Chinese United League (Tongmeng Hui) opened a secret clubhouse at 223 Alexander Avenue.[44] The clubhouse, which Chinese revolutionary leader Dr. Sun Yatsen probably visited in 1911, was part of a global political network that facilitated the flow of member donations to establish a new republic in China.[45] It also functioned to unite worldviews of all its early members. In 1912, the Chinese United League became the Chinese Nationalist League's secret Prairie headquarters.[46]

By 1919, there were 900 Chinese men and women living in Winnipeg, including eight families.[47] By contrast, 400 Chinese lived in Edmonton, and 450 lived in Nanaimo.[48] Winnipeg was the fifth-largest area of Chinese settlement in the nation, after Vancouver, Victoria, Toronto, and Montreal.[49] Interviews with early Chinese Canadian residents suggest that an equal number of Chinese usually lived inside and outside Winnipeg, though there were fewer women in rural areas. Whereas Winnipeg had a small Chinatown, other Prairie locales such as Regina, Brandon, and Saskatoon had Chinatowns that were even smaller – no larger than a couple of city blocks.[50] Newcomers found temporary lodging in Chinatown, and bachelor oldtimers retired there.

Winnipeg residents were predominantly of British ancestry, and almost half the city's total population in 1921 had been born in another country, making it a highly cosmopolitan centre. Gerald Friesen writes:

> To descend from the train at the CPR station in Winnipeg was to enter an international bazaar: the noise of thousands of voices and a dozen tongues circled the high marble pillars and drifted out into the street ... This was not

a polite and ordered society but rather was customarily described as Little Europe, Babel, New Jerusalem, or the Chicago of the North.[51]

Indeed, as Friesen observes, Winnipeg was the Chicago of the North, and some of the earliest Prairie settlers had entered Canada through Manitoba's border with the northern United States and resided in villages and towns near the border. Chinese men regularly made the trip to Winnipeg's Chinatown to pick up supplies and visit with friends at clubhouses. They also attended Chinese mission events at 418-20 Logan Avenue (established by 1917) and went to Bible-study classes.[52] Sometimes they gambled. Chinese men were drawn to and remained in the region because of membership and fellowship found in Chinese political groups based in Winnipeg's Chinatown.[53]

Chinese events were held in Winnipeg to mark the New Year, the Moon Festival, and, after October 10, 1911, the Double Tenth Festival.[54] It was also the place where early Methodists and Presbyterians (before the United Church formed in 1925), who led Prairie Chinese Christian work, had their missions. Thus, Chinese political and religious networks had hubs in Winnipeg and provided significant outreach, support, and also surveillance of the Prairie hinterland.[55]

Relationships formed gradually in Manitoba, providing young boys with mentorship and guidance from elders who were familiar with the province and life in Canada. As a result, Chinese boys raised in Manitoba (such as Frank Chan, discussed in Chapter 3) often became community leaders.[56] Saskatchewan, located on the outskirts of nationalist networks, was different. Its Chinese population was still negligible by 1900; the 1901 Census shows only a handful of Chinese residing there, in contrast to 209 Chinese in Manitoba. In just over ten years, however, almost 1,000 young Chinese men settled in more than one hundred Saskatchewan villages, towns, and cities.[57] By 1911, the number of Chinese migrants residing in Saskatchewan had exceeded the number in Manitoba, who were spread out in only twenty-eight places.[58]

Lacking role models and seasoned mentors of their own ethnicity, early Chinese male settlers in Saskatchewan were also disadvantaged because the province had no large cosmopolitan centre. It had Regina, Moose Jaw, and Saskatoon – all small cities. The absence of a diverse urban centre made Saskatchewan a socially and culturally less attractive place to settle. The harsh conditions of Canadian Prairie life made the cultivation of good human relationships essential. Winter on the Prairies lasted from November to April. People needed each other during the coldest months, when almost all activity was indoors.[59] Most Prairie shops and suites lacked coal furnaces, and winters were spent with frozen windows, floors, and pipes.[60] Settlers slept in beds with others to keep warm and burned wood in cast iron stoves. Prairie winters were lonely: people visited infrequently during months when roads were made impassable by heavy snowfall and ice.

According to Canadian census data, between 1911 and 1921 Saskatchewan experienced the West's largest population surge, from 492,432 to 757,510.[61] By 1921, the Canadian census showed that the Chinese population in Saskatchewan was double the number in Manitoba. In both provinces, the new Chinese settlers were chiefly males between eleven and twenty years old; the youngest newcomers arrived at the age of seven or eight. The rapid increase in Saskatchewan's Chinese population offered little chance for newcomers to visit with experienced elders, build rapport, and obtain assistance from well-established Winnipeg-centred networks and power brokers.[62] Regional differences between the two provinces resulted in different social and legal climates and related settlement experiences.

In Saskatchewan, as in British Columbia, Chinese could not vote for a time and could not employ "white" women.[63] The dominant society feared Chinese men, whom it saw as the "yellow peril."[64] Hundreds of young Chinese boys and men had appeared suddenly, threatening the European status quo. Many of them were merchants and entrepreneurs who inhabited nearly every small Saskatchewan village, town, and city by 1919. Some people imagined that these men, who had no family households, must live as homosexuals. At any rate, the assumption was that a large number of unattached young foreign men could not be good for small-town Saskatchewan.

These men were perceived to be taking away "white" jobs. And some people feared they were making "white" women their slaves.[65] Young Chinese entrepreneurs might become sexually involved with these "slaves" and female employees. This violation of the boundary between "white" and "non-white" society might even be long-term, resulting in "white" women marrying Chinese men and sullying the species with mixed-race offspring. It was fine for Chinese men to marry First Nations or Metis women, or one of the rare Japanese or Chinese women. "White" women, however, risked ruining good reputations and racial purity through interaction with these imagined "yellow" alien sexual deviants. Thus, in Saskatchewan from 1912 to 1969, many towns and cities would not tolerate Chinese hiring "white" women.[66] These forms of institutionalized racism reflected dominant society views of Chinese residents and contributed to other processes of racism.[67] Some

Saskatchewan-born Chinese interviewees remembered seeing the Ku Klux Klan (KKK) erect and then burn crosses across the street from their houses, and being warned not to make trouble. In late 1920s Canada, the KKK made its presence most strongly known in Saskatchewan.[68]

Experiences of racism generally varied by era and by province, settlement region, specific village, town, and city, and on an individual basis. For instance, the Icelandic colony in Baldur, Manitoba, had welcomed and expressed interest in Chinese settlers since the late 1890s.[69] Esterhazy, Saskatchewan, a Hungarian settlement, was a similarly welcoming community, where Chinese and British settlers became popular and prosperous merchants. Both Baldur and Esterhazy were populated by Chinese nationalist men. Community relationships and networking with non-Chinese appeared to reduce racial prejudice by the dominant population and minimize the Chinese man's sense of being hated, excluded, or unwanted.

Although the new networks created by resilient Chinese successfully transformed and reinvented "white" dominant social perceptions and spaces, they nevertheless were constrained by the need for margins, where some Chinese were relegated by nature of gender, geography, religion, and economic status. Rita Dhamoon adds, "Difference ... always implicates power. It is an instrument and an effect of power."[70] To some extent, elite Chinese men used power and networks to indirectly create difference between themselves and those without money or connections.

Many Chinese men, and later families, remained in Winnipeg or Manitoba because they experienced fewer social and legal restrictions than in British Columbia, Saskatchewan, or the United States. Those who lived in Manitoba could vote in municipal, provincial, and federal elections.[71] They could study medicine at the University of Manitoba and could practise as licensed physicians.[72] If they lived in Manitoba and operated a cafe, they could also obtain a liquor licence.[73]

Despite the absence of certain barriers in particular areas, however, Chinese were still discriminated against in Manitoba and Saskatchewan – mostly by non-Chinese, but sometimes also by fellow Chinese. During my interviews with numerous Chinese Canadians who lived during the exclusion era, I heard stories of parents who wanted their children to marry only "pure" Chinese.[74] This was one of the reasons, for instance, that three of Ma Seung's four children returned to China. Even men who had married Ukrainian, French, or British girls confessed to children that though a mixed-race marriage was good enough for them (because there were so few Chinese women in Canada at the time), it was not good enough for their offspring.

Mixed-race Chinese children felt that they were looked down upon by those who had two Chinese parents. Chinese who lived on the rural Prairies were seen as less sophisticated and worthy than those who lived in Winnipeg or Regina. Chinese of the merchant class in Vancouver were seen as superior to those in Winnipeg or Regina. Even today, it is not uncommon to find that Chinese Canadians discriminate against each other, based on wealth, education, profession, class, rurality, southern Chinese, or nationalist or communist affiliation. There is also religious discrimination. Those who are affiliated with Christianity sometimes discriminate against those who are Buddhists, Daoists, and/or more generally associated with "superstitious practices."[75]

Methodology

During the eight-plus years I spent writing this book, I used a combination of embodied ethnography (participant observation fieldwork, interviewing with/without surveys, oral history collection) and historical/archival methods (collecting Chinese and English materials: newspaper articles, letters, postcards, photographs, directories, KMT membership and event registers, United Church clergy records, Chinese Canadian obituaries, and personal scrapbooks).[76] I try to render names, places, and terms following local usage. The everyday language of early Chinese Prairie Canada was Cantonese, though KMT comrades used Mandarin, too. Most Chinese who spoke to me referred to the Chinese nationalists by the Cantonese acronym (KMT), not the Mandarin one (GMD). Where possible, I noted the names of individuals and places in Cantonese as well as English. For most organizations, names, and terms that I discovered through Chinese archival sources, I use the Mandarin Pinyin romanization system. Similarly, Pinyin names appear in parentheses following Chinese names throughout the book. It was nearly impossible to discover how some Chinese names may have been written in Cantonese. I have also included one poem in Chinese with my own English translation.

In the course of researching and writing, I interviewed more than three hundred people both formally and informally. Subjects ranged in age from eighteen to one hundred, but the core participants who provided the detailed information in this book were born between 1912 and 1930. All of them lived through the exclusion era (between 1923 and 1947) in Canada. In addition to interviewing, my research methods included participant observation of events, rituals, and ceremonies.[77] During fieldwork I collected photographs (and used photo elicitation to add to interview and fieldwork notes) and other materials, and photographed events with participants' permission.[78]

Feminist qualitative methods also guided my research.[79] Throughout the research, I drew on interviews that shed light on experiences of racism, racialization, and sexism. I also tried to allow for the contributions of research participants to add to the book in meaningful ways.[80] Several chapters in this book were shown to participants for comment, resulting in further depth and context to the material. The semi-structured interview techniques that I employed were directed by the participants themselves, who were sometimes comfortable with interviews being audio-recorded and transcribed, and at other times wished only for note taking during interviews.[81] As much as possible, I attempted to present details as I found them.

Ethnographic research is complex and time consuming because only part of a researcher's time is spent documenting research experiences in notes. Half of the time is spent in the field and cultivating relationships. When I first began doing fieldwork more than fifteen years ago, I learned that I couldn't simply call people, write them a letter, or email them and expect them to respond and open up to me with their life stories. Webs of relationships have to be cultivated. In 2000, when I moved to Manitoba, I endeavoured to understand the makeup of Prairie society and the history of diversity in this region. Over more than a decade, I attended and participated in all sorts of religious, cultural, and Chinese nationalist events, such as the annual grave custom, Moon Festival, Lunar New Year, and parades and processions throughout Canada.[82] From 2009 to 2012, I also served as a director of the Winnipeg Chinese Cultural and Community Centre (WCCCC). In connection with this directorship, I took on an advisory role as a research contractor for the Canadian Museum for Human Rights' Chinese head tax exhibit. I am not ethnically Chinese, but becoming part of the Chinese community enabled me to develop a more nuanced understanding of Chinese community structures, processes, and adaptations.[83] Through my involvement, I volunteered to help organize and host a number of Chinese community events, and thereby formed relationships.

The other half of my ethnographic research involved setting up interviews, going through the university ethics process, obtaining informed consent, conducting interviews, and transcribing notes and feedback on interview transcripts shared with research participants. Sometimes interviews continued over email, telephone calls, letters, and follow-up meetings.

When I began to examine Chinese settlement patterns outside British Columbia, I found only fragmentary references to early Chinese events, leaders, and Christian involvement in the Prairie region. Although Manitoba began production of its own Chinese community nationalist newspaper in 1915, there are no extant copies of that paper today. There are references to the Manitoba Chinese settlement in the Chinese Freemasons (CKT) publication the *Chinese Times*, as well as in the large collection of materials in the Consolidated Chinese Benevolent Association archives. All of these fulsome collections, however, are skewed toward the telling of Chinese Canadian events from a coastal British Columbian settler perspective. Finding few materials in local, provincial, and national collections, I turned to ethnography and built my own archive.[84] Access to a large number of Chinese and English sources documenting Prairie nationalist lives and activities between 1920 and 1950 helped me write the first chapter. Access to the Ma Seung family archives, written and collected over more than fifty years by six people, enabled me to understand, chronicle, and compare experiences of racism from British Columbia to Manitoba between 1891 and 1935. Ma Seung and his family accounts of religion, racism, and ties within the Prairie affective regime form Chapter 2. The third chapter of this book is also foregrounded in original personal archival material, using Frank Chan's scrapbook (most of it in Chinese), which I discovered on a dusty bookshelf in Winnipeg's Chinatown.

I historicize affect by chronicling relationships and ties in written archival materials, photographs, and established histories. My own experiences of affect – fieldwork, participant-observation experiences, and immersion – enable me to understand and contextualize specific kinds of ties and to gather more materials. By tracing people's historical and emotional connections, I was able to recognize affect because of this ethnographic method of immersion. My interdisciplinary approach counterbalances top-down archival and historical accounts written by scholars, reporters, local historians, and dominant Chinese society. These accounts tended to assign normative meanings to early Chinese male and female interactions within Prairie society from 1870 to 1950. I had to rely on oral history accounts and ethnography to discover more nuanced women's experiences on the Prairies.[85]

Coming to historical research from an ethnographic background led me on an adventure from Quebec to British Columbia in search of stories. It enabled me to ethnographically interpret patterns in the hundreds of stories I heard while sharing dim sum in Winnipeg's Chinatown, drinking tea at the Vancouver Lawn Bowling Club, or touring the halls of Regina's old KMT building at midnight with Sam Gee. These experiences built relationships of trust, and they also instilled in me a tacit understanding of historical and powerful affective ties between Lees and Wongs (the two main Manitoba clans), or the significance of a connection to famous merchant and nationalist Charlie Foo in pre-1950s Prairie Canada. I came to appreciate that Yee Clun's wife, Eng Shee, may have lived entirely as a housewife, but that "she was content being a mom."

Narrative accounts complicated the stereotypes of early Chinese women that linked race and sex. Through the telling and retelling of early women's histories, women became embodied as more than immodest, exotic, unnamed, and unknowable people. I learned what women thought about and why, and what they wanted to do but couldn't because of where they lived on the Prairies or because the singular demands of motherhood prevented them. Life stories remoulded the channels that ranked and chronicled women last, and fathers, husbands, and sons first.[86] Women, as part of the uterine family, were excluded in family genealogies and party and clan lineages. Sometimes they were present only in marginal notations, or mentioned via their husband's clan names. Aside from weaving women back into the historical fabric, narrative accounts showed me what research participants wished they knew about their female forebears. They provided letters, photographs, embroidery, and other artifacts that culturally translated the key moments in women's emotional lives. By historicizing affect through affect, my method and theoretical framework were not only honed in archives, libraries, and in front of books, screens, colleagues, and classrooms; they also evolved out of years of immersion and from my understanding of what Pierre Bourdieu called the "habitus" or "how to play the game" in Chinese Prairie Canada.[87]

Over time, through my interest and involvements, I developed strong and weak ties to various Chinese Prairie groups. The process was an organic one in which my method and theory were guided by interactions and the kinds of stories people wanted to tell. I used my position as a researcher to help the groups and people to whom I was connected by writing grant applications and contributing research to local history publications and other projects. As time progressed, research contacts referred me to others who sent stories, family documents, and photographs. As my archive grew, I emphasized to research participants that I would work with people to write the stories they wanted told and, where possible, to eventually digitize, catalogue, and contribute their resources to public collections. In my interactions with participants and in my writing, I am careful to avoid distancing language and theory, consistent with third-wave feminist methods and theory. I do not avoid first person pronouns such as "I" to create the illusion of a more objective and distanced account. I acknowledge my role, position, and bias in writing and shaping stories. I also share my writing with research participants to ensure that my methods and theories are clear to them.[88] Once the manuscript had been completed and I was confident that I had written the stories that participants wanted, I stepped back from the networks I had joined. I wanted to preserve participant perspectives and voices and to ensure that the book was completed.[89] I also had new research projects and family obligations. I no longer had the time to attend all the events and contribute to community organizations. In doing this, I would sever ties with power brokers and friends throughout various community realms and experience varying degrees of social closure. I knew that research resources (data, invitations, and collaborations) would no longer flow easily to me because of my strong or weak ties.

Both this book and my previous one, *The Way of the Bachelor*, include prefaces written by research participants. This is part of my method. I deliberately shared draft portions of each book with participants to ensure that the theories and arguments I used to write about them and their families were understandable and acceptable. They decided whether they wanted their own names or pseudonyms used in the book. Some people opted to keep their involvement confidential. I didn't want my scholarly work to add another layer of exclusion and domination to the telling of Chinese Canadian stories.

Powerful bachelors, brokers, and merchants between 1920 and 1950 were most often described as patriotic, charismatic, sympathetic, and warm, and as diplomats and senators. The most powerful nationalist merchants tended to marry English-speaking Ukrainian, French, and British wives who had active roles outside the home.[90] When I wrote *The Way of the Bachelor*, I wasn't able to shed light on the women in their lives – their mothers, daughters, sisters, aunts, and especially their wives whose roles were unsung and often unseen. It would take another three years of interviews and research to reveal those stories.

Relying on a rich trove of bilingual documentary, visual, and other unpublished evidence from the exclusion era, this book explores the themes of religion, racism, and gender in the making of Chinese Prairie networks. Religion, which is the first theme, has a prominent place in all of the book's chapters. The cult of Sun Yat-sen, Christianity, and Daoist and Buddhist practice strongly influenced gendered sociability, boundary setting, and agency.[91] The nationalist religious project was in part designed to stabilize Chinese worldviews, interactions, and behaviour. In public, Chinese Canadian men and women dressed, moved, and behaved deferentially in an effort to appear as good Christians and loyal nationalists.[92] Some urban Prairie women's interactions and ties came through Christian involvements and sociality, which led to expansive modern women's networks and less anguish.[93] But many rural women's interactions came through Buddhist, Daoist, or other forms of household religious practice.[94] These religious interactions tied women to deities, symbolically to the past, and to families.

Brokers and other powerful bachelors were free to continue to live relatively ambiguously, as long as they maintained the public nationalist face. In their interactions with Chinese and non-Chinese society, they were free to use a combination of both tactics and strategies to meet competing demands.[95] Chinese Canadian women, by contrast, were at best only indirectly included in nationalist regimes. They were yoked to the home and usually had inferior social positions, which required tactics. Women's religious lives gave them power and a chance for happiness.[96] Throughout the book, I use this first theme of religion to investigate Christian, nationalist, Daoist, or Buddhist affiliations that created weak and strong ties and positions within networks. I aim to show how nationalist propaganda and power brokers, from Vancouver to Winnipeg, fixed new hierarchies and borders of power.[97]

Racism is the second theme in the book. My approach to racism is consistent with critical race theory.[98] I focus on Canadian legislation that virtually banned the immigration of people of Chinese descent, though not people with specific physical traits or skin colour. By excluding women and families, federal legislation forced loved ones to live apart and married men to live as bachelors. This, along with provincially and municipally enacted legislation, helped create a national imaginary of "Chineseness" that was dirty, heathen, untrustworthy, and exotic. Institutionalized racism set up structures of power and understandings of access to citizenship, universities, neighbourhoods, careers, and family life that were based on merchant class and race. It privileged dominant European groups who were free to amuse themselves by dressing up as First Nations, Chinese, Japanese, and Jewish characters in minstrel shows, winter masquerades, school plays, and Christmas concerts.[99] I approach racism and race relations through a focus on Chinese and non-Chinese culture, sports, and entertainment, most notably during events at which "white" dominant European society members disguised themselves as non-dominant society members for fun.

Entertainment in many small towns followed the seasons. Masquerades were favoured during winter curling and hockey rink celebrations, beginning in the 1880s.[100] Often they were organized by church groups. These masquerades and other events where ethnic drag took place functioned as normative commentaries on social and religious hierarchies and the inferior place of newcomers within them.[101] They empowered those who could act, engage, and connect with dominant society, while forgetting, excluding, and making strangers out of others.[102] Masquerades influenced the cultural fabric of Prairie towns, transmitting positive affect for some and blocking its flow for others. They were humorous events to the performers and the spectators, evocative of the dizzy excitement that comes with becoming other than who you are in everyday life. However, ethnic drag was not a form of carnivalesque performance in the way Mikhail Bakhtin has theorized.[103] Masquerades, minstrel shows, chautauquas, Christmas and school concerts, and blackface performances in Prairie Canada were not moments when rigid boundaries between the dominated and dominating broke down and when society was equalized. Asians, blacks, Jews, and First Nations peoples were the stock comical characters of 1910s, 1920s, and 1930s Prairie Canadian ethnic drag.[104] There is no surviving documentary evidence to suggest that the subjects and spectacles of ethnic drag were ever included in the performances or asked to dress up. Even if they had been invited to participate, I doubt that members of these minority groups would have risked precarious community status by dressing up in whiteface or as caricatured uptight Presbyterians. Many Chinese Canadians already lacked the right to citizenship, voting, or entering university professional programs and practising as physicians. They did not enjoy the privilege of performing and imagining race.

Among the dominant culture's favourite costumes was the "Chinaman." It was through newspaper reports about Chinese stereotypes, and not about a Chinese man's everyday life, that one came to learn about Chinese society in Davidson, Saskatchewan. The "Chinaman" costume usually included a pigtail and face paint to accentuate the eyes and wrinkles from long hours of work. It also included long silk dresses that made Chinese men into feminine spectacles.[105] In a description of the Davidson 1909 school Christmas concert, we see reflected the local acceptance of racist masquerading:

A welcome drill by thirty-one girls, parasol drill by sixteen girls. Chinamen drill by ten boys, fancy march by seventeen girls and a clown drill by sixteen boys are just a few of the numbers that are sure to bring down the house at the school concert on Thursday night next. There will be heaps of other amusing and entertaining features.[106]

Newspaper reports described the so-called amusing sight of "white" children masquerading as "Chinamen" and thereby dominating them.[107] They carried descriptions of church women and townspeople dressing up and winning prizes for the best Asian or blackface costume. These stories reinforced local relations of power and the Chinese man's place in "white" society.

I wish to emphasize that occasional race-bridging acts do not mean that there was no racism in a given Christian or community context. Intermarriage, widespread access to integrated education, and one instance in this book in which a Chinese missionary family shared their home with a non-Chinese woman do not negate the fact that Chinese experienced pervasive racism on the Prairies. Christianity may be a multi-ethnic religion in 2014, but before and during the Chinese exclusion era (1923-47), Christianity was associated with Victorian culture and Canada as a nation.[108] Presbyterians, Methodists, Anglicans, Catholics, Baptists, and, later, United Church leaders, ministers, and missionary workers were sometimes racist toward Chinese living in Canada.[109] As I examined the personal letters and reports in the Ma Seung archival collection, I recognized the value of Ma Seung to Chinese missionary work in Canada and that he was warmly regarded by some members of the church, especially by female teachers. But my attention was drawn to correspondence in which leaders used demeaning language toward Chinese and female missionaries. Although I knew that all church workers had low salaries, it was also hard to overlook a pattern of Chinese missionary underfunding.

On the Prairies, Christian churches were the dominant religious institutions whose bells were heard throughout the day and whose pews were filled each Sunday and on Christian holidays throughout the year. Legal jurisdictions historically overlapped with religious ones, where legislation prevented work on Christian holidays and encouraged the use of the Bible to swear an oath. Aside from these processes that held sway over everyday life, Canadian political systems, policies, and leaders were commonly Christian. Ministers, priests, pastors, missionaries, deacons and deaconesses, and others were part of hierarchies that determined priorities, funding, and mission field curriculums. Many missionary workers from England, Ireland, Scotland, and China were newcomers themselves. Most were from well-educated elite backgrounds and also familiar with agrarian life. But missionaries, with the exception of Chinese and other non-Europeans, were seldom newly converted Christians. The multivalence of church and missionary work in Canada and overseas, as foreign policy and local diplomacy, and as cultural translation and imperialism, meant that churches both shaped social reality and were shaped by it. In this way, Christianity was a highly organized structure that influenced inclusion and exclusion.[110]

Webs of power were created by the need for Chinese interactions in a racist world. Chinese organizations and associations were usually male structures that formed as people sought mutual assistance. People needed the networks to survive. They provided the channels along which good feelings, jobs, and other resources flowed. Prairie networks (which had both positive and negative aspects) functioned to decrease racism for Chinese Canadians who were physically, ideologically, and politically close to Winnipeg and nationalism. Racism toward some Chinese non-nationalist men and women remained unchanged, and in some cases it worsened as nationalism swept through overseas communities. Racism was both intentional and unintentional and was reflected in human relationships. Timothy Stanley adds,

> Racialized differences can appear to be naturally occurring, immutable, and self-evident, but they in fact change with time, place and circumstance. What to one person in one time and place is an obvious and fundamental difference is simply invisible to another in a different time and place. This is not to say that how people are seen in terms of racialized difference is unimportant; indeed, it can be a matter of life and death. It is to say that race differences are made through social processes rather than natural or biological ones.[111]

Some Prairie communities, such as Davidson, where Charles Yee lived from 1918 to 1925, displayed ideologies that were much more than mere opinion. In different times and places, these negative feelings became so powerful as to galvanize large numbers of people to behave in discriminating ways.[112] Just like positive affect, negative affect spread in waves and had long-term damaging consequences. In this book, I am interested in understanding the structures, processes, and cultural adaptations that create inclusion and exclusion. I consider the effects of institutionalized racism and also the interactions through sport, theatre, band, church, choir, or clubs that changed this kind of "race-thinking." My research shows that cultural interactions through politics, sport, theatre, and masquerading were as important as, and sometimes more important than, daily work in laundry shops or cafes. Leisure activities were powerful reminders of what early Prairie people did (or were allowed to do) when they paused from work. There wasn't a lot of time for leisurely activities. But most Chinese men were estranged from families, and thus social lives helped them feel connected to Canada and to their trans-Pacific homes. I also consider nationalism and the impact of railway and transportation technologies, which encouraged the flow of people, and of racist and anti-racist acts and ideas, across borderlands, nations, provinces, and rural-urban divides.[113] Institutionalized racism, along with new ideologies, shifted (and continues to shift) networks, cultures, identities, family, and belonging.[114]

Gender is the third theme. Four chapters showcase the lives of male bachelors, ministers, and brokers. Fewer than twenty Chinese wives lived in 1920 eastern Prairie Canada, then populated by more than four thousand Chinese men.[115] During the exclusion era, most wives could not emigrate from China. The paucity of women had a profound impact on affective regimes. Life was lived transnationally for all, especially the men who relied on the KMT for affective links and integration. The absence of these ties in local communities brought devastating loneliness, isolation, and in extreme cases, maternal death.

Masculinity was in some ways re-created to suit the demands of a largely male Prairie society. Men did washing and cooking (women's work) in order to move into the realm of the merchant class. They became manly as masters of the kitchen, having spent formative years as cafe cooks and chefs in Canada. They also became manly through the performance of their affections to home and host nations.[116] When they became involved with the KMT, they were "saving China." These new men were generally second-born sons who were deemed by their families as most capable of surviving life in Prairie Canada.[117] The iconic Chinese man was the quietly noble diaspora gentleman *(junzi)*.[118] Aside from a shared birth order and talent for cooking, however, diaspora gentlemen were not the same. Iconic manhood had martial *(wu)* characteristics, as it was honed in response to Prairie wilderness conditions, and it required innovation and bravery to survive harsh winters and loneliness in a small town without family. For many men I talked to and heard about, manhood had martial characteristics also owing to service in the early Chinese republican army (in the late 1910s) or in Chiang Kai-shek's youth corps (in the mid-1940s). Some men's fathers, or they themselves, had volunteered for military service in the First and Second World Wars.[119] Masculinity had civil *(wen)* characteristics, too. Civility was defined most often through culture, as most men had little more than a Chinese or English elementary school education. This *wen/wu* binary was destabilized by a rich collection of traits such as benevolence, righteousness, loyalty, bravery, and talent, gleaned from traditional Chinese texts.[120]

In some ways, Chinese North American manhood developed in response to racism and exclusion. As David Eng aptly writes:

> The historical period of exclusion was a time when popular stereotypes of Chinese as unassimilable heathens, economic sojourners, and "yellow peril" prevailed. The abstraction and consolidation of the nation's citizenry as an imagined community of whiteness in the nineteenth century depended not only on the rhetoric of these injurious stereotypes; the relative success of the nation-state ... also relied upon the strict management of the cultural terrain and visual apparatus.[121]

The "Chinaman" of which Eng speaks was a popular figure in Canadian advertising campaigns, travelling theatre shows, and popular literature. He was also the subject of exclusionary legislation that targeted migration by the China man, or man from China. This fictional and racialized character persisted long after Chinese Canadian men had cut their trademark queues (pigtails) between 1910 and 1911, and changed their appearance in other ways. After 1911, Chinese men wore Western suits, ties, fedoras, and polished shoes. By this time, large numbers of Chinese men ran cafes, tailor shops, and groceries. They could no longer be associated with dirty laundry and perceived undesirable values. Many early Chinese Canadian men may not have been highly educated, but archival records prove that they were cosmopolitan and sophisticated poets, performers, and Confucians.

Four chapters of the book explore femininity and the lives of extraordinary women *(qi nuzi)*.[122] Traditional Chinese gender stereotypes did not capture the identities of the quietly dedicated wives, mothers, and daughters I talk about in the book. Men had to overcome stereotypes that they were effeminate heathens and homosexuals. But these women had to deal with racist expectations that they were prostitutes.[123]

The first Chinese women to settle on the Prairies were noble, chaste ladies and wives. They were, however, much more than simply traditional beauties *(jiaren)*, described by Confucianism, patriarchy, and represented by bound feet.[124] Only one woman of the twenty-eight featured in this book came to Canada with bound feet. On the Prairies they became exemplary modern girls and new women who favoured short, fashionable bob hairstyles and dresses.[125] Women's talent and roles were traditionally defined by domestic arts such as sewing, crocheting, knitting, and embroidery, and by child rearing. Classes were offered in Canada and in southern China, by Christian and non-Christian women, to teach domestic skills.[126] Patriarchy and tradition linked women to domestic talent. To the Chinese diaspora that started to leave China for global migrant work in large numbers by the 1850s, tradition still defined normative Chinese values, culture, and some aspects of individual identities.[127] As I argue in the book, Chinese Canadian gender, nationalism, and discrimination in many ways revolved around modern adaptations and reinventions of thought, culture, and affect.

Overview

Networks made the fabric of Chinese Prairie Canada. Chapter 1, "Affective Regimes, Nationalism, and the KMT," introduces the organizations, relationships, and ties that determined inclusion or exclusion. Friendships were vital for Chinese Canadian men, who often spent entire lives apart from their families because of immigration laws. Ties developed over the decades and became strengthened by nationalist membership, donations, and roles within the party, proximity to Winnipeg, and gender. To a lesser extent than in British Columbia or elsewhere, affect was determined by clan affiliation.

Chapter 2, "Reverend Ma Seung," presents the biography of a Chinese missionary. He and other low-ranking men shared the network periphery, not because of geography, but because they lacked nationalist involvement and loyalties. By renouncing KMT membership, Ma Seung effectively renounced the power and lifestyle that came through being knitted into the nationalist fabric. Through his biography and exclusion-era experiences, I map Ma's mission work and associations from British Columbia to Ontario.

Chapter 3, "Bachelor Uncles: Frank Chan and Sam Dong," focuses on travelling salesmen who lived across the Prairies and periodically in Winnipeg. Salesmen and KMT operatives, Chan and Dong provided valuable interactions, visiting, and ties to lone Chinese gentlemen and families scattered throughout the Prairies. Chapter 4, "Affect through Sports: Mark Ki and Happy Young," shows two examples of men who adapted to rural life and became symbolic citizens through sports involvement.

Winnipeg leaders are examined in Chapter 5, "Married Nationalists: Charles Yee and Charlie Foo." Yee and Foo lived at the centre of organizations and enjoyed wide-ranging social capital and connections with a large group of people, but they were still bound by the limits of "white" dominant society.[128] Chinese, knowing the power of relationships and good rapport, longed to serve their comrades.

Four chapters provide insight into the lives of Prairie Chinese women. Chapter 6, "Women beyond the Frame," offers a summary of the early Chinese Canadian wife, who often wasn't the only wife, as some men had left another behind in China. In Canada, most Chinese immigrant women couldn't read or write, because they hadn't been educated. In China, a woman had to live in her mother-in-law's home and sometimes also with her sister-in-law. On the Prairies, she lived in her own home without adult female companionship, at least until her daughters became older.[129]

Chapters 7, "Early Chinese Prairie Wives," and 8, "Quongying's Coins and Sword," present a range of stories about early wives in Saskatchewan and Manitoba. As in traditional southern China where they were born, Canadian society was organized by a patriline that assigned women to the domestic and inner sphere. Expected to bear a son within a year of marriage, some wives were also asked to raise children who were not their own, usually of Chinese men and non-Chinese women.[130] Most often, early Chinese wives were traditional women who added status to their respected and admired husbands and provided them with children.[131] Conventional wives remained in the home almost all the time, except on occasional summer outings. Rural wives tended to be more traditional and to practise Buddhist and Daoist rituals in secret. Urban women enjoyed ties to broader Chinese and non-Chinese society through Christian involvements.

Until the 1940s, most people knew these women as "Mrs. Wong" or "Mr. Lee's wife." By the 1950s, women numbered fewer than 10 of the total 434 members of the Manitoba KMT since its formal inception in 1916.[132] Nationalist networks for first-generation Chinese wives were negative, excluding structures. Chapter 9, "Chinese Prairie Daughters," relates the stories of second-generation offspring who enjoyed stronger alliances.

The repeal of the Chinese Immigration Act in 1947 radically changed the quality of life of Chinese men and, especially, women throughout Canada. On the sparsely populated Prairies, this repeal saw waves of women and children arrive within a decade, transforming lonely lives through conviviality and companionship. Family bonds were joyfully renewed, but the social ties and organizations that had so helped the early Chinese adapt and prosper left an indelible mark on Chinese Prairie communities.

1 Affective Regimes, Nationalism, and the KMT

Networks grew out of early global nationalist fundraising campaigns, an imagined modern China, and affections. They were affective regimes that governed, managed, and organized Chinese elite elders, elite members, and the non-elite populace. They were associated with power brokers and were also the voice of the community. Although networks formed from the top down, they spread through grassroots webs of connection and were linked to other Canadian, American, and global configurations. Together, these structures functioned as the de facto Chinese nationalist state until 1949.

Nationalist infrastructure was created through adaptations of traditional Chinese ideas related to governance, human affections, and relationships or *guanxi*.[1] *Guanxi* is a term that is often used to describe the circulation, exchange, and redistribution of material goods, as well as pampering and gifting by both donors and recipients.[2] In traditional Chinese society, people interacted with the Empire and then with the modern republican state after 1911 through the household family unit. Affections and relationships in this traditional system existed within a nested hierarchy.[3] Benevolence guided a father, who provided the family connection to the state. The father was linked to his son. A wife was tied to her husband through maternal rectitude and loyalty, and younger siblings were obedient to older ones. This system of family interdependence and traditional norms was usually not available in Prairie Canada.

Young males often migrated alone, leaving fathers, sons, mothers, daughters, and entire households behind. Those who were fathers could not care for their children when they were young, and sons could not care for their parents when they were old.[4] This was a key reason why Chinese life insurance salesmen, such as Frank Chan, extolled the virtues of being self-reliant in old age.

Prairie nationalists redefined the process of cultivating *renqing* (the closest translation is "human sentiment" or "favour") and affect to suit the needs of their predominantly male populace. Women, who were for the most part

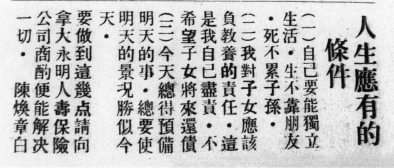

Figure 3 Frank Chan's insurance advertisement, which emphasizes the need for self-reliance during the exclusion era. *Source:* Winnipeg Chinese United Church.

excluded from nationalist interactions, had little chance to cultivate *renqing* beyond the Chinese Canadian household. As a result, friendship, the fifth of five traditional relationships in China, replaced the household unit of interaction.

Affective regimes described nationalist methods to substitute politics for religion.[5] Rebecca Nedostup says, "It was the conviction that such affective regimes existed – and that new ones could be erected, just as a nation's infrastructure could be built and its economy planned – that drove [Sun Yat-sen's] concept of 'psychological construction,' and above all his proclamation that 'to make revolution, we must transform hearts-and-minds.'"[6] Traditional expectations of filial piety to fathers and obedience by younger brothers were largely replaced by service to nationalist friends, leaders such as Charlie Foo, and to Sun Yat-sen, the new father of China. Relationships were vital in Canada, where there was an absence of family but there were strong political Chinese systems. In Prairie Canada, friendships and networks were less bound by traditional rules and customs, and there was a more flexible attitude to social mobility and the assignment of positions within the hierarchy. Nevertheless, imperial and traditional metaphors endured, requiring loyalty and service and uniting local Chinese settlements with the KMT centre (in Canada and China).[7] KMT leaders became the rulers, and lesser-ranking leaders dominated younger or older comrades. KMT leaders and members (not fathers and sons) shared reciprocal relationships.[8] People cultivated goodwill and *guanxi* through friendships, thereby interacting with the mostly male state.

By 1923, racist immigration laws in Canada required Chinese to register and carry head tax and other certificates issued by the Dominion of Canada.[9] Nationalist bureaucracies developed similar observational apparatuses to document and regulate Chinese settlement. By the 1930s and 1940s, nationalists required Chinese males (and later female members) to submit current photographs to their local party office, register using their real (as opposed to "paper") names, and possess certificates issued by the de facto Chinese nationalist government in Canada.[10] These membership registers, which reinvented former Chinese imperial attempts to regulate and govern family units, provided Canadian nationalist leaders with access to a vast amount of largely accurate information (written in Chinese).[11] They documented personal, family, and business relationships, addresses in Canada and China, as well as information related to birth, education, profession, legal and financial status, association membership, connections, and most importantly a personal history of donations to the party.[12] Chinese worked within and through these nationalist state measures that were designed to control and regulate their lives. Depending on their degree of involvement in bureaucratic structures, they had varying amounts of freedom to omit information from certain categories, such as education level.

Thousands of old photographs, membership rosters, nationalist documents, certificates, poems, and newspaper articles (in Chinese and English) bequeathed to Prairie Chinese descendants show the tremendously significant webs of human capital and power that sustained individuals and relationships. Charlie Foo, Frank Chan, and others spent their adult lives dedicated to the Chinese community. Without their efforts, many Prairie Chinese would neither have remained nor survived. Money, guns, opium, people, politics, religion, and culture flowed across and through Prairie webs reaching from Winnipeg east to Quebec, west to Saskatchewan, Alberta, and British Columbia, and south across borderlands into the United States.[13] Lives in Chinese Prairie Canada were made easier through party membership, donations, and nationalist interactions.

Within the last decade of the 1800s, many small towns and villages in southern Saskatchewan had small Chinese settlements. As with early Manitoba settlements, most of the early Saskatchewan Chinese communities were in the southern part of the province and near Regina and Moose Jaw. For

Figure 4 Saskatoon City Nationalist Comrades (Shacheng Guomindang Tongren)
Saskatoon KMT, ca. 1913-14. *Source:* St. Thomas Wesley United Church Archives.

instance, the 1891 census shows that nine individuals in the District of
Assiniboia West indicated that they had been born in China (Assiniboia West
included Medicine Hat, Moose Jaw, Regina, Swift Current, and Walsh).[14]
Those nine respondents were probably just a fraction of the Chinese men
in the region at the time. By 1901, Chinese owned and operated laundries
in Indian Head, Arcola, Maple Creek, Moose Jaw, Prince Albert, Regina,
Roland, Saltcoats, and in several other places in Saskatchewan.[15] In the 1901
census, Buddhist men resided in Yorkton, Regina, and Rosthern. Chinese
Presbyterians resided in Indian Head, Moosomin, and North Portal. By
1911, Confucians living in Saskatchewan were more numerous. Outlook's
Quongs and Lees, Sutherland's Mas and Lees, Rosetown's Mas, Lees, and
Chows, and Regina's Lees and Macks all identified this way. By 1912, there
were up to 170 Chinese residents in Regina alone. That year, men in Saskatchewan reportedly donated a total of $7,900 to the nationalist cause in
China, with Saskatoon men donating $3,600, Moose Jaw men giving
$2,500, and Regina giving $1,500.[16]

Radiating from the main Prairie office of the affective regime's power centre
in Winnipeg were smaller KMT branches in Regina, Fort William, Brandon,

Yorkton, Moose Jaw, North Battleford, and Saskatoon.[17] All of these branches secretly opened around 1912, although they had certificates indicating they opened much later, in 1916. Swift Current (and probably other places with swelling populations) opened a small KMT branch in about 1928.[18] Aside from these formally recognized branches, most eastern Prairie towns and villages came to have Chinese representatives who collected money for fundraising drives, especially from 1931, when Japan invaded northeastern China, and later during the Second Sino-Japanese or Pacific War (1937-45). For their work, Chinese Canadian men resident in these small Prairie locations received certificates stamped by Sun Yat-sen's bureaucrats in recognition of their patriotism and loyalty. Specific Prairie locations such as Saskatoon, Lethbridge, and Edmonton were used for military training and recruitment of an Overseas Chinese Air Corps. Additionally, early troops were sent to China from Canada but never saw active service in the nationalist army.[19]

Nationalist systems were built to serve the nationalist cause, create nationalist subjects, and also provide mutual support. Men used their connections and resources to selectively help clan members and others immigrate to Canada. They couldn't turn their backs on kin or loyal nationalist fictive kin and friends.[20] These men (and their wives) made enormous sacrifices so that newcomers could find a job or a place to live. Elites became brokers who had power that was regionally constituted. Vancouver and the West Coast parts of the network had more power (and rivalry) than Prairie Chinese Manitoban parts. In her study of West Coast power brokers, Lisa Mar explains the complicated lives of powerful men like Frank Chan and Charlie Foo, who led Prairie Chinese communities:

> Chinese power brokers' political world was competitive. They worked hard for the support of Chinese and Anglo constituents, who often had conflicting interests. If one failed, a more effective broker would take his place ... Through brokers, Chinese immigrants actively joined in the central politics of their time: party machines and social reformers, labour and capital, immigration debates, and conflicts over a more interventionist state.[21]

Although Mar's study focuses on famous Vancouver brokers such as Yip On, who possessed far more power and prestige than Frank or Charlie ever had, brokers from both regions shared influence in a common nationalist network. They had the ability to mobilize large groups of men to donate, guide religious and social practices, and sometimes become included in mainstream society, like them.[22] They reduced racism for brokers and others with resources to build bridges between Chinese and non-Chinese communities. They maintained and enabled the flow of positivity and goodwill. But networks were also negative and isolating exclusive structures for those without resources, especially women and non-nationalist members.

Chinese nationalism in the twentieth century emphasized women's talents in the domestic sphere and the virtues that came to them through breeding nationalist heirs.[23] A few women who were married to key Chinese merchants in British Columbia played very peripheral roles in early nationalism as part of the 1902 Chinese Empire Reform Women's Association.[24] Nevertheless, the majority of Chinese Canadian women beyond the BC coast had no chance for political involvement. There is very little evidence that circa 1911 there were any substantial nationalist roles for Chinese Canadian women on the Prairies. By the 1940s, when allowed by their husbands, wives were involved with nationalism, though in limited ways. This was especially true for wives who were born in Britain, France, Ukraine, and Romania, and for the few Chinese Canadian wives with good English skills. They took on supporting roles as translators and mediators for the Chinese community. They sewed and knitted items that were sold or sent to China during the war, and they took care of children.[25] Generally, however, a woman, having few opportunities to cultivate positive affections and relationships beyond her immediate family in Canada or China, had weak *guanxi* and affections.

From the beginning, affiliation with nationalism was the vanguard of acceptability and empowerment for those who sought migrant work beyond China. Friends were willing to serve other nationalist friends who had helped them get jobs and other resources on the Prairies. Brokerage relationships required mutual support. Chinese Canadians continued to be attracted to the Prairies and Winnipeg because of the possibility of establishing rapport with high-ranking executive leaders and becoming merchants. They maintained and strengthened ties between the de facto government and the populace throughout the year's countless social and political events. Chinese brokers hosted and organized events mostly in Manitoba, but also sometimes in Saskatchewan and Ontario.[26] It was therefore not uncommon to find people who knew of, or had been visited by, Charlie Foo (Au Foo) in British Columbia, Alberta, Saskatchewan, Manitoba, Ontario, and Quebec.

Nationalist subjects enjoyed access to the best jobs and the documents needed for cross-border travel. Without party membership, one quickly became an outsider in Chinese society in Canada and in republican China. News travelled quickly throughout Chinese Canadian KMT communities of those who failed to make the expected donations and of those who donated generously. Nationalist papers printed in Toronto, Vancouver, and Winnipeg often ran articles about exemplary members and leaders. Although the Chinese state didn't have complete control over the general population, network leaders were able to banish those who were unwilling to comply or serve to other regions of the network.

Most Chinese nationalists adopted nationalist ideologies. Chinese belonging on the Prairies depended on reproducing "white" society racial discourses and techniques of exclusion.[27] Floya Anthias states, "A liberal multi-cultural framework means that the dominant group within the state is able to set the terms of the agenda for participation by minority ethnic groups and involves a bounded dialogue where the premises themselves may not be open to negotiation."[28] Although becoming a party member did not preclude racism, it certainly lessened it. Chinese men who married "white" European women rose quickly within Prairie nationalist and socio-economic hierarchies.[29]

From 1911 to roughly 1921, nationalists tolerated and sometimes encouraged involvement in Christian mission work. Missions enjoyed moderate success in convincing bachelors of the merits of Christianity during this early period. Nationalist members belonged to Christian organizations and took part in Christian events, and vice versa. Interest waned almost completely after the birth of the Chinese Communist Party (CCP) in China on July 1, 1921. Interest in Christianity also diminished because Chinese Prairie men experienced a reduction in racism following the First World War.[30]

After 1921, nominal Christian identity or baptism were no longer the route to either Chinese Canadian or nationalist success. In order for the republican government and for Sun Yat-sen's troops to be successful, nationalists needed the loyalty and full financial backing of overseas Chinese men.[31] Financial contributions could no longer be shared with Christian organizations. Thus, the drive to separate and distance KMT operations became one that focused on financial contributions that were directed to nationalism, not Christianity.[32] Frank Quo adds that in the post-1921 period, "the party [KMT] assumed the names of various welfare organizations and therefore became involved in the non-political affairs of the Chinese communities. To control the local Chinese associations, as a matter of fact, has become one of the major tactics of KMT operation in Canada."[33] At this point, nationalism became conflated with Chinese respectability. Chinese Canadians had to be loyal and obedient servants of their home nation.

In 1935, a report of the KMT's Vancouver main branch noted that Canada's economy after the stock market crash, and influenced by Saskatchewan's seven years of drought, was worse than the American one, and thus worse for KMT members and all Chinese Canadians. It also noted that the KMT's military efforts, led by Chiang Kai-shek to unify China during the Northern Expedition in 1927, had strengthened the Canadian nationalist project. The Depression, however, had caused the stagnation of donations to and membership in the party. In an attempt to reinvigorate the party and interest in nationalism, the leadership lowered the dollar amount of expected contributions to the party and worked on strengthening KMT propaganda. The report also emphasized that Chinese Canadians needed to remain focused on the nationalist goals of freedom, equality, frugality, being a good person, and having faith in the party. New initiatives to stimulate party membership and nationalist sentiment included training members and leaders who had taken an oath to follow Sun Yat-sen and clarifying the nationalist message in public speeches. In particular, the report noted that whereas some KMT branches were in decline throughout the country, others, and notably those of Winnipeg, and North Battleford, Saskatchewan, were getting stronger. Finally, the main branch of the Canadian KMT reminded members of the need to stay unified, focus on the party goals, and eliminate the communist threat to nationalism.[34]

Related to communism and anti-Christian trans-Pacific sentiments were assaults on Christianity mounted by left-leaning intellectuals and students in China from 1922 to 1927. Guided by Marxist-Leninist doctrine, these activists, as well as the KMT and other groups, mobilized newspapers and other forms of mass media to protest mission education, the YMCA, and imperialism in general. Ka-che Yip adds:

> By the early twenties most intellectuals viewed Christianity as incompatible with modernity. Indeed, by 1924 they viewed Christianity as not only unscientific and outdated, but also as a major obstacle to China's attainment of national independence. Many alleged that it was the vanguard of Western imperialism. These views were, to a large extent, shaped by the nationalist and anti-imperialist campaigns of that decade.[35]

Although the KMT and communists worked together for a few years to fight imperialism and were anti-Christian in China, they don't seem to have been a united front in Canada, and certainly not on the conservative Prairies.[36]

Before 1921, men who converted to Christianity often expressed their decision to convert by referencing Confucianism and its values.[37] Men who were living as bachelors professed familiarity with it, and those few living with families self-identified as Christians. Nationalists admired Confucian qualities of filial piety, loyalty, and decorum. Chinese practised these qualities to gain acceptance by Christians and non-Chinese society. Confucianism as practised on the Prairies was a product of the new Canadian life and the challenges it presented. By 1921, more than 27,000 Chinese Canadians self-identified as Confucian on the census; there were only 1,100 Confucians on the census just two decades earlier. This explosion in Confucian self-identification was in part due to KMT propaganda disseminated through-out overseas Chinese communities.[38] Confucianism was no longer affiliated with the Chinese Empire, which as of late 1911 was dead.[39] It was neverthe-less strongly affiliated with top-down and grassroots Chinese and Canadian nationalism.

Over time, nationalist leaders made broad use of traditional thought and culture to inspire allegiance to Chinese nationalism and the cult of Sun Yat-sen. Sun became an exemplary Chinese man who was familiar with both Western Christian and Confucian customs and ideas.[40] From 1916 until it became an official holiday called Teacher's Day in China (in 1931), com-munities were encouraged by Canadian branches of the authoritative Chinese Consolidated Benevolent Association (CCBA) and the CKT to close KMT and other offices and celebrate Confucius's birthday with teas and banquets.[41]

After 1921, Chinese adopted Confucian identities, especially on the Canadian census and were also nominally Christian. Christian identity was nominal because most of the men neither converted nor accepted baptism, and most men combined Christian and Chinese beliefs. To Christian mis-sionary workers, the Confucian aspect of this belief system was the least offensive and the most similar to Christian doctrine.[42] The rare man self-identified in public as Buddhist.

As diaspora Confucianism progressed, it emphasized male relationships, the reading of classical texts, and Chinese education and culture. Education was essential because few of the Chinese men who migrated to the Eastern Prairies (and rose to positions of political leadership) had attended more than elementary school. Reg Bing-wo Yee (b. 1921), the son of Bing-wo Yee, an early leader of the Lethbridge nationalist community, elaborated: "Dad talked about Confucius. He equated Confucius with the teaching of phil-osophy. He had a very Confucian outlook. Confucius was a philosopher. He taught these virtues to us that he said were basically equal to Christian concepts. He was somewhat of a Confucian scholar. He had Chinese books and spent a lot of time reading." Most Chinese men were familiar with many texts, not through formal education, but through the retelling of teaching stories and their merits by older men educated in China.

Most men had little time to educate boys and sons who accompanied them on the journey to Canada to work in laundries and, later, cafes.[43] The KMT took on that role. Between 1912 and 1949 (and in some places for much longer), the KMT offered Chinese language and culture classes taught by older comrades throughout the country. A 1921 Christian mission report noted the following about Chinese schools in Vancouver:

> Of the eight thousand Chinese living in the city during the winter months at least fifty percent are young men, who for the most part are eager to learn English and our western ways, but who nevertheless cling to their nationalism and to their home religion. Three Public Schools are being operated by the Chinese themselves, with Chinese teachers brought from China, using the Chinese National Readers and distinctly Confucian and Anti-Christian in spirit.[44]

Whereas large numbers of children attended the Chinese schools in coastal areas of Canada, a much smaller number attended them in areas beyond the coast. These classes were populated by a handful of Chinese youths who were born in Canada and the young male labourers brought to Canada. Through the classes, children acquired a rudimentary understanding of regional Chinese languages: Toisanese, Hoiping, or Cantonese. They also practised Chinese calligraphy, customs, songs, poems, and festivals, and became familiar with traditional thinkers such as Confucius, and modern ones such as Sun Yat-sen and Chiang Kai-shek. However, I was told repeatedly by former pupils of these Chinese schools that students took away little from the classes. One research participant was memorable: "I never did learn a damn thing. I went until I was fifteen years old. I listened but did not understand. It was very difficult for me and my siblings. Those were long days as kids." Outside of China, leaders in overseas branches of the KMT encouraged early Chinese Canadian fathers to send their children to these Chinese schools. Leaders imagined that children would memorize and then be able to recite passages from classical texts and thereby intuitively become loyal nationalists. Adults were also encouraged to study Confucian classical texts that inculcated virtues and to become familiar with and memorize the political will that Sun Yat-sen left to his compatriots, explaining the social significance of the three principles of nationalism, democracy, and livelihood.[45] Everyone also read issues of the local and national KMT-produced newspaper.

The 1920s nationalist project had been characterized by a push for modernization. The death of Sun Yat-sen in 1925 made this even more aggressive, with a new campaign to discourage the veneration of anything but nationalism or Confucianism. Ritual reinforced a Chinese man's loyalty to gods and traditional China. Nationalism reinforced his loyalty to Sun Yat-sen and modernity. Eventually, there was no room for both. Offerings went to nationalists, not to unrelated offering halls. As a result, some altar spaces didn't include conventional enshrined deities such as Mazu or Guanyin.[46] These nationalist altars were simply adorned with photographs of the early republic's nationalist leaders Sun Yat-sen or Huang Xing (1874-1916).

Nationalists also discouraged practices that were deemed to be "superstitious" or to detract from party goals. During this period, temples scattered throughout British Columbia lost Chinese community support and were largely dismantled, shifting the allegiance of labourers, who relied on the healing powers of Guanyin and other deities, back to Sun Yat-sen and nationalists.[47] Quongying's coin sword and magic coins (discussed in Chapter 8) belonged to this category of spurned religious practice. When someone in her small Manitoba community discovered her magical ritual instruments, Quongying and her husband installed a special secure door that was kept locked. Although it was acceptable for the small numbers of Chinese women who lived on the Eastern Prairies to use prayer beads, revere Buddhist or Daoist deities, or engage in private ritual practices, this kind of religiosity sullied an otherwise pure nationalist persona. Private rituals and customs belonging to these other modalities could be tolerated only in the farthest back regions of life. If indoors, they had to be practised out of view, in a bedroom or closet, and if outdoors, in a secluded area of the backyard or in the garage.

After the 1920s, Chinese reproduced nationalist world views and ideas that had been circulated top-down and at the grassroots by propaganda and power brokers. Most often this was the Confucianism that nationalists fashioned anew in Canada. In 1940, a *Winnipeg Tribune* reporter who was looking for information about Confucius was told to ask Lee Hip (Li Xie, d. 1977), a Chinese Canadian nationalist and erstwhile Christian (before 1921 and after 1950), who had lived in Winnipeg since the early 1910s.[48] Lee Hip was the Chinese community expert in Confucianism during the 1940s.[49] As the earliest Prairie Chinese were almost uniformly nationalist members and admirers of Confucius, Prairie Chinese nationalist speeches included references to Confucius in the *Analects,* which are based on conversations with his disciples. The children also learned these sayings from the Chinese readers they used in after-school and Saturday morning lessons taught by Chinese community elders. One man, born in 1925 and raised on the Prairies, adds, "I guess they all were Confucian, really. They would have political meetings and they practised by getting together. Confucianism was a way of life, like morality and love of family. It was a social practice, not practised like religion. We were all raised Confucian." Over time, nationalist identities became intertwined with Confucian ones.[50] As a result, men who distanced themselves from nationalism and brokers, and did not become KMT members and serve their comrades, effectively renounced Confucianism.

Given Confucianism's long history, it is not surprising that this school of thought has defined Chinese Canadian identities and gender roles. It has influenced elite culture throughout the Chinese cultural sphere. It has also been associated with Imperial China that ended with the Qing dynasty (1644-1911). The 1911 Wuchang Uprising brought abrupt political, social, cultural, and other changes, but Confucianism survived fashioned anew. Sun Yat-sen, and later Chiang Kai-shek, leader of the KMT after 1926, continued to rely on aspects of Confucian culture as authority.[51]

The People's Republic of China was founded in 1949. Various campaigns initiated by Mao Zedong, the CCP's leader, had taken place since 1935 to reform traditional Chinese thought and culture. Since 1949, when the nationalists and KMT fled to Taiwan, communist leaders have consistently drawn on Confucian ideas to mobilize support for the People's Republic.[52]

Years ago, it would have been a dangerous thing to speak openly and positively about the similarities between communism and Confucianism, such as the shared emphasis on the collective, not the individual, and on meritocracy rather than aristocracy. It is now quite acceptable and even expected. The CCP promotes and crafts new policies based on Confucian virtues related to governance, democracy, learning, and harmony. Confucianism was a strong theme in the opening ceremonies of the 2008 Beijing Olympics, which included passages from the *Analects. Confucius 2010* was a film produced in China, and though not a blockbuster, it received the approval of the CCP. China has been busily promoting the teaching and study of traditional Chinese thought and culture through Confucius institutes that have been set up in universities around the world. It is not unusual for Chinese leaders to quote from the *Analects* and Confucian thinkers today.[53]

Although the governance structures, processes, and subjects of affective regimes formally disappeared some time around 1950, remnants of them can still be found in Winnipeg's Chinatown. Today, the Winnipeg Chinese Cultural and Community Centre (WCCCC) is the main Chinese organization in the city. It is led by people who did not come to the Prairies through historical channels of chain migration and nationalist ties. The new group of leaders came mostly as students, doctors, and professors. A few years after they became settled in their professional careers, they gravitated toward Chinese networks to mobilize and serve the community, provide mutual support, and to lessen racism through various projects related to traditional culture, sport, and entertainment. Although these new leaders have diverse histories, they are nonetheless drawn to Confucianism. An example of this can be seen in the 1980s, when the Winnipeg community worked to revitalize Chinatown. At this time, the leadership aimed at creating a "perfect society."[54] In describing the perfect society, the group drew on Chinese Confucian virtues, such as loyalty *(zhong)*, filiality *(xiao)*, benevolence *(ren)*, and righteousness *(yi)*. The WCCCC foregrounds the virtues of cultivating friendship in a quote from the *Analects* that hangs in its library: "Friends that visit from afar, is that not also a delight?"[55]

2 Reverend Ma Seung

In this chapter I tell the story of Canada's first Chinese Prairie Presbyterian minister, Reverend Ma Seung (1872-1951),[1] and his pioneering efforts to propagate Christianity among the Chinese in Canada.[2]

Ma Seung was born in 1872 in Toisan, China.[3] He was the fifth son in a southern Chinese farming family of six boys and two girls. His father, Ma Tsun-yen, was a gentleman and landowner.[4] Little is known about Ma Seung's mother or any of his sisters. Early family trees and descriptions of lineage typically detailed only male family members' names, dates, and vocations. References to female family members were spotty and limited to their married names (e.g., Ma Seung's older sister married Chu Cut-lay from California).

Ma Seung's unpublished autobiographical materials, found among the many materials collected by his wife and family, recount in English and Chinese his early years in China and his education by his eldest brother, Ma Boon-tsung, who was the school master. Ma writes:[5]

> I entered school in my youth, and after eight years completed the study of the six books (from *Xia Lunyu* to *Da Ya*), and the *Xia Meng*. All of these I was able to recite from beginning to end with no mistakes – my eldest brother being the master of the village school. My father and brother both had high hopes that I would take up a literary career, but I have a wandering disposition and I am fond of playing around, so that when I entered the higher school I spent most of my time in playing around and watching the shows and operas.[6]

China in the 1870s was still under the Manchurian rule of the Qing dynasty (1644-1911), and all Chinese were required to wear their hair with the sides shaved and back worn long in a pigtail. Accordingly, the young Ma Seung wore a queue that he bound up each day when he went to Pui Ying Union Middle School. There, he received a traditional education, studying the

Confucian *Analects (Xia Lunyu)*, the *Mencius (Xia Meng)*, and the major odes from the *Classic of Poetry (Da Ya)*, as well as other classical texts. This prepared him to become a Confucian scholar-official. But Ma, though an exemplary student, was a wayward youth looking for adventure. Families usually sent their second sons for overseas migrant work, or they might choose other offspring who were judged most able to survive on so-called Gold Mountain and to send remittances home. Ma Seung's family realized that he was not suited to the life of a scholar and that migrant work might be a better fit for the restless young man. His older sister, Mrs. Chu, who lived in California, provided the solution and funds. As Pamela Mar notes, "He was on his way to the United States where his elder sister had married and he was going there and the ship docked in Victoria. There was the opportunity to get off the ship and stay there, and that is what he did."[7] It is not known why he chose to disembark in Canada. It was 1891, and he was 18 or 19 years old. Like many others of the Ma clan in Canada, Ma Seung found work as a cook and then a houseboy, or domestic servant.[8]

Throughout the autobiographical notes there are repeated references to the young Ma Seung's internal struggle between the desire for a scholarly life and associated Confucian virtues, and the temptations of a life filled with gambling, "shows and the opera." Ma's father had angrily forbidden him to continue his studies in China and had encouraged him to consider taking up a trade in Canada.

Ma recalls the first year of working life alongside other Chinese bachelors in Victoria's Chinatown. In his memories, we see reflected the experiences of many young Chinese males who came to Canada alone in their teens, laboured in Chinatown's underbelly, and somehow grew into strong, successful men, most often with tight affective ties to friends, not family:

During the first year or so I followed my father's admonitions, and was untouched by any of the vices, and so accumulated a small nest-egg. Following this short period, I was nearly swamped by the four vices, re: women. A certain Ma did tempt and lead me to the brothel's back door. We knocked at the door, a woman came to invite us in, but I was so ashamed that we fled which was indeed a lucky break. Later I again felt the sexual urge and so asked a Ma Wing to lead me, he being a well-known man about town. He not only refused to lead me, but scolded me, saying that though my character was bad at the time, he was not willing to further my downfall. Later I met Chan Duck and Seto Lay and others who were well-acquainted with the red light traffic and were willing to be my guide. After mulling over the offer, I felt that I should keep my body inviolate – why should I follow these women on the downward path and so declined the invitation.[9]

What little free time Ma had was spent in the company of men who belonged to the Ma clan, co-workers, and men he met in Methodist dormitories, as well as in English classes offered by missionaries in Victoria. From these classes, Ma learned to read, write, and speak fluent English.

Ma's notes show a high level of English proficiency and document his early and ongoing battles against vices such as swearing, lust, opium, alcohol, gambling, and opera: "As to the gambling, I was first tempted to play the words game [lotteries], this led later to fan-tan, dominoes, etc., all types of games of chance. In fact on occasions I have gambled with dominoes several nights in succession, neglecting my meals and sleep." Ma was clearly ashamed of his debauched behaviour and lack of self-restraint. He writes:

As to smoking, I have had three bouts with opium. The first two times did not result in heavy addiction, and I was able to stop when I had to work. The third bout was the most severe and I would not have been able to shake off the addiction if I did not become a Christian. In fact had I not been converted at that time I would have been entrapped by opium in the Foo-yung citadel.[10]

Cantonese opera was included on the list of Ma's guilty pleasures in his twenties spent in Victoria's Chinatown. By the early 1890s, Chinese opera, performed by visiting troupes and stars from southern China, was well established in Victoria. Hosted and organized by Chinese of Victoria's merchant class, Cantonese opera offered arias, theatrics, costuming, and acrobatics that catered to a mix of Chinese and non-Chinese audiences.[11]

Cantonese opera was the one carryover from his life in China. Ma writes:

As to the theatre, each month I spent an average of fifty dollars in tickets to the theatre and Chinese operas, together with after theatre snacks usually with several fellow-theatre lovers. Thus after several months, all my savings were used up, and I had not half a cent on me. I had to search for work again, but the daily earnings were not enough to finance my gambling forays. This went on for a year or so, and then I went to Cumberland – guided by the Holy Spirit.[12]

In about 1895, Ma left Victoria's Chinatown after he "finally fell into bad times" and went to Cumberland, 215 kilometres north of Victoria on Vancouver Island.[13] There he hoped that he might find better work and save money. Of the many vices and sins against which Ma struggled, gambling seemed to be the hardest to resist.[14] And Presbyterian missionaries seemed to be aware of the lure of gambling, so they preached in gambling dens. Later, ministers such as Ng Mon Hing (1858-1921) would provide the addresses of these dens to police so that they might raid them and end this "sinful" form of pleasure.[15]

In Cumberland, Ma Seung found work at Union Mines and continued to socialize with men who belonged to his clan. At the urging of a friend who shared Ma's love of and confessed addiction to gambling, Ma Seung attended a gospel meeting at the Cumberland mission house. This moment foreshadowed his eventual conversion:

> When I was asked to go with them to services, I would swear at them. That was before I was converted. Once when I went and listened to passages read from a tract called Questions and Answers on First Steps to the True Gospel I was so incensed that I snatched it, tore it up, and threw it into the fire ... When one slammed the deficiency of the Gospel, I gladly supported his argument. When someone bore false witness against the church, I gladly followed.[16]

Eventually, though, Ma Seung moved into the Cumberland mission house. His notes tell of the evenings that Chinese men spent at the mission house when they were not at work. There were heated arguments between them and Mr. Hall, the head missionary, and Ng Mon Hing, who visited periodically. Verbal sparring continued after the evening's mission classes ended and the female Bible study teachers had gone home. Ma explains:

> At that time, it happened that Mr. Ng Mon Hing a Christian missionary arrived at Cumberland for a preaching session of about a fortnight. I was determined to debate with him, for though I lived at the mission, deep in my heart I still despised the religion and regarded it as so much foreign superstition and so often opposed it and in my self-righteousness often said that if I couldn't win in my arguments with Mr. Ng I wouldn't be a man, and so determined to have it out with Mr. Ng.
>
> That evening after classes I got ready for the fray lining up my forces and my defenses hoping to sweep my enemy off his feet. Mr. Hall sent Miss Doge

home, and he himself stayed to hear the outcome of the argument. Picking up my courage I waded into the argument, pointing my finger at Mr. Ng's eyes and banging on the table with my other fist, I harangued him, accusing him of leaving the ranks of a cultured people and joining ignorant foreign tribes, and of being willing to be abject slaves of the foreigners, tempting our compatriots, etc., with gnashing of teeth, protruding eyeballs, red cheeks and black mane I confronted Mr. Ng and disregarding my own irreverent behaviour I felt that this is conduct fitting for a disciple of the sages.[17]

After Ng returned to Victoria, Mr. Hall, the head of the Cumberland mission, continued to try and cultivate a love of Christ in Ma Seung. At Bible studies, he selected Ma Seung to read passages aloud. A friendship developed between them, and when Ma Seung lost his job at Union Mines, Hall found him one as a domestic servant in the area of Cumberland known as "white town." Most Chinese labourers did not work on Sundays, as this was the Sabbath on which most businesses were closed. This meant that on Saturday evenings after work, Chinese men could stay up late. There was the feared danger that on these evenings they would gather at gambling halls, opium dens, or brothels. As a result, most missions offered activities on Saturday nights, and several Bible and English classes on Sundays when the Chinese had free time. The young men appreciated these free classes and the chance to socialize outside their own circle.

For several months, Hall accompanied Ma home from the Bible study classes to "white town" where he worked and lived. On these walks, Hall would quiz Ma on the meaning of Biblical passages, and through these interactions, Ma began to understand Christian ideas that had previously seemed to conflict with Chinese customs. Ma explains:

> Later I met Mr. Ng again, and this time I assiduously studied the Dao of the bible. I would finish my work in a hurry and go to Mr. Ng and ask him to interpret the bible for me. My desire to know the truth increased and it was at that time that the real battle began. (This is the encounter with the vituperation and scorn of the unbelievers.) At that time, I began to help Mr. Hall somewhat, by helping to read the Scripture [presumably translating it for other Chinese], explaining the passages read and interpreting for Mr. Hall. Several months went by.[18]

To Ma Seung, the *dao* of the Bible was the one truth shared by Christians and Confucians.[19] This *dao* had nothing to do with Daoism, which Ma saw

as a pernicious Chinese superstition. In Cumberland, Ma displayed an am-
bivalence toward Western culture. On the one hand, he reviled the "foreigners" who treated Chinese like slaves lacking culture and civilization. He
resented bigoted depictions of his own background and traditions. On the
other hand, he was educated enough to admire Western Christian teachings,
and especially science. Ma was in Cumberland for close to two years. During
this time he saved money, avoided most vices, and continued to develop his
faith in God. Ma notes, "I was baptized on July 30th 1896 and became a
disciple of Jesus Christ."[20] This made him not only the first Chinese Canadian
Prairie minister, but also one of the first Chinese Canadians to be baptized
in Canada.

March 1897 saw newly baptized Ma Seung return to Victoria to look for
work. Just over a year after his conversion to Christianity, he attended a
conference that included all the Chinese converted to Christianity in British
Columbia.[21] It was at this conference that Ma was chosen by the Presbyterian Mission Board to travel to China and study at the Canton Christian
College Pui Ying, with all expenses paid.[22] Ma recalls:

> In September a meeting was held in Victoria of the BC Presbyterian Mis-
> sion Work Among the Chinese to discuss methods of spreading the Gospel.
> It was decided that we should raise the necessary funds from among our own
> people to establish the foundation of some work at New Westminster and
> send some one [sic] to minister there with us applying for his food and lodg-
> ings. The second decision was to select one person to return to China to study
> for the ministry also to be financed by the Chinese brethren. The decisions
> were made by secret ballot and Mr. Lo Cheung was selected to undertake
> the work at New Westminster, while I was selected to leave for China in the
> month of September.[23]

Being selected from among a group of Chinese converts to attend years of
training in China changed the arc of Ma's life. He was a rising star in the
Presbyterian Church. He embarked on his trip to Hong Kong and then
China with fifteen dollars from his own savings and an additional five
dollars given to him by Reverend Ng. Returning to China, Ma wrote of
his mixed feelings and his fear of what his father and brothers might
think about his conversion to Christianity. At the time, to some Chinese,
Christianity was foreign, Western, and undesirable. This may explain in
part why many early Chinese adopted no more than nominal Christian
identities.

Ma Seung wasn't ashamed of being more than a nominal Christian.[24] And he wasn't interested in attaining merchant status to impress his parents. He simply wanted to display his filial piety with a proper gift of money. In Canada, before this trip to China as well as after it, Ma had continued to uphold his filial duties and send money back to his father and mother. But as a Chinese missionary, he was paid too little to give his parents a gift that adequately reflected his respect and love for them. He writes:

Among my audience was a preacher Mr. Eng Kam Sing [who] advised me to pray for myself, and also for my parents, and I [would] be sure to have no difficulty in facing them. A few days later, I travelled down river homeward bound. I reached home in the evening, and found everyone happy at my return especially my parents who assumed that I had acquired some unexpected riches. However after I had explained my presence instead of being saddened by my lack of money they were glad and felt lucky to be able to meet again.

The next day early in the morning I returned to Canton. I was home for only eleven hours. I have been instructed not to tarry long at home since I must hurry back and immediately enter school to take up some lessons that I had missed or else I would not be able to be promoted to the next class. While at school I made rapid advances in my studies and managed to make the top of the list in all my examinations, which was a source of great satisfaction to my teachers.[25]

This short visit with his parents and brothers appears to be the last recorded family one. Requests for return visits to see his dying parents were denied by the Presbyterian Foreign Mission Board.[26]

Ma had proved himself to be a remarkable student when he studied at Pui Ying Union Middle School years earlier. This time, however, he was being re-educated in China as a Christian at a college run by Westerners.[27] And after his formative experience at the Canton Christian College, he was able to use his comparative religious expertise to convert Chinese men to Christianity. Following his conversion, he continued to be inspired by Christianity and a desire to rid his fellow countrymen of their shameful and sinful habits, and their "worshipping of all kinds of idols and following of all sorts of false gods."[28] To Ma Seung, the worship of idols and gods such as Mazu, in China and in Canadian Chinatowns, was a Daoist practice. Confucianism, however, was not a religious practice like Daoism or Buddhism, and therefore posed no threat to what he referred to as the *dao*, or way, of Christian doctrine and practice. His son, Peter, explains: "In Christian circles the word *dao*, hoary

Figure 5   Ma family. Left to right: Andrew, Hong Lin, George (in front), Peter (behind), Ma Seung, Jacque (seated), Cumberland, 1913. *Source:* Jacque Mar.

with age old use by the Chinese and later adopted by the Daoists, and meaning the way, has been adopted by Christians [to mean] 'Christianity.'"[29] Throughout the collection of Ma Seung's notes, there are scattered references to Confucian texts, virtues, and ideas. At one point, Ma refers to himself as a "disciple of the sages."[30]

While studying in China, Ma Seung looked for a suitable girl to marry who might share his Christian values and interest in missionary work. In 1899, he met his future wife Yeung Hong Lin, who was then at the Anglican Ladies College in Canton, studying midwifery and nursing. Pamela Mar recalls: "When he was in China he knew that it was essential he should find a Christian wife. So he went to Christian schools to find a Christian wife ... The mother or teacher head arranged for Jacque's mother and father to meet casually in the garden of the school, and if they liked each other, that was fine. They met in the garden and all was well."[31]

Even men who had immigrated to Canada as boys returned to China for an arranged marriage, or welcomed brides who had been selected and sent to them by their parents.[32] As early as 1900, however, young women who had received a Christian missionary education or who had attended Anglican schools in Hong Kong followed more modern Western marriage customs. This was Ma Seung's preference. Therefore, he and Hong Lin had a Western ceremony "conducted according to Christian rites (modern as against the old ancestral rites)."[33] Jacque adds, "Father clearly adored Mother. She was a Christian. Her Ama [nursemaid in China] had been a Christian. She was from a sufficiently wealthy family and raised in Canton."[34]

The Boxer Rebellion came a year later in China. Ma Seung was asked to return to Victoria before he had completed his studies, where he would take up the position of assistant catechist to Reverend Ng:

> In the year 1900, the Boxer Uprising began, and in Canton province, as elsewhere, considerable trouble developed and destruction of churches often occurred. Also at that time, my projected training period of three years was about up, so that after receiving permission from our Superintendent of Chinese Missions ... I returned to Victoria.[35]

Ordination as a minister within the Presbyterian Church would have to wait until Ma Seung could return to finish his training. Because they returned to Canada as a married couple and part of the church hierarchy, both Ma Seung and Hong Lin were exempt from paying the head tax, which in 1900 was still fifty dollars. Christian affiliation and religion sometimes trumped race. Chinese missionaries may not have been European-born, or bred with an understanding of Continental customs and values, but they shared a European faith in God. Church affiliation, however, did not help Chinese missionaries become citizens or vote, and it did not guarantee exemption from the requirement under section 18 of the Chinese Immigration Act, 1923, that "every person of Chinese origin or descent in Canada, irrespective of allegiance or citizenship" must register with the government or risk being fined.

Ma Seung's notes contain careful outlines and summaries about the early activities and leaders of the Presbyterian Church and mission in Victoria. Presbyterian mission work was started through the urging of the British Columbia Synod and Presbyterian leaders in Manitoba and British Columbia in the early 1890s. It was met with considerable resistance at first, as work done in China with the Chinese population was judged to have more value. In the end, the Foreign Mission Board, which oversaw Chinese mission work in Canada as well as in China and elsewhere, became convinced of the need to open a Victoria mission to serve the several thousand Chinese men in the city, who were deemed to be "more accessible" than the "Indians":

The Chinese Presbyterian Church began in 1893 as Victoria Presbyterian Gospel Hall, in a store in the 1490 block of Government Street with Dr. Winchester as the minister. Night school, Church Services and open air gospel meetings were conducted [in] 1893. The following year, 1894, Mr. C.A. Colman, a catechist who had spent eight years in S. China, and could speak the language, was added to the staff. The work was terribly discouraging. The men wanted English, but were not interested in the Gospel message.

In 1893 the first Chinese minister was appointed. This is his story. As a boy in San Francisco Ng Mon Hing had been a leader of a gang who used to break up outdoor religious meetings. Converted on shipboard, during a visit to China, he became an ardent worker for Christ in his native village. While there he met Dr. Winchester who had been sent to South China to learn the Cantonese language. He was invited to come to Canada to work amongst his own people. He arrived in 1893, but spent most of his twenty-five years until retirement in Vancouver. The Rev. Ng Mon Hing was a great man and a great missionary. A church and a school were erected in his native village, as a memorial to him, and all the money was raised in Canada ($1500 gold).[36]

The Victoria mission became the First Chinese Presbyterian Church on January 22, 1899, offering Christian Scripture in Chinese, a boys' day school, evening school, and women's missionary outreach. Miss Carrie Gunn came from Barrie, Ontario, in 1899 to lead the women's missionary work. The work was difficult, as most of the women knew little English and, guided by Chinese tradition, remained in their homes. When Reerend Ng was transferred to Vancouver in 1904, Ma Seung, assisted by Miss Gunn, was promoted to head of the mission. In this same year, a Christian Boys Boarding School was also opened.[37]

The Presbyterian Church regarded Chinese pastors as better able to convert Chinese to Christianity than "white" pastors. The number of conversions and baptisms a preacher chalked up was seen as a benchmark of success.[38] It was the justification that the Presbyterian leaders required to maintain operations in different Canadian regions. Missionaries were continuously under pressure to prove the value of their Winnipeg, Edmonton, Cranbrook, or Cumberland work. Being familiar with Daoism or Buddhism, Chinese church workers could easily compare these religious ideas with "white" Christian ones.[39] Confucian values, usually not perceived by Chinese as religious, provided a basis for understanding Christianity. To the church, Confucianism made early Chinese immigrants appear accessible and more open to conversion.

The Presbyterian Foreign Mission also relied on Chinese men like Ma Seung for their much-needed linguistic and cultural fluency in Canada's various mission fields. He and many nameless others were appreciated for their work. Yet, letters and autobiographical pages in the Ma Seung archive also show a tendency of the Presbyterian Foreign Mission Board to ignore his work and delay furloughs and payment of invoices for reimbursement of mission and outreach expenses.[40] Winnipeg's United Church Archives contain similarly incomplete and scanty references to Ma Seung and his family, and thus fail to properly document the eighteen-year contributions made by Ma to the mission there and to Chinese Canadians from the Kootenays to northern Ontario in the same period.[41] Perhaps the absence of references to Ma Seung in Protestant records has to do with the tendency to overlook the value of Chinese missionary work in smaller and less populous Prairie and eastern locations.

At the same time, Canadian mission work (Presbyterian, Methodist, and Anglican) privileged "white" men and the British Empire and its culture.[42] Oriented toward reinforcing dominant ideologies, mission work was necessarily focused on the most obvious threats to dominant culture. Chinese men who were perceived to be trapped in sinful Chinatown lifestyles needed missionary help. Chinese women had to be rescued from imagined prostitution, slavery, and concubinage in 1910s Canada.[43] Ma Seung wrote several letters to the Foreign Mission Board, identifying the need to reach out to lone Chinese beyond Chinatown and coastal British Columbia.[44] The Foreign Mission Board may have lacked interest in converting Prairie Chinese merchants who didn't fit Chinese stereotypes. Despite his commitment to early Presbyterian mission work, and his eventual service and dedication to Chinese men scattered from British Columbia's Kootenays to Lake Superior, Ontario, Ma continued to encounter obstacles in his dealings with the Presbyterian Foreign Mission Board. Nonetheless he proved his worth by innovating with street preaching and chautauquas (entertainment and lecture series that toured to towns, villages, and cities).[45] Recognizing the value of ambient or indirect exposure to religion through such outreach, he also organized Prairie soccer and other Chinese athletic leagues and involvements.[46] For a short time after the First World War, the Chinese conversion rate improved, at least outside British Columbia.[47]

But by 1921, nationalism was spreading quickly. Nearly every Chinese man belonged to the party by this time, as a Presbyterian Church report indicates:

Figure 6   Chinese mission picnic, annual wheelbarrow races, Winnipeg, ca. 1920.
Source: Jacque Mar.

During the twenties and thirties the focus of the Church was not only to evangelize, but to bridge the gap between cultures. There was a very strong sentiment of 'China for the Chinese.' Many Chinese men were tempted to take advantage of the job opportunities in China at that time especially, in light of the anti-Chinese sentiment in Canada, and treatment as non-citizens. So there were programs for those who might return to China and those who were likely to remain in Canada.[48]

Although Ma Seung and sons Peter and Andrew made regular trips to visit Chinese men and boys scattered throughout small-town Manitoba, northern Ontario, and some of Saskatchewan, this wasn't enough to create strong bonds. They couldn't compete with the large number of Chinese nationalist leaders who were doing the same. Chinese missionaries travelled by train and needed room and board once they arrived, as well as donations. In return, they offered conversations highlighting similarities between Christian and Confucian doctrine and, if the men were baptized, salvation. Few of the men ever converted, and though they enjoyed their conversations and professed nominal Christian identities in public (for example, on tax rolls and the census), they didn't see the efficacy of conversion or of being more than weakly affiliated with Christianity.

By contrast, Chinese nationalists such as Frank Chan and Sam Dong (discussed in the next chapter) arrived in the newest and most fashionable automobiles, wearing three-piece suits, silk ties, fine shoes, and fedoras. They represented the modern Western Chinese merchant who made enough money and had enough social capital and ties to be accepted into dominant society. Nationalists also asked for donations and for men to become party members. In return, they occasionally offered a prestigious-looking certificate stamped with Sun Yat-sen's Chinese chop or seal. The recipient could then boast of being the nationalist representative for his small Canadian town. Members were invited to grand banquets, teas, and picnics attended by powerful business leaders from dominant Chinese and non-Chinese society. Most of the time the events took place in Winnipeg, but sometimes they were held in smaller places where there was a KMT branch. Not only did membership lend status, power, and positions in powerful Chinese and non-Chinese organizations to newly immigrated Chinese men, but it also led to merchant status.[49] Chinese missions and ministers could not compete with the powerful nationalist infrastructure and webs of connections that were forming across Canada by the 1920s: they did not belong to them.

Institutionalized racism also didn't help. The Chinese Immigration Act of 1923 virtually ended the emigration of any newcomers from China, making it difficult for Canadian missions to grow any larger. By 1924, Ma had been transferred to Edmonton, and a year later, when the Presbyterians and Methodists merged to form the United Church, he was sent to Calgary.[50] The following year saw him go to the Kootenays. By 1927, the nationalists were putting increasing pressure on Chinese men (especially labourers suspected of communist leanings) to sever their Christian and other religious ties, dedicate themselves to Chiang Kai-shek, fund the Northern Expedition in China. By this time, KMT offices were firmly established across Canada. In addition to discouraging superstitious practices, nationalists also opposed people who promoted the merits of communism in Canada.[51] Documentary and oral history evidence suggests that nationalist offices throughout Canada circulated information about overseas members and communities by code.[52] An RCMP letter sent on February 8, 1927, said:

Sir, I have been informed by the General Superintendent of the Government Telegraph Services that he has received a letter under date of 29th January, to the effect that it has been noticed that the Chinese Nationalist League in Vancouver is sending out quite a number of messages in code to various Chinese in the Cariboo and northerly districts.[53]

By 1928, the labourers began to experience less pressure from nationalists, possibly because most had joined the KMT or hidden their left-leaning views. Nevertheless, communism continued to be treated as a threat to KMT Chinese Canadian respectability.[54] The 1929 stock market crash further weakened nationalist membership drives and fundraising for struggling missions. In 1930, many Chinese moved out of larger centres like Winnipeg into smaller villages and towns, and their grown children returned to China in search of work or to join the nationalist army. It also seemed that the once-burgeoning business of Christianity was failing. As Ma's son Peter wrote in a 1931 report,

> Today there are about six families, three of which are mixed marriages. Of these, we may perhaps be the last family to leave Winnipeg since:
>
> 1 The older children cannot hope to make Canada their home;
> 2 Improving conditions in China; and
> 3 Depression in the price of silver.
>
> I need not dwell on the effect of the anti-religious propaganda. Its effects are too well known. Suffice it to say that our Winnipeg branch of the Nationalist League happened to be quite radical in their outlook and since their membership takes in the majority of the Chinese population our work was greatly affected.[55]

Peter's remarks proved to be true. Decades-long nationalist leader Charlie Foo and his family moved to Plum Coulee, Manitoba, where there was a business opportunity for Foo, though he returned after a year. Several Chinese bachelors working in Winnipeg around the same time also drew on strong nationalist connections and partnered with men in small nearby towns to operate businesses. Many Chinese never returned. Other families left Canada altogether. Older Chinese men and sometimes their families returned to China in the mid-1930s in part because the Chinese nationalists had advertised that they would help fund return trips for men wanting to "save China."[56] They also left because of scant employment opportunities for Chinese children born in Canada. Many businesses were unwilling to offer non-"white" youth even blue-collar jobs. Still more families returned to China so that their children could marry Chinese.

To return to the story of Reverend Ma Seung, in Victoria, he continued to conduct his street preaching, visited Chinese in their homes and shops, and preached to Chinese men with leprosy in the D'Arcy Island Leper Colony, and to those who were generally ill and poor.[57] As well, under Ma's leadership after 1904, the Victoria mission continued to emphasize Christian education with evening Bible classes and three Bible classes on Sundays. Ma's wife taught Miss Gunn Chinese. Once Gunn had learned enough of the language, she was able to organize classes in Chinatown for a small number of "little girls."[58]

From the beginning, Ma Seung had found it difficult to support his wife and himself on his salary, which in 1902 was raised to forty dollars a month after the birth of their first son, Peter. Mrs. Ma was paid five dollars a month for teaching Miss Gunn Chinese, but the lessons and additional income ceased within a year. Gunn continued to live with the Mas and to pay rent.[59] After the birth of the Mas' second son, Andrew, in 1905, it became increasingly difficult for the family to afford life in Victoria, though it would be another two years before they left and settled in Cumberland.

In 1906, Ma Seung wrote to Reverend Armstrong, then head of the Foreign Mission Board in Toronto, requesting a transfer. He wished to return to Cumberland, where he had been baptized, and proposed an exchange of postings with Mr. Hall, who would come to Victoria as lead missionary:

> I should like to go to Cumberland not only for myself but for the sake of others working and for the Chinaman too, because there is only a white missionary in the place and the Chinese boys to help him. The work is hard because a white missionary cannot have the intercourse with Chinamen that a Chinaman can, and the Chinese have not the same confidence in him, so it is hard for the work to grow. Anyone acquainted with the work at either Cumberland or Vancouver would believe this. There are many Christian boys here and some of them could help with the mission work. The Chinese have nothing to read in the way of newspapers or newly translated good books and their minds are very unenlightened and this makes a barrier to the entrance of the Gospel, and so if I were sent there I could not only preach the Gospel, but would hope to attend to this other important thing. The conditions there are not the same as in Vancouver or Victoria. In these places there have been Chinese missionaries preaching many years but in Cumberland there has been nobody and the ground is still in its wild state with so many people needing to be looked after. So I feel that the work there is more important than at other places.[60]

By 1907, Ma Seung and Hong Lin had moved to Cumberland, where they had two more boys, George in 1910 and Jacque in 1912. Each of the four boys

Figure 7   Ma Seung, Cumberland mission, ca. 1912. *Source:* Jacque Mar.

was given an English name, three of which were chosen because they were the names of Jesus's disciples – Jacque is French for John but spelled without the "s." In addition, each boy was given a Chinese name. Jacque's middle name means "Christian grace."[61] The boys were raised in a strict Presbyterian household and weren't allowed to smoke, swear, or go out with girls (though Jacque confided that his mother sometimes found his father having a "puff" of a cigarette behind the furnace).

In Cumberland, Ma continued his missionary work with the Chinese community, many of whom he knew from having lived there a decade earlier. He organized mission picnics, travelled on missionary chautauquas, and preached to Chinese men who worked in the mines, restaurants, and laundry shops. But he deliberately remained outside nationalist society. Jacque notes that though his father did not approve of getting involved in Chinese politics, he was a supporter of nationalism and Sun Yat-sen: "In 1911 Father and Mother created a nationalist flag in Cumberland – the five-barred one. So he would have been a supporter in that sense."[62] At home, the boys spoke

Chinese with their mother and English with their father. Jacque adds, "Father gardened vegetables. Food was important." It was in Cumberland that the Ma boys became known as the "Mar" boys, because the name was easier for non-Chinese to say and remember.

Having become part of the family, Miss Gunn followed the Mas to Cumberland and lived with them.[63] After ten years in Cumberland, Ma requested a posting in Winnipeg so their four boys could receive professional university education, which they couldn't get in British Columbia, as racist ideologies barred Chinese from many professional faculties there.[64] Jacque notes, "Father wanted his sons to be educated in the sciences of the new world and to bring this back to China."[65] Peter, who was born in 1903, was one of the first Chinese Canadians to be accepted into and graduate from any university in Western Canada.[66] Once the Mas moved to Winnipeg, Miss Gunn resigned from the church, retired, and moved back to Barrie, Ontario. She sent regular letters and Christmas presents for the boys.[67]

Jacque remembers travelling from Cumberland in 1917, first to Victoria and Vancouver to visit friends, and then taking a train to Winnipeg and a horse-drawn taxi to their new home. And he remembers being struck by the city, which in comparison to Cumberland farmland was very developed and large. They took up residence at 296 Ellen Street in a two-storey house around the corner from the Chinese mission on Logan Avenue.

The home was an improvement over their former residence in Cumberland, where the rotten roof tiles leaked every time there was a hard rain.[68] But as Peter reports, the family encountered new difficulties with life in Winnipeg, especially prohibitively expensive heating costs. Peter wrote:

The house was a two storey frame structure with dining room, living room and kitchen on the ground floor, four bedrooms and bathroom above and a full basement, in which was installed a large galvanized iron tank (for catching the rain water – our only source of soft water for washing). Of course, to us at that time it was much more spacious and comfortable than the lean-to we had at Cumberland. It took just one winter to bring us to a realization of what we had to cope with. Rental on the house was thirty dollars, which was nearly half of Father's meagre stipend, whereas no rental was charged at Cumberland. In BC, fuel was practically free. All we had to do was to climb the hill immediately behind our back yard for small pieces of wood, while members of the church would periodically roll in cross sections of fallen trees from the nearby hills, and we always had more than enough for both the church and home use, free of charge ... It seemed that no matter what we did we could not keep the cold out, despite the double windows and doors, keeping the furnace on all night, closing off most of the rooms and huddling around the stove in the kitchen. Often during the middle of winter we would wake up in the morning and besides finding it impossible to look through the ice-covered windows we would see streaks of hoary frost around some hitherto unnoticed cracks on the floor of the blocked rooms. The parlour was rarely used in winter, unless on special occasions when we had guests who gave us prior notice of their visit.[69]

Growing celery and other fresh greens in a home garden, which they had been accustomed to doing in Cumberland, was hard work. They now had only a few summer months and land that Ma Seung referred to as Manitoba's "clay gumbo," as opposed to the "rich black loam which was easily worked" in British Columbia.

In Winnipeg, Ma Seung ministered to approximately nine hundred Chinese in the city and about the same number outside of it in smaller towns and cities. Throughout the week, he visited Chinese men in their shops and homes, and also those who were "ill and housebound." In his spare time (and to fund his mission work and family expenses) he became an amateur photographer, shooting immigration photographs for the Chinese community. Pamela Mar notes, "He set up a studio at the back of the house to take pictures of the Chinese for head tax certificates and later so that they could register with the government."[70] Ma Seung had apparently learned photography when he had first come to Canada, from a well-known Chinese photographer in Vancouver named Yucho Chow.[71]

Ma also opened the Winnipeg Chinese Young Men's Christian Association and visited two Sunday afternoon classes each week in rotation at Winnipeg's Youth Methodist Church, Grace Methodist Church, St. John's Methodist Church, the Pentecostal Assembly of God, and St. Paul's Presbyterian Church.[72] The St. Andrew's Chinese class was held in the mission building at night, for which Ma provided a regular Sunday evening sermon at 7 p.m. "as part of the Forward Movement."[73] In addition, he continued to encourage athletic participation and indirect Christian practice through weekly gym classes that were held at the YMCA and the Winnipeg Chinese Athletic Football Club (a soccer team). Winnipeg also had a Boy Scout troop as part of the Chinese church, with boys from twelve to sixteen years old. Jacque Mar explains that this "Chinese Boy Scout troop was one of the first in Canada."[74]

Figure 8 Jacque, Andrew (Scout master), and George Mar, Winnipeg, 1920.
Source: Jacque Mar.

As aforementioned, Ma Seung also organized annual picnics, beginning in 1917. Unlike Chinese nationalist picnics that were first organized a year later in 1918, these Chinese Presbyterian picnics were supposed to be exclusive congregational events. Ma Seung was careful not to get involved with the nationalists or to co-sponsor events with them.[75] He also arranged for Christmas trees for the local Chinese children.[76] At 8:30 p.m. each Sunday there was a prayer meeting. In addition to holding Sunday evening services, Ma read and explained Scripture in English classes taught by a former missionary to China on Tuesday, Thursday, and Saturday evenings, when there were as many as twenty-two Chinese men in attendance.

Ma's son Andrew also used to help one of the local Winnipeg lawyers, acting as an interpreter and clerk. Though the Mas were not a merchant family, their ties to both the Presbyterian and Chinese communities, coupled with their English proficiency, enabled them to gain limited access to "white" society – for instance, as census takers in 1921.[77]

The Mas found Winnipeggers to be much more welcoming than the people they had met in Cumberland. Shortly after they arrived in August 1917, they were invited by Mr. and Mrs. Jones to their home at 877 Winnipeg Avenue.[78] This was only the third time that the family had ever been invited into the home of a non-Chinese family, having been inside Reverend and Mrs. James Hood's home once in Victoria, and inside Reverend Colman's home in Winnipeg only upon arrival from the train station. Peter recalls, "We were surprised when we got to the Jones' home to find a group of Chinese boys and girls there, quite at home, joining an equal number of young Canadian men and women in a social hour, and singing besides hymns from the hymnals, secular songs from the One Hundred and One Songs."[79] In addition to socializing at picnics, singsongs, socials, annual banquets, and concerts with Mr. and Mrs. Jones, the Mas spent time with the Holmes, Ross (Old Rossy, as well as Daisy and Molly, Lily and Agnes), and Morton families, and with Frank and Wesley Chan, Wesley Lee, Lee Hip, Gordon Lim, Frank Wong, and Jessie Lee and Lily Chan.[80] Only male members (both Chinese and non-Chinese) of the Christian community were included in the Young Men's Chinese Christian Association rosters, even though the group included a near constant assembly of non-Chinese female teachers and a few dedicated converts such as Jessie Lee and Lily Chan.

Within four years of the Mas' arrival in Winnipeg, the Foreign Mission Board decided that Ma Seung, though he had not completed his theological training at Canton College, now qualified for ordination as a Presbyterian minister. In 1921, at St. Andrew's Presbyterian Church on Elgin Avenue, at a ceremony attended by many in the Winnipeg Chinese community, Ma Seung was ordained.[81] This made him Canada's first Chinese Canadian Prairie Presbyterian minister.

Figure 9 Ma Seung's
ordination, 1921. *Source:*
Jacque Mar.

Ma received a salary of 60 dollars a month (720 dollars annually) for his work. It was well known that ministers and missionaries earned little and that church work depended on their innovations, fundraising, and the donations of wealthy congregants.[82] His salary was less than what most Chinese labourers earned. Non-Chinese Winnipeg-based Presbyterian deaconesses and pastors of the era all received higher salaries. Ma also appears to have been paid less than lone Chinese church workers: for instance, Victoria's Chinese missionary and widower Ng Mon Hing received a salary of forty dollars a month in 1895.[83] Ma also had to pay rent and for missionary chautauquas that he and his two older boys conducted throughout Manitoba, Alberta, and to the east side of Saskatchewan and Lake Superior in Ontario.[84]

During 1922 and 1923, Ma Seung spent a year in China on furlough, during which time sons Peter and Andrew helped (often without pay) with the Winnipeg and Manitoba mission work.[85] Hong Lin suffered from terrible arthritis in her arm, was often sick from the cold, and like most Chinese women living in Manitoba at the time, abhorred the winter. For years, she was effectively a single mother, solely responsible for the care of sons George and Jacque, as well as Henry, whom she adopted from an orphanage in the early 1920s when he was an infant.[86] Once he had returned from furlough, Ma Seung pleaded with the Foreign Mission Board not to separate him from his wife and family, who needed him. Nevertheless, he was sent away from 1924 to 1925 to live in Edmonton and Calgary, and in 1926 he was sent to the Kootenays to stay in Cranbrook for several months.[87]

Unable to afford a car, or drive, most Chinese missionaries travelled by rail. Ma Seung travelled for more than thirty-five years in Canada on the railway branch and main lines. His correspondence and family notes are clear that he experienced considerable racism on the railways. Racism and bigotry were common on trains, which were culturally dominated by "white" British values and customs. Members of the church who travelled by train qualified for certificates that would enable them to buy tickets at half price. For Chinese missionaries and ministers, these certificates were essential because they had very little money and because even though they spoke fluent English and were familiar with Western customs, train conductors and conductresses sometimes treated them like "heathen Chinamen." There is evidence that the board failed at least once to give Ma Seung the half-fare mission worker's certificate to prove his identity. In these instances, Ma and others were unable to persuade train ticket agents that they were Chinese pastors (not regular passengers). They ended up paying full fare to avoid trouble, as evidenced by this 1924 letter sent from Ma Seung to Reverend MacKay of the Presbytery:

April 12 1924

Dear Rev. MacKay,
I am enclosing herewith a report of my trip.

Arriving in Vancouver on March 12th I was asked by Rev. Smith to stay in that city to await instructions from the Board. I received a letter from the Board on March 21st and left for Calgary on March 22nd where I stayed for two Sundays. I left for Edmonton on March 31st where I spent a week and on the 7th of April I left for home. Because your ticket terminated in Edmonton

I was forced to add money to complete the passage to Winnipeg because in that way I could save quite an amount of freight expenses, as the Trans Pacific limit is 350 dollars while the overland limit is only 150 dollars[;] if I did not do that I would have to pay freight for excess baggage of 200 dollars from Edmonton to Winnipeg.

Going from Calgary to Edmonton that [sic] was a lot of trouble between the conductor and because I was unable to show him the half fare certificate I didn't get to Edmonton until after a series of quarrels with him and [he] even threatened to put me off. Because of these troubles I was afraid that the same trouble might happen so I didn't stop at Saskatoon, Regina, etc., but went straight home.[88]

Church reports confirm that Winnipeg's Chinese mission work was poorly funded and disorganized.[89] Mr. Ewing of the Foreign Missions Committee considered Chinese food to be cheaper than Western food. Ma Seung, when challenged on his accounting of family food expenses, went out of his way to document and compare the equal costs of both Chinese and Western tastes in a letter to Reverend MacKay in 1905, subtly exposing the racism in such comments.[90] At the time, Reverend MacKay was secretary of the Foreign Missions Committee. He considered Ma Seung a "native preacher and helper" who was thus vital to the success of mission work.[91] Ma Seung's papers show a frustrated man. As a "native preacher and helper," he accepted that his congregants would have to fund much of his outreach work, sometimes in its entirety. When he and other Chinese missionaries visited places where they had no connections, they paid their own expenses. The Presbyterian board repeatedly delayed or complained about the reimbursement of his own and his son's expenses.

Peter Ma served as a Manitoba College summer volunteer to "enlist recruits for the ministry."[92] After he graduated from the University of Manitoba in 1922, Peter was sometimes paid to do that work during the time his father was on furlough. Chautauquas or missionary lecture and visiting circuits were gruelling journeys in midsummer heat. Ma Seung and sons Peter and George volunteered their time, funds, and own connections to help make these chautauquas possible. Jacque Mar's wife, Pamela, added, "He was lucky if somebody put him up and it didn't cost him anything. He had to pay for his accommodation and things like that so you would hope that you would be entertained because the amount of money the church gave you was so little."[93] In a 1921 report, Peter Mar documented his summer trip through southern Manitoba:

Report of the Chinese Work In Villages and Towns of Manitoba July/August 1921 Peter Mar

To the Members of the Presbytery of Winnipeg, Manitoba

Dear Sirs,

While at the Students summer conference at Lake Carlyle, Saskatchewan I was notified by a letter from Rev. Dr. Roddan, that at a meeting of the Presbytery on July 6th, 1921 I was appointed to make an itinerary of Southern Manitoba.

Following instructions given in the letter, I left the Conference on July 6th arriving at Souris that afternoon. Next day I began my work. From Souris I went on the CPR to Brandon, Oak Lake, Elkhorn Virden; then on the C.N.R. to Hartney. From Hartney I went to Napinka and Melita, and then along the Napinka-Winnipeg line to Plum Coulee stopping at Deloraine, Boissevain, Ninga, Killarney, Cartwright, Crystal City, Pilot Mound, Manitou, Morden and Winkler. From Plum Coulee, I went north to Carman, stopping at Roland on the way. After leaving Carman, I visited Elm Creek, Rathwell, Treherne, Holland, Cypress River, and Glenboro, returning to Winnipeg via Boissevain, visiting in all twenty-seven towns.

As I had no knowledge beforehand of the numbers of Chinese in the towns, the time that I spent in these places varied very much, according to the hospitality extended, as I wished to cut down expenses. At towns where there are any Chinese at all, I have visited but I spent more time in some places while at others I did not spend enough time to finish my work, this being due to the fact that in some places I obtained some of my board or meals free, in which case I stayed a little longer, allowing perhaps a day for towns where I was not entertained.

The number of meetings and services addressed was eighteen, number of restaurants, cafes, etc., visited was twenty-nine, laundries twenty. Besides the seventy-eight Chinese in Brandon which I visited on Brandon Fair Day ... outside of Brandon, I visited and interviewed 124 Chinese. Of this number 100 are not connected in any way with the Church or any kind of Church work, they being either indifferent or tied down by business responsibilities. Of the remaining twenty-four, six are young lads between ten and eighteen years who attend Sunday Schools or receive instructions in English in private homes. Five are young men seeking educational help in the Church or in the homes and the rest [are] attendants or supporters of the Church.

In general I have been well received everywhere. As a large number of ministers in the towns were away on their vacation, or moving, or had just moved in, some difficulties were encountered, but I was generally able to obtain the information that I required. Where I was not entertained in Canadian homes, I sought accommodation in Chinese restaurants or laundries and if they [lacked] space I went to the hotels. At several places my board and lodgings were provided free by the Chinese.

Chinese in these towns were mostly middle-aged or elderly men and most of the younger men have learnt enough English for their business. Therefore the usual methods of work through the English classes cannot be very well applied in the cases of the towns in which the Chinese population is very small.

In endeavoring to do what I could for the Chinese, my method was to find out the conditions under which they lived and which Canadians adopted towards them. Most Chinese complained of the treatment meted out to them.[94]

From her conversations with husband Jacque and five other Ma family members, Pamela recalls that "this is how the Chinese made progress. They spent time with the men. They did what they did, stayed up late talking, and ate breakfast early in the morning. It was the Chinese way to invite and entertain guests from afar. In the summer Andrew and Peter used to travel to various towns like the chautauquas with plays and things. Peter would do talks on science and Andy did similar things – on a travelling basis."[95] A letter written in 1922 expressed that the board was very unhappy that Peter had been paid sixty-five dollars for three months of work, when he had completed only two months of work. This meant that Peter at the age of twenty was being paid just over twenty dollars a month, which was less than what some Chinese workers had been paid to build the railway in 1885. Andrew had presumably volunteered to accompany Peter on these trips. The letter suggested that the difference would be taken out of Ma Seung's wages.

By 1927, when Prairie nationalism was in full swing, Chinese men, though they admired and appreciated Ma Seung's efforts, chose political membership over conversion. At this point, Ma Seung appears to have been able to return from Cranbrook to his posting in Winnipeg. Sons George, Jacque, and Henry were then seventeen, fifteen, and six years old, respectively. Ma Seung had spent five years apart from his wife and sons. Hong Lin had been wanting to return to China for a decade, since she had first moved to Winnipeg.[96] Winnipeg's Chinese women hoped that she would never leave. She organized events under the guise of domestic training and in keeping with Foreign Mission Board goals. As discussed elsewhere, the women didn't

Figure 10 Ma Seung and family, ca. 1934. From left to right: Rev. Ma Seung, Dr. George Mar, Dr. Peter Mar, Dr. Jacque Mar, Mrs. Mar, and Andrew Mar.
Source: Jacque Mar.

need this re-education, but they appreciated the chance to socialize. Hong Lin's interest in women's mission work was transnational. For years, she talked to her husband about the prospect of continuing her work overseas and helping a brother, Dr. Yeung Shiu-Chuen, who was very involved in rescuing Chinese women in Hong Kong.[97] Ma Seung's request for retirement to China was finally granted seven years later in 1934, and passage of two hundred dollars was given to each of his children, his wife, and him.[98]

After forty-three years in Canada, nearly four decades spent in service to the church, Ma Seung had merited only brief mention in Presbyterian and United Church minutes and reports. Most of his contributions to Chinese Canadian communities from Flin Flon and The Pas in northern Manitoba, to the Manitoba-US border, west to northeast Saskatchewan, east to Lake Superior, as well as in Edmonton, Calgary, and the Kootenays, were overlooked. One of Ma's sons, in a 1934 interview with the *Winnipeg Tribune* about the family's departure from the city, responded to a question about world events that had affected the United Church Board's Chinese mission in Winnipeg. He said that the family was used to being "looked down upon by Chinese here since these things began ... Father keeps plugging away despite his hindrances." The reporter noted that the last sentence of the comment was "added with a shy smile."[99]

In Hong Kong during the Pacific War (1937-45), the Mas had to barter for food and spend their life savings. Ma Seung died in 1951 from heart disease at the age of seventy-nine, and Hong Lin died in 1962 from complications of a broken hip at the age of eighty-two. The Mas were buried in Hong Kong's Kowloon cemetery, and their photographs were placed on the gravestones, as is Chinese custom.

Chinese Canadians quietly and nobly lived under a severe shadow of discrimination, and it is possible that the shy Mar son mentioned above was also referring to the church underfunding and under-appreciation experienced by Reverend Ma. Left out of nationalist alliances, Ma Seung and his family suffered through the combined influences of religion and racism. In the next chapter, I discuss nationalist bachelor uncles Frank Chan and Sam Dong, who came to Canada in their youth, learned English, and made their way to the Prairies. Their vocations enabled them to reach countless numbers of lone Chinese men who lived on the Prairies and convert them to nationalism (not Christianity).

3 Bachelor Uncles: Frank Chan and Sam Dong

The patriotism that swept through overseas Chinese communities transformed Frank Chan and Sam Dong (whose stories I tell below) into merchant nationalists. Frank and Sam came to Canada as young men, joined the Kuomintang (KMT, aka Chinese Nationalist League), attained merchant status. Then they returned to China to marry and have children. When they returned again to Canada, the enactment of the Chinese Immigration Act in 1923 condemned their wives and children to remain in China while they themselves lived, grew old, and died in Canada. In fog, rain, and especially in snowstorms, these salesmen's lives were filled with long stretches of solitude and loneliness. Forced to live as bachelors, they formed significant emotional bonds by serving as uncle figures to sons of close friends.

Frank Chan (aka Chan Tok Wah, Chan Shan, Frank C. Fun, 1901-52)

Frank Chan was born August 18, 1901, in Toisan, China. A Chinese newspaper that printed a biography of Chan's accomplishments in the Chinese community noted that he arrived in Canada at the age of ten in 1911 with his father and brother.[1] When he reached adulthood, Chan followed custom and returned to China to marry and start a family.[2] He left his wife, son (Gerald Chan), and daughter (Mae Woo) in China, sent money back, and visited every few years.[3] He also had a brother, married with children in New York City.

Friendly and well-dressed, Frank was described as a uniformly kind man. Though a merchant and power broker, he had less clout than others in Vancouver or New York because his circle of influence was not as far-reaching. He also had fewer rivals. Power brokers made and kept ties between home and host nations, facilitating channels of immigration by selecting favoured relatives and friends to come to the Prairies. They helped these male newcomers by using their resources and connections to find them jobs and lodging, with the standing promise of returned favours if needed. Successful merchant gentlemen like Frank used skill, privilege, and new transportation technologies to position themselves in close proximity to, and sometimes even inside, the perimeters of "white" British Christian society.[4] In creating their own positions of influence, they mitigated racism for the entire group of Chinese Canadians. In the words of many Chinese Canadians I interviewed, merchants became "big shots," whereas labourers, missionaries, and Chinese wives languished in a less privileged world that was more racist and less accepting.

Having come to Canada at a relatively young age and spent his youth working in small-town Chinese cafes, Frank spoke English well. A supporter of traditional Chinese education and language training, and a collector of Western art, he contributed to a book called *Inspiring Chinese Experiences (Zhen Huayue)*. He was a supporter of Winnipeg's Chinese newspaper. In 1916, when Frank was a teenager, he joined the Manitoba KMT. At that time, he probably worked as an assistant in a restaurant in Swan River, Manitoba.[5] He and many others drove or took the train to Winnipeg's Chinatown to attend monthly nationalist meetings. A year later, Frank joined the Young Men's Chinese Christian Association of Winnipeg. The association was not unique to Winnipeg as there were similar groups in Victoria, Calgary, Edmonton, Toronto, and Ottawa. Prominent members of the executive and leadership were long-time friends of the Ma Seung family, L.A. Jones, and wealthy Winnipeg power broker Mah Joe. Chinese Presbyterian community photographs dating to the late 1910s show that Frank was a frequent participant in mission community events.[6] With his own children growing up on another continent until 1949, Frank served as a loyal uncle figure in Canada. On many of his longer trips, he took along Charlie Foo's son, Wally, for whom he was a favourite uncle. Wally and Frank travelled to Kenora, Ontario, where Frank visited with Gin Ham, who owned the Ken Richa Cafe. Sometimes Wally accompanied Frank to Fort William, Ontario. As uncle to Chinese Canadian children, Frank enjoyed swimming and sometimes paddling a canoe during the summer months at Twin Lakes, Grand Beach, Lake of the Woods, and Lake Winnipeg.[7] He also enjoyed picnicking at Fort Garry Park and craw fishing along the Assiniboine River in Winnipeg.

After 1925, Frank became increasingly active in the local and national Chinese Christian communities and in the activities of the Chinese United Church (Jidu jiao Xiehehui). When other Chinese Canadian United Church communities had events, Frank was often the member sent from Winnipeg to represent the group.[8] He was also one of the organizers of Winnipeg's Three Principles Youth Group (Sanmin zhuyi qingnian tuan), which opened on June 25, 1944. Similar youth clubs were created around the same time in

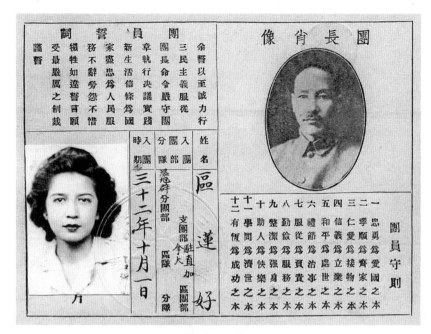

Figure 11   Helen Foo membership card, featuring Chiang Kai-shek, Winnipeg Three Principles Youth Group, 1943. *Source:* Helen Wong.

the United States and in Ottawa, Toronto, and other major Canadian cities.[9] By 1945, Frank was drawing on his own affective ties to fundraise for a Chinese United Church in Winnipeg's Chinatown.[10]

Frank was also closely associated with Winnipeg and Vancouver's amateur opera company, Wake Up the Soul Opera Troupe (Jinghun jushe) (Chinese Dramatic Society [CDS]), which formed in 1921.[11] According to Wing Chung Ng, the 1920s were the golden age of Vancouver's Cantonese opera, which was put on by professional troupes.[12] Chinese communities farther away from the coast enjoyed operas that were mounted and produced by the same travelling professionals who performed in San Francisco, New York, Vancouver, and Manitoba. Whereas documentary evidence suggests that Winnipeg's amateur opera troupe formed in 1921, a photograph dated 1906 (Figure 12), shows a much earlier tradition of opera in Manitoba. Three Cantonese opera performers in traditional costumes travel on horseback as part of Brandon's Dominion Day parade.[13]

Frank's involvement with Winnipeg's local amateur troupe wasn't unusual: Charlie Foo, long-time Manitoba nationalist leader, as well as David and Isaac Farn, and Ma Seung's second son, Andrew Ma, attended, sang, and

Figure 12 Cantonese dramatic troupe travels on horseback past Kuong Yuen Merchantile at 25 Twelfth Street, the location of Brandon, Manitoba's Chinatown in 1906. *Source:* John W. Hotson Collection, Daly House Museum.

played music in, and occasionally even produced local Winnipeg operas.[14] Preliminary research indicates that Winnipeg's CDS members were from a number of different clans, with greatest representation from the Lees, Wongs, and Woos.[15] Interviews with old-timers and long-time amateur performers strongly suggest that Winnipeg's amateur troupe clubhouse was a space to which men seeking non-religious and non-political involvements were drawn. Drama clubhouses did historically have altars, with the first opera teacher as the enshrined deity to whom offerings and incense were given before practices and performances, but otherwise, the CDS members were not usually KMT associates, and the clubhouses were a religiously neutral (and non-Christian) space.[16] As one research participant put it, "People didn't care if you were Christian, Buddhist or a Jew."[17] The club had no rules per se, but everyone who became a member understood that this was not a place

Figure 13 This 1938 list of Winnipeg KMT staff shows that executive committee members Charlie Foo and Frank Chan were responsible for group training and publicity, respectively. *Source:* Winnipeg Chinese United Church.

where politics, racism, or religious (Christian) discussions were welcome. The men still admired Sun Yat-sen and thus displayed his photograph and sometimes his will on the wall. Like other overseas dramatic troupes, they admired Chinese traditions and history, and the "engage[ment] in the arts for moralistic and altruistic purposes."[18] Though merchant-class men and power brokers organized and produced some of the operas, Winnipeg's opera clubhouse was seen by the community as a valuable site for free social expression. For Chinese who were trying to get away from Winnipeg gambling clubs, and who weren't interested in Saturday evening Bible study and other mission excursions, the clubhouse was the place to be. Bachelors arrived after they finished their shift at a Chinatown cafe or wash house. From midnight to dawn, they performed historical arias from the late Ming (1368-1644) and contemporary ones about laundry workers and migrant life.[19]

In 1944, Winnipeg's troupe marked its twenty-second anniversary. Mr. Wong (Wang Chuting) opened the anniversary celebration, followed by Mr. Lee (Li Biaoyi). There was a full house in attendance, including Frank Chan, who was representing the KMT and CPL, and Mr. Watson Chan

(Chen Rongguang, d. 1945), a Chinese schoolteacher.[20] After telegrams and speeches were read, the crowd enjoyed an amateur performance of an opera in which many people at the event participated, including Frank Chan. The party continued into the early morning, with guests becoming tipsy. The hosts organized impromptu games from the stage, entertaining the guests with riddles and other guessing games.[21]

Though Frank had ties to Presbyterian and opera groups, his strongest connections were nationalist. Fiercely anti-communist, he believed in Sun Yat-sen's Three Principles (Sanmin zhuyi) and a government structure with five councils who balanced constitutional powers.[22] Frank had travelled widely for business, to solicit donations to "save China," as well as to visit family and friends all over North America.[23] He was a multiple-time Manitoba KMT chairman, vice-president party affairs, and publicity and overseas commissioner.[24]

When Frank was about to make a return visit to China, his fellow nationalist, comrade, and friend, Guan Dongxian wrote a poem in his honour. It conveys many traditional Chinese themes related to friendship and masculinity. In overseas affective regimes and during historical periods of Chinese disunity and exile, people wrote poetry about bonds mediated by politics, music, and the landscape.[25] Guan's poem runs as follows:

送陳煥章同志歸國 "Sending off Comrade Frank Chan Who Is Returning to China by 關動賢 (Guan Dongxian)

其一	*Verse One*
瞻韓欣有路	I longed to meet you, and was lucky to have the chance
幸獲識高賢	What great fortune that I came to know so worthy a man
分手將三月	We now part company for three months
初逢恰二年	While it is exactly two years ago that we met
才聞遷上苑	A talent so famous you were transferred to the Imperial Garden
又報整歸鞭	Then came news you were preparing to return
翹首揚帆處	You look up and set sail for lands across the sea
臨風一惘然	But facing the wind you find only disappointment

其二	*Verse Two*
天涯同作客	We both were guests at the ends of the Earth,
邂逅一相逢	It was just by chance that we came to meet
忘年許過從	Forgetting our age difference, you took me as a friend
交情惟道義	And showed me only righteousness in our dealings
處世尚雍容	Your deportment was nobly dignified

服務平生志	Serving others was your life-long ambition
精誠夙所宗	Perfect sincerity was your constant goal

其三   *Verse Three*

徵賢拜輔導	Soliciting the worthy to seek their guidance
萬里迎歸軺	You travelled thousands of [Chinese li] miles to meet returning worthies
抱負正堪展	What you have to offer can now finally be displayed
壯懷未許消	For you never let your stern resolve wane
匡時襄建設	You will rectify the evils of our time, and help rebuild [the nation]
戡亂戡紅潮	But once disorder and the Red Tide [of communism] are controlled
漫 作林泉想	You will turn your thoughts to the forest and streams[26]
飛騰上九霄	Where you can soar to the highest heavens
投袂從公日	You never dallied while working on official business
辛勞志不休	Through the bitter toil you never relinquished your ambition
愛羣懷太德	You love the common flock and cherish the highest virtue
策馬故鄉去	Now, urging on your horse, you go off to your native home
姓名海國留	Though your name will remain in this nation across the sea
知君衣錦日	I know you sir will some day don imperial brocade
得意勝封侯	And find satisfaction greater than that of being enfeoffed a lord.[27]

Guan's poem reminds us of the strength of the valuable male bond in a world where men grew up largely alone and without fathers, brothers, and other close kin. Poems expressing close affections would have been published in newspapers, posted on clan and dramatic clubhouse walls, and performed there, too. Guan's verses describe Frank Chan as a worthy, righteous, sincere, virtuous, and nobly dignified guest who suffered and served others. Employing conventional Chinese poetic techniques and the pentasyllabic form, Guan aptly demonstrates the erudition and sophistication of many early modern Chinese Canadians.

Guan's tribute also highlights the significance of new kinds of friendship in Chinese Canadian society. Friendship was not based on age. It was determined by emotional connections and righteous behaviour. As men cultivated affective ties to like-minded nationalists, Christians, or Chinese dramatic performers, they came to inhabit parts of the network near their friends. Likewise, as men congregated with labourers, merchants, entrepreneurs, and salesmen, they took on other traits such as wealth and status of varying degrees.

Frank and many other nationalist men were outwardly defined by their clothing and cars. Most of the men drove themselves, whereas others had cousins and associates who chauffeured a family. Those who were too poor took the train.[28] Automobiles were polarizing influences in 1910s Prairie Canada. Many men who lived in populated coastal British Columbia and Chinatowns didn't need cars. Prairie nationalists did – patriotism spread via new forms of technology.

Interviews with more than twenty Chinese Canadians born between 1912 and 1930 confirmed that Chinese in Manitoba, Saskatchewan, and northern Ontario bought life insurance from Frank and other Chinese men and women who were employed by Wawanesa Insurance and Sun Life Assurance in Canada.[29] Frank's Chinese advertisements for Sun Life acknowledged the difficulties of life in Canada, where Chinese bachelors were made to stand alone and could not depend on friends or kin, though tradition dictated that fathers could expect to rely on family in old age. Life insurance became a way for trans-Pacific fathers and husbands to provide for their wives and children after they died.[30]

Besides selling insurance, Frank also took part-time jobs. He worked for the Canadian Pacific Railway (CPR) as a ticket agent and interpreter, where he was sometimes called upon to act as a go-between for Chinese passengers and immigration authorities.[31] Frank listed the KMT dormitory where he lived as his ticket agent address. Railways moved Frank and others even closer to the vanguard of Prairie Canadian power. The CNR issued train passes to men who were hired as Chinese passenger agents. These agents

CANADIAN PACIFIC
RAIL AND STEAMSHIP LINES

FRANK CHAN,
CHINESE REPRESENTATIVE,
211½ PACIFIC AVE.
WINNIPEG, MAN.

E. A. McGUINNESS,
GENERAL AGENT. PASSENGER DEPT.
WINNIPEG, MAN.

W. HORDER, GENERAL PASSENGER AGENT, WINNIPEG, MAN.

W. C. CASEY, STEAMSHIP GENERAL PASSENGER AGENT, WINNIPEG, MAN.

Figure 14 Frank Chan ticket agent address from his scrapbook, ca. 1930s.
Source: Winnipeg Chinese United Church.

were responsible for certain regions of Canada, such as Ontario and Quebec or Manitoba and Ontario. The title of Chinese representative of the Canadian National Railway brought many benefits, such as season tickets to exhibitions organized and hosted by the railways.[32]

Frank's links to nationalism, Christianity, and railway and insurance companies gave him valuable merchant status and friendship. But these connections could not trump the racist law in place between 1923 and 1947 that barred him from bringing his wife and family to Canada. In 1949, Gerald and Mae came to Winnipeg to live with Frank and a nanny. In 1952, Frank became sick with meningitis and died. He was fifty-one years old.

Sam Dong (aka Dong Sum and Dong On, 1891-1960)

Sam Dong first appears in Manitoba and Saskatchewan in August 1913. Everyone knew Sam as soft-spoken, kind, dignified, and always smiling. Conversations with Sam's many "nephews," "nieces," and friends suggest that he was in Canada years before he came to the Prairies. The 1916 census records a man who was probably Sam arriving in Canada in 1909. At this time, Sam resided and worked with Merry Dong (who was a year younger), whose name is very close in meaning to Happy Young, Sam's life-long friend, who was from the same Dong/Young clan and Chinese village. I suspect that Sam worked in Battle River, Alberta, with three other Dongs before he came to Saskatchewan and Manitoba.[33] By the time Sam reached the Prairies in the early 1910s, he spoke English well and was familiar with Canadian customs. Sam's webs of connection, like those of Frank Chan, were defined through his interactions as a nationalist uncle and cafe owner, then travelling salesman and merchant. Also like Frank, Sam was an occasional interpreter for the railways and courts.[34]

By 1913, at the age of twenty-two, Sam had opened and was operating a cafe in Esterhazy, Saskatchewan: "The Canada Cafe will be open for the public on Main Street opposite the hotel on Monday next when Charlie (Dong Sam) will put up a first class meal at any old time. Ladies will note that bread, chocolates, ice creams are some of the necessities Charlie will handle."[35] For the next few years, Sam ran the Esterhazy cafe, building a rapport with local patrons and with Chinese living and working in nearby towns and villages. His popularity was such that in January 1914, it was reported that he was "the Prince of Celestials."[36] By June that year, it was reported that Sam had acquired a sewing machine. The writer of the article mused that this item portended the arrival of a spouse: "The wife must be coming and the bells will ring Ding Dong."[37] Two years later, Sam's "cousin" Happy Young took over the Esterhazy cafe and would remain in Esterhazy for another thirty years, building on the good feelings people had for Sam.

By the late 1910s, Sam was approaching thirty years old and probably left the Prairies to return home for an arranged marriage. Many Chinese men went home around the age of thirty, when they had accumulated enough money to marry and start a family. By 1922, Sam was in Elphinstone, Manitoba, presumably running a cafe there.[38] He and thousands of other Chinese men saw their prospects of a family life as husbands and fathers disappear with the enactment of the Chinese Immigration Act one year later. By 1924, Sam became a travelling merchant, selling candies, tobacco, and for a time slot machines to Chinese cafes in Manitoba and Saskatchewan. He ran the business out of the Carlton Cafe, owned by his good friend Sam Wong.[39] Until the 1950s, when he moved to Winnipeg, Sam travelled through webs of Chinese cafes, taking orders, arriving with supplies, and making friends. By that time, Sam was tired. He was in his sixties and wanted a quieter life.

Happy Young (who still resided in Esterhazy) went into business with Sam to buy Harry Chan's curio shop, Oriental Arts Emporium, on Osborne Street in Winnipeg. Sam moved into the Chinese residence at 76 Yale Street.[40] This was the Chinese community house purchased for Chinese consul general Weng, who arrived in 1944.

Vaughan Baird, a non-Chinese lawyer and art collector who knew Sam from the 1940s until his death in 1960, recalled Sam as a "favourite friend" with whom he could discuss anything from art to politics.[41] Aside from Vaughan and other friends Sam met as a salesman and through the shop, he had a large circle of Chinese chums. Frank Chan was also his good friend. They had both lived at the Winnipeg KMT dormitory. They met at KMT clubhouse meetings and had friends in common. Sometimes they fundraised throughout the Prairies together. Through this activity, Sam and Frank experienced the ebbs and flows of nationalist affect. Before the Depression, fundraising drives had gone well. However, in the late 1930s, Sam and Frank went on a less fruitful trip across the Prairies. During this odyssey, they sold over $1,125 in nationalist bonds and received donations of clothing. Among the most generous donors in Manitoba was Mr. Wong (Huang Rongsheng), who had been one of the province's earliest KMT leaders and secretary in 1917.[42] Still, a report published in a Chinese Canadian newspaper noted that funds raised in 1939 were half the amount that had been drummed up in the previous year. Sam and Frank, who had used their own vehicles for the project, resigned from their positions, presumably out of embarrassment.

Because Sam's wife and children were forced to remain in China, Sam, who was part owner of a house in Brandon at 321 Tenth Street, doted on Sam Wong's sons, Walker and Westley. Sam Dong took Walker with him when he went on long trips to Saskatchewan and to the summer fair. He gave Walker presents at Christmas such as boxing gloves and a motion picture projector. When he died, he bequeathed special items to Walker, who had travelled with him throughout Chinese eastern Prairie Canada, "all across the Prairies to Regina, and Oxbow and all over Number 2 Highway to Winnipeg and down to Killarney, and Deloraine."

Sam died of cancer in 1960.[43] He didn't want to be buried away from his ancestors and family in the Prairie cold. Returning his ashes to China would be cheaper than flying his body back. So before his death, Sam decided on cremation, which was rare for a Chinese man at that time. Close friend and lawyer Vaughan Baird travelled to Hong Kong to deliver the ashes.[44] The story of Sam Dong's life shows a successful man who had ties to the broader Chinese and non-Chinese community.

I end this chapter with an account of Sam's trip with twenty-year-old Westley Wong (1922-2004), Sam Wong's eldest son. Here we see Sam, a beloved Chinese uncle, and Wes travelling along the established Prairie Chinese routes:

My Story: "Wes Goes West" by Westley Wong, May 4, 1942.

We left Brandon at five minutes past three in the afternoon and proceeded west on number one highway ... We got to Griswold about 4 o'clock and stopped there for about ten minutes ...

On to Virden. Past Oak Lake, the road winds on the southern crest of the Assiniboine Valley ...

Ah, Virden at last. It was 5 o'clock now. We parked the car in front of the Star Cafe. Sam went in while I went to the drug store ...

Sam and I then went to the Virden Cafe and had tea there. I also read about dad [Sam Wong] in the Free Press but didn't find any picture. The local laundry man, a wizened, white-haired old fellow, typically Chinese, I recognized as one who often comes to Brandon.

I drove to Elkhorn, twenty-two miles northwest ... We reached Elkhorn 45 minutes later and I parked ... in front of Queen's Cafe. I woke Sam up (poor boy was tired) and in we went. The two Chinese were having supper at the time. We were invited so we promptly sat down and helped ourselves ...

After gratefully thanking our hosts for the supper, we continued our journey ... We crossed the Saskatchewan border at about 9:50 p.m. ... At 10:25 p.m. we arrived in Moosomin where we checked in at Queen's Hotel and we had a little lunch at the Royal Cafe, Sam playing the role of cook. I retired to my room early, leaving Sam at the store. He returned later when I met him in the writing room filling out the orders ...

May 5, 1942

By 10:30 a.m. we left Moosomin and proceeded northward. Our next port of call was a little hideaway town named Welwyn, which is right back on the Saskatchewan-Manitoba border. The main street looked something a little better than a ploughed field. Sam went into the only cafe of an elderly Chinese, who I learned used to work at the City Cafe at Brandon.

Back at the cafe, we had dinner. Sam fried the two big beefsteaks which he had bought at Moosomin. Mmmmmm!

After Sam's business, about 2 o'clock we returned to the highway and went to Whitewood where my good friend Wong Hoy greeted me.

At 6:30 p.m. we headed north to Esterhazy ... Half an hour later we arrived at Esterhazy. A genial elderly Chinese there owns the Canada Cafe. Happy Young was his name. When I introduced myself as Sam Wong's son, he thought I was Walker whom he had seen about five years ago. "Has he grown that tall?" he gasped. We had supper together, the three of us.

An hour and a quarter later, we started out west again for a place named Lemberg ... We stayed at the local hotel for the night.

May 6, 1942

Around noon we started for another town about 10 miles farther west, a place called Abernathy. After a brief stop there we continued toward Bincarres where we had pork chops for dinner. Our next stop was ... the quaint little French-Canadian town of Lebret, hidden in the Qu'Appelle Valley ... Our next station was Fort Qu'Appelle, which is only three more miles on. It had the most modern cafe I had seen along the whole trip. After a little lunch, we left Fort Qu'Appelle to resume our westward journey. Qu'Appelle and then McLean. Here we left the gravel road ... We entered Regina. The streets were very narrow and bumpy but there were many impressive buildings. We stopped in front of the Kitchener Hotel where we checked in. A decent hotel at last! Someone had told Sam's cousin and he phoned the hotel promptly. We had supper at the Peek-Inn Cafe, owned by Sam's cousin. Bacon and eggs this time!

After supper we called on this cousin [Mr. Dong], whose wife is a young Canadian-born Chinese woman, very attractive and well-mannered. They have a young baby girl of 11 months [Lynne Dong]. We then went to the Silver Dell where we met Jean Tai and Mr. Tom Wongmow ... Len, his dad, Sam and I went to the Asia Chop Suey house after midnight and it was around 3 o'clock in the morning before we got to bed ... The "Asia" does not compare with the Winnipeg Chop Suey houses for style and food.

May 7, 1942

Around two we had dinner at the Exchange Cafe [associated with Yee Clun] ... I met some interesting people from Vancouver – an insurance salesman (Sun Life) and his wife and another young lady. The couple had a son named Wesley. The wife is the former Rose Wong, cousin to Effie Wong and therefore cousin to me! ... All of them will be down to Brandon in two weeks, they promised ... We had supper at Whitewood and from there gave an air-force man a lift to Virden. We stopped off at Maryfield [Tom, Jean, David, and Isaac Farn] for half an hour. At Virden we had a little lunch, ham sandwich Sam Dong style and coffee. And now fifty-five miles more to Brandon.[45]

This charming account of a sales trip aptly illustrates how the Chinese of the Prairies gave each other sustenance, both social and physical. Bachelors Frank Chan and Sam Dong filled their time in Canada with work, nationalism, and as uncles who travelled the Chinese Prairie pathways and had broad and varied interactions. In the next chapter, the attention shifts to Mark Ki and Happy Young, merchants and bachelors who inhabited the rural borderlands and drew on similar systems to integrate.

4 Affect through Sports: Mark Ki and Happy Young

By reflecting on the experiences of travelling salesmen Frank Chan and Sam Dong, I came to recognize Chinese culture, structures, and processes that expanded well beyond Chinatowns and cities. Affections and people traversed highways and main and branch rail lines, forming networks that by necessity were loosely patterned after "white" routes. People (usually men) established strong social capital and ties with friends whom they met through national and international Chinese associations, trade guilds, and business interactions. Participation in sports provided the opportunity for connection and integration outside political channels. When Chinese newcomers in rural Manitoba and Saskatchewan were allowed to participate as team sponsors, players, or fans, they also learned Western ways of moving and behaving in groups.

In this chapter, I map the emotional connections that were created and sustained through participating in broader society, aside from being Boy Scouts or band or church members. I look at participation on curling teams and in gun clubs, and as hockey fans and team sponsors. At the end of the chapter, I tell the stories of Mark Ki and Happy Young, who were welcomed by rural Prairie communities through sport involvement.

Athletics were in many ways a crucible in which Canadian identities were formed and cultivated. The broad social appeal of segregated sports and performance in "white" settler society and British Columbia has been studied, but much less is known about non-segregated sport involvement and performance in dispersed Prairie settlements.[1] Although sport (or other cultural) participation could help young Chinese men fit in, athletic involvement wasn't a guarantee of acceptance. Sometimes, in uniting team members, sport competition promoted exclusionary, intolerant behaviour or even violence.[2] Often, team victories and coaches led players to believe that winning a game meant they were superior to their opponent(s) – a mindset of discrimination. Other times, participation in sports wasn't possible, or it inflamed racist attitudes.[3]

Figure 15 Tennis players. Left to right, back row: Goo Wong and Don Ton. Front row: unknown and Andrew Mar, Winnipeg, ca. 1920. *Source:* Jacque Mar.

In some cases, lack of participation was owing to a shortage of leisure time for team practices or games, or money to buy uniforms. Their average size in height and weight also kept Chinese from playing hockey or football. But in other cases, I was told that the Chinese had not been welcomed onto the teams and fields and into the clubs.

Thus, there is little evidence of sport participation by people of "colour" in late nineteenth-century Manitoba or Saskatchewan. As Varda Burstyn notes,

For many of the founding sport associations of the late nineteenth century, "amateur" athletics meant "gentlemen's athletics." Women, workers and people of colour need not apply. While class and colour barriers were to prove permeable by the social and economic developments of professionalism in sport in the twentieth century, gender barriers have been more resistant.[4]

Chinese Canadian men who were welcome to participate and move out of the shadows of Prairie life mostly chose sports such as curling, tennis, or baseball. They often, but not always, rejected those, such as hockey, lacrosse, or football, that were deemed too uncivilized, brutish, or violent for their culture.[5]

The earliest forms of Prairie Chinese sport participation appear to have been in tennis. During the 1910s, Jacque Mar and brothers Peter, Andrew, and George played tennis at parks from an early age. They also played tennis with non-Chinese children who participated in Chinese community mission events. Reg Bing-Wo Yee remembers: "I played sports. I was never very good at any of them. I spent a lot of time on the tennis court. They let me onto the tennis court. I was welcome into tennis clubs, but golf was a rich man's game." Older Prairie men also interacted with local youths by making and flying kites.

Making kites wasn't a team sport, and it didn't necessarily help Chinese men overcome bigotry or move toward the centre of the Prairie power circles. But it did bring Chinese men who were separated from their own families in China into contact with local children. Alameda's Sam Long (in the early 1900s) and Lee Sing (d. 1955), who came to Windthorst, Saskatchewan, in 1930, were notorious kite makers and laundrymen.[6] Lee Sing "was a popular and familiar figure in our village. He was an expert kite maker. Many Saturdays he was the 'Pied Piper' leading the children to the hill past the rink for an afternoon of kite flying."[7]

In Regina's Chinatown, the Salvation Army operated a gym class for the small Chinese community. Gin Farn (the husband of Jung Farn, whose story appears in Chapter 7) was part of Regina's 1915 five-man Chinese basketball team organized by the local Salvation Army.

Similar athletic activities were offered in the 1910s by the YMCA in major cities all over Canada. Gin Farn's son also remembers seeing a few photographs of his father as a young man in the YMCA gym. About the Winnipeg YMCA, which was located at Alexander and Fountain, Lai Man Cheng states: "They provided space for the weekly meeting of the Chinese rotating credit association. Every Saturday people went to the [racially] White YMCA for exercise; they took baths there and played [basket]ball. On Saturdays, tens of people from the laundries would go to the White YMCA."[8] Winnipeg's Chinese community was roughly five hundred by 1912. As with Regina, this number included Chinese men from outlying regions. Chinese, who were classed as "coloured," could play soccer in leagues or attend weekly gym classes put on by the YMCA.[9]

Christian Prairie groups used athletics to entertain men who came to rural picnics or who lived in Chinatown dormitories and wanted more social opportunities. In Vancouver, Regina, and Winnipeg between 1910 and 1930, there were many opportunities to get involved in field days and play on segregated tennis, baseball, and soccer leagues and teams.[10] The YMCA, Christian Fellowship Associations, and the KMT organized basketball games among Chinese men. All of these sporting activities offered valuable opportunities to cultivate identities and sociability defined by more than race and colour. Ma Seung's boys played sports in high school and in the early years of university, before course work and part-time jobs became too demanding. Jacque notes, "I played hockey with a league. I curled and I played baseball. All of us played." He and his three brothers were welcome to play on Winnipeg's sports teams and to participate in the realms of mainstream society.

By 1917, Winnipeg Chinese boys could participate in a number of sporting activities put on by the Chinese Young Men's Christian Association. That year, the association had thirty-nine Chinese male members who played in leagues against Chinese and non-Chinese teams.[11] Elderly research participants reminisced about Winnipeg's Chinese Athletic Club Football [Soccer] Team Champions and their grand victory in 1918.[12] The *Manitoba Free Press* reported:

Chinese YMCA Footballers Win Dingwall Cup by Trimming N. Leaguers 2 to 0. Uncovering a brand of play that was indeed a revelation to a large crowd of enthusiasts at River Park Saturday afternoon, the Chinese YMCA pigskin-punting eleven administered a 2-0 defeat to the representatives of the Chinese National League in a grand revival of the national pastime of the Empire of China. Contrary to expectations, it was a real game that the Chinks put up, their playing being of a surprisingly high-class order, and their team work, well-nigh perfect. Winnipeggers who witnessed the game were most favourably impressed with the contest and the truth of the statement that the great game of football was indeed originated in the Orient was brought home to one and all.

Arrayed in regulation uniforms and looking anything but a crowd of shirt manglers, the Chinese boys opened the game at a fast clip and maintained the pace throughout the entire hour's play. The YMCA team had a considerable edge on matters all the way and were greatly assisted by some remarkably good playing on the part of Gordon Lum, their star centre-forward man. Gordon led the YMCA attack and bore right in on the nets time after time to keep the National league goalie pretty busy ...

When the smoke of the battle rolled away and the YMCA boys were proclaimed victors, they were presented with the Dingwall Cup, a handsome silver trophy donated for the big event by the well-known local jeweller. It is not often that a soccer team, newly organized and just getting into the game can win a trophy after their first victory but that unique distinction went to the YMCA Chinks, and on the merits of their playing they certainly deserved the honour. Joe Evens of the YMCA refereed the game satisfactorily.[13]

Athletics were a common part of missionary offerings by the Salvation Army, Presbyterian and Methodist missions, and the YMCA in both Canada and China.[14] By 1924, soccer, which had been established as a YMCA sport in England years earlier, was highly regarded by YMCA representatives in Winnipeg.[15] Groups encouraged soccer and other kinds of sport participation to control the sexual appetites of men who lived largely without women. A Winnipeg Presbyterian mission report dating to the early 1920s listed four categories of mission work: social, educational, physical, and religious. Under the category of physical, the report included YMCA gym activities each Saturday afternoon as well as outdoor sports and [Chinese] Scout training.[16]

Missionaries and church leaders also used athletics to curb gambling and opium use, to substitute Chinese opera (deemed sinful and illicit) with sport, and to inculcate good, clean virtues appropriate to Christianity and Western civilization.[17] As Talal Asad has noted, Christian dispositions have been perceived in those who employ their bodies in Christian ways such as fasting and praying.[18]

But beyond the Christian and religious meanings of athletic involvement, there were other, more social ones. Watched by entire communities, games that included Chinese Canadian participants served to unfix identities and stereotypes defining iconic "white" manhood.[19] Sporting events sent commonsensical media messages to audiences that conveyed and reinforced sport as an inclusive forum for participation.[20] As people watched local curling bonspiels that included Chinese curlers, they came to see these participants as members of their own community. Community pride swelled when local boys played sport, regardless of whether they were Chinese or non-Chinese. When the team won an end, the spectators cheered for the whole rink (four-man team). Chinese men and youth blended with other teammates by wearing new curling, hockey, and other uniforms. When they curled, shot the puck, or kicked a ball, they sent spectators the message that they looked and acted the same way as their teammates. Through sport, Chinese came to be seen as those who shared mainstream values and identities.[21] These were deliberate tactics and strategies that Chinese newcomers used to adapt to life in a "white" Christian normative social context.[22]

Curling was the most significant sport in which Prairie Chinese men and boys were welcome to participate. Newspaper accounts suggest that Chinese men could be curling sponsors and players in both Manitoba and Saskatchewan. In the 1920s, Billy Dong, Charlie Yee, Wing Dong, and countless others were avid and respected curlers who operated Chinese cafes in small Saskatchewan and Manitoba towns and villages.[23] Newspapers reported on the weekly progress of individual curlers and rinks with members from the religious, military, and business communities. One 1920s report from Esterhazy, Saskatchewan, mentioned the town's affections for Billy Dong: "Billy Dong is some curler. Three times a week he has attended the local bonspiel."[24] A different account from Morden, Manitoba, noted, "The noise of the Spiel was amply provided by a rink composed of Wing Dong, Rev. Chapman, Tom Morris and Colonel Pigott, skip, who provided an exciting mixture of noise, good curling and hilarity."[25]

Chinese were reportedly less welcome to join hockey teams and leagues. People played hockey outdoors and curling inside. Whereas curling is linked to balance and precision, hockey is typically associated with toughness, stamina, and physical strength. Brian Pronger adds: "The athletic world of power, speed and pain is an expression of the masculine ideals of our culture."[26] Hockey socialized boys and young men: it taught them about roles, belonging, team loyalty, and fair play, as well as about the harshness of Prairie winters. But unlike many other Canadian games, hockey was a violent contact sport. It also was not a small man's sport, thus excluding all but mixed-race, larger Chinese boys and youth from the ice. Discussions with research participants suggest that those who played hockey needed to spend long stretches of winter days practising on the ice. Mixed-race Chinese boys, such as Tommy Chow from Moose Jaw and William Yee from Winnipeg, of Romanian Chinese and Ukrainian Chinese ancestry respectively, were bigger and welcomed onto hockey and other "white" teams during the 1920s and 1930s.

Because of the limitations they faced with regard to playing, Chinese Canadian men in rural areas were mostly sponsors or fans of hockey. They thereby became associated with new notions of iconic Canadian manhood that ascribed to them the desired traits of courtesy, persistence, loyalty, generosity, and community pride, and especially an emerging and ambiguous Canadianness.[27]

As mentioned, migration separated boys from fathers, brothers, sons, and entire families. They missed the usual life-stage rituals that defined traditional Chinese masculinity.[28] These boys led lonely, monotonous lives and needed parental and male role models. Male teams provided essential fellowship, father figures, and other absent roles. Sports and group activities (encouraged by early voluntary associations and Christian groups) also led to intercultural understanding and the building of early communities. Chinese gentlemen or boys whom everyone knew as typically wearing suits, ties, and dress shoes became acceptable as more than just that: now, sometimes, a Chinese male could be dressed in the team jersey and appear as "one of the guys" in the locker room.[29] Newcomers began to seem less strange and exotic as team players learned acceptable and, in the words of Marcel Mauss, new "techniques of the body" so that they were seen to be like everyone else.[30] The bachelors were aware that in order to fit in and be accepted, they had to both appear and act in ways that were socially appropriate, civilized, and racialized as "white."[31]

Evidence of Chinese Canadian sport participation in Manitoba and Saskatchewan dramatically increased during and following the First World War. Such activity became an important way in which Chinese bachelors could balance pressures from dominant British society to conform with fulfilling their own social, economic, political, and familial needs. Through sport, Chinese men moved beyond their own cultural fields and onto teams, making the transition from weak, feminine, uncivilized "Chinamen" to strong, masculine, cultured community boys who sometimes won curling or even hockey trophies. As Bruce Kidd remarks:

> Almost everywhere, sports were meant to be masculine, a training ground for those qualities of physical artistry and strength, courage and stamina, ingenuity and loyalty that gave men their claim to the greatest share of the social surplus. They were usually played in all-male institutions, and audiences were largely male as well ... In part, sports were promoted to sustain the mystique of male superiority at a time of first-wave feminism. At the same time, sports were taught as an antidote to the "feminization" of young boys ... In the 1890s, churches and YMCAs began to offer sports as a way of reversing the exodus of young men from their services and programs.[32]

Participation in the realms of sport and entertainment allowed newcomers additional economic, social, and cultural resources through which they could gain power, change perceptions, and join the bourgeoisie.[33] Varda Burstyn confirms, "It remains true that the culture of big-time sport generates, reworks, and affirms an elitist, masculinist account of power and social order, an account of its own entitlement to power."[34] Through athletic interactions,

Chinese immigrants made non-Chinese friends and were less inward-looking. Sports participation also made Chinese Canadians into symbolic citizens, as demonstrated by the stories of Mark Ki and Happy Young.

Large and powerful clans – Lees, Wongs, Yees – dominated major Canadian Prairie cities.[35] This opened up territory in between for Woos, Choys, Chows, Gees, Dongs (aka Youngs), and Mas (aka Mah, Mar). Men such as Happy Young (from the Young/Dong clan) and Mark Ki (from the Ma clan), who came from less prominent families, could open rural washing shops, groceries, tea houses, and restaurants near those with shared clan and village ties and affections. This ensured that friends could provide essential mutual support during the long winter months or when the businesses needed extra assistance during curling bonspiels, church picnics, or sports days.

Happy and Mark had travelled east by the 1910s and acquired passable English. Participation in curling leagues, gun clubs, and fandom enabled them to integrate in their host country, with varying degrees of success. Lone Chinese settlers remained only in regions where they could establish good rapport with the local non-Chinese community and ties to other Chinese men. As I have outlined, these ties formed through visiting with clan members, itinerant missionaries, or non-Chinese clergymen, or with nationalists they met at political meetings, who came to see them on fundraising trips.

Mark Ki

Mark Ki (1883-1957) (Cantonese: Mark Sea Kee) had a wife (Cantonese: Mark Chin Ki), a son (Cantonese: Mark Kin Hoon, aka Bill), and a daughter (Ham Ham), all living in China.[36] But for most of his adult life, he lived apart from them in the Mennonite town of Morden, Manitoba. Morden is just thirty-five kilometres from the American border (by highway) and has always had a small number of Chinese men operating cafes, laundries, and tailor shops. Morden was attractive to the Prairie's earliest settlers not only because of its milder climate (in a region that research participants called the "apple belt") but also because it was located roughly 135 kilometres from Winnipeg, allowing for convenient periodic trips to the city. It is unknown when Mark came to Canada. What we do know is that, while based in Morden, he made regular trips to see friends and associates in Winnipeg and elsewhere. Every few years, he also returned to China to see his family. He was a merchant and nominal Christian.

In 1919, at the age of thirty-five, Mark Ki arrived in Morden to open a grocery.[37] Like many other Prairie bachelors, by the time he opened his business, he spoke very good English, having presumably worked his way across Canada or the United States before that. This was not a very welcoming year for Chinese residents of Morden. In December, for example, Charlie and Bill Dong were denied a hotel licence by Morden City Council. Morden's Dong clan already ran the town laundry.[38] The council defended its decision by stating that a hotel managed by the Dongs would not be suitable for the Morden general public. However, Mark Ki was able to open his grocery the same year.[39] The fact that Mark came to Morden in 1919 and left more than thirty years later in 1951 strongly suggests that he overcame the bigotry that had been an obstacle for others.

Within a few years, Morden also had a Chinese tailor shop, a laundry shop, and a Chinese cafe, initially also run by the Dongs, called the New York Cafe.[40] By 1925, it was clear that Mark Ki's grocery was run in partnership with so-called brothers. Most Chinese Prairie businesses, assumed to be operated by one individual, were actually operated, at least at first, with partners, and with the help of Chinese from the labouring class. These labourers almost always shared the shopkeeper's surname (i.e., Mark), spoke little English, and interacted only intermittently with townspeople.

Within just over a decade, in 1930, despite the Great Depression, Mark's success as a merchant enabled him to join the Morden gun club.[41] As he hunted for red fox and coyotes in the Prairie hinterland with non-Chinese patrons, his popularity soared. When he celebrated the arrival of King George VI and Queen Elizabeth in 1939, along with other merchants throughout the Prairies, his employees entered him in a grocery magazine contest for the best-decorated store window.[42] He won. A year later, Mark appeared to be a highly regarded member of the business community, representing the region at a late spring Retail Merchants' Association of Canada meeting.[43] He could never have flourished in Morden if he had not been recognized as one of Morden's citizens. In the words of Engin Isin, affiliation with the gun club had made Mark Ki a "citizen without frontiers."[44]

After 1923, Mark Ki and all men and women of Chinese descent who were residing in Canada were required by the Chinese Immigration Act to register with the government, and though as a resident of Manitoba he was able to hire "white" women and vote, he did not have full legal rights.[45] With merchant status, and by becoming a member of the gun club, however, he was able to pass through nationally, legally, and culturally imposed obstacles and enter into the realm of citizenship. In 1948, he received a citizenship award from the president of Morden's Kinsmen Club for years of good deeds in the community, including his payment of a long-time patron's hospital bill. The event honouring Mark was appropriately held in Morden's United Church lecture room, recognizing his affiliation not only with citizenship but also his weak ties to Christianity.[46] (Although Mark Ki was recognized for his interest in the Freemasons' Hospital, I found no evidence that Chinese had belonged to fraternal orders such as the Masons, the Orangemen, the Oddfellows, and the Rebekah Lodge.)[47] Mark's funeral was officiated by a Lutheran minister. Along with other members of the Winnipeg Chinese community, Mark was buried in the Chinese section of Winnipeg's Brookside Cemetery.[48]

Happy Young

Happy Young (1890-1956)came to Canada from the District of Toisan, China.[49] In 1918, he arrived in the Hungarian town of Esterhazy to take over Sam Dong's Canada Cafe, which had opened five years earlier, in 1913.[50] Esterhazy had been very welcoming toward Sam Dong, and it extended the same courtesy to Happy. Happy's Canada Cafe prospered as the town meeting place, frequented by businessmen who loved his steaks, and by families and children wanting his delicious apple pie, chocolate bars, and ice cream.[51] Happy had a wife and two children, a son and daughter, who lived in China. Like many Chinese men, however, he spent most of his life as a bachelor. When his family died during a 1940s Japanese bomb raid, the remainder of Happy's life was spent as a widower. Like Frank and Sam, he adjusted by becoming an uncle to Chinese and non-Chinese children. He formed strong friendships and became a beloved Chinese and Canadian citizen. Mark Ki and Happy were long-time popular and successful merchants in their respective towns, recognized at the end of their lives as favourite town citizens.[52]

Happy worked nearly all the time, allowing for little athletic involvement. His support for local teams, however, was legendary. Through fandom and sponsorship, he acquired considerable cultural capital.[53] His fan identity and community connections intensified as he travelled the same routes as fans and shared spaces with them on trains, buses, in ticket lines, in his seat, and during first- and second-period intermissions of hockey games. Through these related interactions, Happy and many other Chinese Canadian fans and sponsors came to have positive masculine and Western identities, and weak ties to hockey and Canada.

Happy sponsored the town hockey team, and he cared about the youth who served as soldiers in the war, to whom he sent regular care packages and letters.[54] His prize possessions, bequeathed to Moon Dong, his nephew

Figure 16 Happy Young in Canada Cafe window, Esterhazy, ca. 1930s.
Source: Moon Dong.

who joined him late in his life, included photographs of himself seated in the centre of Esterhazy's prize-winning junior hockey teams, which he had sponsored for three decades. When newspapers reported on the poor refereeing of a game, they asked Happy to comment: "Happy [was there] on Friday and says [our] boys would have won if he had refereed."[55] He was also an ardent supporter of the curling club and its annual bonspiel.[56]

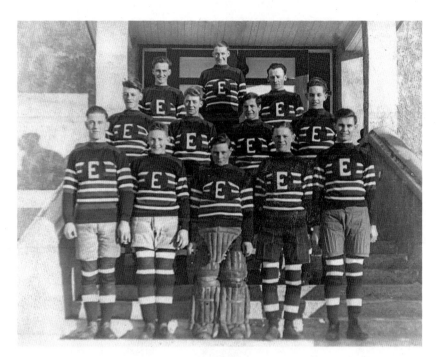

Figure 17   Happy Young's hockey team, Esterhazy, ca. 1940s. *Source:* Moon Dong.

Over the decades that Happy lived in Esterhazy, he established strong friendships with prominent local residents Dr. Christie, Reverend Jim Brown, and the Gardiners.[57] Like other Chinese men in Canada, Happy was part of a large Chinese network of friends, clan members, and associates all over North America. Once a month he took a brief leave from Esterhazy and travelled by car, not to Regina or Moose Jaw, which were relatively proximate, but to Brandon and Winnipeg, where he attended KMT meetings and associated with nationalist comrades. The waitresses looked after the cafe during these absences. Along the way, Happy visited with clan members and close friends Sam Dong and Jim Dong (d. 1973), Sam Wong, Charlie Foo, Frank Chan, Harry Chan, and countless others on the urban and rural Prairies. Jim Dong's granddaughter Lyn married Sam Wong's son Chuma, displaying the strong bonds of fictive kinship (relationships that took on kin-like status) and networking of Chinese Prairie Canadians.

Throughout the 1920s and 1930s, Happy Young became an increasingly integrated part of the small Esterhazy business community.[58] He contributed to local ladies' fundraisers that featured his Chinese cuisine and music.[59] And his business prospered, enabling him to renovate his cafe in 1934.[60]

When the war finally ended in 1945, Happy, now widowed, celebrated for his two nations. Children, now grown men, reminisced of Happy tossing candy and boxes of firecrackers to them from the cafe's second floor, where he had his bedroom. When Happy retired in 1950 after thirty-two years, the *Esterhazy Observer* reported: "This week Happy Young is leaving Esterhazy after spending thirty-two years of his life as a beloved citizen of this community."[61] As a Saskatchewan-based Chinese merchant, Happy did not have full legal rights. But to his patrons and friends, he had become a beloved citizen.

Happy died from a heart attack a few years later. His nephew, Moon Dong, arranged a simple funeral for Happy and his burial in the Brandon cemetery. For many years, Moon Dong, who moved to Winnipeg, maintained Happy's grave. As he aged, the yearly trip from Winnipeg to Brandon became too difficult, and he sent money to Brandon's Chinese community so that it could maintain the grave. When I completed this chapter, I thanked Happy by making offerings at his grave.

In this chapter, I have explored some of the processes and activities that reduced racism and enabled integration. Athletic involvements were historically relevant. They had economic and social benefits that enabled Chinese Canadian men to participate in the realms of dominant society, to belong and to transcend national and cultural boundaries of citizenship.

5 Married Nationalists: Charles Yee and Charlie Foo

For decades, the KMT, along with Christian organizations, had provided younger and older migrating males with necessary connections to Canada and China. In the paragraphs that follow, I focus on the centre of Chinese political Prairie life and nationalism in Winnipeg, recounting the history of nationalist groups there, and later the life stories of two of Winnipeg's leaders, Charles Yee and Charlie Foo.[1]

In 1950, Winnipeg was still the KMT Prairie headquarters, with a leadership dominated by men from the Au (Foo), Chan, Choy, Lee, Ma, Yee, and Wong clans and a provincial membership as high as 425.[2] Surviving evidence indicates that women had begun to join the Manitoba KMT only in the 1940s. Reporting to this main office were numerous KMT branches, including one in Regina whose membership between 1950 and 1951 was roughly sixty-five, including Yees (twenty-four) and Lees (nine).[3]

Winnipeg's KMT offered vital mutual support in a racist "white" world. I often heard that Winnipeg or Manitoban Chinese were more conservative than their BC brothers. Nationalists thrived there; anecdotal evidence suggests that more communist and left-leaning settlers fared less well. They either left the province or moved to rural areas where they existed on the periphery of life and culture, keeping their feelings for communism hidden. Once settled in the rural borderlands, they did not renew their nationalist memberships. Manitoba's earliest nationalist leaders belonged to the Lees and Wongs, who controlled leadership in other regions. After the 1920s, however, Winnipeg leadership was dominated by an Au (Charlie Au Foo) for almost two generations (until 1975). Today, Winnipeg's largest Chinese association, the WCCCC, is led not by a Lee, Wong, Ma, or Chan. It is led by Dr. Du, a Vietnamese Chinese Canadian.

Charles Yee (1887-1954)

Charles Yee was a one-year-old infant when his father and mother died from an unknown disease, leaving their only son in the care of paternal grandparents who were wine merchants in Toisan, China. Life in Canada would transform this lone orphan into a tough merchant Chinese national-ist, philanthropist, husband, and father.

Being relatively affluent, Charles's grandparents decided to send him, then a young teenager, to California to study engineering. He travelled to San Francisco, studied for a diploma in engineering, and was then called back to China because his grandfather had died. In 1901, Charles returned to North America, this time going to Vancouver under the sponsorship of an uncle who ran a Chinatown grocery store. He paid the head tax and was recorded in the General Register of Chinese Immigration as Yee Kee.[4] Over the next several years, Charles lived as a bachelor and worked hard to repay the money he had borrowed to come to Canada. For a time, he worked with his uncle in the grocery, one of Chinatown's more than sixty businesses at the time, and then the two opened a Vancouver popcorn factory, an enterprise that ultimately failed.[5] Later, Charles briefly returned to China, married, and started a family. The arc of his life shows a resilient, disciplined, and re-sourceful modern Western Chinese Canadian who developed strong ties and connections.

From Vancouver, Charles travelled to Moose Jaw, where he worked as a cook and lived with two other men named Yee: Yee Brown and Yee Wing.[6] By 1912, Charles had become active in the KMT, which was opening branches in Regina, Yorkton, North Battleford, Saskatoon, Brandon, and Winnipeg. Figure 18, which dates from that period, shows Charles Yee front and centre among a group of well-dressed men who have cut their traditional queues (braids), and are wearing formal suits and ties. Behind the group hang the two flags of the early Chinese republic – the five-barred flag and a blue flag with a light-coloured rectangle, inside of which is a white twelve-pointed star. The caption above the group reads: "A Photograph of the KMT Canada's Yorkton Comrades."

By 1918, Charles Yee had given up his share of the Moose Jaw business and moved to Davidson, Saskatchewan, a town located north of Moose Jaw and east of Yorkton.[7] As owner and operator of the Union Hotel and Cafe, he offered first-class meals as well as ice cream, soft drinks, candy, cigars, cigarettes, tobacco, and fresh fruit. The relationship between the Chinese and non-Chinese residents in Davidson was unusual. Many eastern Prairie towns had a succession of cafes opening around 1895, but docu-mentary evidence suggests there had been only one Chinese-owned and -operated cafe for five years before Charles arrived. It was called the Owl Cafe, which in 1921 was run by Jimmy Mee.[8] In the mid-1920s, proprietors

Figure 18 KMT Canada's Yorkton Comrades, 1912. *Source:* William Yee.

of the Owl Cafe hosted curling banquets.[9] In Davidson, Chinese athletic involvement as a sponsor, unlike in Esterhazy and Morden, did not seem to correlate with greater acceptance of Chinese by the community.

Like the many men who were forced to live as bachelors after the 1923 Chinese Immigration Act, Charles Yee, though married, was now also confined to life in bachelor society. Unfortunately, available documentary evidence up to August 1925 (when he left) suggests that he enjoyed little goodwill in Davidson. However, his connections to Chinese society were strong.

Being a devoted KMT member, Charles travelled to attend small monthly meetings of outposts in Moose Jaw or Yorkton. Although others in this small Chinese community returned to China every few years (presumably to visit their growing families who were unable to migrate), Charles is known to have gone only once from Davidson to Vancouver, in May 1925.[10] Most men who went to Vancouver were en route to China.

After seven years in business in Davidson, Charles decided to leave. In August 1925, the *Leader* reported that he had leased the Union Hotel and Cafe to Yee Wing, Yee Quinn, and Yee Foon.[11] He had gotten to know Yee

Wing when he lived with him in Moose Jaw in 1911. Unfortunately, the building burned to the ground in the early 1930s, and Charles lost his investment. Cafe and hotel fires were commonplace in this era, and many men lost their livelihoods through these tragic events.

Between 1925 and 1928, Charles worked his way across the eastern Prairies until he reached Roblin, Manitoba. In Roblin, he became the owner and operator of a cafe, bakery, and grocery. In Manitoba, unlike Saskatchewan, Chinese men were free to hire "white" waitresses and didn't need to apply for a licence. It was through this that Charles met his future wife, Pauline, who had immigrated to Canada from Ukraine at the age of four. When she was thirteen, her mother died while giving birth to a seventh child. A year later, Pauline left home to escape what had become, following her mother's death, a very hard life. She worked in Dauphin as a waitress and later came to Roblin at the age of seventeen, where she found employment in Yee's cafe. Even though he already had a wife and a daughter in China, he was free to marry Pauline in Manitoba.[12] It is unknown if Pauline (a Catholic) was aware that Charles was already married and had a child when she married him in 1929, and later when they had two children (Margaret in 1930 and William in 1931) in Roblin. But Pauline and her children certainly discovered this when Charles's daughter's son came to Winnipeg. As for Charles's wife in China, she and most wives accepted a husband's remarriage in Canada, though for them divorce and remarriage were taboo.

It was difficult to make a living in Roblin, and the family moved in 1932 to Winnipeg's May Street, located northwest of Chinatown. It was there that George, the couple's third child, was born in 1935. Eldest son William Yee explains that the Yees also adopted a child named Jimmy when he was only a few months old: "A cousin of my father, Fatty, gave Jimmy to us to look after. What relationship Jimmy was to Fatty is unknown but [he] may have been his son. Jimmy was the same age as I was and I loved him [as] more than a brother. Jimmy died at the age of ten of rheumatic fever. Jimmy will always be in my heart and memory."[13]

Family life and ties sustained Charles, and through them he established webs of connection to Chinese and non-Chinese society. In Winnipeg, he hit his stride with the Moon Cafe. As sole proprietor of this new venture, he became very successful by offering Ukrainian food to predominantly Ukrainian customers. Most of the time, Pauline did the cooking, preparing a delicious selection of *kartoplia solimkoi* (fried potatoes), *holubtsi* (cabbage rolls), pierogies, and jam-filled doughnuts. Charles, having worked in Prairie cafes for most of his Canadian life, baked an assortment of fine apple, raisin, lemon, and cream pies. The Moon Cafe became a prosperous business because of its food and the good feelings the broader community had for Charles and Pauline.[14] During the Depression, Charles offered free soup and bread to those who were hungry and could not afford to pay. But the cafe also became well known for other reasons.

The Moon Cafe at 177 Henry Street was in a bad neighbourhood. Charles had been robbed and assaulted outside of it in 1934 on his way home from work early one morning.[15] One Sunday afternoon eleven years later, a man was attacked outside of it and rushed to the hospital with a fractured skull.[16] Soldiers were not allowed to go there, because there were too many violent fights inside and outside the Moon Cafe.[17] Research participants told me that when Bob Hope was in Winnipeg once, he used the cafe in one of his jokes, describing how things got a little rough there.

Once the Moon Cafe was established, Charles opened State Cleaners on his own, and the National Hotel in partnership with Pauline's uncle. Uncle Bill, a favourite of the Yee children, helped him manage the business.

Charles was smart and determined, and he had to be. His efforts were focused on meeting practical needs and ensuring that his children received a good education so that they could succeed. Thus, aside from socializing with Yee clan friends from the Prairies and Ontario, including Fatty Yee, Jimmy Yee, and Skinny Yee, and the Yees from Thunder Bay, he did not spend much time at Winnipeg's Chinese gambling clubs or the Chinese Dramatic Society. And if there was a KMT or United Church banquet, picnic, or other event, he wasn't interested in going unless he could take his family. He had very little time for socializing, and the free time he did have was spent with them. He relished his life as a married family man.

Every weekend Charles took Margaret, William, and George to a Winnipeg Chinatown chop suey joint. Initially, they went to the Nanking. Later, they went to the Shanghai Restaurant.[18] When the kids were older, he hired a taxi on Sundays to take them to a park, where they had picnics and spent the day together. Every year, Charles took his family to the Chinese community Decoration Day, around Father's Day, to pay their respects to old Chinese friends buried at Brookside Cemetery. The custom was observed in the swampier part of the cemetery, where most of the Chinese were buried. People brought incense sticks and flowers and visited the graves.

Charles Yee paid his taxes, voted in all the elections (all Chinese naturalized citizens living in Manitoba could vote), and was always interested in what was happening in China. He bought buildings for his community in Toisan. And during the Second World War, he distinguished himself with an enormous contribution of ten thousand dollars to support the nationalist Chinese troops.[19]

Through his wife, Pauline, Charles also became connected to a large Ukrainian family and its traditions. Unlike Charles, who had no religion and who had never interacted with Chinese missionaries or lived in missions, Pauline was Catholic. The children became Catholic, took catechism classes, and went to confession. They also went to the KMT Chinese school on the weekends with the other kids from Chinatown. Their father's wealth and generosity to Chinese community fundraising campaigns ensured that the good feelings nationalists had for Charles included them.

Charles's life ended abruptly in 1954.[20] Six months before his death, he had been diagnosed with diabetes, and the family had assumed it was under control. One day, he suddenly needed to go to the hospital for treatment. He died three days later at the age of sixty-six or sixty-seven. The family was in shock.[21] Since Charles wasn't a Catholic, Jimmy Yee looked after the funeral, which was held at the KMT building. The hall was packed with loyal friends who came to say goodbye and hear the eulogies for Charles Yee, who had given so much to Chinese and Canadian communities during his two decades in Winnipeg and more than fifty years in Canada. Through the support and kindness of his wife, Pauline, and through his own hard work and alliances, he overcame the obstacles of poverty and bigotry to achieve success and ensure the success of his children.[22]

Charlie Foo (1894-1980)

The third son of a migrant worker, Charlie Foo was born on November 13, 1894, in an Au clan hamlet called East Lake (Dong Huli) in Hoiping, China.[23] Although he was an Au, he became known in English Canada by the name Foo, which was given to him on the General Register of Chinese Immigration when he came to Canada in 1919.[24] Charlie, like Charles Yee, first landed in Vancouver. Making his way to Winnipeg, he would make the transition from ordinary Chinese immigrant to nationally revered political leader, merchant, jazz club manager, husband, father, and citizen.[25]

People who knew Charlie in the Canadian Chinese community called him Mr. Foo (Au Xiansheng). A research participant explains: "It was always Mr. Foo. Basically people honoured him. There is no other explanation for it. People just did it. There was always a great deal of respect." As the Prairie affective regime's leader, Foo was a model Chinese gentleman who expected and earned respect and loyalty.[26]

When Charlie was three years old, his father, Au Jock, went to Hawaii, where he managed a large plantation and sent money home each month to cover the family's expenses. Au died there seven years later when Charlie was ten years old, leaving him, his mother, and his two brothers, as well as an adopted daughter, with Charlie's paternal grandparents. After the death of Charlie's father, the family survived on the remittances he had sent in the past and through the generosity of relatives. A family member adds: "Mrs. Au's brother always saw that when the harvest came in they got a sack of rice. He always saw that her children got food. My grandmother had a brother who was very caring." Kind maternal uncles figured prominently in all the period's stories told to me by Prairie Chinese settlers. Life could not have been easy for the Au family after that in China, and eventually all three boys left to become migrant workers. The adopted daughter immigrated to Canada a year before Charlie to marry a Chinese Canadian man (Sam Wong), but within two years she was dead. Charlie's mother died in the 1940s, during the war.

Charlie received a good education in China and was known to keep very careful personal and family records. Later, when he became a political leader in Manitoba, he was known for his neat calligraphy and accurate note keeping and files documenting the entire Prairie Chinese community. When he needed letters written in English, however, he asked his daughters to write them or had them typed.

Charlie arrived in Vancouver on March 8, 1919, and according to the immigration documents he used to travel, he came at the relatively older age of twenty-one (though he was actually three years older). At first he worked as a laundryman in Vancouver. Later, in Winnipeg, he opened a shop called Practical Tailors. His mother had been a fine seamstress in China and had educated the village girls in all sorts of needlework. It is possibly at her side that Charlie learned to operate a sewing machine.[27] He was drawn to Manitoba because his adopted sister had moved there, and he could develop connections through her and her husband, Sam Wong.

Like Charles Yee, Charlie was able to hire "white" women to work in his tailor shop because he lived in Manitoba. And so he, too, met his non-Chinese future wife, Frances Mary Victoria Phillips (d. 1992), when she came to work for him. In 1920, Frances had left England and her marriage, sailing to Canada with her young daughter, Pat. Frances impressed Charlie with her poise, fine needlework, and disposition. He fell in love with her

Figure 19 Twin Lakes, Manitoba, swimming and picnicking, ca. 1930s. Left to right: (front row) Charlie Foo, Fred Foo, Louis Pak Tong, Dick Lim, and Jack; (back row) Mrs. Frances Foo, Lily Foo, Pat Low, two unidentified men, and Wally Foo. *Source:* Helen Wong.

despite their differences in language, religion, and culture. Frances divorced her husband in England, and the two were married by an Anglican minister in early 1924. Charlie adopted Pat and showered her with affection. Helen was born later that year, followed by Fred, Wally, and Lily.

Frances and Charlie, at the request of good friend Frank Chan, also adopted a fifth child, Harold, whom they treated and raised as their own son. Harold was nine months younger than Wally and was the son of Frank's friend. The adoption was an informal one, and Harold's father, Mr. Ying, who owned a Winnipeg Chinatown restaurant, would periodically drop by the Foo house in north St. Vital with clothing for Harold.[28]

The Foo children grew up in the glow of their father's prominence in Prairie and Chinese Canadian society. They attended after-school and Saturday morning Mandarin classes taught by comrades at the KMT building. They also went to the Fox or Starland Theatres on Saturdays to see productions by the local Chinese Dramatic Society. Periodically, they would be treated to a performance that included their father in a cast of seven, wearing a long beard and a beautiful silk robe. In addition to seeing opera in the 1920s, 1930s, and 1940s, the Foo children enjoyed going to the annual nationalist picnics held in Winnipeg's parks.[29]

Foo family events always included bachelor uncles and friends whom Charlie met through nationalist involvements. Everyone was connected early on through the cult of Sun Yat-sen and later through devotion to nationalism and Chiang Kai-shek. On summer weekends, Charlie and Frances would take their children to Assiniboine Park or to a picnic spot along the Assiniboine River.[30]

Christmas holidays and Western New Year were big events in the Foo household. The family would be joined by a large community of nationalist gentlemen and bachelors. Bachelors Frank Chan, Sam Dong, and Happy Young were part of these gatherings. As one of Charlie's children remembers: "They were our uncles. It was a real community and those men didn't have families. They watched us grow up and got the sense of family from us. It was something that some of them really needed and it was great for us to have all those uncles around. There was a closeness to that." During Christmas holidays, there could be so many of these uncles visiting the Foo home that extra seating would be set up. They would have two dining tables, one in the front room and one in the dining room. For Charlie, it was community first, family second; he never missed a political meeting on Sunday.

In the late 1920s and following the 1929 stock market crash, Charlie's small tailor shop could not compete with larger ones. His family and others moved out of Winnipeg to work in and operate the hundreds of Prairie cafes beyond Chinatown. Drawing on his ample social capital built through years of Prairie nationalist leadership, Charlie soon heard about a cafe for sale in Plum Coulee, Manitoba. He bought it with partners and moved his family there for a year. Soon, however, he sold his share in the business, and he and his family returned to Winnipeg. He took a job as a salesman for Western Packers, a meat supplier to Chinese and non-Chinese Winnipeg restaurants. Being an innovator, he noticed that Chinese restaurants needed seafood, too, and so began selling that as well.

Charlie was a notorious nationalist and an admirer of Sun Yat-sen. As an Au, he belonged to one of the less dominant clans (i.e., not a Lee, Wong, Ma, or Chan) in the Chinese Canadian community. Although he helped many of his cousins and relatives to come to Winnipeg over the years, there were still comparatively few Aus in Manitoba, even by 1950. When Charlie was elected chairman of the Winnipeg KMT in 1925, he was seen to be independent from the most influential clans.

In the 1930s, under Charlie's leadership, Winnipeg's Chinatown clan groups, associations, and the KMT all moved into the Johnson Building on Pacific Avenue. At the time, there was a shift in the way that "white"

Winnipeggers perceived the Chinese community. In 1930 a *Manitoba Free Press* report of Chinatown, Chinese men were depicted as subhuman thugs and gang members:

> It was shortly before midnight that five members of the Nationalist league strolled down King Street in the heart of Chinatown. Nearly 30 other Orientals, members of an opposing group, lurked in the darkness, armed with axes and heavy clubs. Suddenly, with wild, high pitched screams, they sprang from their hiding places, set upon their rivals and beat them unmercifully.
>
> Axes swung dangerously, baseball bats crashed against human skulls and the Chinese, maddened with rage, fought like tigers, kicking, biting, slashing, and battering, with no thought to life or limb. From all sections of Chinatown, further warriors, attracted by the din, rushed to the scene and joined in the fray. As fast as police tore them apart, they would clash again and resume hostilities the moment the backs of the officers were turned.[31]

Winnipeg's Chinatown, if one is to believe this racialized and cartoon-like account, was a violent, dangerous place filled with Chinese "barbarians" who battled for control of gambling dens during the year following the crash of the stock market.[32] It was true that there were Chinese gangs in Winnipeg. These were clan-based factions that vied for power in Canadian Chinatowns. There were also politically based factions. From the beginning in Winnipeg, the Chinese nationalists were in control, though it had been the CKT who arranged for the visit of Sun Yat-sen to the city in 1911. But after Sun Yat-sen visited in April that year, the KMT ascended in power, and the CKT dwindled.

Many men gambled before or after political meetings in Chinatown. Gambling was a serious part of some bachelor lives, either as owners or part-owners of gambling dens or as addicts. There were ample opportunities to join partnerships and open businesses in conjunction with cafes to serve the men who wished to play fan tan, paigow, chuck a luck, or mahjong on the weekends.

For most, however, surviving life on the Prairies was already a game of chance. Long-term gamblers moved on or died. Presbyterians, Methodists, and, after 1925, United Church ministers and missionaries focused on gambling as a clearly defined vice.

But nationalism, the Depression, and Charlie's strong leadership changed Chinatown. By 1935, assisted by Frank Chan and other prominent Chinese men, he had forged strong connections with the broader non-Chinese community. He didn't encounter much opposition from other power brokers in the city. He was held in high regard. Nor did he face much rivalry from his few clan members who were attracted to Winnipeg through his efforts. When KMT dignitaries arrived from Vancouver, Montreal, or China, Charlie was there to greet the crowd of well-dressed businessmen and entertain them. Heeding main branch propaganda and training strategies for educating members and the public, he and others gave talks to students at the University of Manitoba on nationalism and Chinese culture. Along with Frank Chan, then party affairs commissioner, Charlie explained to students the aims of the KMT and why the party needed donations.[33] He also visited colleagues, from Nanaimo to Montreal.

When asked by Charlie to donate to various nationalist military campaigns in China, Chinese Prairie nationalists gave generously. As donations flowed from coast to Prairie, and from north and south to Winnipeg, various intersecting nodes within nationalist Prairie systems developed. One research participant said, "People respected Mr. Foo and he really deserved and needed that respect. I think money came far, far second to him. Respect was right up there. He loved meeting people who were influential. Influential people were more important to him so that he could take care of his people. He had a great need to do that." Some Chinese Canadians, like Charles Yee, became rich merchants with ties to Chinese and non-Chinese society. Charlie Foo's wealth was measured by amity rather than monetary status.

Sun Yat-sen was the catalyst for the development of Prairie nationalism. But it took Chiang Kai-shek as the military general and leader of the KMT to refocus the men's gaze back on China and Japanese aggression, first in 1931 through invasion of the northeastern province of Manchuria and then six years later. The Marco Polo Bridge Incident on July 7, 1937, marks the beginning of the Japanese war with China. During the incident (in Wanping, near Beijing), a small number of Japanese troops and the KMT shot at each other. The war became the catalyst for renaming KMT organizations the Chinese Patriotic League (CPL) that same year.[34] Charlie Foo was the league's president. Local, national, and international fundraising campaigns and KMT propaganda became more aggressive after 1937.[35]

The *Winnipeg Free Press* reported:

Called in special session to review events in the Far East which have thrown their country into a life and death struggle with Japan, meetings of the Chinese Patriotic League and the local branch of the Kuo Min Tang [KMT], attended by the entire Winnipeg Chinese population, were held Sunday at the league headquarters, 209 Pacific Avenue. A complete spirit of unity among all local Chinese organizations and a readiness to do all in their power to aid their homeland, were the keynotes of the meetings. While as yet no appeals from China for financial assistance have been received; a committee in [the] charge of Charlie Foo and W.J. Yuk, key men in the Winnipeg Kuo Min Tang, was named to receive funds to assist homeless civilians and wounded soldiers in the battle-scarred war areas. Four teams each with four men will begin systematic campaign in cash and kind, next Friday. Similar action is being taken in all cities in Canada and the United States, with Canadian headquarters at Vancouver, BC. A resolution seeking confirmation of a recent press dispatch in which it was stated the Kuo Min Tang government wanted all Chinese aviators resident overseas to join the air force was passed and will be sent immediately to China. Another resolution pledging wholehearted support of the local branch, requesting latest news from the front and particularly urging information on the numbers left homeless by the war, will also be forwarded. In addition, the Winnipeg Kuo Min Tang has undertaken to assist financially any local Chinese who desire to return home to join the air force or army, or assist in any other capacity. To date, no such applications have been received, officials stated.[36]

In December 1937, Charlie met with leaders of the non-Chinese labour community and raised more than $360 in donations. Acting as the lead nationalist in the province and in accordance with nationalist propaganda, he encouraged the group to boycott Japanese-made goods.[37] Chinese groups throughout overseas communities did the same. During the next six years of fundraising for war relief, Chinese restaurants were asked to donate a day's earnings. Women's organizations held rummage sales and requested in-kind donations of knitting and clothing. Charlie, along with Frank Chan, Wong Yuk, and other brokers, ran multiple fundraising drives that solicited donations from party members in Winnipeg and beyond in rural Canada. These campaigns were to assist the wounded, sick, and families of the dead in China. After the war ended, groups continued to support nationalist soldiers in China who were fighting against the communists. The lieutenant governor of Manitoba had an open house, and sports teams held events to raise money.[38] Similar community campaigns were led by the local Chinese men who ran cafes or groceries throughout the rural Prairies.

On Nationalist Day 1939, the CPL coordinated the branches' fundraising activities and invited the community through a message placed in the *Winnipeg Tribune* to join it in a celebration of the republic.[39] The ad was written in both Chinese and English. It was a rare and bold act for the community to use its own language in a Western newspaper. It was even rarer for it to invoke racist stereotypes to refer to Chinese and the Japanese in public advertisements, which it did four years later. The Chinese community now enjoyed strong support from mainstream society, now its ally in war and in Canada. It could afford to be bold. August 11th's advertisement advised: "We've got a Chinaman's Chance. Let's take it."[40] Three days later a new one had the headline: "Blot out Jap infamy. Give help to China."[41] During this and other campaigns for donations to the war-relief fund, writers emphasized the need for liberty amid the suffering of Chinese who were imperiled by the ravages of Japanese aggression.

Until the early 1950s, Charlie continued to be an active leader of the CPL and an organizer of picnics, banquets, and other events for China War Relief, the Chinese Community Chest, and the Chinese fund.[42] In 1944, for instance, he organized a benefit performance of an opera about Emperor Ming to assist the Navy League. The performance was attended by five hundred people.[43] Charlie also organized book drives for the Manitoban Chinese community, which became so popular, that he once ran out of books.[44]

The bombing of Pearl Harbor on December 7, 1941, mobilized Manitoba Chinese and non-Chinese communities to work closely together. Charlie, acting on behalf of the CBA, issued a press release to announce a badge campaign that would symbolically unite China and Canada as allies against the Japanese. Wearing a badge was also a way for Chinese to announce to would-be assailants that they were not Japanese. In Foo's bold remarks, prepared by his lawyers and read out at the press conference, he noted: "We are all fighting in common cause as brothers in arms ... We salute our flags and we pledge our undying faith in the noble cause for which they fly."[45]

By 1943, the Manitoba headquarters of the Chinese War Relief Fund, whose creation had been authorized by the War Charities Act, included honorary patrons, such as the premier, chief justice, and lieutenant governor of Manitoba. Those listed as patrons included a similarly distinguished group of Christian ministers, a rabbi, Manitoba mayors, the editor of the *Winnipeg Free Press*, and other dignitaries. The executive committee comprised a judge, the chief of police, and prominent Winnipeg lawyers and businessmen. In the end, the relief fund raised a total of $124,000.[46] The success of the Chinese War Relief Fund was proof that Chinese had been welcomed and accepted by non-Chinese in Winnipeg and Manitoba.

Charlie Foo, acting as an agent of the Winnipeg Chinese community and the CBA, went to Ottawa thirteen times during his life. Most of these visits to the nation's capital were to lobby for the repeal of the Chinese Immigration Act, which occurred in 1947 and has been attributed in part to the efforts of Madame Chiang Kai-shek. For many men, the repeal came far too late. Vaughan Baird tells of a conversation with long-time Prairie bachelor uncle Sam Dong after 1947. He wanted Sam to bring his wife to Canada: "I said, 'Sam, we can bring your wife over.' And Sam showed no surprise or emotion. I asked, 'Sam, aren't you excited?' He replied, 'No, she's too old now.' And he had a very glum look on his face." Sam died before he had a chance to be reunited with his wife.

After 1949, when the nationalists had been defeated in the civil war against the communists, Charlie continued to bow to the portrait of Sun Yat-sen in the KMT clubhouse before meetings and at other times. One Chinese community elder remembers that once, a KMT member came to the clubhouse and announced to Charlie that he was visiting China, not Taiwan, where the KMT had fled. The cult of Sun Yat-sen had not died out, and Charlie, upon hearing this, turned his head toward the portrait of Sun Yat-sen that had always hung on the wall. With his head lowered, Charlie bowed and then apologized to Sun for this member's transgression. Until 1975, when he moved to Vancouver, Charlie Foo held executive positions in the KMT, CPL, and CBA as chairman, vice-chairman, overseas party commissioner, and in many other roles.[47] The overseas party commissioner was a very high-ranking position that was offered to loyal party elders. Charlie reported directly to the nationalist government.[48] In 1952, once the KMT had fled to Taiwan, and after his good friend and comrade Frank Chan had died, Charlie was part of the overseas Chinese branch.[49] Figure 20 shows Canadian members meeting with Chiang Kai-shek in Taiwan. Charlie is on the far right, seated in the first row. Chiang Kai-shek is in the centre.

Charlie Foo was known to every person whom I interviewed in the course of my research. Often when I collected photographs from families who had lived in rural parts of Manitoba or Saskatchewan, he was in them.

In 1945, he became a partner in Chan's Cafe at 426 Main Street with Harry Chan (1895-2001), Wing Chan, and Jim Chan (the chef).[50] Twelve years later, the third-floor Moon Room opened and showcased nightly performers from the Chicago and Minnesota jazz circuit.[51] Chan's Moon Room became one of the first integrated nightclubs in the region, where people of all colours were welcome.

In 1974, the cafe was sold, and the following year Charlie and his wife moved to Vancouver, where they retired. At the age of eighty-five, he died on May 25, 1980, in Vancouver. A service was held at the CBA hall, and

Figure 20   Charlie Foo (seated), far right) at a meeting with Chiang Kai-shek (centre), Taipei, Taiwan, ca. 1952. *Source:* Manitoba KMT.

donations were requested to be sent there in his memory. An article about Charlie in the *Winnipeg Free Press* referred to him as the "unofficial Mayor of Winnipeg's Chinatown."[52]

Charles Yee and Charlie Foo lived at the centre of rural and urban Chinese Canadian society. Attractive, well liked, and married to Ukrainian and British women, respectively, they had strong nationalist ties. They also had connections to non-Chinese communities. Foo and others depended on their labouring brothers for votes to elect them to top executive positions and for smaller donations to display their different loyalties and affections in nationalist networks. The labourers depended on them, too. Nationalist affective regimes began to disintegrate once the communists came to power in China, and by 1950 the battle had started for control of Canadian territory. After the 1950s, and once the Chinese Communist Party took over as the ruling

Figure 21 Chan's Cafe banquet, Winnipeg, December 1961. Standing at back (left to right): Unknown man, Jim and Betty Ward (née Chan), Frances and Charlie Foo, Wing Chan, Harry and Mary Chan, and unidentified couple. Front and centre: Roy Petty, jazz performer, and date, sitting at the KMT table with Louis Paktong and others. Right side: Bernie Shaw Trio members with dates. *Source:* Barry Chan.

party in China, Chinese Canadian KMT leaders and groups burned their KMT memorabilia, removed photographs from walls, and destroyed evidence of affiliation and membership. On fieldwork trips from Nanaimo to Montreal, I heard the same thing. Fearing a communist backlash, KMT leaders torched the documents and files in their possession. But Winnipeg's Charlie Foo (and many other Prairie Chinese) never did.[53] Conversations with early Chinese Canadian settlers in Manitoba suggest that he was a staunch traditionalist and believer in documenting and preserving the past. Charlie was largely responsible for preserving the history and legacy of the Manitoba and Prairie KMT – vital threads of the Chinese affective fabric.

6 Women beyond the Frame

In the next four chapters, I focus on women. I move out of the symbolic centre of Prairie Chinese power inhabited by powerful married men, affable bachelor uncles, interpreters, and travelling salesmen. I shift my attention away from scrapbooks, newspaper articles, diaries, letters, speeches, and political, dramatic, and Christian association membership rosters that document male involvements and ties. Instead, I focus on oral histories, fieldwork, collected handicrafts, and other items often resorted to only when the valuable material of written texts is unavailable. These materials vividly reveal women's affect and domestic and religious ties. Narrative accounts gathered over time and across Canada were accurate. Research participants corrected the names, dates, and places in documentary material I had found in archives. Narrative accounts were further enriched and expanded by photographs, recordings of a grandmother's voice, embroidery, and religious paraphernalia that I discovered or that was shared with me during ethnographic research. Accounts corroborated each other, enabling events, people, and facts in life stories to take shape and overcome perceived memory fallibility.[1] Looking into the shadows of Chinese Canadian life, I combine this interdisciplinary approach with intersectional analysis to research and write about women.[2] Early Chinese Prairie women led mostly quiet, hidden lives. Their experiences have remained largely undocumented.[3]

During the research for this book, I collected information about twenty-eight women, the wives or daughters of Chinese men, who were born between 1875 and 1944 in China or Canada. It was not easy to find twenty-eight women for whom I had enough information. It was similarly difficult to obtain permission to have some of their life stories revealed in this book. Half of the women in this study lived in Winnipeg, and half lived beyond Winnipeg in rural Manitoba (five), Regina (six), or rural Saskatchewan (three). The information was gathered during interviews with children born in the 1910s, 1920s, and 1930s, and a few grandchildren of Chinese Canadians who at one point had lived on the Prairies.

Chinese women and men sailed from Hong Kong to Vancouver or Victoria, a voyage that took about four weeks. If they arrived in Vancouver, they disembarked and reported to the immigration hall, where (after 1903 and if they did not have merchant or other special status) they had to pay the head tax of five hundred dollars. They were subjected to medical examinations and had to have their hearing and vision checked. A clerk would examine their papers, compare their appearance to their immigration photograph, and note (after 1910) their intended final Canadian destination on the General Register of Chinese Immigration.[4] From there, they would be corralled into the CPR detention hall and sometimes detained. This experience could be particularly traumatic and life changing for women.

In Victoria, some early Chinese women were detained for hours, days, or weeks in what family members described as the immigration "prison."[5] Although it was considered acceptable for non-English-speaking Chinese women to be held there for long periods, it was seen as an unacceptable hardship for women and children of European origin to "wait in the Canadian Pacific or Canadian National station all day."[6] Railway immigrant halls and prisons were potent reminders that Canadian rights and privileges were graded by gender and race.

Detainment was followed by a long journey in a third-class "Colony" rail car to what was often a small Prairie town. A Chinese Canadian female passenger would probably have been the only woman of her own ethnicity riding on the train. The railway in some ways remained a "white" British space of the Canadian state, where Chinese could be seen as heathen prostitutes if female and bachelor opium-smoking "Chinamen" if male.[7] Conductress reports and other accounts of Chinese on board trains until the 1920s and 1930s often referred to large "herd-like" numbers of Chinese passengers with disparaging and racialized language that was dehumanizing.[8] Special cargoes of Chinese on board trains were a threat.

Owing to sixty-two years of institutionalized racism, traditional values, and the requirement to pay the head tax of five hundred dollars after 1903, there were very few Chinese women in Prairie Canada. Many families in China could afford to send only their second son, who was usually judged to be the best family representative (after the first-born heir) and the most able to thrive as a migrant. Tradition was also a factor in wives and families remaining in China.[9] As a result, by 1911, Prairie cities such as Winnipeg and Regina had only a handful of Chinese women.[10]

These women were largely unknown creatures. Unlike their husbands, who worked outside the home in laundries or cafes, learned English, and had the chance to mingle with dominant society, Chinese women were isolated. They were an enigma to "white" society. Moreover, Canadians who had any inkling about Chinese women in Canada generally associated them with British Columbia missionary rescue homes for prostitutes and slaves.[11] Although there were Chinese prostitutes or slaves in that province – roughly seventy of them in 1885 British Columbia – the number had dropped greatly by the turn of the century.[12] Interviews with early Chinese Prairie settlers suggest that among the handful of first families who settled in Winnipeg, Regina, or Moose Jaw, none had Chinese slaves, concubines, or maids.[13]

The Women's Missionary Society opened the first Chinese Rescue Home in Victoria in 1887. Its function was to rescue and domesticate Chinese women who were assumed to be slaves or prostitutes.[14] Marilyn Whiteley explains, "Christian missionaries of the Chinese Rescue Home were also cultural missionaries. They took upon themselves ... the imperial task of civilizing, as well as evangelizing, the residents. They aspired to lift the girls not only from sin, but also from the habits that respectable 'white' women saw as common to those of the girls' race and class."[15] The very existence of missionary-run rescue homes perpetuated false stereotypes (and negative affect) that Chinese women were sinful beings.

In late nineteenth-century Victorian Canada, evangelical Christians who aimed to convert Chinese newcomers were overwhelmingly "white" and of British heritage. Individuals within Christian institutions sometimes differed with and even challenged church and Dominion of Canada policies that made Chinese integration impossible until after 1947.[16]

My research demonstrates that the Presbyterian, Methodist, and United Churches were among the most accepting of Chinese newcomers in their small Prairie communities. Missionaries may have hoped their efforts would break down racial and ethnic barriers. They wanted to help immigrants assimilate to British culture, as well as be saved. But ethnohistorical research shows that rescue and other missionary facilities, however well intentioned, reinforced the perception among mainstream Canadians that Chinese women had loose morals. Chinese women were made aware of this perception and stereotyping as soon as they arrived in Canada.

According to the General Register of Chinese Immigration, fewer than twenty Chinese wives (born in China or Canada) resided with their husbands in either Saskatchewan or Manitoba before 1920.[17] Gender, racism, nationalism, and traditional Chinese values determined different levels of "free emotional expression" and "access to specific realms of Chinese and non-

Chinese dominant society."[18] The absence of women (and families) for decades in areas populated by thousands of Chinese men strengthened connections to nationalism and the cult of Sun Yat-sen.

By 1921, sixteen females, only two of them girls, had indicated Saskatchewan as their destination on the General Register of Chinese Immigration.[19] In addition to Chinese-born wives and girls in Saskatchewan, I heard about a few Canadian-born Chinese women who married and joined husbands in the province. The number of women staying on the Prairies was unstable. Within the next decade, some of these women had moved to other provinces, returned to China, or died giving birth. In the course of my research, I heard about three Chinese women in Manitoba alone who died during childbirth between 1913 and 1929.[20] Although this number seems low, consider that by 1920 there were still fewer than ten Chinese Canadian wives resident in Manitoba. Maternal death was a serious risk for all Prairie Chinese women, whether of high or low standing, urban or rural, because they had difficulty accessing midwives who spoke their language and were familiar with their birthing customs.

In some ways, life in Canada was better than that back home. A wife didn't have to reside in her husband's home village, as in China, but in Canada she usually had to live in a place where everyone knew and admired her husband and viewed her as alien or exotic. She may not have had to please a demanding mother-in-law and sister-in-law, who would have been central to her social circle in China. She did have to live with other challenges, including the traditional expectation that she would give her husband an heir and first-born son and continue to fill the home with children.

Most Chinese women did not speak any English when they arrived. Once they landed, they became pregnant and raised children. They lived above cafes that were isolated from other homes. In most cases, interactions with broader society were rare and fractured, given language and cultural barriers. Women came to depend entirely on their husbands and the non-Chinese Christian midwives and nurses who helped them through their often yearly pregnancies and sometimes their stillbirths and miscarriages.[21]

Moose Jaw had more Chinese residents than other small Prairie cities, yet the size of a settlement didn't always determine the likelihood of Chinese wives living there. Smaller cities such as Brandon, Manitoba, had no Chinese women at all until 1918.[22] Regina had three Chinese women by 1920, but Moose Jaw had only two, who had arrived in 1922 to join their husbands.[23] These towns, either because of the predominance of low-paid jobs and racism

(Moose Jaw) or because of isolation from Winnipeg (Brandon), appeared to be more predisposed to a bachelor society. Kinship ties, relationships with non-Chinese businessmen and Christians, proximity to the border, and wealth – either earned in Canada or brought there – determined whether a man was able to become a naturalized citizen and apply for head-tax exemption as a merchant, in order to bring a wife to Canada. Among the cities and small towns examined on the eastern Prairies, Winnipeg had the largest women's community. In Saskatchewan, the absence of established structures and elders did not help the small number of women to integrate.

On the whole, life was very difficult for the widely dispersed Chinese women who lived beyond coastal areas of Chinese settlement. Unlike in Vancouver, Victoria, or Nanaimo, there was no Chinese woman next door with whom they could establish rapport while hanging out the laundry. And there were seldom enough women for a game of mahjong or any other sustained social activity or interaction, at least before 1947. Chinese women adjusted to life in Canada, loneliness, and alienation outside larger coastal communities, but they were not happy or fondly regarded. To say that women who lived under the harsh conditions of cold Prairie life were miserable would not be an overstatement. Most husbands had lived in Canada for years. As bachelors, they had become attached to networks of friends and business associates. Women, once they arrived, were bound by native traditions that their husbands enforced and with which they sometimes disagreed. Some women who were fortunate enough to have social lives and to be active in a women's community did so only after they had raised their families or their husbands had died.

Unlike their husbands, who were almost always members of the KMT, women couldn't become members until the 1940s.[24] Donations to the party, the purchase of bonds and certificates, and awards that were issued to faithful party members were all in the names of husbands, even if the women had personally contributed. When trips were made by nationalist leaders from Manitoba to Saskatchewan, Ontario, and Vancouver, they were made entirely in the company of men and sons. Girls and women weren't allowed (or rather, paid) to come. On these junkets the men stayed up late into the night at dining room tables, organizing fundraising events and discussing nationalism and ways to eliminate communist threats to it. They crafted strategies to pressure the government to repeal the Chinese Immigration Act or to end general infringements on Chinese human rights in Canada. Women were not permitted to share in this powerful fellowship.

Fathers and grandfathers, though good and loving men, sacrificed to serve the broader Chinese community, and wives often bore the burden. According to the children I interviewed, Prairie Chinese husbands had abounding affection for their wives.[25] But as much as women were cherished in the family, it was made clear to many that they could not attend most community events.[26] Women took care of their children and families, hoping that if they survived this period of intense detachment, better times would come.

Nationalism was better for men than women in China and in overseas communities. Sun Yat-sen was regarded as the father of modern China – a republic where all ideally had the right to vote. But voting and citizen rights were gendered. By 1920, women in China were still unable to vote.[27] In Canada, most Chinese women did not have the right to vote until after 1948.[28] During the republican era, nationalist values replaced family ones. A father's ties and loyalties were now shared with the state. The male citizenry, though sovereign, accepted new systems of power. Men had to submit to power brokers (not emperors) and to Sun Yat-sen and Chiang Kai-shek, who were more suited to govern.[29] In this new nationalist scenario, traditional family roles, the expectation of Confucian loyalty to the family, and filial respect for parents and grandparents were ideally to be replaced by loyalty to party elders, the Chinese Canadian community, and to Sun Yat-sen.

On the whole, Chinese Canadian women tended to be more religious than men. As I hope to show, this was in part due to the women's community and network of connections that came through religious (Christian, Daoist, and Buddhist) interactions in Canada. Half of the women I interviewed became baptized Christians, and the other half were nominally Christian, which meant that they had Christian ministers officiate at their weddings or funerals and that they professed a Christian identity in public.

Only three of these women had completed a year or more of university, and another three had attended a technical school. The earliest college attendee, Hong Lin, had been to an Anglican Chinese Christian college in 1900. She had been trained as a modern nurse and as a more traditional midwife. Once in Canada, whether a woman worked outside the home or alongside her husband in the family business was determined by the husband's wealth and adherence to Chinese tradition. Wealthier, more traditional husbands wanted their wives to live strictly domestic lives. As one interviewee noted, "Grandfather would not have had her work. She had no English ... and they started their family just about as soon as she arrived. And then she was busy with child rearing." Ukrainian, French, and British

Figure 22   Chinese family mission picnic, Winnipeg, ca. 1918. *Source:* Jacque Mar.

wives were not bound by the same rules. They were usually Christian, not Confucian. Within Chinese Canadian communities, families were identified in terms of those who were purely Chinese and those who were mixed-race Chinese. Although mixed-race Chinese families were headed by KMT leaders and often possessed the most power in a community, pure-race families were seen to be superior, according to tradition.

After 1947, wives, daughters, and sons arrived in Canada and joined husbands and fathers who had been estranged from them for decades. Life at this point improved for all Prairie Chinese women. Marriages continued to be arranged on the Prairies, as Seth, who was raised as a Buddhist, notes, "My wife and I had met because our fathers were friends. She had lived with her family in a small town in Alberta that had 200 people and where her father had operated a cafe." Two of the wives in this study were raised in British Columbia. Girls raised in British Columbia came to the Prairies with good English skills that were very useful to husbands. Usually, these girls had received a Christian upbringing.[30] The remainder of wives had come to the Prairies from China, Quebec, England, or Ukraine. Often, the brides who came from China before 1920 had received little education and were not proficient readers or writers in Chinese, let alone English. Without an education, it was difficult for a woman to maintain direct ties to her family living elsewhere.

At least one-quarter of the women cared for adopted Chinese or mixed-race children. These families took in children who were sick and miserable in orphanages or languishing in the family home of their "white," unmarried mothers. Most of the time, adoptions were informal ones, with payment required in exchange for boys. Girls were freely given to anybody who was willing to take them. Sometimes payments were a lump sum, and in other cases they were intermittent. Fathers visited periodically at best, and when they had money, they gave it. Birth mothers vanished and were never mentioned in the telling of stories to me. All of the adopted children, I was told, were treated no differently than the Chinese family's biological children; children enjoyed loving ties with adoptive mothers and fathers. In my discussions, there was no evidence that the women resented raising the additional children. On the contrary, I heard repeatedly from several research participants that mothers and siblings cherished these new additions to the family. Adopted children were given university educations when there was money for that, though sons usually received the education. I never heard of a single Chinese Canadian adopted child who was treated as a slave or maid. Children, both adopted and Canadian-born, became in the words of Karen Dubinsky, "symbolic children cross[ing] geographic borders, political spectrums and historical eras."[31]

Two of the adopted boys died before the age of twenty. One drowned and the other died from typhoid fever. Two other adopted boys became estranged from their adoptive families in adulthood and spent their careers in both the Canadian and the Chinese nationalist army.[32] Their families expressed good feelings about these boys through references to their loyalty, bi-national citizenship, and patriotism.

Belonging or not belonging to key organizations determined power, difference, the strength of affective bonds, and degrees of exploitation and exclusion by mainstream Chinese and non-Chinese. Racism was not a topic that interview subjects discussed easily. Stories about violent racist acts and general discrimination, if mentioned at all, came after the third or fourth conversation and sometimes several years after. Racism was discussed at the farthest reaches of, in the words of Erving Goffman, the backstage.[33] In public, most Prairie Chinese said that they expected but did not dwell on discrimination. Helen Wong, the eldest daughter of Winnipeg leader Charlie Foo, now in her late eighties, remarks, "Racism was not something you concentrated on. You just took what came." Parents worked hard to shield their children from racist acts by developing their own affective bonds to Chinese and non-Chinese leaders and by taking on roles that led to greater social mobility and power.

Between 1912 and 1920, nationalists worked with Christian missionaries and ministers (both Chinese and non-Chinese) in the Canadian network-building project. The two groups appeared to co-host events where nationalist fundraising took place, and most nationalists took on a public or nominal Christian identity, while continuing to practise traditional customs in private. Leaders in the 1930s and 1940s used social connections and affections to anchor themselves to the centre and maintain difference from the margins. Their daughters benefitted from this, as the story of Mamie and Katie Yee in Chapter 9 shows.

One of the most significant modes in which social boundaries were maintained and regulated by dominant male Chinese society was through the annual grave custom. Performed only by men until after 1950, this custom reinvented traditions and used offerings to celebrate and demarcate the boundaries of early Chinese Prairie nationalist society. Early labouring male ancestors who wore pigtails and tunics were recognized, as were more modern merchant nationalist leaders. New grave customs shifted the understanding of ancestral ties away from the family and toward the nationalist community, with Sun Yat-sen as father and chief deity. As Confucian identity, beliefs, and practices moved front stage, non-Confucian ones moved backstage. In addition to reinventing Chinese customs, nationalists in Canada adapted traditional forms of observational apparatus and propaganda to control and regulate Chinese Canadian life.

By the 1930s, several men who were active in the KMT were married to non-Chinese women, displaying a trend among the elite to encourage the integration of leaders into the non-Chinese economic, political, and social fabric. Active KMT members and donors Charles Yee (owner of the Moon Cafe) and Harry Chan (owner of Chan's Cafe) were married to Ukrainian women. Wong Yuk, secretary of the KMT and a merchant, was married to a woman of South American descent. Charlie Foo, a merchant, was married to Frances, who was of British descent. Being married to a non-Chinese woman offered a chance at family life, as well as English skills that could, so to speak, be learned "on the pillow." Mixed marriage provided access to someone who could help draft Chinese community press releases, speeches for banquets, picnics, and universities, or communications with diplomats. It could also be used to become closer to "whiteness" and Canadian society.

The experiences of Chinese Canadian merchant and labouring classes, as well as women, varied greatly on the Prairies. Labourers, ministers, and women lacked the power that came with belonging to affective regimes.

Despite the claims of Western affective theory, women had negative emotional associations.[34] I repeatedly heard stories about the loyalty, honour, charisma, and goodness of male bachelors who "made it," but I never heard the same about women, though men needed women not only for companionship but for status as a husband, father, and family man. In the 1930s, Mr. Howard (aka How Min Yet; Hou Minyi) was one such bachelor.

He lived at 529 Gore Avenue in Vancouver's Chinatown. This was the address of the KMT office and dormitory. Although Howard enjoyed a high-ranking position within the Canadian KMT, he paid ten dollars to the Robe Cross Dance School at 518 West Hastings Street for dance lessons and presumably companionship.[35] He also received a non-transferable ticket for ten private ballroom dancing classes and presumably etiquette skills he might need as an executive member of the KMT.[36] One research participant's comments summed up what was often said to me about these powerful, companionless Chinese men, many of whom lived entire lives apart from wives and families: "Most Chinese men living apart from wives had girlfriends." These girlfriends were often Ukrainian waitresses who worked in their restaurants, or restaurants frequented by the bachelor society. Some of them, as mentioned earlier, became wives.

As we've seen so far, many Chinese Canadian men earned the affections of non-dominant society through their political involvements and status; others did so through food. Bachelor cafe owners were warmly regarded by local children, who later reminisced about their raisin pies. The children of men who were fortunate to enjoy family life in Canada also remembered them through the good food they made such as lemon snow pudding or bird's nest soup. I never heard the same description of racialized Chinese women. People who grew up in towns with a cafe seldom saw them. Family members didn't remember much about them. Children grew up hearing about a father or grandfather's heroism – his work, sacrifices, success, and Chinese and Canadian contributions. Framed awards and letters hung on the wall, attesting to the greatness of these men. Stories of women in the period 1903-50, told to me by daughters, sons, nieces, nephews, and grandchildren, were almost always negative. Sometimes daughters-in-law and granddaughters sympathized with the elder members of their uterine family and understood the reasons for a woman's unhappiness in Canada, such as being sold as a young girl to pay for a brother's passage to Canada and head tax fees, raped by Chinese communist soldiers, prevented from entering Canada, or having endured poverty and loneliness.

A man's strong ties weakened a woman's ties. Sons, grandsons, and others never knew enough about their Chinese mother, grandmother, or aunt to question what they had heard or experienced with her when they were small: She was grumpy. She was not warm. She never integrated. She complained all the time. She was sensitive and a hypochondriac. She was lazy and embittered.

I wanted to write about Chinese women who lived beyond coastal areas of settlement. But I refused to write only an account that reiterated and reinforced a negative impression of early Chinese women.[37] I knew the extent of women's sacrifices and worth in society. Brides had come from either British Columbia or China. In almost all cases, marriages had been arranged and life on the Prairies was foreign. The often disparaging tone of stories I heard about women was the first obstacle I encountered. I didn't blame the people who gave me these accounts. I had the sense that something was missing from the recollections passed down to them, and that I would have to recover this missing information. The second obstacle I faced was also related to omission. When I began gathering data on early Chinese Prairie settlement in 2005, I noticed that some research participants had no interest in talking about women, and others were very guarded when they spoke about mothers or grandmothers. Often I was asked to remove or adjust any negative comments about women and grandmothers from my research notes, which I did. I continued to interview Chinese Canadians and aimed to unearth stories of mothers, wives, and daughters. Although I had been able to interview hundreds of Chinese Canadians, I could present here only a fraction of my findings that pertained to women. The stories in the subsequent three chapters represent the range of available Chinese women's experiences I learned about on the Canadian Prairies.

7 Early Chinese Prairie Wives

Early Chinese Prairie wives physically resided with their husbands and families but were symbolically located on the margins of nationalist and "white" society. Urban wives experienced belonging and sociality in Christian networks. Rural wives tended toward individual Buddhist or Daoist practice that provided ties to deities, China, and the past, but created much greater detachment. Neither group, as aforementioned, directly benefitted from nationalism.

Early Winnipeg Women: Jessie Lee and Ma Yeung Hong Lin

Among the earliest wives to come to Manitoba were Mrs. Lee Mon (née Wong, b. 1875), who came in 1910 with two daughters, and Mrs. Mah Joe, wife of Winnipeg's General Hospital chef, who came to Winnipeg in 1905.[1] Aside from photographs and passing references in conversations, I came across very little documentary evidence on Mrs. Lee. The same was true for Mrs. Mah Joe. Both women were affiliated with Winnipeg's early Chinese Christian community. Beyond that, I was unable to determine the strength of their bonds to the larger community or to their husbands. Below, I present the life story of Mrs. Lee's daughter Jessie Lee (aka Lee Tong Duey), who came to Winnipeg in 1910.[2]

Jessie Lee (1897-1992)

Thirteen-year-old Jessie made the voyage with her mother, Mrs. Lee Mon, and elder sister, Mary (aka Lee Ten Hee), from Nam Toon, Toisan, China, to Winnipeg in 1910. Thirty-three Lees and Wongs would make this same journey from that village to Vancouver and then to Winnipeg between 1910 and 1923. The majority of these Lee and Wong clan newcomers were labourers; two were grocers; one, Jessie's mother, was a merchant's wife; and the remainder were children and students. Jessie's younger brother, Gilbert (1911-97), was one of the Lees who came to live in Winnipeg in 1920 and

Figure 23 Left to right: Wong Kim and child, Jessie Lee, Mrs. Lee Mon, and Hong Lin Ma, Winnipeg, ca. 1918. *Source:* Jacque Mar.

join families already resident there.[3] Jessie and her family were drawn to the Prairies by her father and processes related to chain migration.

Jessie, her mother, sister, and her brother were part of a small group of Chinese Canadians who were exempted from paying the head tax, which was then five hundred dollars. The exemption was granted because the sponsoring husband and father, Lee Mon (b. 1871), was a merchant. According to the 1911 census, Lee Mon owned a general merchandise store at 261 King Street. This address was beside the offices of the KMT at 263 King Street in the 1910s.[4] Lee and his family were active participants in Winnipeg Christian events in the 1910s and 1920s. Lee would also have been heavily involved in the Manitoba KMT and one of the Prairie affective regime's earliest leaders.[5] Lee Mon, who arrived in Winnipeg in 1903, was among those who lived there the longest.

Jessie, Mary, and their mother, Mrs. Lee Mon, arrived in Canada before photographs were appended to head tax certificates. The three women later had to have C.I. 36 certificates issued to replace the former C.I. 5 certificates, which had no photographs. These photographs became an important aspect of the Chinese immigration process. Once Chinese were registered under the 1923 Chinese Immigration Act, immigration photographs were also required to identify people of Chinese descent, even those who were born in Canada. Winnipeg Chinese residents had photographs taken at Ma Seung's studio after 1917.[6]

Jessie, her mother, and sister are the earliest documented Chinese female Winnipeg residents in this study.[7] Many children and families who lived in

Figure 24 Front row, left to right: Miss Houston (white-sleeved shirt), Miss Stewart, and Jessie Lee at a Winnipeg mission picnic, ca. 1920. *Source:* Jacque Mar.

Manitoba during the 1910s, including those of Winnipeg General Hospital chief cook and power broker Mah Joe, returned to China in the 1930s.[8] Jessie and her brother Gilbert, however, remained in the province throughout their lives, demonstrating strong ties and affections in the region, which, as I show, came through Christian religious and nationalist involvement.

On the 1911 and 1916 census, Jessie and her entire family self-identified as Methodists. Bachelors who lived in dormitories and worked together, by contrast, self-identified as Confucians. Living with a woman or in a family situation changed self-identification from Confucian to some form of Christian. Before Presbyterian missionary and minister Ma Seung and his family arrived in Winnipeg in 1917, the Chinese community was served by the Methodist mission. Once Ma Seung and his family arrived, both Gilbert and Jessie participated in Presbyterian mission activities. Having come to Canada as a young girl, Jessie went to school and learned to speak English well, as did her brother.

Mrs. Lee Mon's husband was wealthy and influential enough that she didn't need to work. But like a few early and more modern Chinese Winnipeg women, she nevertheless chose to work. In Winnipeg, Mrs. Lee Mon grew and sold bean sprouts.[9]

From the beginning, Jessie was active in the Methodist, then Presbyterian and, after 1925, United, Church. She attended the community picnics, socials, concerts, teas, and afternoon Bible classes along with other Chinese Canadian Youths at the Logan Avenue United Church. She was also active in the Chinese Dramatic Society (CDS) and participated along with other women in various community events, such as the 1949 Chinese community float to mark Winnipeg's seventy-fifth anniversary. When the Chinese United Church celebrated its seventy-fifth anniversary in October 1992, Jessie was there along with her brother Gilbert to cut the cake.

In 1925, when she was twenty-eight years old, Jessie married Thomas (Tom) Tsutin, and four years later the couple were living in Morden, Manitoba, where they ran the Home Restaurant. One research participant noted: "If you wanted to see Chinese things for sale in Morden you had to go over to the restaurant. There was a woman [Jessie Lee] there. She had those red banners with Chinese writing [New Year's couplets] on them." Life was good for Jessie and Tom in Morden. Jessie, having benefitted from her mother's modern upbringing and her own Christian involvements, enjoyed socializing.

Morden had a small Chinese community that included the affable and generous Mark Ki, merchant and owner of the long-standing local grocery (discussed in Chapter 4), and another Chinese man who was the tailor. There, Jessie and Tom ran the cafe and raised a son, Douglas, and a daughter, Eunice. In 1949, Jessie and Tom moved back to Winnipeg, after Douglas died in a car accident. Four years later, Tom also died. Helen Wong recalls that Jessie and her husband had bought a house in Winnipeg right near her parents, Charlie and Frances Foo: "They moved to Winnipeg next door to Mother and Dad. Jessie spoke fairly good English and socialized quite a bit with my mother. Mother and Jessie would go to the show once in a while. Jessie was tiny and mother was very tall – five-foot-ten and a half." Jessie married Bing Kwan (aka Kwon, Quon) after her husband's death.[10] Jessie Lee Tsutin did not have a mixed-race marriage that enabled her connections to broader society, yet her Christian interactions helped her move easily between urban and rural Chinese life and from maiden, wife, and widow to wife again. In many ways, her modern Christian background shares much in common with that of Hong Lin, who was seventeen years older.

Yeung Hong Lin (1880-1962)

Yeung Hong Lin, or Mrs. Ma, came to Victoria, Canada, at the age of twenty in 1900 during the Boxer Rebellion.[11] As recounted in this book's chapter on Ma Seung, Hong Lin arrived in Canada as a devout Christian and new wife.

She had a strong command of English, having been educated at an Anglican Christian College in Canton and raised in a wealthy Chinese family by a Christian nursemaid.

Hong Lin connected to Chinese culture and heritage through the traditional family household unit, rather than nationalist ties. In her household, loyalty was to her husband and five children, and they felt the same toward her. In this important way, she defined her connection to China and available routes for belonging. Living off her husband's meagre missionary or minister's salary was difficult. To supplement the family's income, she grew bean sprouts in the basement of the house, which she sold to neighbours and nearby restaurants. Presbyterian congregants showed their affections for Hong Lin and the family through yearly gifts. These gifts were especially memorable signs of community affection for young Jacque: "During the Christmas season we would get so many turkeys that we would have to keep them outside in the snow. There was always a turkey in the pot." Cultural and social interactions were also defined outside of affective regimes. There was always music in the house, though only Andrew in the family may have been involved with the CDS while they lived in Winnipeg. Ma Seung had an especially large collection of 78 rpm Chinese records, which he played on the family gramophone. Hong Lin loved music too and awakened the household each Easter morning with the song "Hail the Day That Sees Him Rise."

Hong Lin was warmly regarded by the Winnipeg Chinese Christian community and non-Chinese leaders within the Presbyterian "social gospel" movement. She provided an essential service to women. In his youth, Jacque was privy to many conversations that took place among the Winnipeg Chinese women's society.

He would also accompany his mother on her women's missionary and other church work. He remembers when she started a "maiden house" to welcome BC-born Chinese girls who wished to travel to Winnipeg by train and meet a merchant husband. Hong Lin also acted as a go-between for men who were searching for a good wife. Marriageable women were in high demand, especially after 1923, when virtually all Chinese-born emigrants were denied entry to Canada.[12] Jacque recalls that several girls came to look for husbands in Winnipeg, including Nanaimo's Ma Bingkee's two daughters, Florence Ma and Emerald Case, who came to stay with the Mas short-term in the 1920s.[13] Girls from Victoria, Nanaimo, and elsewhere in British Columbia were looking for husbands who were not coal miners or labourers, and who instead owned businesses and could provide them with a comfortable life.

Winnipeg did not have the BC problems of Chinese prostitution or slavery, and for this reason it had no need for women's rescue homes. But the Chinese women did benefit from the events that Hong Lin organized and hosted. She also started a class to teach young married and unmarried women how to sew and do fine needlework, as well as other domestic arts. Jessie Lee was part of this group. Connecting to women through needlework and weaving was a traditionally appropriate activity, common in the southern Chinese villages from which many girls had migrated. Hong Lin's focus on teaching domestic arts was partly influenced by these Chinese traditions and by Presbyterian foreign mission boards, who highly valued this kind of "girls' work." An education in the domestic arts and needlework was believed to impart skills that would help women who were not "white" or European to become good mothers.[14] Sewing groups like Hong Lin's became emblematic of church efforts to prepare women for marriage and running a household. Some girls had already received domestic training from their mothers in Canada and in China, but they appreciated Hong Lin's work and match-making. Kenneth McDonald adds, "Through church activities women could establish social networks of their own and through the church, a legitimate sphere of female influence, women would enter into the larger world of economic and political discourse."[15]

Beyond urban Winnipeg, most Chinese women had few opportunities to socialize outside the home. Hong Lin saw a need for women's activities in the community, and so she organized an annual mothers' picnic during the 1920s for the five Chinese wives in Winnipeg and the few who by then were scattered beyond it.[16]

In Winnipeg, merchant and labour-class wives and daughters were fortunate to have Hong Lin, who, as discussed earlier, provided domestic re-education that they didn't need and valuable opportunities to socialize, which they did need. They didn't want her to leave. In 1927, when her husband finally returned to Winnipeg, the family's thoughts turned to China. They hoped to retire once the boys had been educated at the University of Manitoba (Peter graduated in 1922, Andrew in 1927 and Jacque in 1935) and at Columbia University (George).[17] Hong Lin, Peter, Andrew, George, and Henry returned to China in 1934. Becoming connected to Christian networks and self-identifying as Christian helped women fit in and feel less lonely. Women who lived outside Winnipeg and in Saskatchewan focused on family, having little access to mothers' picnics and sewing groups.

Figure 25 Chinese girls' sewing class and mothers' picnic, Winnipeg, 1920.
Source: Jacque Mar.

Figure 26 Hong Lin's sewing group at the back of her home. Winnipeg, 1920.
Left to right, front row: "Big Rossy," Unknown, Jessie Lee, and Unknown.
Source: Jacque Mar.

Saskatchewan's Eng Shee Yee, Jung Farn, Wong Low Sam Mui, and Esther Lew Yee

Eng Shee Yee (1897-1954)

Eng Shee Yee was the wife of a famous Chinese Canadian named Yee Clun (1881-1967).[18] Yee Clun was born in Pak Yim village (a Yee clan village), Hoiping, China, and immigrated to Victoria in 1902 at the age of twenty-one, paying the hundred-dollar head tax. Within four years, he had migrated east; the 1906 census shows a Yee Clun working as a domestic servant in Tyvan, Saskatchewan. A year later he was working in Rouleau, Saskatchewan, possibly in a laundry.[19] Between 1908 and 1912, he operated Rouleau's BC Restaurant.[20] By 1916, Yee Clun was in Regina. He was part owner of Yick Lee Lung Company, a Chinese grocery and supply shop. Like many Chinese merchants in Canada, he was a prominent KMT leader and part owner of multiple businesses, including the Exchange Cafe.[21] Around 1919, when he was almost forty years of age, Yee Clun's thoughts turned to marriage. Presumably, his parents in China arranged for him to marry twenty-two-year-old Miss Eng.

Yee Clun and Eng were married in China in February 1919. Once the wedding celebrations had concluded, the couple made the four-week voyage on the *Empress of Asia* to Canada, arriving in Vancouver on October 22, 1919. Upon arrival, Mrs. Yee presented her papers to the immigration clerk. He recorded her as Ung Shu, a twenty-two-year-old female from Wing Hing Lee village, Hoiping District. She was exempted from the five-hundred-dollar head tax payment as a "merchant's wife" (his business being the Yick Lee Lung Company).

Eng Shee Yee was from a poor family in China and had little education. She came to Canada knowing that her life there would be better than life in China. Within months of being wed, she became pregnant. Sadly, the first-born son, Harry, died a year later at the age of two months. A daughter, Ruby, was born later that same year, but she also died, at age seven and a half. She was accidentally burned during a Victoria Day celebration. In 1923, another daughter, Mamie, was born, and William, born the same year, was adopted. Eng Shee continued to bear children every year or two. Katie was born in 1925, followed by Dan Hin in 1926, Irene in 1928, and Ann in 1929. By 1929, Eng Shee, now thirty-two years old, had given birth to seven children in nine years. One might imagine that she was tired and lonesome. But her daughter Katie says, "She got used to living in Canada, and we didn't hear her complain.

Figure 27 Yee Clun family, Regina, ca. 1927. Standing, left to right: Yee Low (Yee Clun's younger brother), Jack Yee (Yee Clun's nephew, son of Yee Yin), Yee Yin (Yee Clun's older brother). Seated, left to right: Yee Clun, Katie, William, Ruby, Mamie, Eng Shee, and Dan. *Source:* Yee Clun Family.

She lived entirely as a housewife and enjoyed summer outings. She was content being a mom."[22]

Eng Shee typified the modern Chinese Canadian wife, except that she didn't sew, embroider, or knit. She also appeared to have no religious involvements. She wore Western clothing and her hair was cut short in a fashionable modern-girl bob. On family outings or on rare special occasions, she wore hats. She didn't drive and was entirely dependent on her husband for most things. She enjoyed Chinese opera, but Regina, unlike Winnipeg, didn't have its own amateur troupe. The community was too small to support one. She had no time for anything but housework and taking care of the

family, but at least she was spared most of the cooking. Her husband prepared the family meals, having spent many years of his young adult life
working as a domestic servant and cook. Their daughter Mamie adds:
"Mother had little contact with the English-speaking community. She would
socialize with other Chinese families: the Bing-wos, the Tais and the Louies.
Her main contact with the outside world was a Caucasian woman who had
married a Yee. We called her Yum Mo, or Mrs. Yee Yum. She was the one
who introduced us to activities organized by the Salvation Army. We would
help with translation from English to Chinese, and vice versa."

Joining thousands of other Chinese families in the early 1930s, the Yee
family left Canada in 1932. They returned to China when Saskatchewan's
drought and related economic conditions forced many Canadians into
poverty. Even though Yee Clun had become a naturalized Canadian in 1925,
the family hoped to remain in China, where they could raise their children.
Yee Clun, now in his fifties, could also retire. But by 1931, Japan had invaded
northeast China, and in 1937, Japan attacked China. Life became increasingly difficult and dangerous for the Yees in late 1930s China, and news
probably reached Yee Clun that Canada's Depression was over. He and his
son, William, returned to Regina in 1936. The rest of the family followed five
years later, in January 1941.

The Yees remained in Regina until 1947, when they moved to Vancouver.
Eng Shee died of lung cancer in Vancouver in 1954. Her story shows a woman
who lived in Canada at a time when women were excluded from political
organizations, and urban Chinese Christian involvements were not available. All accounts suggest that Eng Shee, though busy with domestic work,
enjoyed positive ties to her family that were enough to sustain her life in
Canada. She enjoyed visiting with the few Chinese women scattered throughout Saskatchewan and trips with her family through North America.

Jung Farn (1903-?)

Jung Farn was born in Suey Hop, Toisan, China.[23] Chain migration and an
arranged marriage brought her to Canada. A modern woman, she was both
Christian and a nationalist. She resembled most other Prairie wives of the
era, having cut her long hair into a short, stylish bob. She wore Western
dresses. To her family, she was known as Jung, but to everyone else in town
she was just Mrs. Farn. Jung came to Canada in 1922 when she was almost
twenty. She had married Gin Farn (aka Gin Fon) in a Western ceremony in
China, although the marriage had been arranged.[24] Jung gave birth to a son

within a year of her arrival in Canada, and another son was born in 1925. Baptized Chinese Canadians routinely gave children born in Canada Biblical names, and thus Gin and Jung named their first-born son David and their second son Isaac.

By 1923, Jung and Gin Farn had bought and opened the Maryfield Cafe in Maryfield, Saskatchewan. The long distance from Winnipeg and from Regina meant that the Farns, if they wanted to survive Prairie life, had to make connections with the broader community and beyond nationalist networks. Maryfield is nestled in the southeastern corner of Saskatchewan and located roughly 8 kilometres from the Manitoba border, 100 kilometres north of the American border, 120 kilometres west of Brandon, and 331 kilometres west of Winnipeg. Maryfield, though fairly distant from the KMT geographical Prairie centre, was still close enough for visits from merchant nationalists Sam Dong and Charlie Foo.

The new Chinese cafe in Maryfield was initially met with opposition. It presented competition to the hotel, which also offered meals. It also opened at a time when Saskatchewan law prohibited Chinese cafe owners from hiring "white" waitresses. This law was in effect until 1969.[25] Maryfield businessmen organized to deny the Farns' request for a cafe licence, and the Farns successfully petitioned, having gathered 102 names, to have the licence reinstated.[26] Eventually, they became highly respected members of the business community in Maryfield.

Like everyone else, however, they felt the pressures of life during the Depression and Saskatchewan's seven years of drought. They returned to China between 1932 and 1935. Returned overseas Chinese families such as the Farns were welcomed back to maternal or paternal villages but nevertheless maintained ties to Canadian Chinese communities and business partners.[27] They lived with Gin's parents in a village called Thai Ning Lee. During that time, they rented the Maryfield Cafe to someone else. When Saskatchewan's economy improved in 1936, the Farns (and Yee Clun and William Yee) returned to Canada.

They remained in Maryfield for another six years after that, living above the cafe that they owned and operated. Gin and Jung Farn never hired local "white" girls, because Saskatchewan's laws prevented them from doing so without obtaining a licence. Jung continued to serve and interact with customers. Gin cooked and baked. Every month, sons David and Isaac were in charge of decorating the cafe windows with streamers. Like their father, the boys were always dressed for work in white shirts, ties, dress shoes, and

Figure 28   David and Isaac Farn at Maryfield, Saskatchewan, 1928. *Source:* Isaac Farn.

short or long dress pants, depending on the weather. Sports, band, and Boy Scout participation for the Farn boys allowed them to vary this uniform.

Although there had been at least one Chinese-owned and -operated laundry in Maryfield since 1907, its owners had resided in Canada without their wives. As a result, Jung was the only Chinese woman in Maryfield. She didn't have the help or company of other Chinese women in the community, and initially life was lonesome. But over time, she learned English, adapted, and became quite comfortable in Maryfield. Her son Isaac suggests that she didn't mind the cold Prairie climate, and that, unlike many women, she wasn't skilled in Chinese domestic arts: "My mother didn't weave, sew or embroider. She had no time." On Sundays, the family was welcome to attend the Maryfield United Church and became part of its regular congregation. Occasionally, the Farns went on outings to Regina to visit with Yee Clun, Eng Shee, and their six children, and to Brandon to visit with Sam Wong, Quongying, and their five children. But since Gin Farn didn't drive, the family always had to find a driver for these trips. In addition to working in the restaurant and attending church on Sundays, Jung became an active member of the Maryfield Homemakers Club and later the local Women's Aid group. She was the only rural woman in this study to establish such extensive connections to the broader community.

In 1942, the Farns sold the restaurant. They moved to Winnipeg, where David and Isaac attended the University of Manitoba. A few years later, the

cafe was destroyed in a fire. Now Winnipeg merchants, Gin and Jung operated a Chinese grocery on Main Street. They were immediately accepted into
the Winnipeg Chinese community and took part in KMT, Chinese United
Church, and CDS events. David and Isaac also became the third and fourth
Chinese Canadians to be married in the Winnipeg Chinese United Church.[28]
When David took a job in Toronto, Gin and Jung moved with him and his
wife. With David's help, they purchased a house in Port Credit, Ontario,
where they lived until they died.

Wong Low Sam Mui (1904-93)

Radville, Saskatchewan, is about 74 kilometres north of the United States
and 136 kilometres south of Regina.[29] Similar to many towns and villages
located near the American border, Radville had a small early Chinese settlement. Jake Wong (also known as Wong Tong and Tom Wong, 1889-1960)
came to Canada from Hoiping, China, as a labourer in 1905, and by 1911 he
had joined cousin Joe Wong running a cafe in Radville.[30] Jake was a merchant's
son who had laboured in a Nanaimo lumber mill.[31] He self-identified as
Confucian on the 1911 census and had a wife and two sons who lived in
China. Like other Chinese husbands, he was presumably planning to bring
his family to Canada once he had earned enough money, but the 1923 Chinese
Immigration Act ended that dream for him. In 1920, Jake heard about his
future wife Wong Low Sam Mui in Victoria from a matchmaker.[32] Sam Mui
was almost twenty years younger than Jake. She had come to Canada after
her mother had been tragically bitten by a cobra in China and died.

Sent to Canada to live with relatives at the age of sixteen, Sam Mui worked
but did not go to school when she arrived in Victoria, possibly because of
the era's special requirements for segregated Chinese education or because
from 1922 to 1923, there was a year-long Chinese students' strike in Victoria.
This strike was organized by the Chinese Consolidated Benevolent Association (CCBA) and other key members of the Chinese community in response
to the forced segregation of Chinese students by the Victoria school board.[33]

In Victoria, Sam Mui worked as a seamstress. She was introduced and four
years later married to Jake, in 1924. Lil Chow, their daughter, emphasized
that "all the Chinese wives knew their husbands had first wives in China."
Within months, Sam Mui was pregnant and gave birth to her first child, Lil,
followed by another girl, Jean. In 1927, the couple adopted a son, Henry. Lil
Chow describes adopted Henry (d. 1947) as a "chosen boy": "As was the
custom, he was adopted because Jake did not have a son and the boy needed
a home." The boy was also presumably adopted to provide the family with a

male heir who could take over the business and continue the family lineage in Canada. In 1933, Peter, the son of Jake's cousin King Wong from Moose Jaw, also came to live with Jake and Sam Mui, Lil, Jean, and Henry.[34] Henry attended the University of Manitoba but sadly drowned in 1947.

Lil Chow describes her mother, Sam Mui, as a "modern lady." She was known to the broader community as Mary Wong and wore the fashionable uniform of Chinese Canadian wives. Her hair was kept in a short pageboy haircut, and she favoured Western dresses and shoes. Having spent four years in Victoria before she came to Radville, she knew more English than most Chinese women in Canada. Lil adds that she was also skilled in the domestic arts: "When she came to Victoria she worked in a tailor shop. She was very crafty in the sewing and with people. She mixed with everybody too." Sam Mui did not cook or work in the cafe. Jake would not allow that. He was not the master of this household kitchen, however, and he did not cook, either. He had no cafe experience, having previously laboured in wash shops and in a 1911 Nanaimo lumber mill.[35] He had simply earned enough money to purchase a share of the Radville restaurant and eventually buy out his partners. Unlike Maryfield's Gin and Jung Farn, Jake had been able to hire "white" waitresses and other staff to work in his restaurants and cook for his family.

Mary died on August 17, 1993. She is buried in the Laurier Cemetery in Radville.[36] Jake belonged to the CKT, and he and his wife, like many Chinese Canadians, had a Christian minister (Anglican), who presided over their funerals.

In the final story of early Chinese Saskatchewan wives below, I show another Christian Chinese woman who came from British Columbia and thrived on the rural Prairies.

Esther Lew Yee (b. 1902)

Bing-wo Yee (b. 1882) arrived in Victoria in 1903 from Shang Jow (Cantonese: Shar Joy), San Wui (Xinhui) District, China, at the age of twenty-one.[37] Bing-wo paid the hundred-dollar head tax that was required of all immigrants of Chinese descent.[38] By 1913, he was owner and operator of Lethbridge, Alberta's, Bing Wo and Company, Vegetables, a firm that sold his market garden vegetables.[39] By 1916, he was Lethbridge's nationalist leader.

Within two years of living in Lethbridge, Bing-wo had applied for and become a naturalized citizen in the province of Alberta and the Dominion of Canada.[40] In 1920, he also prepared a sworn declaration so that his son Yee Quai Sing could come to Canada. Bing-wo's application was successful, and Yee Quai Sing arrived in Vancouver in May 1921. In this same period, Bing-wo met and married his second wife, Esther Lew.[41]

Esther was one of many Chinese girls raised in British Columbia who later came to the Prairies to live with Chinese husbands. She was also one of a handful of young Chinese women I heard about who had strange early family backgrounds. According to her eldest son, Reg Bing-wo Yee, Esther Lew came to Canada as a child with an aunt who then abandoned her in Cranbrook, British Columbia, for unknown reasons.[42] Reg explains:

> My mother was brought to Canada by her aunt. This is the dicey part of our history ... A Scottish Presbyterian family named MacKinnon, who were practising Christians, adopted her. My mother was brought up as one of their daughters. She was just a young girl. We don't know when she came. My mother never talked about family in China. She was quite secretive about it. Females were of lesser value. They were expendable. There were no letters home to family.[43]

Reg's recollection of his mother's early history makes clear that the MacKinnons adopted her. Transracial adoptions in Canada and elsewhere reveal that though adoptions were motivated by compassion, they were also sometimes motivated by colonialism and a desire to Christianize.[44] Like many girls who were rescued in Victoria, Esther was given a Christian name by the MacKinnons.[45]

Raised as one of the MacKinnon daughters, she went to school and learned to speak English fluently. She became a good Presbyterian girl. News spread throughout the Chinese Canadian community when she reached marriageable age. Chinese Canadian girls provided a rare chance at family life. In 1920, Bing-wo was thirty-eight years old, but he was still a handsome and well-connected KMT leader in Alberta. He probably heard about the young Esther through another Yee and KMT member, and went to meet her. Bing-wo and Esther were married, and a year later their first son, Reginald, was born. The couple went on to have another two boys and two girls. The Yees were a typical couple – almost twenty years apart in age. Esther raised the children as Christians, and because she spoke fluent English, she developed friendships with other women with whom she socialized and went to church. She helped her husband in his business, and then in the 1930s the family moved to Regina in search of a better market for the vegetables they grew and sold. Eldest son Reg adds, "She did beautiful embroidery. She was a good sewer and good mother. She did the washing using the wash board and cooked. She was a very good Chinese cook of all types of family meals, like salt fish and pork with stir-fried vegetables."

As I documented these early female Prairie settlers, I came to see that religious involvement and education gave women such as Esther and Jung Farn agency, valuable interactions, and status in a community. Sometimes, however, as I demonstrate in the next chapter, self-empowering religious involvement was not Christian or public. Instead, women found freedom and happiness through private religious practice.

8 Quongying's Coins and Sword

Decades of institutionalized racism meant that there were fewer than twenty Chinese wives resident in 1920 eastern Prairie Canada, then populated by more than four thousand Chinese men.[1] As discussed in the previous chapter, brides who came to Canada from China before 1920 usually had little education and were not proficient readers or writers in Chinese, let alone English. They came to Canada and quickly changed into modern dress, adopting pageboy hairstyles. Prairie Chinese wives' quality of life was influenced by whether they lived in Saskatchewan or in Manitoba. Life was easier for women who joined successful merchant husbands than for those who married left-leaning labourers. But most of all, a woman's quality of life was determined by nationalism, her gender, and her outsider status.

Traditionally, Chinese women are alien to the family. They enter it from outside the male descent line and have the potential to bring biological instability and pollution through menstrual blood, hormonal fluctuations, and impurity. They also have the potential to destroy a family's lineage if they cannot bear male children. Gary Seaman explains:

> In societies like China, where descent is based almost exclusively on the male line, women's rights and the way women are incorporated into their husbands' lines are fraught with danger, threatening male solidarity. To preserve the solidarity of the male-oriented ... line, a rationalizing ideology develops that subordinates the role of women to that of men ... For husbands, who are parties to the difficult political negotiations involved in taking brides, the absence of 'wives' rights' ... is not difficult to rationalize.[2]

When Chinese wives came to the Canadian Prairies, they knew there were few countrywomen there, and they knew they were coming to join husbands who were, in almost every case, between ten and twenty years their elder. They also knew that the traditional expectations for childbirth in China and

Canada were the same. Brides had to produce children, preferably males, within a year or two of marriage.

Women and brides in pre-1950s southern China, and even in present-day Taiwan, routinely prayed to village temple goddesses and other deities.[3] These deities included well-known goddesses Guanyin and Mazu and male gods Lü Dongbin and Huang Daxian (Cantonese: Wong Tai Sin).[4] Women prayed to them for children, male heirs, and for success during childbirth. Most of these deities were either Daoist or Buddhist and were associated with repro- . duction and the family. There is no reason to presume that the era's non-Christian women behaved differently. Village temples and altars in the late Qing and early republican periods were still intact. They would not have been destroyed yet by invading Japanese troops during the war (1937-45) or during the civil war in the 1940s. I have never heard it confirmed, but I surmise that young women, before they left for Canada and after they had been married, went to their village temples. They would have prayed to their local goddess for good fortune, sons, or at least children. Many of these women may have learned that they could not take these religious beliefs with them to Canada, as there were few Chinese temples beyond coastal regions. They probably also learned that these practices would have to be hidden because of pervasive nationalism.

Every one of the twenty-eight women documented in this study gave birth to a child. Not every woman or child survived that birth. In this chapter, I provide a window into one woman's cloistered practices in 1920s Prairie Canada. Life in Prairie Canadian society was dominated by the religious demands of mainstream "white" society. Chinese residents in Prairie Canada felt pressure to be baptized, or at the very least to self-identify as Christian on tax rolls or the census. Those who did otherwise risked being branded as heathens. There were also expectations of proper religious behaviour in Chinese Canadian Prairie society. In addition to being nominal Christians, people were expected to behave with propriety.

Nationalist leaders tended to have traditional wives who taught daughters how to crochet, embroider, and sew or who instilled in the children an appreciation of Chinese thought and culture as well as nationalism. Fathers and husbands quoted to their families from the Confucian *Analects* and the political will of Sun Yat-sen, emphasizing the merits of traditional learning and normative Chinese behaviour. Although the men were working for the reduction of racism toward all Chinese, women and traditional wives often didn't benefit from this reduction. Racism toward them was too severe. Dominant society members rarely had a chance to interact with Chinese wives, who seldom left the home. As I discussed earlier in this book, women on the 1920s Prairies were misunderstood, alien creatures, sometimes assumed to be prostitutes.[5]

Belonging to or being excluded from key Chinese nationalist structures determined the strength of affective bonds as well as degrees of exploitation by mainstream Chinese and non-Chinese societies. Chinese Canadian men enabled the successful integration of their children, but nationalist architecture prevented them from helping traditional wives.

Nationalists had envisioned a place for women in the new Chinese republic and in overseas Chinese communities with greater social roles and mobility.[6] Judy Yung notes, "The cause of women's rights would be raised during each epoch of China's continuing fight against feudalism and imperialism – through the 1911 Revolution, the 1919 May Fourth cultural revolution, and the War of Resistance Against Japan (1937-45)."[7] However, I did not find any evidence to show that women's rights increased in Canadian nationalist society until the 1930s and 1940s, and especially after 1950, when more women arrived.[8]

The story of Sam Wong's two wives in 1920s Prairie Canada portrays women who were hinged by family ties, excluded from nationalist systems, and unable to become party members or attend meetings but sometimes able to find agency through interior lives and religiosity. In this chapter, I describe a first wife who was transformed into a jealous spirit by her bad death and birthing experience that also killed the baby. I also provide a window into the life of Lim Quongying (1900-93). This second wife, according to four family accounts, came from a tradition of Daoists and arrived in Canada as the daughter of a geomancer. Geomancers are Daoist religious functionaries and mediums with lower social status than priests, but they are often wealthy because they perform popular fortune-telling, exorcisms, and rituals that change bad luck to good.[9] Later research on Daoist practices in the region where Lim lived indicated that daughters of geomancers sometimes became Immortal Born Ladies (Xiansheng). Immortal Born Ladies were not full spirit mediums who became possessed by spirits, but they were familiar with the ways to use magic coins, charms, and swords, and they knew how to perform ritual exorcisms. Though most women practised Buddhist and Daoist customs daily, in 1920s Canada they, along with others, were encouraged to keep all but Christian religious practices secret.[10]

Miss Au (aka Ow Shee) was the first wife of Sam Wong. Born in the village of Chuck Suey and raised in East Lake Village (the same village as Charlie Foo), Hoiping, China, she was twenty-eight when she came to Canada in

1918.[11] She had been adopted into a family with three boys but no daughters. Although infant girls were typically adopted and intended for marriage to sons, the circumstances here were different.[12] Miss Au's adoptive mother was a well-off widow who taught local girls domestic arts such as sewing and needlework in her spare time. She decided to informally adopt one of the girls in her sewing class, who was poor and needed a home. This girl was not intended as a slave, maid, or future wife for her boys, as often happened in southern China, but as a daughter. Au was born in 1890 and her adoptive brother Charlie Foo was born four years later. When her boys began to leave for migrant work in other countries, Au's mother prepared her daughter to go, too. Au waited past her mid-twenties before an opportunity to go to Gold Mountain appeared.

Much of Au Wong's life is a mystery. But it is known that she came to Canada to marry Sam Wong when she was a relatively older bride, in December 1918.[13] By all accounts, Sam, though her elder by just over a decade, was a model husband who was kind, caring, and considerate of women. He was a good marriage choice for Au, who had poor marriage prospects. The two had a traditionally arranged marriage using a matchmaker in China, and Au was sent to Canada as Wong's bride. She was the first Chinese woman to live in Brandon. The nearest woman, Mrs. Lee, had bound feet and lived an hour and a half away by car in an even more remote part of the Prairies; Au was alone, without kin or friends.

Within a year after she arrived, she became pregnant with a boy. She had a difficult labour, and with only her husband and a male doctor in attendance, she and her son died on February 19, 1920.[14] According to Chinese tradition, this was Lunar New Year's eve (the year of the white metal Monkey) and a time for gathering and celebrating with family, not mourning the loss of an heir.[15] Au Wong's reportedly horrible death remains largely undocumented and forgotten. Her clothes were burned and I was told that the family didn't even keep a photograph of her. She was buried in a simple grave. Beside her grave was a cross, which presumably marked the place where the baby son was buried.[16]

Sam Wong's friend and nationalist brother, Mr. Lim, heard of this terrible loss and offered his own daughter in marriage. Within two years, his daughter, Quongying, seized upon the chance to come to Canada as a new wife. She came during Ghost month – an inauspicious time to travel.[17]

Quongying had a way of speaking that was often difficult for people to understand. This may have been related to her hearing deficit, which progressed to near deafness in her later years. Such communication difficulties would have drastically reduced the pool of families who might consider her as a bride for their son. Perhaps more detrimental to her future as a bride, however, was the fact that she was the daughter of a geomancer and socially of lower class in the republican era. Sam Wong, who was a kind, older widower, was an excellent marriage choice for the young and beautiful Quongying.

More fortunate than many Chinese emigrants journeying to Canada for the first time, Quongying travelled in second class, not in steerage. There, she enjoyed the comforts of a cabin and had her own bed. She shared bathing facilities with one or more roommates. She was able to go to the second-class dining room for her meals and enjoy many of the ship's activities. Quongying's steamship, the *Empress of Russia*, docked in Victoria on September 5, 1921. Quongying had paid the higher second-class fare, yet when she arrived in Canada she and other Chinese passengers were segregated by race, not cabin class. As a result, once she stepped onto the pier, she was sent to the line for Chinese emigrants, the majority of whom had travelled by steerage.

Although she had travelled in second class, was the fiancée of a merchant, and was freshly showered and in clean clothing, she was assumed to be dirty.[18] While inside the detainment chamber, she was forced to undress in front of a non-Chinese-speaking stranger; depending on the day, this could have been either a man or a woman. Standing naked in the immigration hall shower stalls, she would have been sprayed with water and told to wash. After she had showered, she would have been told to dress in clean clothing and was then led into a room. Here she would undergo an extensive medical examination to ensure that she did not have tuberculosis or other diseases. More questions would have followed. Some Chinese immigrants would next pay the head tax and leave the building. Other women, such as Quongying, were sent to the "piggy hut" (literally, log cabin or *muwu*), the name used by the Chinese community for the immigration sheds at Victoria's old detention hall.[19] Quongying's head tax certificate is stamped, signed, and dated October 12, 1921. This means that for more than a month, from September 5 to October 12, she had been forced to reside in one of the immigration hall cells.

Carved into the walls of the immigration rooms in Victoria were poems that David Lai was able to transcribe from pieces of the building when it was demolished decades ago.[20] Chinese men performed poems expressing private feelings in opera clubhouses.[21] Frank Chan's friends published poems about him in newspapers (one of which is translated on pages 73-74). Poetry expressed separation and loneliness, and a desire for closer ties and affections.[22] Quongying had received a good education and probably read these poems, describing the horrors of confinement and racism.

There are two possible reasons to explain Quongying's five-week detainment. The most common reason for detainment was an inability to pay the five-hundred-dollar head tax, which at the time was the equivalent of two years' wages in Canada. As Quongying's fiancé was a wealthy, well-connected merchant and she came from a rich family, this seems unlikely.[23] The other common reason, and especially for the detainment of Chinese women, was that they were seen as drastically different from the women of mainstream society. They were suspected of being prostitutes, or *mui-tsai,* sent from Hong Kong to work in North American brothels. By 1900, the incidence of Chinese prostitutes in Canada was rare. Still, these stereotypes persisted and mainstream society in the West tended to view Chinese women as vaguely defined victims of Chinese patriarchal society. Many were thus associated with women's rescue homes.[24] As Jacque Mar, other research participants, and archival research confirmed, the Prairies had no need for rescue homes.[25] There were no Chinese prostitutes, slaves, or concubines. Quongying had arrived in Canada to replace a dead wife and join a husband.

Once she was released from the piggy hut, she and Sam Wong were married in Victoria and afterward enjoyed marriage parties and celebrations in British Columbia. From Victoria, the newlyweds travelled to the Prairies.

As the daughter of a Chinese Canadian merchant, Quongying did not have bound feet. Being modern, she had left several unworn traditional outfits in her trunk.[26] Her choice of Western dress upon arrival in Canada signalled liberation from Sam's mother and traditional networks that governed women's lives in the family home.

The first half of Quongying's Canadian life, until the 1950s when more Chinese women and families emigrated, was lonely. Aside from her husband and children, she seldom talked with anyone. Her speech pattern made her difficult to understand. Although there were Chinese women who lived in Brandon short-term in the 1920s, she had no Chinese women friends. A popular, affectionate father and ardent nationalist who ran a prosperous business, Sam took time out to cook the meals and eat with his family.

Every day in Brandon, Sam ran all the household errands and also dropped off and picked up the children from school. On spring and summer weekends, he took his family to parks and lakes for picnicking and swimming. Photographs show that Quongying clearly enjoyed these times. The family went on sporadic summer outings to visit with families who lived in the

Figure 29 Quongying Wong and family, Brandon, 1934. Front row, left to right: Walker, May, and Irene on Quongying's lap. Back row, left to right: Sam, Charles (Chuma) and Westley. *Source:* Helen Wong.

region, including the Farns of Maryfield, Saskatchewan, the Yees in Regina, the Dares (aka Der) in Neepawa, and the Foos in Winnipeg. Sam ensured that Quongying, whom he always introduced as a lady ("My wife is a lady"), was provided with the best Western dresses, furs, and hats purchased from the Eaton's catalogue. She was spared any kind of menial labour. In this way, Quongying was different. I had heard about only three Chinese Canadian women during this period whose husbands had discouraged them from doing any work at all. Jake Wong, Mah Joe, and Sam Wong were all wealthy enough that their wives did not need to work. These same men were also more traditionally Chinese.

Quongying was the rare educated second daughter, who sent not only remittances but also family news.[27] Through her letters she maintained ties to her family in China, but her ties in Canada seemed weak.

Quongying had known that she would have an inauspicious beginning in Canada, involving a journey during Ghost month and then a desolate life in a home with the jealous spirit of her husband's deceased first wife. Miss Au's bad death was linked to the spilled blood, violent labour, and polluting influences that had brought about the death of the baby.[28] The fear of bloodshed during childbirth is common in Chinese and many cultures and religions.[29] Many religions associate women with blood, impurity, and vaguely articulated social taboos that require female social and familial regulation and subjugation.[30] Pregnant and birthing mothers in traditional and Chinese Canadian society had the potential to upset and defile social harmony and hygiene, to open a bloody pathway for unseen bad omens, and to disrupt and trouble masculinity and the patriline.[31] Jealous spirits resided in the Lake of Blood but were believed to wander and try to make their way back to homes and husbands through dark, enclosed spaces, such as closets and basements.

Ninety years after Quongying had entered Canada in 1921, I accompanied eighty-seven-year-old Walker Wong up the stairs of his old Brandon family home and down the hall to his mother's bedroom, largely untouched since she had died eighteen years before, in February 1993 (Walker lived downstairs and the upper floor was used mostly for storage).

We entered Quongying's bedroom, opened the closet door, and found the trunk that had been locked for virtually all of Walker's life. We unlocked the trunk, lifted out a rectangular silver box, and opened it. Inside were hundreds of very heavy, old round coins with square centre holes. The coins dated to the reign of Qianlong, an eighteenth-century Qing dynasty emperor. They were commonly used as heavenly treasury money to restore destiny.

As I looked more closely, I could see that some coins still had red thread joining them to other coins.[32] These specific coins were used to prevent family members from being pulled apart and to prevent someone from leaving his or her present position within the family, be that dead or alive.[33] The red thread bound family members together and kept ghosts and spirits such as Miss Au in the Lake of Blood. Quongying had been performing her own rituals of inclusion and exclusion. According to traditional beliefs, Au would

Figure 30   Eighteenth-century Qing dynasty coins with red thread.
Source: Alison Marshall.

have tried to become reborn, escape from the Lake of Blood via the closet, and then possess Quongying.[34]

Beneath the box of coins was a coin sword. The coin sword was approximately eighteen inches in length and five inches wide, with twenty-three coins forming the central axis. The coins were sewn together with red thread. I was told that at one point there had been four coin swords in the home. It is highly likely that Quongying had brought these Daoist talismans to keep herself and her family safe from the supernatural threat of Miss Au.

On the basis of interviews and subsequent conversations with specialists in the field and four research participants, I offer the following as a preliminary hypothesis. Someone close to Quongying had ensured that she received enough religious education to enable her to deploy the swords, position the coins, and utter the chants and prayers needed for protection, repayment of the debt to Miss Au, and exorcism.[35] As mentioned, these kinds of rituals gave Quongying a sense of personal power and control. They also gave her cultural rootedness and her own ties, not to affective regimes, but to old country traditions. These traditions were highly frowned upon in 1920s Chinese Prairie Canada.

Four family members revealed that during the 1920s and throughout the 1930s, when all of Quongying's children were growing up, there had been a three-foot by five-foot wall of coins and swords hung in the cafe apartment's master bedroom closet. In the early 1930s, a Chinese person from outside

Figure 31   Coin sword. *Source:* Alison Marshall.

the family went into the closet and saw the magic swords and coins. After that, the family installed a special door with a large lock to keep people out of the ritual space. A woman could not allow anyone but her husband to know about these powerful ritual implements, even though many of the overseas nationalist male leaders were themselves positively disposed toward these illicit practices. One decades-long Manitoba Chinese nationalist leader kept a figurine of a Chinese deity by his bedside and prayed to it.[36] Public religious practice unrelated to Christianity was seen to be a blight on the image of modern Chinese. Thus, it had to be concealed.[37]

After we examined these objects and the various kinds of coins, we continued looking through the other layers of the trunk. We found unused, folded black clothing and silk embroidery that had accompanied Quongying to Gold Mountain. The scarves, comb holders, and change purses were pink, green, yellow, purple, blue, and orange, and were embroidered with similar colours of thread. They were not red. These items did not appear to have been intended for a wedding or birth.[38] Many of them appeared to never have been used. Brigitte Baptandier adds that these may have been "ex-voto given to mediums to thank their *benshen,* or original spirit gods, [for granting] their vows."[39] I have to wonder if Quongying had brought these votive gifts, along with the other bridal clothing and coins, to ensure that life went smoothly on Gold Mountain and that the gods (who presumably included Guanyin, associated with women and children) granted her wishes. Each silk piece was embroidered with a different Chinese couplet. The first couplet described how the embroidered item brought clarity of perception: "The bewildered eye may see a thousand li [miles] clearly."[40] The second item

Figure 32
Locket with
image of Miss
Au Wong.
Source: Alison
Marshall.

brought illumination: "The precious mirror of radiance."[41] The third brought understanding and appropriate affections: "The host understands feelings and behaves [accordingly]."[42]

I photographed the items and returned them to their section of the box. When I found the silk embroidery, I had no idea of its meaning or significance. Eager to re-examine the coins, I returned to the upper section of the trunk to take another look. Mingled with the coins were nationalist pins, one red and blue with the twelve-pointed star, and another entirely blue. Both were corroded with age. I kept digging around in the coins to see what else might be there. I found Sam Wong's daguerreotype copper plate, dating to around 1919, that he had used to make prints for Canadian immigration and nationalist membership photographs. I continued sifting through the mound of coins to see if there might be anything else. Then I noticed a locket. There was no chain in the box. I motioned to Walker to come over and see what I had found. We opened the gold clasp and discovered a very old photograph of an unknown young woman, whom we now presume is first wife Au Wong. Before this day, none of Quongying's children or family members had ever seen a photograph of Au, even when they had searched the trunk before me. No trace of Miss Au had been publicly displayed or made known to Sam Wong's children while they were growing up.

Quongying never told her children about her private rituals. But we presume she set to work, using many coins she had brought with her to Canada for protection, based on Miss Au's birthdate, which she had learned from

Sam. Miss Au would have recognized and been attracted to the early image of herself in the locket and to Sam's daguerreotype plate kept in the box. But the magic coins and swords (which were often dipped in blood for extra power) would have bound her spirit. Quongying was now married to her husband and was indebted to Miss Au. The coins repaid her debt and kept Au from harming Quongying and the family. In Quongying's mind, these powerful ritual instruments had efficacious power. In some ways the information on Quongying's coins and sword presents only slim evidence of a woman's interior religious life. But, as indicated by repeated interviews with four research participants, these secret practices do seem to have provided comfort during the difficult first half of her life in Canada.

Over the months that followed the remarkable discovery in the trunk, I repeatedly interviewed family members about Quongying. I was told that she used to utter Chinese chants and prayers in the master bedroom. I was also told that her husband, Sam, not Quongying herself, had been the one who knew the old Chinese recipes and about special foods to cure colds or other ailments. Quongying, I was told delicately and with affection, had been somewhat of a hypochondriac, who in her fifties had insisted that her husband take her to the doctor every day. She seemed to know nothing about medicine. She knew about needlework, however, and she liked to read. Youngest daughter Irene recalls: "She did a lot of knitting. That's where I got my training. She taught me to knit and crochet, and she created beautiful things, mostly handiwork." She also read Chinese books and Chinese newspapers. Irene continues: "I had little readers and I spent a lot of time with my mom reading Chinese stories – any little child's cute stories. She had gotten them from China."[43]

Quongying's life went as well as it could have. She had given birth to a son, Westley, and then Charles, another son. After that came two girls and a boy, May, Walker, and Irene. Quongying had provided Sam Wong with a first-born son who would be the head of the clan in Canada, as well as two additional boys. Interviews with family members confirmed that, like most Chinese Canadian women living on the Prairies, she gave birth at home, not in hospitals, with a midwife and doctor present.[44] Whether or not she consulted her father, who was a geomancer, is not known. I suspect that she would have contacted him to ask for religious guidance and that she would have given birth in a specific location of the house, and would have faced a certain direction. I also suspect that all of her actions during childbirth would have been determined by *feng shui* and southern Chinese customs.

With Quongying, Sam Wong was assured that any bad fate or karma associated with his first wife had been used up. Given her limited interactions with broader society, time before 1950 was passed alone, reading, sewing, embroidering, knitting mittens, socks, and toques, or crocheting items such as baby clothes and doilies that literally filled her home in piles. By being an extraordinary husband and father, Sam Wong had unintentionally made it very difficult even for family members to recognize and appreciate the goodness and talents of their own mother and grandmother. Sadly, as she aged, her hearing loss became severe, further affecting her ability to communicate and making it nearly impossible for all but family members to understand or interact with her.

Until the repeal of the Chinese Immigration Act in 1947, when more women immigrated to her small Prairie city, Quongying had interacted with her children, grandchildren, and husband, and rarely with other women. Quongying, who displayed special affection for her daughters and granddaughters, cared for the children when they were not at school, but otherwise she had little to do. Others recall that much of the time she simply lay on her bed.

Some time in the late 1960s or 1970s, Quongying developed a very special friendship with a woman named Mrs. Frank. Mrs. Frank took her under her wing, and together they enjoyed spending time at the local seniors' centre, where Mrs. Frank introduced her to other people. Having such an advocate, Quongying showed an outgoing side that surprised many of her family members. One day, she came home from the centre and reported that a nice man had asked her to dance. When she replied that she didn't know how, the gentleman told her that was all right. He would help her – she just needed to listen to the music. When she related the story to her family, she said, "I listen. I listen. Listen what? I don't know." Owing to her hearing loss, she probably could not hear or sense the rhythm to the music, thus finding the experience rather confusing and frustrating. However, she described it with good humour and pleasure in having been asked to join the fun. Dancing "lessons" from her daughter-in-law were given to help prepare her for the next invitation.

Quongying's affect was very different from other kinds I had heard about. The arc of her life had changed because someone had died. That negative affect had enabled her to leave China and migrate to Canada. Once she arrived in Canada, she (and others) must have continued to be stirred by that death. It was in the past, never spoken about, but somehow always a part of the fabric of her own and her children's lives. I can only imagine how Quongying felt during the long quiet days that she lay on her bed. Perhaps sometimes she heard the floor creak or the downspout fill with rain. I wonder if those moments agitated her, drawing her attention toward Miss Au.

For decades, Quongying made sacrifices for her husband, a leader and power broker, so that he could mobilize support for nationalist causes. Excluded from nationalist architecture, and living in a region where so few Chinese women resided, she behaved appropriately all her life, dressing well, staying indoors, and keeping her life as an Immortal Born Lady closeted. Her daughters and other Chinese Canadian women had very different alliances, loyalties, and webs of connection. I recount some of their stories in the following chapter.

9 Chinese Prairie Daughters

Chinese Prairie daughters, as second-generation Canadian-born children, escaped the marginal lives of their mothers. In this chapter, I tell the stories of daughters who were born in Manitoba and Saskatchewan before the repeal of the Chinese Immigration Act.

Mamie (aka Minnie) Yee (b. 1923) and Katie Yee (b. 1925)

Mamie and Katie are the two eldest daughters of Yee Clun and Eng Shee Yee. Yee Clun was a Chinese entrepreneur, KMT leader, and interpreter in Regina who ran the Exchange Cafe with various partners over the years. In 1924, he was denied a licence to hire "white" women to work as waitresses in the Exchange Cafe. A law restricting the employment of "white" women in Chinese shops had been enacted in 1912 Saskatchewan.[1] Yee Clun challenged the Regina legislation and sued the city. He had the support of many local businessmen and Christians. In 1925, his lawsuit was successful, though the law remained in place until 1969.[2] Although Yee Clun experienced considerable political barriers in Regina, his children grew up unaware of them.

Yee Clun and his wife, Eng Shee, raised their children in a strongly nationalist environment. The family home at 1821 Osler Street was next door to the Chinese nationalist clubhouse in Regina, and Yee Clun was its leader.[3] The Yee children didn't attend nationalist regular meetings. They did attend KMT and Chinese Benevolent Association (CBA) teas and other functions, such as the Western New Year (observed by Chinese nationalists) and nationalist or Double Tenth (October 10) Festival celebrations. Thirty people or more from Regina and surrounding areas would be present.

Long tables with chairs around them would be set up in the big room on the ground floor of the clubhouse in preparation for these events. Mamie and Katie do not recall whether Chinese food or Western-style food was served at the lunches. Katie adds:

Our Dad would have us make speeches on Chinese Nationalism to the crowd. We were uncomfortable doing this, a little shy and reluctant to speak, and when we spoke we would just basically praise the KMT. There were sometimes other young people in attendance, such as the Yee children – Isobel, Norman and Reggie. We also remember Mr. Chan, Mak Foon Ping, and Charlie Yee, among others. These events were rather boring. We weren't too interested in the proceedings.

Mamie, Katie, and their brother Dan remember that at all KMT events they, along with all the Chinese men, would recite Sun Yat-sen's political will and sing the Chinese nationalist anthem. Meetings throughout Canada began in the same way.

The clubhouse held many events, but it didn't have a Chinese language school. Regina's Chinese community had too few children and teachers to support one.[4] Systems of integration, such as those that forged cultural rootedness for Winnipeg's Chinese children, did not exist in Regina. Before the family returned to China in 1932, Mamie and Katie learned to speak the Hoiping language at home. But it was only when they lived in China that they learned to read and write it.

The children were also encouraged to develop ties to the broader community through church services and Salvation Army events, as well as camp from 1923 to 1932. Mamie remembers that Violet Yee, the daughter of Yim Mo, a mixed-race woman who married a Yee, encouraged them to go to camp. Through the camp, the children formed relationships with Chinese and mixed-race children, some of whom they knew from Strathcona Elementary School. Sometimes, Mamie and Katie would also go to the Sunday morning service at Knox United Church and then enjoy lunch at their father's Exchange Cafe. Yee Clun and Eng Shee were "atheists," according to their children, and professed nominal Christian identities.

The Yees had strong family bonds. The girls were predeceased by an infant brother named Harry (d. 1920), and their sister Ruby (1921-29), who as previously mentioned had died from serious burns. The accident happened while Ruby was lighting a firecracker during Regina's Empire Day celebrations in her front yard on Victoria Day weekend in 1929. Katie's son, Clarence, adds: "The *Regina Leader* reported that her funeral procession was accompanied by fifty cars, and that her funeral was attended by most of the Chinese people of Regina, and many other citizens." Mamie and Katie have two other sisters, Irene (or Ileane) and Ann, and youngest brother Dan, in addition to William, who was adopted in 1923. Their mother, like most of the Chinese

Canadian mothers I heard about, had a non-Chinese midwife to help with each of the births.

The Yee family left Regina on November 19, 1932, to return to China. Several Prairie families went back to China in the 1930s, including the Farns of Radville, Saskatchewan, Winnipeg General Hospital chief cook Mah Joe and his family, and Canada's first Chinese Prairie minister, Ma Seung, and his family. Mainly, families returned because of the financial pressures brought on by the Depression. Many of them also wanted their young children to get to know aging grandfathers and grandmothers, and to have a Chinese education. Parents also wanted their children to have a chance at a good job (as opposed to becoming a cafe or wash shop labourer) and to marry a Chinese spouse. Many fathers were decades older than their young wives, and for them returning to China meant retirement. For a time, Yee Clun, Eng Shee, and the children lived in Yee Clun's natal village of Bak Yim, and after a month they moved to Canton City. Mamie adds: "We moved to Hong Kong in the late 1930s with at least three other Yee families. Together we shared one floor in an apartment building, with a common kitchen and washroom. But there was only one bedroom per family. Six of us slept in one bed! After a while we all moved to a new apartment building located closer to the Kowloon airport." Following 1936, and during the Pacific War, the family returned to Bak Yim village, where they shared a house with Yee Clun's mother and elder brother. Here, the girls felt that they "had become Chinese," as they spoke only the Bak Yim village language and Cantonese.

The children never met Yee Clun's father, who was presumably dead by then. The family was able to survive on money provided by Yee Clun. Once the Japanese invaded the village in 1938, the family embarked on a three-year odyssey that led them to Macao, where they slept in a barn with hay, and then on to Hong Kong, where the five kids shared one bed with their mother in a room they rented in a cafe suite. The family was fortunate to get on one of the last CPR boats from Hong Kong to Vancouver in January 1941. Upon arrival in Canada, they all had a much-needed week's vacation in Vancouver. Mamie and Katie enjoyed sightseeing, as well as having their hair permed and attending a Cantonese dramatic opera show.

When the family returned to Regina in 1941, Mamie was eighteen years old and Katie was sixteen. Instead of sharing their home with three other families, the Yees had an entire house to themselves, which Yee Clun paid to have renovated after the tenants moved out. While the renovations were being completed, they lived atop the Exchange Cafe, as it was part restaurant and part rooming house.

The children, who had spent a few years in school in Canada before they left, could now hardly speak English. Initially, they were put back into Strathcona Elementary School. Mamie says,

> It was embarrassing to be in the classroom with the smaller children, but we don't remember being teased or ridiculed. We quickly adjusted to life back in Regina, and became much more Western than Mother. We had to re-learn how to be Canadian, but it did not take long. We were somewhat different from the local-born Chinese, or those who had not spent any time in China. While we spoke both the village dialect and Cantonese, and could read and write Chinese, others could not. They had learned only the village dialect of their parents.

The girls studied hard and advanced grades. Within a year, they were attending Balfour Technical School. There were a few Chinese and Japanese kids at the school, but none in their classes. Mamie carried around a Chinese-English dictionary and studied French for three years, in preparation for university.

After they returned to Regina, Mamie and Katie worked for a short time at the Silver Dell along with their cousin Jack Yee, brother Willie, and friend Jean Tai, whose father helped operate the Exchange Cafe. Mamie recalls: "We checked coats. It was a 'dine and dance' place where banquets would be held. Live music would be provided by big bands. We even had some visits from some Hollywood stars [Patric Knowles, an English actor in Hollywood]." During the war, the Silver Dell was a place where the Regina community (including Armed Forces soldiers and Chinese) interacted. It was a fun place to work. There would be teacup readings by Edgar Chan, who had come from Ontario. Chan's wife Effie (Wong) and her sister Emma would come from Moose Jaw to visit. Travelling salesman Sam Dong, along with Westley Wong, visited the Tais and Wongs at the Silver Dell in 1942. The Silver Dell was Regina's version of Chan's Cafe, which Charlie Foo managed in Winnipeg.

Mamie graduated from Balfour Technical School in 1945 and then went to the University of Manitoba for a year in 1946.[5] At university, she drew upon her family's Manitoba and Saskatchewan connections. In 1944, the family had taken a trip to Manitoba, including Winnipeg Beach and Clear Lake, to socialize with other Chinese families in Brandon (Sam and Quongying Wong, discussed in the previous chapter) and Neepawa (the

Figure 33   Yee family trip to Los Angeles, 1947. Back row, left to right: Mamie, Katie, and William. Front row: unknown, Yee Clun, Irene, Anne, and Eng Shee Yee Clun. *Source:* Yee Clun Family.

Dares and Lees).[6] They also spent time in Winnipeg, visiting with Charlie and Frances Foo. Mamie lived in Winnipeg with close family friends, the Farns, who had moved from Maryfield, Saskatchewan, to Winnipeg. David and Isaac were also at the university. University was difficult for Mamie, who had had to relearn English after living in China for nine years. She was enrolled in the Faculty of Arts and took courses in literature and math. After one year, she decided to return to Regina and join the family when they moved to Vancouver.

In 1947, the Yees moved to Vancouver. Yee Clun decided to turn the trip into a family vacation through the United States. The journey took the Yees through Montana, Wyoming, Colorado, Arizona (Eng Shee's brother, Kay Quong, lived in Ely, Nevada, and Yee Clun's niece lived in Phoenix), New Mexico, and then up through California, including stops in San Diego, Los Angeles, and Berkeley.

In Vancouver in 1947, Mamie worked at an import-export company.[7] In 1953, Katie married C.K.L. Sihoe. He subsequently introduced Mamie to her future husband, Ding Wong, who came from Hong Kong to attend the University of British Columbia. Today, Mamie and Katie remain close. Growing up in exclusion-era Prairie Canada and wartime China, the sisters were aware of discrimination and suffering but had no personal experiences of them. Instead, their memories reveal solid foundations in nationalism and family life that enabled them to escape racism, famine, and poverty in both Canada and China.

Shifting the discussion from Regina and the Prairie hinterland, we return to Winnipeg and the geographical centre of the KMT in Canada. It is there that Charlie Foo and his wife, Frances (who was not Chinese), raised their family.

Helen (Foo) Wong (b. 1924)

Helen Wong is the eldest daughter of Charlie and Frances Foo. Most children of nationalist leaders met each other at some point in their lives and became well accepted because of their fathers' service to the community. Helen had met Mamie and Katie when they, along with their father, Yee Clun, visited Winnipeg and Charlie Foo in 1944. Helen also knew Mamie and Katie's good friends David and Isaac Farn, who moved to Winnipeg from Saskatchewan to attend the University of Manitoba. Chinese Prairie Canada was a small world.

Helen had an older half-sister, Pat (1919-86), from her mother's previous marriage in England, and younger siblings Fred, Wally, Lily, and Harold, who was adopted. There were very few Chinese kids during the time Helen grew up in Winnipeg.[8] On Saturday mornings, she went to Chinese school with some of these children. In the 1930s, Winnipeg's Chinese school was the only one on the eastern Prairies, though it was not actually a school, per se. It was run at the KMT clubhouse by older men in the Chinese community who had obtained a grade five or six education in China. The pupils memorized and recited passages from old books, learned how to hold a brush and use ink, and practised calligraphy. Although many of the students became proficient in Chinese calligraphy and learned Confucian and nationalist sayings and songs, few of them came away from the classes with more than a rudimentary knowledge of a few characters.

Helen was often in Chinatown to see her father, who was very involved with the Chinese nationalists and often at meetings and other Chinatown events. Helen says, "I was so used to going to these events with my father that I didn't think anything of them. Once I went into a building on Pacific Avenue (near the clubhouse) where some Chinese fellows were living. They were cooking in the basement and I remember how good it smelled. Chinatown was familiar to me and I didn't feel out of place." But Helen didn't grow up in the Chinatown enclave. Even in the 1920s, Chinatown tended to be inhabited by bachelors. The few other Chinese families in Winnipeg when Helen was growing up tended to live outside Chinatown. Ma Seung and his family lived on Ellen Street, Charles Yee and his family lived on Henry Street, and for most of Helen's life her family lived farther from downtown, in either North St. Vital or St. Boniface, where they were the only Chinese family.

Many Winnipeg Chinese fathers, who were nominally Christian, involved their children in church activities and Sunday schools to give them a social outlet, to help them learn Canadian values, and possibly also because their children wanted to go. In 1920s Winnipeg, there were more than fifteen Chinese Sunday schools, held at Zion Presbyterian Church, St. Stephen's Presbyterian Church, Knox United Church, St. Matthew's and St. John's Anglican Church, as well as in other churches. These Sunday schools were mostly for the young boys who lived apart from parents and siblings in China, and who had come alone to Canada to labour in a cafe or laundry. Chinese families, however, usually sent their children to the Logan Street mission for afternoon classes taught by a number of teachers and women over the years, including the well-known Ross sisters (Daisy, Molly, and Lily), and the older "Big Rossy," as well as the Morton sisters, Mrs. Milne and Mrs. Holmes (see Figure 34). Although Chinese had complicated relationships with churches and missionaries, Ma Seung's archive shows that the community enjoyed close, sometimes family-like, bonds with these teachers.

Charles Yee's children went to Catholic mass in their neighbourhood, and the Foos attended St. Philip's Anglican Church in St. Boniface. Helen's parents were married in this church, and the Foo children were baptized there.

Helen and her family lived on Carriere Avenue in North St. Vital, Winnipeg. All the children went to King George the Fifth School from grade one to grade nine. For high school they attended Norwood Collegiate Institute. Helen doesn't remember much racism in St. Vital: "If there was an issue I

Figure 34   Teachers at the annual picnic of the Chinese Sunday schools of Winnipeg, June 18, 1921. *Source:* Jacque Mar.

talked to Mother about it. She never made a fuss about it. You were strong and you were who you were." She does recall one time when her brother, Harold, was teased by children in the playground: "The kids were taunting Harold, saying things like 'Chinky, Chinky Chinaman.' Harold broke into the circle around him and joined in the same taunt, hollering it with the other children, and broke the hands of two people. He hollered at the top of his voice and nobody ever bothered him again."

In her spare time, Helen liked to embroider, sew, crochet, and knit. She came from a long line of women who did fine needlework. Her mother sewed all of the children's clothing. Helen remembers: "Often I would come home from school ... and coming down that last block I could always see Mother in the window at the sewing machine. She loved that sewing machine." Charlie Foo's mother in China had also sewn and given sewing classes to the village girls. When Helen was a young girl, her father bought her a sewing basket. It was a special present, which she still has today. She adds, "I remember when I was eighteen. I was embroidering a pillow case and getting ready by preparing things for my hope chest and I remember my father saw the pillow case and started to cry. He was so touched that I could sew like that and ... he related it to his mother in China."

Helen's early life was also defined by Cantonese opera and by family and community outings. She has fond memories of going to the opera with her granny, her mother's mother, who came to stay with the family until Wally was born in 1930. One time, Helen and her grandmother went to Winnipeg's Chinatown to see a Cantonese opera. She was startled to see that her father was in the performance. He was wearing a black skull cap, a long moustache and beard, and a bright satin robe embroidered with blue and green designs. Helen adds that the CDS costumes were made in China and then shipped to Canada. Many men in the Chinese community and even nationalist leaders such as Charlie Foo, who weren't formally part of the troupe, participated in opera performances. Helen says, "He sang in a falsetto voice and he had a very nice voice."

On Sunday afternoons, there were Foo family outings with the Chinese community along the Assiniboine River at Roblin Boulevard. Christmas and New Year's were other special times. Chinese nationalists didn't observe the Lunar New Year and instead celebrated the Western New Year. Accordingly, the Foos marked each New Year at the New Main Cafe, which was owned by Mr. Liu. Here, they, Chinese uncles, and other close family friends would enjoy a turkey dinner with all the trimmings.

In terms of post-secondary education for Chinese Canadian daughters, aside from Mamie Yee's one-year stint at the University of Manitoba, none of the daughters discussed in this chapter obtained a university education. I asked Helen, who had been a good student in school, why she hadn't gone to university. She answered that neither she nor her parents had made the decision: "When it came time to decide in grade nine whether you would go to university or go into the commercial stream, I was shunted into the commercial stream." Helen adds that her husband, Westley Wong, who had been given the chance to go to university, was surprised that the school administrators had made that decision for her. As a result of what she perceived to be a sexist, but not racist, decision, she ended up going to Manitoba Commercial College on Portage Avenue. After that, she got a job at the Winnipeg General Hospital as a bookkeeper through her Chinese family connections. She also worked briefly for Chinese consul Weng when the Chinese consulate opened an office in Winnipeg in 1944.[9] When she was twenty-one years old, in 1945, Helen got married. She elaborates: "The first time I was aware of Westley was when he was about twelve and I was about ten. Westley's father had been married to a lady [Au Wong, discussed in the previous chapter] that my father considered as his sister." Westley was the eldest son of Quongying and Sam Wong. Sam, like Charlie, was an ardent nationalist.

Figure 35   Frank Chan and Helen Foo, outside the Chinese Consul House, Winnipeg, 1944. *Source:* Helen Wong.

Figure 36   Helen and Westley Wong wedding, Winnipeg, 1945. Left to right: Sam and Quongying Wong, Westley, Helen, Frances and Charlie Foo. *Source:* Helen Wong.

After they were married, Helen and Westley moved to Toronto so that Westley could complete his graduate training at the University of Toronto. Later, they returned to Manitoba.[10] Unlike the women in the generation before her, Helen did not feel much pressure to have children right away; her first son was born in 1948. Her school friends and her father's friends visited and sent presents. Happy Young from Esterhazy (discussed in Chapter 4) also visited and gave her son a stuffed animal.[11] Throughout her life, Helen has enjoyed strong ties and affections through her father's and later her own connections. She adds, "I was well-accepted I think because of my father's place in Chinatown. He had his friends, Frank Chan, Sam Dong [discussed in Chapter 3], Happy Young [and many others], and they all supported one another. They were here in a different country and they had to make their mark. The sad part was so few had wives or families."

Marcelle (Choy) Gibson (b. 1944)

I end this chapter with the story of an adored adopted daughter of a laundry shop owner. Unlike other vignettes in this book, this one begins in Winnipeg (where Marcelle was born in 1944) and ends in Toronto, and is thus weakly linked to the processes and structures that helped shape early Chinese Prairie Canada. But in other ways, the story shows how positive interactions led to intermarriage and other connections, which drew this family away from the Prairies. The daughter of travelling Cantonese opera performers, Marcelle was adopted by Lee Choy (1882-1958) and his wife, Liliane, who was French Canadian. They married so that they could become eligible to adopt Marcelle.[12] Being poor and starving, the performers were unable to care for their three children – a boy and two girls. The boy was sold but the mother was willing to give the girls away for free. Lee Choy was thrilled to have a chance to be a father and to have a daughter. During our conversation in June 2011, and in subsequent emails, Marcelle made it clear that her father was the "light of her life."

Lee Choy came to Canada from Toisan, China, in 1902 when he was twenty years old. Like Charles Yee (discussed in Chapter 5), he had lost his family in some kind of plague. Marcelle recalls:

When I was growing up, my father said over and over again he earned two dollars a month when he first came to Canada. He thought that was good pay and he thought it was alright. He talked about China sometimes. He had lived through a plague in China where he was assumed to be dead and put in a mass grave. He would say, "I made them scared. I woke up." Everybody had been sick with some kind of illness and then everyone had died and been buried. My father never wanted to talk about his family in China. He said he had never been back to China. I don't think he had a wife there.[13]

Lee Choy had said to Marcelle when she was growing up: "You don't know trouble." He had lived his entire life doing hard labour. After working in northern British Columbia in logging and other work, he made his way across the country to Toronto, labouring in wash shops and cafes. By the 1940s, he was working as a Winnipeg Chinatown cook. He adopted Marcelle when he was sixty-one years old. When he heard of the opportunity to buy a laundry shop on Dundas Street in Toronto, and thus provide a better life for his daughter, he bought it.

Lee was also a devoted CDS performer, who distanced himself from politics and religion, but he was somewhat guided by nationalism. He owned a nationalist flag, read the nationalist newspaper, and told Marcelle as a child that Chiang Kai-shek was a good man. At the same time, he did not attend nationalist meetings, and he was not involved in any church groups. He did not want his adopted daughter to learn Chinese or be involved with nationalist society. But he appeared to condone her exposure to Cantonese opera. Disconnected from the nationalist structures and processes that for others led to belonging, Marcelle grew up feeling ashamed of being the daughter of a laundryman:

> My father was so dignified. People made me feel like being a laundryman was an undignified life. I still dream about my parents every night. They were so elemental in my life. But my dad was not unlike a religious figure. He was so steady and such a rock and the fact that he was Chinese was such an elemental part of me. He was a gentleman who lived such a silent life with never an expectation.

Marcelle adds:

> My father started the laundry so that he could have a business and show that he could support me and my mother. It was hell – absolute hell. Running restaurants was much better. He had to get up at four in the morning to start the coal stoves. We lived above the laundry and there were three coal stoves downstairs and one up. So the one upstairs was to keep us warm. There were two coal stoves in the laundry drying room and one in the laundry proper.

So he would have to start the fires in the heat of summer and they would have to be lit to dry the clothes. There were two cycles of laundry Monday, Tuesday, Wednesday and he would deliver on Wednesday to the Jewish neighbours there. And also he would pick up dirty laundry and then cycle again Thursday, Friday, Saturday[;] he would deliver and pick up from different families. He had a delivery route. By 1950, he drove a Chevrolet. It was a pretty big one. He would always say that we liked Chevrolets. He took very good care of his car. Everything in the laundry was bare wood and dark brown. There was nothing fancy. There were ironing tables and a wooden tub that my mother would put me in when I was little and the ringer that when I was bigger I could operate. There was also a huge mangle that would iron the sheets. I now hate the heat. No matter where you went, you could be scorched.

After Lee Choy bought the laundry, he would occasionally be asked to fill in at a friend's restaurant as a cook for the day. He would take Marcelle with him on these days and also whenever he visited Chinatown gambling houses to see his friends. These outings with her father to Toronto's 1940s and 1950s gambling joints were among her favourites:

> To me it was a huge place with all these people talking and the noise of mahjong and the roar of people talking, and smoking. There was always stuff going on and there were all men. Because I was a little girl [being taken out with my father] they would think I was lucky for their gambling. I might help them win the game. I was always happy to go because I would get a nickel or quarter, which was candy for me.

Lee Choy doted on his daughter. In his spare time, he sat with her, watching Roy Rogers. And he, too, was the master of the kitchen, making all the meals, cutting vegetables and meats on an old tree trunk he used as a cutting board for decades.

Marcelle's mother and family friend Kep used to take her to the Cantonese opera when they found out that her real dad, who was part of a travelling dramatic opera troupe, was coming to Toronto to perform in a show. Those who knew her birth father called him something that sounded like "Bal Ahn Kooey." To Marcelle, it seemed an unlikely Chinese name, but she wasn't allowed to learn Chinese. From a young age, Marcelle loved the opera performances, but she didn't understand that they were not part of mainstream Toronto life. She explains:

Figure 37   At left, Marcelle (Choy) Gibson, father Lee Choy, and mother Liliane at a birthday party, Toronto, 1950. *Source:* Marcelle Gibson.

Once a year the travelling Cantonese opera came to the Toronto casino where they performed on Sundays. There were strippers and weird things in fish tanks. It was very strange but I really enjoyed going. I didn't learn until years later that my real dad was a performer in Cantonese opera. Apparently my birth father went to the United States at some point.

Marcelle did well in school and spoke English there, French with her mother, and Chinese with her father. She grew up in a Jewish part of Toronto; her friends were all Jewish, and she thought she was Jewish, too, until about grade four, when the school asked. It wanted to know if she was Christian and if so, whether she was Anglican, part of the United Church, or Catholic. Religion wasn't a topic that was discussed in her house, and they never went to church. Her mother was French Canadian and not religious. Her mother said to tell the school that the family was "Christian and nothing else."

Lee Choy typified the careful Chinese Canadian man who lived on the Prairies. He didn't drink or gamble. He'd probably seen too many men lose their homes and businesses that way. He relished family life and served his friends, but he didn't cultivate brokerage relations. Family friend Kep, who had lost everything to gambling, lived with Marcelle and her family. He slept under the kitchen table in the suite above the laundry shop. When the family ran into financial problems from time to time, Lee Choy would draw on weak ties to the Lee Association and ask for a loan, which he always paid back.

When Marcelle was eleven, Lee had a heart attack. He tried to carry on working but could not. After he experienced several consecutive heart attacks, the family was forced to give up the laundry shop and move. Marcelle finished high school at fourteen and then went to work. Her parents had used up all their savings, so she supported the family. Lee Choy died shortly after, at the age of seventy-five. Neither Marcelle nor her mother had any idea how old he was when he passed away. But they knew how much they meant to him. His father's last words were: "My wife. My daughter."

Conclusion

In the Introduction, I discussed the necessity and merits of this book's ethnohistorical approach. Finding few published archival and historical sources on Chinese settlements beyond the coast and Chinatowns, I used ethnographic research methods to gather oral histories, immerse myself in Chinese Canadian society, and build an archive. From the outset, my goal was to uncover the stories of people who hadn't merited attention in written documents. I aimed to recount the stories of women in a way that was sensitive to the kinds of stories families wanted told. I emphasized to research participants that I wasn't interested in telling their dirty secrets or exposing painful memories. I wanted to use my work to restore the humanity of their mothers and grandmothers and to include them in a broader Chinese Canadian story beyond Chinatowns.

The stories in this book present the networked fabric of the Prairie Chinese, centred on affective regimes. I historicize affective ties documented in scrapbooks, diaries, membership rosters, photographs, letters, and many other materials, through my own understanding of the fields and operations of personal connections. Fieldwork enabled me to understand and become connected to Charlie Foo's family, friends, and political allies. Through these relationships, I became familiar with dominant Chinese societal and political ties, alliances, and taboos. I cultivated connections beyond this dominant frame as well. These relationships enabled me to understand the experiences of outsiders who had more distant ties to power brokers, such as rural labourers and women in Saskatchewan and Ontario. I immersed myself in Prairie Chinese culture, and in the process caught glimpses of historical networks still teeming with affect that made it possible for families to be welcomed and accepted in Prairie Canada, and remain for generations. Religious affect enabled women, especially, to live spiritual lives away from China. Patriotic affect transformed lone bachelors into resolute Chinese nationalists and Canadian citizens.

The act of writing this book brought with it many surprises, from the discovery of Frank Chan's scrapbook to the mysterious 1917 photograph found nailed and hidden beneath the Winnipeg Chinese Dramatic Society's enshrined image of the first teacher of opera. Six years after I first learned about Esterhazy's Happy Young, I came to realize that although he had spent thirty years in small-town Saskatchewan, he cultivated brokerage relations far beyond it. Helen Wong, daughter of Charlie Foo, recounted to me how close friend Happy had given her a stuffed toy puppy when her first son was born almost sixty-five years ago. Helen's granddaughter now had that cherished toy, appropriately named "Happy." Ma Seung's youngest son, Jacque, contacted me as I prepared to launch my previous book, *The Way of the Bachelor*, offering interviews and hundreds of documents and photographs that helped me piece together the entire Prairie network.

As I travelled along the old Chinese networks from Montreal, to Toronto, and through the Prairies to British Columbia, I was able to meet and get to know remarkable Chinese Canadians. In spite of the discrimination and bigotry they had experienced, they continued to love Canada. Some encouraged sons to volunteer for military service in the Second World War – even in Saskatchewan and British Columbia, where Chinese couldn't vote. Through a research contact, I met a relative of Yee Clun who then introduced me to Yee Clun's three children. I came to learn that Yee Clun had never told his children about his successful challenge to a racist Regina law.

In this book, I have tried to demonstrate the roles played not only by the people but by religion, racism, and gender in the Chinese Canadian nationalist project by tracing the webs of connections and affections that flowed through Prairie pathways. These pathways and ties emerged as Chinese arrived. They coalesced in 1909 as settlements stabilized. They buzzed with energy when the last dynasty ended in 1911 and nationalist clubhouses dotted the globe in its wake. From the 1910s to the 1940s, nationalist clubhouses facilitated the flow of donations to save China. And while nationalism was led by economic need, it was anchored by human passion. Although the nationalist dream of a modern China ended in 1950, the embers of nationalist affect, preserved in stories, song, poetry, and performances, still glowed almost sixty years later.

Seeking a better life in Prairie Canada between the 1880s and 1950, male Chinese settlers aimed to work, but not in mining, logging, or factories. At first, they were dishwashers or labourers in rural towns or in Winnipeg's shops and laundries. Later, they were owners of cafes and groceries. Newly arrived Chinese men, mostly from the North American west and south, found free lodging and meals at Prairie KMT clubhouses and affiliated restaurants.[1] Newcomers with better English skills quickly moved out of low-paying labouring positions and became itinerant, well-paid salesmen of meat, produce, slot machines, and life insurance to cafes, shops, and Chinese on the rural Prairie. The especially lucky ones became railway ticket agents, interpreters, power brokers, and sometimes family men. Life beyond urban Chinatowns was not defined by gambling or opium gatherings, but rather by affect, the common nationalist cause, and shared worldviews. It was for many a mutually supportive society, further defined by sporting and other interactions with broader society. Through sport participation, mostly in rural regions, Chinese men took on new identities as hunters, anglers, fans, curlers, soccer players, and sometimes even hockey players. Athletic involvement confirmed a man's rugged Canadian manhood and his loyalty to a place. It also helped his business.

From the 1910s to the 1940s, intersecting channels invigorated by affect became networks and reinforced the architecture of inclusion and exclusion. Nationalists and travelling merchants Charlie Foo, Frank Chan, and Sam Dong visited Chinese in towns and villages. Calling in on others kept alliances strong and rural Chinese men such as Happy Young and Mark Ki connected. Life was forged through balancing the demands of intertwined ties and cultures. Life was also lived between rural and urban areas by necessity. Chinese Canadians who lived in Winnipeg didn't necessarily "make it." Often, those who lived in Winnipeg or in a larger city with a Chinatown experienced too much economic or clan competition to ever become financially well off.

Networks were also forged through religious activities and institutions. Chinese Canadian men and women were almost uniformly Christian in public until 1920. A man's non-affiliation with the KMT was effectively non-affiliation with traditional Chinese culture and its positive social attributes. Chinese Canadian children were usually encouraged by their parents to participate in church and Christian activities. Ma Seung and his sons Peter and Andrew conducted missionary work that saw them visit scores of small Prairie towns and villages where Chinese lived. But privately, women and sometimes men practised Buddhist and Daoist rituals and other customs. Quongying's ritual use of the mystical sword and coins threatened the nationalist project in Canada but may have saved her family by keeping her strong. It was this secret part of her existence that gave her power in a world where Chinese women had very little influence and almost no ties to others. Her actions confirmed that Chinese Canadian Prairie lives and women, as much as they may have appeared ordinary, were far from it. Prairie women were tremendously resourceful human beings who, in the background, made family and status possible.

With so few women in the early Prairie community, wives before 1950 often had very limited social opportunities. They spent the prime years of their adult lives caring for children and doing housework, alone, while their husbands had rich social interactions beyond the home. For women who were fortunate enough to live where other Chinese women resided, life was happier. They could gather to talk in their own language and share embroidery, sewing, and weaving patterns, childcare duties, and even gossip. Through these friendships and Christian involvements, they could lessen the pain of estrangement from their own far-off families in China.

Other Chinese girls were Canadian-born and wanted to marry Prairie merchants. Coastal Chinatowns were some of the most racist places for a Chinese woman.[2] Chinese residents in Manitoba were not prohibited from voting, practising as doctors, or joining other licensed professions that were linked to citizenship and voting rights. Canadian-born Chinese girls wanted a husband who made enough money to support them and their children and to possibly negate their need to work. Marriages were ultimately about power, status, and family alliances in a period in Canadian history when many people (of all ethnicities) were newcomers, and a significant number were bachelors. Through these marriage alliances, various clans from different districts came to populate different regions of Canada.[3]

The rural Prairies were as important to Chinese Canadian experiences of racism as Chinatown. On the rural Prairies, a Chinese man lived alone and had to learn English. He had to live ambiguously, shielding the public from Chinese dress, foods, politics, music, or religious practice, which might be seen as too foreign. He also learned the benefits of athletic involvement in places where access to team sports as player or fan was unrestricted by colour or race. If he managed to get to the top of Prairie hierarchies, he might have a chance at family life and advancement in the local KMT. Throughout his life, he and his family relied on and were shaped by nationalist systems and adaptations. The reinvention of cultural, religious, and political processes knitted the various strands of Prairie life into the global nationalist fabric.

It cannot be emphasized enough that there was less racism in Manitoba and certainly in some parts of Saskatchewan. Unlike in Vancouver and other regions of coastal British Columbia, Chinese were welcome to attend nonsegregated schools, live on the margins of better neighbourhoods, play on sports teams, and go to church. In part, this was because there were far fewer Chinese on the Prairies and less competition with "white" businesses. Prairie populations were small, and communities wanted to grow. Winnipeg, being the Prairie centre, was more welcoming due to its relatively cosmopolitan and diverse population base and workforce. But most of all, the Prairies were a better place to live because of the individuals who made the region that way.

The Canadian Prairies still beckon to migrants who seek a better life. Drawn by promises of less competition, higher quality of life, and business opportunities, migrants are returning to the Prairies. In the 2010s, Chinese families bought farmland in Prairie borderland regions.[4] Today there are fewer cultural and legal barriers to integration, but Chinese still rely on elders, networks, and camaraderie to establish their businesses and maintain their connections. Unlike Prairie networks of the past, these networks are unaffiliated with religion or politics, and they are not all-male.[5] Today, in part through the influence of early Chinese migration, Canada is a highly secularized society. But connections are still essential. Networks today, as in the past, link newcomers to seasoned mentors and elders who are familiar with politicians and Prairie systems and processes.

As more Chinese migrate, they will adapt and the rural towns will adapt to them. New businesses will emerge as Chinese bring family into the region through chain migration. Urban Prairie Chinatowns will be reinvigorated as well. Asian shopping malls that provide expected goods and services to entrepreneurial Chinese may emerge in Chinatowns, stimulating economies and core areas. Throughout this process, Chinese networks and the structures of migration will become transformed by affect.

In the past, as men served their nationalist friends, they defined the texture and contours of Chinese Prairie Canada. Networks had edges and centres where people were drawn or repelled by forces of culture and blood, Christianity, Daoism, or poverty. Networks contributed to belonging and exclusion, power and weakness, social interactions and loneliness. They destroyed some lives. For an elite few, they fulfilled dreams of greatness. No Chinese Prairie resident was untouched by these threads of human connection that still shimmer in the fabric of culture and memory.

Appendix

KMT register indicating the clan names of 254 Manitoba members. Total number of party members starting from 1943 *(Dangyuan zong mingce, Zhonghua Mingguo sanshier nian yuanyue li* 黨員總名冊,中華民國三十二年元月立). Forty-one clan names are listed in the order in which they appear in the register. These names have multiple English translations. See Glossary on page 230.

黃	42	關	6	彭	5	容	1
李	33	謝	5	雷	1	曾	1
余	22	鄧	5	劉	3	模	1
陳	14	何	4	馮	2	譚	1
甄	8	高	5	魏	1	衛	1
袁	7	胡	6	區	4	任	2
伍	5	宋	3	敖	1	朱	1
麥	7	林	3	呂	2	張	1
馬	19	周	2	裴	1		
蔡	11	王	4	鄭	1		
曾	9	吳	3	潘	1		

Notes

Introduction

1 The story of eastern Prairie settlement was largely omitted from a book and project commissioned by the Citizenship branch of the Department of the Secretary of State in 1982, led by Edgar Wickberg and W.E. Willmott at the University of British Columbia. Ron Con and Frank Quo had been asked to conduct ethnographic research on Chinese communities in Regina, Saskatoon, and Winnipeg but had encountered unexpected obstacles and challenges. Correspondence – General (1970-79), Chinese Canadian Research Collection, UBC Archives. See Harry Con et al., *From China to Canada: A History of the Chinese Communities in Canada* (Toronto: McClelland and Stewart in association with the Multiculturalism Directorate, Department of the Secretary of State and the Canadian Government Publishing Centre, Supply and Services Canada, 1982).

2 Raymond Williams's term "structure of feelings" provides one of a number of ways to examine affect and interactions just as they are taking shape. Raymond Williams, *Marxism and Literature* (Oxford: Oxford University Press, 1977). In my work I was seeking to historicize sentiments and the relationships they led to, and to reflect on the waves of human passion that wove a certain kind of Prairie fabric. One of my obstacles was convincing people that I could analyze past affect, or as Huehls refers to it, the "not yet formed." See Mitchum Huehls, "Structures of Feeling: Or, How to Do Things (or Not) with Books," *Contemporary Literature* 51, 2 (2010): 419-28.

3 According to the *Book of Rites* (*Liji* 禮記), a well-known Chinese classical text, there are seven human affections. These range from happiness to desire and are inborn. See "Commentary and Subcommentary to the *Book of Rites* (*Liji Zhushu* 禮記注疏)," in Ruan Yuan, comp., *Commentary and Subcommentary on the Thirteen Classics* (*Shisan jing zhushu* 十三經注疏) (Beijing: Zhonghua shuju, 1957), "The Uses of Rites (*Liyun* 禮運)," 18. Allen Chun's explanation of the systems that create links between human affections and ties was particularly helpful: "I do not know of any actual *guanxi* tie that is not at the same time an attempt to cultivate *renqing*, no matter how instrumental its intent. It is more difficult on the other hand to state when *renqing* is actually an attempt to cultivate *guanxi* (as personal connection) or just a friendly act, since it is a value judgement." See Allen Chun, "From Culture to Power (and Back): The Many 'Faces' of *Mianzi* (Face), *Guanxi* (Connection), and *Renqing* (Rapport)," *Suomen Anthropologi* 27, 4 (2002): 19-37, and 23. See also Mayfair Mei-hui Yang, *Gifts, Favors and Banquets: The Art of Social Relationships in China* (Ithaca: Cornell University Press, 1994), 28. Affective theory is discussed in greater detail in the next chapter of this book.

4 See Baruch Spinoza, "Ethics," in *Complete Works*, ed. Edwin Curley (Princeton, NJ: Princeton University Press, 1985), Part 3: 1. Brian Massumi notes that emotion is for the "personalized content, and affect for the continuation." Affect is what creates the threads and ties of the networked society that I discuss in this book. I use ethnohistorical methods to discover the networking and channels through which human affections flowed. See

Brian Massumi, *Movement, Affect, Sensation: Parables for the Virtual* (Durham: Duke University Press, 2002), 217.

5 For a similar treatment of graded affect in a Chinese context, see Clara Wing-chung Ho, "Male Expression of Emotions: Observations from Collections of Birthday Greetings and Bereavement Messages for Women in Late Imperial and Republican China" (Paper presented at the Association of Asian Studies annual meeting, San Diego, March 22, 2013).

6 Following Sara Ahmed, my research also turns "to the question of how we can theorize positive affect and the politics of good feelings." Sara Ahmed, "Happy Objects," in *The Affect Theory Reader*, ed. Melissa Gregg and Gregory J. Seigworth (Durham, NC: Duke University Press, 2010), 30. Using ethnohistorical research methods, I investigated the lives of people for whom the Chinese community had "good feelings." Those who experienced negative affect, such as women and labourers, were often shunned or silenced and omitted from written accounts. I did not intentionally ignore those for whom there were bad feelings, but it was difficult to discover their stories.

7 Chinese living in Canada and across the Prairies were subject to institutionalized racism enacted by the federal Chinese Immigration Act. This legislation required most Chinese entering Canada to pay a head tax ranging from fifty dollars in 1885 to five hundred dollars after 1903. The head tax was so expensive that most men with wives and children had to leave them behind in China. The tax did not apply to merchants and their families, teachers, diplomats, or missionaries. The degree of exclusion worsened when the Chinese Immigration Act, revised and in force from 1923 to 1947, denied entry to almost all people of Chinese descent, especially wives and children. This had the effect of separating some families permanently. The act also required that Chinese register with the government and obtain certificates.

8 Chinese males were often known as bachelors, though many of the older ones had wives in China. For studies on coastal British Columbia Chinatowns, settlements, religious and political cultures, and the Chinese diaspora, see Timothy Stanley, *Contesting White Supremacy: School Segregation, Anti-Racism and the Making of Chinese Canadians* (Vancouver: UBC Press, 2011), and "'Chinamen, Wherever We Go': Chinese Nationalism and Guangdong Merchants in British Columbia, 1871-1911," *Canadian Historical Review* 77, 4 (1996): 475-503; Edgar Wickberg, "Chinese Associations in Canada 1923-1947," *Visible Minorities and Multiculturalism: Asians in Canada*, ed. K. Victor Ujimoto and Gordon Hirabayashi (Toronto: Butterworths, 1980), 23-31, "Vancouver Chinatown: The First Hundred Years" (Paper presented at the workshop "The Vancouver Chinatown: Past, Present, and Future," Institute of Asian Research, UBC, April 21, 2001), and "Overseas Chinese: The State of the Field," in *Chinese America: History and Perspectives* (San Francisco: Chinese Historical Society of America, 2002), 1-9; Peter Ward, "The Oriental Immigrant and Canada's Protestant Clergy, 1858-1925," *BC Studies* 22 (Summer 1974): 40-55, and *White Canada Forever: Popular Attitudes and Public Policy toward Orientals in British Columbia* (Montreal and Kingston: McGill-Queen's University Press, 1978); Kay J. Anderson, *Vancouver's Chinatown: Racial Discourses in Canada, 1875-1980* (Montreal and Kingston: McGill-Queen's University Press, 1991); and W.E. Willmott, "Some Aspects of Chinese Communities in British Columbia Towns," *BC Studies* 1 (Winter 1968-69): 27-36.

9 Winnipeg's earliest documented Chinese settlers arrived in 1877 from Chicago to open a laundry shop. This was one year before the first Chinese settlers arrived in Toronto. Connections with Chinese settlers throughout Canada and across the border were continually maintained by men who were familiar with North American terrain, cultures, and global networks. For a re-enactment of this settlement pattern, see Stanford University's Spatial History Project Model: "The Chinese Canadian Immigration Pipeline, 1912-23," http://www.stanford.edu/.

10 Large numbers of Chinese passengers frequently travelled north from the United States into Canada along rail lines, usually as prisoners travelling in bond. See "Local and Personal: Eighty Chinese Passengers Passed through the City," *Brandon Daily Sun*, November 1901. These railway lines would have been well known within the North American Chinese community and used for legal and illegal trans-border migration. In the 1880s and 1890s, immigrants arrived in southern Manitoba and parts of Saskatchewan through familiar crossings between Canadian and American borderlands and pastures. Later, branch lines extended northward across the American border and into Canada via Estevan and Weyburn to Moose Jaw, Saskatchewan (which all had consistently good-sized Chinese populations). See Bill Waiser, *Saskatchewan: A New History* (Saskatoon: Fifth House, 2005), 52 and 64.

11 Motivated by a desire for a better life in a less racist environment, low-paid miners, loggers, ship builders, ditch diggers, railway, factory, ranch, and construction workers, and cooks and domestic servants moved out of Chinatowns and less welcoming communities, aiming at a merchant's life and opportunities.

12 One of the exempt classes of Chinese immigrants were "merchants as defined by such sections as the Minister may prescribe" under section 5 (c) 1: of *An Act Respecting Chinese Immigration* (Ottawa: F.A. Acland, 1923). However, all of the married Chinese Prairie merchants in this study lived apart from wives and family after 1923. They did not appear to have been exempted. The Poys were among the few dozen merchant Chinese who were allowed into Canada during the exclusion era (1923-47). Blessed by good fate, merchant status, and Poy's quarter-Irish heritage, the family escaped the Pacific War and exclusion from Canada and went on to have remarkable success. Adrienne Poy (Clarkson) became Canada's first Chinese Canadian governor general in 1999.

13 In 1977, Frank Quo noted in a government report that people on the Canadian Prairies were less hostile toward Chinese immigrants than were those who lived elsewhere in Canada. These observations were confirmed in discussions with Frank Quo by telephone in 2010, and in multiple interviews with Jacque Mar (1912-2012), the ninety-nine-year-old son of Winnipeg's first Chinese minister, who lived in Winnipeg from 1917 to 1935. Jacque's father, Ma Seung, being an itinerant minister from 1900 to 1935, had travelled to many Prairie cities and towns and had noticed that Manitoba was more welcoming than other places. In Victoria and Cumberland, British Columbia, the family had not been able to interact with non-Chinese people, but in Manitoba the family had friends who, in the words of Jacque, were "white, black, and yellow." See F. Quei Quo, "Chinese Immigrants in the Prairies," Preliminary Report Submitted to the Minister of the Secretary of State (Simon Fraser University, November 1977), Chapters 1, 2, and 4. Racism and anti-Chinese sentiments in British Columbia are well documented. See, for instance, Patricia Roy, "British Columbia's Fear of Asians," *Histoire Sociale/Social History* 13, 25 (1980): 161-72, *A White Man's Province: British Columbia Politicians and Chinese and Japanese Immigrants, 1858-1914* (Vancouver: UBC Press, 1989), and *The Oriental Question: Consolidating a White Man's Province* (Vancouver: UBC Press, 2003). See also Peter Ward, "Class and Race in the Social Structure of British Columbia, 1870-1939," *BC Studies* 45 (1980): 17-35; and Con et al., *From China to Canada*. Manitoba was the least hostile to Chinese newcomers, and parts of Saskatchewan were the most. See Alison R. Marshall entries in the Bibliography.

14 For a detailed look at the life of early Chinese wash shop owners and labourers, see Hoe Ban Seng, *Enduring Hardship: The Chinese Laundry in Canada* (Gatineau, PQ: Canadian Museum of Civilization, 2003).

15 Rebecca Nedostup's work has been very influential in the way that I have come to perceive Chinese Canadian nationalism and transnational society. In this book, I use her term

"affective regimes" to describe Kuomintang (KMT) networks that enabled Chinese to connect transnationally through modern nation-state infrastructure, culture, and the reinvention of religion. See Rebecca Nedostup, "Ritual Competition and the Modernizing Nation-State," in *Chinese Religiosities: Afflictions of Modernity and State Formation,* ed. Mayfair Mei-hui Yang (Berkeley: University of California Press, 2008), 91, and "Affective Regimes," in *Superstitious Regimes: Religion and the Politics of Chinese Modernity* (Cambridge, MA: Harvard University Press, 2009), Chapter 7. See also Michel de Certeau, *The Practice of Everyday Life,* trans. Steven Rendall (Berkeley: University of California Press, 1984), xi-xxiv. Marcel Mauss and Pierre Bourdieu's notion of the "habitus" is helpful in understanding the social processes that created nationalist structures, subjects, and cultures. According to Bourdieu, the "habitus" unconsciously follows a "logic of practice" to negotiate power and improvise organizational processes. Pierre Bourdieu, *Outline of Theory of Practice* (Cambridge: Polity Press, 1972), 78. See also Marcel Mauss, "Les techniques du corps," *Journal de Psychologie* 32 (1934): 3-4, repr. in Mauss, *Sociologie et anthropologie* (Paris: PUF, 1936).

16 Manitoba and Saskatchewan also had branches of the Chinese Freemasons (Chee Kung Tong; Zhi Gongtang 致公堂 [CKT]), but the CKT held less power on the Prairies.

17 The Victoria branch of the CBA was known as the CCBA (Consolidated Chinese Benevolent Association). The Victoria group was the "official voice for all Chinese across Canada for twenty-five years (1884-1909) before the Chinese Consulate General was established in Ottawa in 1909." It functioned to unify Chinese Canadian thought and culture. See David Chuenyan Lai, *Chinese Community Leadership: Case Study of Victoria in Canada* (Singapore: World Scientific, 2010), xxvi.

18 In this book, I use quotation marks for racialized terms to highlight the subjective nature of these categories.

19 This book's Prairie settlers came from Toisan (Taishan), Hoiping (Kaiping), San Wui (Xinhui), Canton City, and Zhongshan County (Sun Yat-sen's native county), which shared borders in Guangdong province, China. Chinese who came to all Canadian regions can be traced to specific districts (Taishan [Sunning], Kaiping/Hoiping, Xinhui, Enping, Panyu, Nanhai, and Shunde) and Zhongshan County. See "Canada," in Lynn Pan, *The Encyclopedia of the Chinese Overseas,* pref. and intro. Wang Gungwu, 2nd ed. (Singapore: Nanyang Technological University Press, 2006), 235.

20 In 1880s Victoria, Chinese Canadians were first able to visit offering halls dedicated to Confucius at the Chinese Benevolent Association Building. This building housed one of the earliest Canadian altar rooms that in addition to Confucius, featured major gods of the early Chinese diaspora, such as Mazu. Chinese Canadians could visit halls during important festivals throughout the year. By 1911, Vancouver's Chinatown had overtaken Victoria's as the largest site of Chinese settlement in Canada, with 3,559 settlers. See Chinese Canadian Research Collection, box 20, Interviews with Leaders, UBC Archives. See also David Chuenyan Lai, *The Forbidden City within Victoria: Myth, Symbol and Streetscape of Canada's Earliest Chinatown* (Victoria: Orca Books, 1991), 4-11.

21 The CBA was relatively weak on the Canadian Prairies. Although the CKT was seen as the earliest provincial association, the Victoria head branch had always been recognized by the Canadian government as the face of the Chinese community in Canada. This, however, had not been the case in Winnipeg, where the CBA often operated in the shadows of the more powerful KMT. Led by Mah Yuk, the CBA opened an office in Winnipeg in 1914. See Wing-sam Chow, "A Chinese Community in a Prairie City: A Holistic Perspective of Its Class and Ethnic Relations" (PhD diss., University of Manitoba, 1981), 110. On September 18, 1918, the government declared the KMT illegal, along with twelve other ethnically based political organizations. KMT offices, as well as the Winnipeg CBA,

closed from September 28, 1918 to April 2, 1919, when Order-in-Council PC 2384 was repealed. RG 13, Justice, series A-2, 1940, file: Chinese Nationalist League, Library and Archives Canada (LAC). The Winnipeg CBA reopened in the early 1920s under the leadership of Charlie Foo (interviews with exclusion-era research participants, Manitoba KMT Archives [private collection]). See also Allan Rowe, "'The Mysterious Oriental Mind': Ethnic Surveillance and the Chinese in Canada during the Great War," *Canadian Ethnic Studies* 36, 1 (2004): 48-70.

22 The Magnuson Act of 1943 repealed the Chinese Exclusion Act but limited the number of Chinese immigrants who could come each year to the United States. The privileging of "white" voting rights in the United States began with the 1790 Naturalization Act.

23 As Erika Lee reports, northern and southern border crossings, "beginning in the 1890s, had indeed become a reality ... Both American and Canadian newspapers located in the border regions regularly and actively covered the smuggling of Chinese from the north into the south." Erika Lee, "Enforcing the Borders: Chinese Exclusion along the US Borders with Canada and Mexico 1882-1924," *Journal of American History* 89, 1 (2002): 66-67. For a study of Chinese-Mexican border crossings and merchant businesses facilitating cross-border trade, see Grace Delgado, *Making the Chinese Mexican: Global Migration, Localism, and Exclusion in the US-Mexico Borderlands* (Stanford, CA: Stanford University Press, 2011); Victor G. and Brett de Bary Nee, *Longtime Californ'; A Documentary Study of an American Chinatown* (Stanford, CA: Stanford University Press, 1986), 22; and Stuart Creighton Miller, *The Unwelcome Immigrant: The American Image of the Chinese, 1785-1882* (Berkeley: University of California Press, 1969). The United States enacted the Geary Act (1892), requiring Chinese to register and obtain residence certificates within the year. Canada's Chinese Immigration Act (1923) also required registration and for Chinese to obtain certificates. The Geary Act enabled the American government to collect photographs and vast amounts of personal information about Chinese residents.

24 This borderland's history has been covered in Sheila McManus, *The Line Which Separates: Race, Gender, and the Making of the Alberta-Montana Borderlands* (Edmonton: University of Alberta Press, 2005).

25 Brothels and prostitution rings operated in the mid- to late-1800s by American Chinese gangs known as *tongs* (*tang* 堂 or hall) helped perpetuate the false perception that all Chinese women were prostitutes and that Chinese men were corrupt opium merchants or dirty labourers. Ronald Riddle provides a window into the shadowy world of San Francisco Chinatown and these stereotypes. See Ronald Riddle, *Flying Dragons, Flowing Streams: Music in the Life of San Francisco's Chinese* (Westport, CN: Praeger, 1983), 97-116.

26 State agents also used borders to collect taxes and regulate citizenship. See Kornel Chang, "Enforcing Transnational White Solidarity: Asian Migration and the Formation of the US-Canadian Boundary," *American Quarterly* 60, 3 (September 2008): 673. See also Bruno Ramirez with Yves Otis, *Crossing the 49th Parallel: Migration from Canada to the United States, 1900-1930* (Ithaca: Cornell University Press, 2001).

27 The 1875 Page Law worked along with the later 1882 Exclusion Act to close American borders to Chinese female immigration. See Leti Volpp, "Divesting Citizenship: On Asian American History and the Loss of Citizenship through Marriage," *UCLA Law Review* 53 (2005): 411, http://scholarship.law.berkeley.edu/.

28 Riddle, *Flying Dragons, Flowing Streams*, 5.

29 Renqiu Yu, *To Save China, to Save Ourselves: The Chinese Hand Laundry Alliance of New York* (Philadelphia: Temple University Press, 1992), 21.

30 Even today, when I discuss Chinese male groups with others, people immediately think of gangs, *tong* wars, and the Chinese Six Companies, which is another name for San Francisco's Chinese Consolidated Benevolent Association. The Chinese Six Companies

was indeed powerful. As Victor G. and Brett de Bary Nee note, it was headed by merchant power brokers: "In the early days of immigration, their power had emanated out of their positions as brokers and contractors who extended credit and negotiated employment for impoverished peasants seeking passage to America." See *Longtime Californ,'* 67.

31 See Anthony Chan, *Gold Mountain: The Chinese in the New World* (Vancouver: New Star, 1982), 50-51.

32 Ethnohistorical research shows that Chinese Manitobans were free to associate with and marry non-Chinese in churches and outside of them, unlike in the United States, where there were anti-miscegenation laws preventing Chinese and non-Chinese marriages, or in Saskatchewan, where "white" women could not freely work in Chinese shops. In March 1888, Anne Chan married Simon Weidman in Winnipeg (Registration Number 1888-002177, Vital Statistics, Province of Manitoba). I cannot help but wonder if Sam Dong (discussed in Chapter 3), who later became a travelling salesman with Weidman Brothers, established his business ties to that company through some kind of Chinese connection or whether the connection came as a result of mutual good feelings between the Chinese and Jewish communities in Manitoba, which I had also heard about. In 1911, Lee Fang presented his naturalization papers at a Winnipeg police station in application for a marriage licence to an American girl. *Manitoba Free Press*, April 28, 1911.

33 I am grateful to Paul Gilmore, who grew up in several Franco-Manitoban towns and pointed this out to me.

34 See Garry Enns, *Window on the Northwest* (Gretna, MB: Village of Gretna History Committee, 1987), 82-85. See H.H. Hamm, *Sixty Years of Progress, Diamond Jubilee, 1884-1944: The Rural Municipality of Rhineland* (Altona, MB: D.W. Friesen and Sons, 1944), 13.

35 Department of Agriculture correspondence, August 3, 1892, RG 17, series I-1, 731, 84229, LAC.

36 See Alison R. Marshall, *The Way of the Bachelor: Early Chinese Settlement in Manitoba* (Vancouver: UBC Press, 2011).

37 Census data show that in the District of Assiniboia West (a region that included Medicine Hat, Moose Jaw, Regina, Swift Current, and Walsh) there were nine Chinese-born individuals. See Census 1891, 1, 112, and 362. See also Li Zeng's entry in *The Encyclopedia of Saskatchewan*, confirming that Chinese settlement in that province began in the 1880s. Li Zeng, "Chinese Community," *The Encyclopedia of Saskatchewan* (Regina: Canadian Plains Research Center, 2005), 170. See David E. Smith, ed., *Building a Province: A History of Saskatchewan in Documents* (Saskatoon: Fifth House, 1992); Waiser, *Saskatchewan: A New History*; and John H. Archer, *Saskatchewan: A History* (Saskatoon: Fifth House, 1980).

38 See, for instance, History Committee of R.M. of the Gap 39, *Builders of a Great Land: History of the R.M. of the Gap 39 Ceylon and Hardy* (Altona, MB: Friesens, 1980). Interviews with research participants who lived during the exclusion era provided evidence of additional early Chinese settlements in Lake Alma, Tuxford, and Maple Creek, Saskatchewan.

39 The research findings presented here are somewhat different from those of Peter Li, who analyzed fifty-five case studies of Prairie Chinese who came to Canada between 1910 and 1923. Li's research focused on the social and economic marginality of his participants. My research concentrates on the networks of transnational individual, family, and political lives, as well as the multiple overlapping social, economic, and cultural identities and people's roles as labourers, merchants, and power brokers in Prairie Chinese Canada. My research, based on ethnography and Chinese and English archival materials from 1890 to 1950, shows that experiences of exclusion varied across the Prairies (and Canada), owing to discriminatory legislation enacted nationally, provincially, and municipally, and to Chinese webs of connection. Parts of Manitoba were more welcoming of Chinese

Canadians, and parts of Saskatchewan were much less welcoming. Peter S. Li, "Chinese Immigrants on the Canadian Prairie, 1910-47," *Canadian Review of Sociology and Anthropology* 19, 4 (1982): 527-40.

40 It was only after speaking with Tim Stanley, who first mentioned this settlement pattern in conversation in May 2011, that I examined the addresses of key Chinese Prairie nationalists and realized that they, too, lived only on the perimeter of better neighbourhoods.

41 Ma Seung and his wife, Hong Lin, decided that their sons should take the surname "Mar," not Ma, when they were registered for school in Cumberland. They believed that this name sounded less Chinese and would help them fit into mainstream society.

42 Large-scale migration and (re)settlement patterns in Manitoba were largely formed by 1921, making Manitoba the first settled Prairie province. New Manitobans generally arrived directly from Europe and not via the United States, as was the case for many Saskatchewan and Albertan migrants. Manitoba's unique Prairie settlement history produced a more tolerant "ethnic mosaic," according to Philip Keddie. See Philip Keddie, "Changes in Rural Manitoba's 'Ethnic Mosaic,' 1921 to 1961," *Manitoba Historical Society Transactions* 3, 31 (1974-75), http://www.mhs.mb.ca/.

43 The 1916 membership roster of the KMT reflected the clans that were dominant in Manitoba at that time. Of the 65 members, 13 were Lees, including the president, 11 were Wongs, including the secretary, and another 5 were Chans and Hongs. Manitoba KMT Archives, unpublished. Within a year, membership had more than doubled to 132. Now, Wongs (22 percent) dominated the group, followed by Lees (14 percent), Yees (13 percent), and Hong/Fong (7 percent). By 1943, there were approximately 254 documented members in the Manitoba KMT, with the Wong clan (16.5 percent) dominating, followed by the Lee (13 percent), Yee (9 percent), and Ma (7.5 percent) clans. See Appendix at the end of this book. I suspect that the absence of Mas in earlier KMT groups is due to the missionary influence of Ma Seung. Chain migration of cooks and kitchen staff to the Winnipeg General Hospital happened because of connections to Mah Joe, an early Christian and one of the few early Ma clan members in the region. Both Ma men and their families left Winnipeg in the mid-1930s, but chain migration and marriage alliances have continued to the present day. In addition to the KMT, the Lees, Mas, Wongs, Yees, and others had their own clan and district associations to which they belonged.

44 The Chinese United League formed in 1905. In the *International Chinese Business Directory*, the clubhouse is listed as Hong Wah and Co. Chi. and Ja. Bazaar. Given the pattern of businesses in the core area of Winnipeg's Chinatown, and basing my conclusions on interviews with elderly Chinese, I am quite certain that this was the secret location of the Chinese United League Manitoba branch. It is also where Sun Yat-sen would have visited when he arrived in Winnipeg in April 1911. Wong Kin, comp., *International Chinese Business Directory of the World for the Year 1913: A Comprehensive List of Prominent Chinese Firms and Individuals (Wangguo jixin bianlan)* (San Francisco: International Chinese Business Directory, February 10, 1913), Winnipeg.

45 Sun Yat-sen came to Canada three times: in July 1897, February 1910, and from January to April 1911. Throughout the years, Winnipeg was visited by many important Chinese nationalist political figures.

46 The *International Chinese Business Directory for the Year 1913* was published February 10, 1913. It included information about KMT branches in Canmore and Medicine Hat, Alberta, as well as Brandon, Manitoba. By combining information in this directory with other information from interviews, newspaper articles, photographs, and through fieldwork at the Manitoba KMT clubhouse, I was able to determine that Canada's KMT branches opened in 1912, though most received branch certificates only in 1916. Wong, *International Chinese Business Directory*, 1372, 1375, and 1383.

47 Winnipeg Chinese had usually lived in rural Manitoba or Saskatchewan before they moved to the city. A search of clergy records documenting Prairie exclusion-era Chinese shows ties to Vancouver, San Francisco, Bismarck, ND, Edmonton, Ottawa, New York, Toronto, Hong Kong, and China, among other places. Winnipeg Chinese United Church, Clergy Records, unpublished.

48 A 1924 report completed by Reverend Ma Seung on the 1,100 Chinese living in Calgary and 450 in Edmonton showed that there were ten merchant families residing in Calgary and six in Edmonton. Chinese were employed most often in wash shops, of which there were fifty in each city. Ma Seung noted that Calgary Chinese were more predisposed toward Christianity than were Edmonton Chinese. The second and third most popular Chinese businesses of the time in these two cities were cafes and tailor shops. Ma Seung Fonds, unpublished. The General Register of Chinese Immigration showed that five women had come to Edmonton as wives (one Wong, Ma, and Pon, and two Fongs), and eleven had come to Calgary by 1924 (one Lim, Fun, Der, Quong, Jung, and Ma, two Wongs, and three Louies). Census data showed that by 1921, 182 women (daughters and wives born in China and Canada) resided in Alberta.

49 By 1921, census data indicated that Montreal had a Chinese population of 1,735 people. There are intermittent references to Montreal's population size and character in Chan Kwok Bun, *Smoke and Fire: The Chinese in Montreal* (Hong Kong: Chinese University Press, 1991). There were 4,000 Chinese residents in Victoria, 7,000 in Vancouver, and 3,500 in Toronto. See United Church Archives of Canada, Winnipeg, G7a, 107; Population of Selected Cities in Canada ca. 1919 (passim in report), in S.S. Osterhout, "A Religious and Missionary Survey of the Chinese (being a report on the work of the Methodist Church among the Chinese in British Columbia, Alberta, Saskatchewan, Winnipeg and Toronto)," Vancouver, Superintendent of Oriental Missions, 1919, 21 pages (typescript unnumbered).

50 Moose Jaw was atypical of Chinese Prairie settlements and experiences. Even to this day, the city perpetuates images of Chinese who dwelled underground in tunnels and lived the life of heathens in opium dens, laundries, and gambling joints. I aimed to write about everyday Chinese Canadian experiences and thus did not examine Moose Jaw settlement in detail. Chinese settlement there seems to have been more racialized, imagined, and distorted, and thus I leave this city for others to discuss in more detail. None of my research participants had much involvement with Moose Jaw, though non-Chinese participants were quick to try to steer me there. Urban myths circulated that there were also tunnels in Winnipeg's Chinatown; however, this is untrue.

51 Royden Loewen and Gerald Friesen, eds., *Immigrants in Prairie Cities: Ethnic Diversity in Twentieth-Century Canada* (Toronto: University of Toronto Press, 2009), 37; and Gerald Friesen, *The Canadian Prairies: A History* (Toronto: University of Toronto Press, 1987), 243. See also Li, "Chinese Immigrants on the Canadian Prairie, 1910-1947"; and Hoe Ban Seng, "Adaptive Change and Overseas Chinese Settlements, with Special Reference to a Chinese Community in the Canadian Prairies" (Master's thesis, Department of Sociology, University of Alberta, 1971).

52 The founding of the Logan Avenue mission appears to coincide with the 1917 arrival of Ma Seung in Winnipeg, though joint Presbyterian and Methodist mission work was performed by Mr. Colman (Presbyterian missionary) in this city prior to Ma Seung's arrival. The Methodists provided the start-up funds to purchase the building, but mission operations were funded by the Chinese and non-Chinese members of the Chinese Young Men's Christian Association and by dedicated baptized and nominal Christian Chinese in the Winnipeg community. The Presbyterians contributed a small salary to Winnipeg's missionary and later minister, Ma Seung, but it was never enough to fund the region's operations or to cover living expenses for him and his family.

53 Extensive archival and ethnographic research shows that by 1910, Winnipeg Chinatown businesses and activities had been well established for a decade. But it would take a clubhouse to which all settlers were drawn to unite and anchor the region. See also Chow, "A Chinese Community in a Prairie City."

54 October 10, 1911, was the Wuchang Uprising. Winnipeg was additionally the site of political meetings and national KMT conventions in 1936 and again in 1943. In 1943, members from forty-five Canadian branches converged at the western regional head office of the party. *Winnipeg Evening Tribune,* May 18, 1943, 2.

55 Canadian Chinese society was not defined and contained by Chinatown. Chinatowns may have dominated early coastal British Columbia, but the situation differed on the Prairies. Ethnographic and archival research shows that Winnipeg's Chinatown, though essential, was a hub in a large network of Prairie relationships and settlements, most of which were located outside Winnipeg.

56 Ethnographic research suggests that Frank Chan grew up in Somerset, Manitoba, but a search of the Somerset local history revealed no men or businesses associated with him. See Somerset History Book Committee, *Reflections-Reflets: Somerset and Area* (Altona: Friesens, 2000).

57 The General Register of Chinese Immigration from 1910 to 1949 listed 112 Saskatchewan destinations where Chinese settled. This was roughly the same number of destinations listed in the register for British Columbia. Local histories and census data show that Chinese men and women settled in many more destinations than those indicated on the register. The additional towns and villages where Chinese settled are too numerous to list, but here is a selection: Allan, Bateman, Buffalo Horn Valley, Coteau, Driver, Edenwold, Elstow, and Fosston.

58 Census data, though largely unreliable because Chinese residents were missed by the census taker or because Chinese tended to be unwilling to self-identify by race, show general trends. Saskatchewan's Chinese population was small, but these Canadians lived under a more severe shadow of discrimination, similar to those who lived in British Columbia. Between 1910 and 1923, 569 Chinese Canadians who paid head tax indicated on the General Register of Chinese Immigration that they intended to settle in Saskatchewan. In the same period, 589 individuals indicated that they would settle in Manitoba.

59 See Adele Perry, "Hardy Backwoodsmen, Wholesome Women, and Steady Families: Immigration and the Construction of a White Society in British Columbia, 1849-1871," *Histoire Sociale/Social History* 33, 66 (2000): 343-60; and Andrew Nurse, "Regionalism, Citizenship, Identity," *Canadian Diversity* 2, 1 (2003): 43-44.

60 In coastal British Columbia, coal was sometimes freely available along the routes where miners returned home (for Chinese males who could afford a furnace). Interview with Jacque Mar.

61 Canada Census 1911 and 1921. See also Donica Belisle, *Retail Nation* (Vancouver: UBC Press, 2011), 32.

62 Lisa Mar presents extensive documentation of power brokers in British Columbia. There were power brokers far beyond the coast as well. Lisa Rose Mar, *Brokering Belonging: Chinese in Canada's Exclusion Era, 1885-1945* (New York: Oxford University Press, 2010). Power brokers were regulators of migrant state or nationalist interactions. Dorothee Schneider refers to these regulators as "facilitators" and as the third party in the processes of migration. Dorothee Schneider, *Crossing Borders: Migration and Citizenship in the Twentieth-Century* (Cambridge, MA: Harvard University Press, 2011), 49. Vilna Bashi refers to these agents as "hubs" who create ties to spokes and entire networks dependent on the flow of mutual assistance. See Vilna Bashi, *Survival of the Knitted: Immigrant Social Networks in a Stratified World* (Stanford, CA: Stanford University Press, 2007).

63 Under Saskatchewan law, Chinese were denied the provincial right to vote from 1909 to 1947. Saskatchewan Chinese Canadians voted for the first time on June 8, 1948. See "Chinese to Exercise First Franchise June 8, 1948," *Leader-Post*, April 15, 1948, 10. British Columbia denied Chinese residents the provincial right to vote from 1872 (and in subsequent acts in 1902, 1908, and 1939) to 1947. According to the 1900 Dominion Elections Act, a provincial loss of voting rights automatically meant a federal loss of voting rights. The only other province in which Chinese were denied the right to vote was Saskatchewan. See Constance Backhouse, "White Female Help and Chinese Canadian Employers: Race, Class, Gender and Law in the Case of Yee Clun, 1924," *Canadian Ethnic Studies* 26 (1994): 34-52, and *Colour-Coded: A Legal History of Racism in Canada, 1900-1950* (Toronto: University of Toronto Press, 1999). Chinese men did enjoy some freedoms that British Columbian Chinese did not. In early Saskatchewan towns, men were able to purchase lots from the CPR and build laundries. See D.E. MacIntyre, *Prairie Storekeeper* (Toronto: Peter Martin, 1970), 38.

64 Saskatchewan society and leaders were particularly inclined toward racist thinking and the categorization of society based on colour and race. This is consistent with global classifications that interpreted Chinese as "white" until 1775 and "yellow" after that. See Michael Keevak, *Becoming Yellow: A Short History of Racial Thinking* (Princeton, NJ: Princeton University Press, 2011), Chapter 5.

65 "Slave-girl" stories were well known in 1880s British Columbia, where various Chinese groups vied for control of funds generated by girls who were kidnapped and sold as prostitutes. See Roy, *A White Man's Province*, 266.

66 According to *An Act to Prevent the Employment of Female Labour in Certain Capacities, 1912*, 2 Geo. V. c. 17, which was in effect in various forms until 1969, Chinese men could not freely hire "white" female employees from 1912 to 1919, and between 1919 and 1969 could not do so without a licence. Yee Clun challenged the act's requirement in 1924 to apply for a licence to hire "white" women and won a year later.

67 The research presented here builds on previous studies of historical and current racism in Canada. See Sherene Razack, "Making Canada White: Law and the Policing of Bodies of Colour in the 1990s," *Canadian Journal of Law and Society* 14, 1 (1999): 159-84; and Barrington Walker, ed., *The History of Immigration and Racism in Canada* (Toronto: Canadian Scholars' Press, 2008). See also Adele Perry, *On the Edge of Empire: Gender, Race and the Making of British Columbia, 1849-1871* (Toronto: University of Toronto Press, 2001); and Backhouse, "White Female Help and Chinese Canadian Employers," 34-52, and *Colour-Coded*.

68 Constance Backhouse and others have written about the strength of the presence of the KKK in Saskatchewan, in particular from 1927 to 1929. See Backhouse, *Colour-Coded*, 163-64. See also Martin Robin, *Shades of Right: Nativist and Fascist Politics in Canada, 1920-1940* (Toronto: University of Toronto Press, 1992); Julian Sher, *White Hoods: The Ku Klux Klan in Canada* (Vancouver: New Star, 1983); and Timothy Messer-Kruse, "Memories of the Ku Klux Klan Honorary Society at the University of Wisconsin," *Journal of Blacks in Higher Education* 23 (Spring 1999): 83-93.

69 See Marshall, *The Way of the Bachelor*, 79-82.

70 See Rita Dhamoon, *Identity/Difference Politics: How Difference Is Produced and Why It Matters* (Vancouver: UBC Press, 2009), 11-12.

71 A search of available voters' lists from 1895 to 1947 shows that Chinese Manitobans living in rural and urban centres have always been able to own land and vote at all levels of elections, even after they were required by law to register with the government in 1924. Wong Chan, a "laundryman" in Brandon, was on the voters' list from 1895 to 1907. See City of Brandon, List of Electors. Wah Lee, a "laundryman," and Queen Wong, a grocer on Winnipeg's Elgin Avenue, voted in 1924. See 1924, List of Electors, City of Winnipeg,

Province of Manitoba, Ward 2, Polling Division 24, 42. Charles Yee and his wife, Pauline, the operators of Winnipeg's Moon Cafe, voted in 1939. See 1939, List of Electors, City of Winnipeg, Province of Manitoba, Ward 2, Polling Division 31, 26.

72 Chinese also came to Winnipeg to study at the Winnipeg School of Art in the mid-1910s.

73 City of Brandon General Permit 10s 12016 expires March 31st, 1952. The permit entitled H. (Happy) Young to purchase alcohol in Brandon and listed his Brandon home at 321 Tenth Street as his place of residence. The liquor was presumably brought back for use at Happy Young's cafe in Esterhazy, Saskatchewan. I met Happy's nephew, Moon Dong, through a research contact in 2009. Throughout the years, I interviewed Moon Dong and scanned and catalogued his large archival collection documenting Happy Young's life in Saskatchewan. I later obtained permission to digitize and include this collection in the Canadian Historical Recognition Program Chinese Canadian Stories Project at the University of British Columbia, Moon Dong Fonds, Chinese Canadian Stories, UBC Archives.

74 Winnipeg's Chinese community tended to be racially divided between "pure" Chinese and mixed-race Chinese. According to this system, in the 1930s there were seven "pure" Chinese families, those of Ma Seung, Mah Joe, Lee Mon, Wing Dong (formerly of Morden), Lee Hong Hui, Wong Git, and Ma Hon. There were four mixed-race Chinese families, those of Wong Yuk, Tony Quan, Charlie Foo, and Charles Yee. Children from these families, as well as the young Chinese labourers who lived as orphans in Canada, would be at the yearly nationalist picnics. By 1928, there were between twenty-five and thirty Chinese families who came to the picnics, half of them coming from Winnipeg, and the other half beyond it in rural areas. Nationalist involvement, business skill, and charisma determined status and wealth. Though Mah Joe and his family were "pure" Chinese and part of the wealthy merchant elite, in terms of social status, Charlie Foo, because of his involvement in nationalism, and Charles Yee, because of his extraordinary wealth, were ranked higher within nationalist systems of power. The highly educated family of Ma Seung lacked wealth and nationalist connections, and thus had the lowest social status within the community. Both Ma Seung and Mah Joe would take their families back to China by 1934. As Peter Mar reported in 1931, families were leaving Canada around this time due to the Depression and perceived better economic and social prospects in China (Peter Mar, 1931 Report to Presbyterian Board, Ma Seung Fonds, unpublished.) I confirmed these names and this information with several research participants who grew up during the exclusion era in Winnipeg. As mentioned elsewhere, elderly research participants had excellent memories of people, places, and events. Without their interviews, I would have had to rely on incomplete and inaccurate written accounts, mislabelled photographs, and archives with general omissions. By 1943, several other Winnipeg men and families had left the city and now resided in Hong Kong, including Lee Sun, nationalist leader and former owner and operator of Winnipeg's Nanking Restaurant, Tong Wong, Lee Wing, Carl Thom, Walter Lee, Yee Bon, Wesley Lee, and Dr. T.L. Quong, who had formerly been a Winnipeg physician with the King Edward Hospital and the Winnipeg General Hospital. Lee Sun remained an active KMT member in Hong Kong. *Winnipeg Free Press,* October 22, 1943.

75 Such practices include fortune-telling and the use of magic charms and spells to bring good luck.

76 Oral history has been very useful in documenting a largely undocumented group of people living on the margins of "white" society. I have corroborated information discovered through oral history with extensive archival and historical research. As Peter Li has noted, "Oral history is ideal for sorting out the folk version of events as an additional source for reconstructing social reality." Peter S. Li, "The Use of Oral History in Studying Elderly Chinese-Canadians," *Canadian Ethics Studies* 17, 1 (1985): 75.

77 James Clifford and George E. Marcus, *Writing Culture: The Poetics and Politics of Ethnography* (Berkeley: University of California Press, 1986); John Van Maanen, *Tales of the Field: On Writing Ethnography* (Chicago: University of Chicago Press, 1988). All quotes in the text without sources/citations were drawn from interviews. Some research participants chose to remain anonymous.

78 Fieldwork was conducted throughout Canada and also in southern China, Taiwan, the Philippines, and Singapore. Steven Feld and Keith H. Basso, eds., *Senses of Place* (Santa Fe: School of American Research, 1996); John Collier, *Visual Anthropology: Photography as a Research Method* (New York: Holt, Rinehart and Winston, 1967); and Patricia van der Does et al., "Reading Images: A Study of a Dutch Neighborhood," *Visual Sociology* 7, 1 (1992): 4-68.

79 See Ruth Behar and Deborah A. Gordon, eds., *Women Writing Culture* (Berkeley: University of California Press, 1995); Mary Margaret Fonow and Judith A. Cook, *Beyond Methodology: Feminist Scholarship as Lived Research* (Bloomington: Indiana University Press, 1991); Shulamit Reinharz, *Feminist Methods in Social Research* (New York: Oxford University Press, 1992); Jill Vickers, "Methodologies for Scholarship about Women," in *Gender, Race, and Nation: A Global Perspective*, ed. Vanaja Dhruvarajan and Jill Vickers (Toronto: University of Toronto Press, 2002), 64-92; and Gayle Letherby, *Feminist Research in Theory and Practice* (Buckingham: Open University Press, 2003).

80 Mary Field Belenky et al., eds., *Women's Ways of Knowing: The Development of Self, Voice, and Mind* (New York: Basic Books, 1997); Janice Ristock and Joan Pennell, *Community Research as Empowerment: Feminist Links, Postmodern Interruptions* (Toronto: Oxford University Press, 1996); Fay Ginsburg and Anna Lowenhaupt Tsing, eds., *Uncertain Terms: Negotiating Gender in American Culture* (Boston: Beacon, 1990).

81 Julie Cruikshank, *The Social Life of Stories: Narrative and Knowledge in the Yukon Territory* (Vancouver: UBC Press, 1998); Mihaly Csikszentmihalyi and Eugene Rochberg-Halton, *The Meaning of Things: Domestic Symbols and the Self* (Cambridge: Cambridge University Press, 1981); Sherna Berger Gluck and Daphne Patai, *Women's Words: The Feminist Practice of Oral History* (New York: Routledge, 1991); Henrietta L. Moore, *A Passion for Difference* (Bloomington: Indiana University Press, 1994); and Patricia E. Sawin, *Listening for a Life: Bessie Eldreth, a Dialogic Ethnography* (Logan: Utah State University Press, 2004).

82 Although the discussion refers to Chinese community celebrations, it is worth noting that Chinese, Japanese, Vietnamese, and Korean communities observe the same Lunar New Year, and related Asian community celebrations would have taken place at the same time.

83 Here, my role came close to that of an "indigenous anthropologist," though I am not of Chinese descent. See James Clifford, *The Predicament of Culture: Twentieth-Century Ethnography, Literature, and Art* (Cambridge, MA: Harvard University Press, 1988), 59.

84 From January 2011 to 2012, I worked with the WCCCC and co-project manager Tina Chen via the Canadian Historical Recognition Program to arrange for more than a thousand documents, photographs, and oral histories that I had collected since 2005 to be uploaded to the UBC Chinese Canadian Stories project. I was unable to upload my entire collection of more than four thousand files, some of which I include here.

85 David D. Dunaway and Willa K. Baum, *Oral History: An Interdisciplinary Anthology* (Walnut Creek, CA: Altamira Press, 1996). Discovering women's emotional lives required me to look beyond the frame and margins of most scrapbooks, diaries, membership rosters, photographs, letters, and newspaper articles. Oral history and unwritten materials (such as photographs or crocheted doilies in their aggregate) usually provided a better window into a woman's ambiguous life. Through life story collection, I became familiar with a woman's central position in traditional households and network edges. I drew on my personal connections, developed through feminist ethnographic methods, to question

and make sense of, link, and contrast past theories, materials, and linguistic and cultural patterns with present ones.

86 Donna Haraway, "Race: Universal Donors in a Vampire Culture. It's All in the Family: Biological Kinship Categories in the Twentieth Century United States," in *The Haraway Reader* (New York: Routledge, 2006), 251-56.

87 My theoretical approach follows that set out in Pierre Bourdieu, and Loïc J.D. Wacquant, *An Invitation to Reflexive Sociology* (Chicago: University of Chicago Press, 1992).

88 See Natasha Pinterics, "Riding the Feminist Waves: In With the Third?," *Canadian Woman Studies* 21, 4 (2001): 15-21. For Bourdieu, see note 15.

89 I allowed participants to comment on and edit their own stories but not the stories of others.

90 Charlie Chow, who lived in Moose Jaw, Saskatchewan, was an exception. He married a Romanian girl. The interactions and affections of labouring men were limited by linguistic, social, and economic barriers as opposed to gender. For these reasons, labourers and women often had only supporting positions in the various Chinese Canadian circles.

91 Throughout the book, I draw on two decades of research and training in the field of East Asian Studies and understanding of thought and culture in Canada and throughout the Chinese cultural sphere. The cult of Sun Yat-sen refers to the way in which many earlier settlers, and especially nationalist KMT members, worshipped Sun Yat-sen like a god. See Marshall, *The Way of the Bachelor*. Religion as practised in Guangdong, Hong Kong, and throughout Canadian immigrant communities has unclear boundaries. Sometimes these practices are labelled "popular religion," based on the three traditions: Buddhist, Daoist, and Confucian. The reality is that Chinese religious practice has taken a blended form since at least the late Han dynasty (206 BCE-220 CE). See Adam Chau, "Efficacy, Not Confessionality: On Ritual Polytropy in China," in *Sharing The Sacra: The Politics and Pragmatics of Inter-communal Relations around Holy Places*, ed. Glenn Bowman (Oxford: Berghahn Books, 2012), 80n4. Religious practice is also defined through actions in front of household altars. Here, individual families choose which deities to enshrine and how to make offerings to them. They host these deities, who become guests in their homes. See Adam Chau, "Household Sovereignty and Religious Subjectification: China and the Christian West Compared," in *Religion and the Household, Studies in Church History*, No. 50, ed. John Doran, Charlotte Methuen, and Alexandra Walsham (Suffolk: Boydell and Brewer, 2014), Chapter 33.

92 For an incisive discussion of customs designed to enforce normative domestic and marital expectations in pre-1950 Canada, see Pauline Greenhill, *Make the Night Hideous: Four English-Canadian Charivaris, 1881-1940* (Toronto: University of Toronto Press, 2010), 21-24.

93 In this book, I refer to the modern period as beginning in 1900. See Kam Louie, "Defining Modern Chinese Culture," in *The Cambridge Companion to Modern Chinese Culture*, ed. Kam Louie (Cambridge: Cambridge University Press, 2008), 1-19; Immanuel Hsu, *The Rise of Modern China*, 6th ed. (New York: Oxford University Press, 2000); and Tan Sor-Hoon, "Modernizing Confucianism and 'New Confucianism,'" in Louie, *The Cambridge Companion to Modern Chinese Culture*, 135-54.

94 By household religious practice, I am referring to the customary use of home altars (special wooden shelves on which deities are placed) by people throughout the Chinese cultural sphere. Chinese typically treat gods and ancestors as guests in their homes to whom food, incense, and other offerings are made. The altar may be a very traditional one, with the figurines of Guanyin (the goddess of mercy) or the Kitchen God. Altars also include images of deceased ancestors going back four generations, sometimes represented by memorial tablets (that have been blessed by a Daoist or Buddhist priest) or vertical strips of wood engraved with the names of the deceased. Sometimes an altar might be only photographs with no gods present. See note 91 above as well.

95 For a discussion of these tactics and strategies, see Alison R. Marshall, "Homosociality, Ambiguity and Efficacy in the Everyday Practices of Early Chinese Manitoban Settlers," in *Everyday Religion*, ed. Liza Debevec and Samuli Schielke (Oxford: Berghahn Books, 2012), Chapter 3.

96 Michel de Certeau's everyday practices, ranging from reading to cooking, come close to the kind of everyday doing and affect that this book aims to understand. See de Certeau, *The Practice of Everyday Life*, xi-xxiv.

97 They also intentionally and unintentionally maintained margins of difference within emergent and intersecting Chinese and non-Chinese political, Christian, and business networks. See A. Dirlik, "Asians on the Rim: Transnational Capital and Local Community in the Making of Contemporary Asian America," in *Across the Pacific: Asian Americans and Globalization*, ed. E. Hu-DeHart (Philadelphia: Temple University Press, 1999), 30-31; see also M. Boyd, "Family and Personal Networks in International Migration: Recent Developments and New Agendas," *International Migration Review* 23, 3 (1989): 638-70; James T. Fawcett, "Networks, Linkages and Migration Systems," *International Migration Review* 23, 3 (1989): 671-80; and Henry Yu, *Thinking Orientals: Migration, Contact and Exoticism in Modern America* (New York: Oxford University Press, 2001).

98 See, for instance, Dhamoon, *Identity/Difference Politics* and Sunera Thobani, *Exalted Subjects: Studies in the Making of Race and Nation in Canada* (Toronto: University of Toronto Press, 2007).

99 According to my ongoing Social Sciences and Humanities Research Council of Canada-funded study of nearly five hundred communities and the complete collection of local histories in the province, roughly 15 percent of all communities in Manitoba practised some form of ethnic drag. Almost 80 percent of this ethnic drag, or performance of race, up to the 1940s took place in predominantly British and Protestant church communities. Blackface and related "Chinaman" performances were sometimes even organized and hosted by church groups. See Josephine Lee, *The Japan of Pure Invention: Gilbert and Sullivan's "The Mikado"* (Minneapolis: University of Michigan Press, 2010), xii.

100 The *Brandon Sun* told of an upcoming carnival at the rink in 1882 and announced that prizes would be awarded to those deemed to have the best costume. Prizes would be given to those dressed in uniforms of dominant society or racialized, effeminate ethnic drag of the late nineteenth century: chief of police, CPR station agent, and "Chinaman." *Brandon Sun*, December 26, 1882.

101 Ethnic drag, a term popularized by Katrin Sieg, refers to the performing of race in "Chinaman," blackface, and other kinds of racialized and imagined ethnic costumes. See Katrin Sieg, "Ethnic Drag and National Identity: Multicultural Crises, Crossings, and Interventions," in *The Imperialist Imagination: German Colonialism and Its Legacy*, ed. Sara Friedrichsmeyer, Sara Lennox, and Susanne Zantop (Ann Arbor: University of Michigan Press, 1998), 295-319, and *Ethnic Drag: Performing Race, Nation, Sexuality in West Germany* (Ann Arbor: University of Michigan Press, 2002).

102 See Patricia Ticineto Clough, *The Affective Turn: Theorizing the Social*, ed. Patricia Ticineto Clough and Jean Halley (Durham: Duke University Press, 2007), 1-33.

103 See Mikhail Bakhtin, *Rabelais and His World* (Bloomington: Indiana University Press. 1984).

104 A 1913 newspaper report shows these four "clown" figures: "Immense Crowd at Masquerade Carnival. Financially, numerically and for all round good fun, Friday night's masquerade carnival was a grand success. Fay Easter dressed as a Japanese Girl for which she won a box of chocolates. Willard Thompson dressed as a colored jockey and won a clock. Myrtle Winkjer [sic] dressed as a Chinaman and won a watch." Others mentioned in the report included Herbert Willner who dressed as a 'little Jew.' *Davidson Leader*, March 13, 1913. See also *Davidson Leader*, March 25, 1926, 4; and *Davidson Leader*, February 25, 1927, 1.

105   See, for instance, James S. Moy, *Marginal Sights: Staging the Chinese in America* (Iowa City: University of Iowa Press, 1993), 83.
106   "Local Happenings," *Davidson Leader,* November 1909. See also *Davidson Leader,* March 24, 1906.
107   See the description of the Children's Missionary Alphabet, conceived and organized by two women from a Presbyterian church in Scotland. The program was seen to be a useful way of introducing mission work to children. The performance offered racist and demeaning descriptions of a different character in ethnic drag for each of the letters of the alphabet. *Davidson Leader,* December 1918.
108   See Lamin Sanneh, *Disciples of All Nations: Pillars of World Christianity,* Studies in World Christianity (London: Oxford University Press, 2007); and Lori G. Beaman, ed., *Religion and Canadian Society: Traditions, Transitions and Innovations* (Toronto: Canadian Scholars' Press, 2006), 8-9.
109   Missionary workers chose a life of financial and other hardships. They established close relationships with, and made many sacrifices for, the people they served in their various missionary fields. Not only were they involved in the cultivation of Christian values and the civilization of newcomers, but they were also important agents in imperial cultural translation and colonialism. See Isabel Hofmeyer, *The Portable Bunyan: A Transnational History of "The Pilgrim's Progress"* (Princeton, NJ: Princeton University Press, 2004), Chapter 1.
110   See Brett Christophers, *Positioning the Missionaries: John Booth Good and the Confluence of Cultures in Nineteenth-Century British Columbia* (Vancouver: UBC Press, 1998); Myra Rutherdale, *Women and the White Man's God: Gender and Race in the Canadian Mission Field* (Vancouver: UBC Press, 2002); Alvyn J. Austin, *Saving China: Canadian Missionaries in the Middle Kingdom, 1888-1959* (Toronto: University of Toronto Press, 1986); Ruth Compton Brouwer, *New Women for God: Canadian Presbyterian Women and India Missions, 1876-1914* (Toronto: University of Toronto Press, 1990); and Robert A. Wright, *A World Mission: Canadian Protestantism and the Quest for a New International Order, 1918-1939* (Montreal and Kingston: McGill-Queen's University Press, 1991).
111   Timothy J. Stanley, *Contesting White Supremacy: School Segregation, Anti-Racism, and the Making of Chinese Canadians* (Vancouver: UBC Press, 2011), 8.
112   See Hannah Arendt, *Imperialism: Part Two of the Origins of Totalitarianism* (New York: Harvest, 1968), Chapter 2.
113   Chinese contract workers en route to New York, Boston, Cuba, Mexico, Trinidad, or South America travelled in special secure rail cars, sometimes in chains and with bodyguards. The men were referred to in newspaper articles as "Chinamen travelling in bond." Early Chinese described these cars as having steel mesh screens on the windows. The doors on either side were locked so that the men could not escape. Guards were posted outside the doors. CPR immigration officials arranged for Chinese grocers to provide Chinese foods (sausage, cured fish, tofu, and Chinese vegetables) to the men (and the rare woman) on the journey. Each of the cars also had a stove, so the men could prepare a hot Chinese meal and/or tea. Ko Bing Hong, Oral History Interview, Dorothy Choy, tape C-1157, lines 179-230, Manitoba Archives. For a fictionalized account of railway labour life based on a Chinese man's personal journal, see Paul Yee, *I Am Canada: Building the Railway, Lee Heen-gwong, British Columbia, 1882* (Toronto: Scholastic, 2010). See also Richard White, *Railroaded: The Transcontinentals and the Making of Modern America* (New York: W.W. Norton, 2011).
114   Technologies, from horse-drawn carriages to automobiles to the Internet, change the speed and quality with which people experience life. Faster travel and communication might be more convenient, but they have the potential to create weaker ties to people and places. See John Lutz, "Riding the Horseless Carriage to the Computer Revolution:

Teaching History in the Twenty-First Century," *Histoire Sociale/Social History* 34, 68 (November 2001): 427-35.

115 After 1912, networks expanded and became sharply gendered as thousands of young Chinese, mostly between the ages of eight and twenty-two, emigrated and moved beyond Chinatown. Forty years after the first Chinese settled on the Prairies, there were still very few families, or women. As mentioned, I use interdisciplinary methods to gather materials and data. I combine data published in the General Register of Chinese Immigration and the census with estimates given in unpublished research participant interviews and reports gathered through ethnographic research. Interviews and unpublished reports enabled me to determine the number of Chinese on the Prairies up to 1920. The number of Chinese increased from 1920 to 1923; however, interviews and reports did not supply enough information for me to provide an accurate assessment of this period.

116 Manliness was re-created through labour practices as well as network building, where power brokers dominated. See R.W. Connell, *Masculinities,* 2nd ed. (Berkeley: University of California Press, 2005), 76-81.

117 Steven Nunoda mentioned this observation about Japanese Canadian immigration patterns, and then I noticed the same pattern of second-born Chinese sons coming to Canada.

118 Wenying Xu, "Masculinity, Food, and Appetite in Frank Chin's *Donald Duk* and 'The Eat and Run Midnight People,'" *Cultural Critique* 66 (Spring 2007): 78-103.

119 Sam Gee Papers (private collection).

120 See Susan Mann, ed., "Gender and Manhood in Chinese History," Forum of Five Contributions, *American Historical Review* 105, 5 (2000): 1559-1667. See also J. Chan, *Chinese American Masculinities: From Fu Manchu to Bruce Lee* (New York: Routledge, 2001); and Yen Ling Shek, "Asian American Masculinity: A Review of the Literature," *Journal of Men's Studies* 14, 3 (2006): 379-91; Kam Louie and Louise Edwards, "Chinese Masculinity: Theorising *Wen* and *Wu*," *East Asian History* 8 (1994): 135-48, and *Theorising Chinese Masculinity: Society and Gender in China* (Cambridge: Cambridge University Press, 2002); and Joanne D. Birdwhistell, *Mencius and Masculinities: Dynamics of Power, Morality, and Maternal Thinking* (Albany: State University of New York Press, 2007).

121 David L. Eng, *Racial Castration: Managing Masculinity in Asian America* (Durham, NC: Duke University Press, 2001), 66.

122 By using this term, I am referring to the general idea of the woman who becomes noteworthy (and no longer silent) through being a good weaver and virtues such as maternal rectitude, chastity, loyalty, and filial piety in traditional Chinese culture and society. See Liang Duan, ed., *Biographies of Virtuous Women and Supplementary Notes* (*Lienü zhuan buzhu* 列女傳補註). (Shanghai: Zhonghua shuju, 1933), 1.11. See also Lisa Raphals, *Sharing the Light: Representations of Women and Virtue in Early China* (Albany: State University of New York Press, 1998), 33-35. Women learned about these and other stories through folk tales about Tang dynasty powerful beauties such as Wu Zetian (624-705) and Yang Guifei (719-56).

123 This assumption was evident in Presbyterian and Methodist mission materials of the exclusion era and was confirmed by several research participants who had lived through it. An Act Respecting Chinese Immigration, 1923, included language specifically targeting and excluding women who were prostitutes. Under Section 8, Prohibited Classes, subsection (d) explicitly associates women and girls of Chinese descent with prostitution and immorality. *An Act Respecting Chinese Immigration* (Ottawa: F.A. Acland, 1923).

124 See Susan Mann and Yu-Yin Cheng, eds., *Under Confucian Eyes: Writings on Gender in Chinese History* (Berkeley: University of California Press, 2001); and Vivian-Lee Nyitray, "Treacherous Terrain: Mapping Feminine Spirituality in Confucian Worlds," in *Confucian Spirituality,* vol. 2, ed. Wei-ming Tu and Mary Evelyn Tucker (New York: Crossroad, 2004), 463-79. See Allan G. Johnson, *The Gender Knot: Unraveling Our Patriarchal Legacy*

(Philadelphia: Temple University Press, 1997); Sherry J. Mou, *Gentlemen's Prescriptions for Women's Lives: A Thousand Years of Biographies of Chinese Women* (Armonk, NY: M.E. Sharpe, 2004); Jinhua Emma Teng, "The Construction of the 'Traditional Chinese Woman' in the Western Academy: A Critical Review," *Signs* 22, 1 (1996): 115-51; Susan Brownell and Jeffrey Wasserstrom, *Chinese Femininities/Chinese Masculinities: A Reader* (Berkeley: University of California Press, 2001); and Susie Lan Cassel, "Footbinding and First-World Feminism in Chinese American Literature," *Journal of Asian American Studies* 10, 1 (February 2007): 31-58.

125 See Sarah E. Stevens, "The New Woman and the Modern Girl in Republican China," *NWSA Journal* 15 (Autumn 2003): 82-103; and Yen Hsiao-pei, "Body Politics, Modernity and National Salvation: The Modern Girl and the New Life Movement," *Asian Studies Review* 29, 2 (June 2005): 165-86; and Alys Eve Weinbaum et al., eds., *The Modern Girl around the World: Consumption, Modernity, and Globalization* (Durham, NC: Duke University Press, 2008).

126 Confidential interviews with research participants. See individual chapters for stories about domestic training and talent.

127 Confucianism is broadly defined by traditional and modern Chinese thought and culture. Although Confucianism takes its name from Confucius, it refers to older ideas that were associated with a group called Emerging Scholars (Ruists). Hu Shi (1891-1962), a modern Confucian scholar, described Emerging Scholars as experts in the early arts of rites, music (performance), history, archery, and numbers associated with the *Classic of Changes*. Confucian and Christian identities were often combined by nominal Christians and devout ones such as Reverend Ma Seung. Ma Seung's youngest son, Jacque, had framed images of four of the Emerging Scholars' five arts on the wall of his living room until he died. He inherited these images from his brother, Peter, who was a devout Christian. Hu Shi, incidentally, visited Winnipeg's KMT office in 1933. "Dr. Hu Shi Urges Fellow Chinese to Have Patience," *Winnipeg Free Press*, August 4, 1933.

128 Canada's Multiculturalism Act (1985) and section 27 of the Canadian Charter of Rights and Freedoms protected Canadian rights to diversity. But that diversity was still one that privileged the "white" Christian majority. For a discussion of multiculturalism, see Will Kymlicka, "Ethnocultural Diversity in a Liberal State: Making Sense of the Canadian Model(s)," in *Belonging? Diversity, Recognition and Shared Citizenship in Canada*, vol. 3, ed. Keith Banting et al. (Montreal: Institute of Research on Public Policy, 2007), 39-86. See also Himani Bannerji, *The Dark Side of Nation: Essays on Multiculturalism and Gender* (Toronto: Canadian Scholars' Press, 2000).

129 In general, life on the harsh Prairie frontier required women to be less *yin* (passive) and more *yang* (aggressive). But just as manhood was defined by much more than simplistic *wen* and *wu* binaries, femininity was defined by much more than cliché notions related to female passivity or aggressiveness. See Robin Wang, ed., *Images of Women in Chinese Thought and Culture: Writings from the Pre-Qin Period through the Song Dynasty* (Indianapolis: Hackett, 2006); Susan Mann and Cheng Yu-Yin, eds., *Under Confucian Eyes: Writings on Gender in Chinese History* (Berkeley: University of California Press, 2001); and P. Sangren, "Female Gender in Chinese Religious Symbols: Kuan Yin, Ma Tsu, and the 'Eternal Mother,'" *Signs* 9 (1983): 4-25.

130 Adoption is covered in greater detail in Chapter 6.

131 Chinese Canadian women joined husbands in foreign worlds where they needed to be demure good spouses (*haoqiu* 好逑) and adhere to understandings of appropriate indirect and public displays of affection, maiden identities, and courtship according to Chinese tradition. Chinese traditions surrounding the idea of a good wife date to the *Classic of Poetry*'s famous first poem, "Calling the Ospreys" (Guanju 關雎, ca. Zhou dynasty 1027-221 BCE). The authoritative *Classic of Poetry* contained verses describing normative

traditional models of pure, morally superior maidens and ladies associated with Confucianism. As Mark Laurent Asselin observes, this poem "is a celebration in song of finding a good and fair maiden as a match for a young gentleman." See Mark Laurent Asselin, "The Lu-School Reading of 'Guanju' as Preserved in an Eastern Han Fu," *Journal of the American Oriental Society* 117, 3 (1997): 427. This is the dominant interpretation of the poem, which is based on a mid-second-century BCE dynasty commentary. See also Zuyan Zhou, *Androgyny in Late Ming and Early Qing Literature* (Honolulu: University of Hawai'i Press, 2003), 72. Later prose and poetry showed different Buddhist and Daoist-inspired iconic women such as Wu Zetian, China's infamous Tang dynasty empress, and the dazzling beauty Yang Guifei.

132 Only one of those women, Mrs. Lee, had joined before 1946 (in 1941); the remainder joined after 1946. Two of these later female members were students, and the rest were the wives of prominent men. Manitoba KMT Register, total number of party members starting from 1943 (*Dangyuan zong mingce, Zhonghua Mingguo sanshier nian yuanyue li* 黨員總名冊,中華民國三十二年元月立). This register of membership includes information related to gender, hometown, vocation, education, family members, date of joining the party, and the party member introducing the member. Occasionally, register pages of members also include marginal notes indicating, for instance, that people had died (and/or their cemetery plot numbers), moved back to China, or moved to a new address in Canada.

Chapter 1: Affective Regimes, Nationalism, and the KMT

1 The ties examined in this chapter both privileged and were strongest for male bachelors and brokers. Mayfair Yang assigns gendered meanings to *renqing* and *guanxi*, associating the former with the feminine and rural, and the latter with the masculine. See Mayfair Mei-hui Yang, *Gifts, Favors, and Banquets: The Art of Social Relationships in China* (Ithaca, NY: Cornell University Press, 1994), 320. For a different and Western gendering of affect, see Leela Gandhi, *Affective Communities: Anti-Colonial Thought, Fin-de-siècle Radicalism and the Politics of Friendship* (Durham, NC: Duke University Press, 2006), 6-7.

2 Allen Chun et al., "The Lineage-Village Complex in Southeastern China: A Long Footnote in the Anthropology of Kinship [and Comments and Reply]," *Current Anthropology* 37, 3 (June 1996): 429-50; and Mayfair Mei-hui Yang, "The Gift Economy and State Power in China," *Comparative Studies in Society and History* 31, 1 (January 1989): 39.

3 Traditional rules and customs guiding governance and interactions were derived from the doctrine of the rectification of names (*zhengming* 正名). According to this doctrine, a ruler had to behave and serve others like a ruler, a father had to behave and serve others like a father, and so on, according to the five relationships; ruler to subject, father to son, husband to wife, brother to brother, and friend to friend. This doctrine is articulated in the Confucian *Analects, juan* 12.19 and 13.3.

4 Between 1942 and 1945, when remittances between China and Canada were blocked, fathers could also not support wives and families.

5 The term "religion" is not native to China. It came to China in the late 1800s through Japan. By using this term, I am referring to practices that came to be understood by overseas Chinese as "religion." These practices include those related to Confucianism, Daoism, Buddhism, and Christianity.

6 Rebecca Nedostup, "Ritual Competition and the Modernizing Nation-State," in *Chinese Religiosities: Afflictions of Modernity and State Formation,* ed. Mayfair Mei-hui Yang, (Berkeley: University of California Press, 2008), 91.

7 See Stephen Feuchtwang, *Popular Religion in China: The Imperial Metaphor* (London: Routledge, 1991).

8   Diaspora Confucianism represented the shift toward the relocation of traditional liturgical (rituals performed by Chinese specialists), cultivational (i.e., meditational), and immediate practical (i.e., divination) modes (as defined by Chau) to the backwaters of life. See also Adam Chau, "Modalities of Doing Religion (Zuo Zongjiao de Moshi)," *Journal of Wenzhou University (Wenzhou Daxue Xuebao) Social Sciences (Shehui Xue)* 22, 5 (2009): 18-27.

9   Chinese (including naturalized citizens and all people of Chinese descent, even those born in Canada) had to provide photographs and register with the Department of Immigration of the Dominion of Canada by June 30 of that year. Those who failed to register and provide photographs were threatened with a five-hundred-dollar fine and deportation. July 1, celebrated throughout the country as Dominion Day, became known by the Chinese community as "humiliation day," and the 1923 Chinese Immigration Act was henceforth known as the Exclusion Act.

10 Some early Chinese immigrated to Canada as sponsored sons, using fake birth certificates. These men became known as "paper sons." Participant observation fieldwork in Alberta, Manitoba, Ontario, and Saskatchewan.

11 Chinese empires and states have traditionally used forms of household registers to monitor family activities. Nationalist registers required members to submit similar types of personal information to leaders. See Martin C. Yang, *A Chinese Village: Taitou, Shantung Province* (New York: Columbia University Press, 1945).

12 This information has been gathered through interviews, oral history, photographs, and document collection.

13 Chinese bodies were similarly transported through these railway lines and then shipped to China. The transportation was often financed and/or organized by Chinese voluntary organizations. Sometimes the transportation was arranged through the assistance of the Red Cross. Peel 4915: Hanna, David Blythe, ed., *Trains of Recollection: Drawn from Fifty Years of Railway Service in Scotland and Canada, and Told to Arthur Hawkes* (Toronto: Macmillan, 1924). Peel's Prairie Provinces. Opium similarly travelled along these webs of connection. In 1919, Lee Sing from Fort William, Ontario, was caught making preparations to ship opium by rail to Brandon, Manitoba. *Brandon Daily Sun,* February 13, 1919, 1.

14 See Census 1891, Vol. 1, 112 and 362.

15 For instance, Arcola was established in 1900. Young Sing was a Chinese laundry operator there in 1901. Arcola Kisbey History Book Committee, *Arcola-Kisbey Golden Heritage: Mountain Hills to Prairie Flats* (Arcola, SK, 1987), 151.

16 "Chinamen the World Over Will Assist in Raising $300,000,000 for Needs of Chinese Republic," *Morning Leader,* August 10, 1912, 1. I was unable to locate financial information in newspapers and published archives for Manitoba's nationalist contributions. I did not have the consent to publish other findings discovered through ethnographic research.

17 North Battleford in 1917 had a membership of thirty-five men, with sixteen of them from the Chow clan (Zhou 周). Membership roster: Chinese Nationalist League North Battleford, Sask., Canada, Saskatchewan Archives Board. This list of branches over which the Winnipeg office had control is based on archival documents found at the Manitoba KMT clubhouse, scrapbooks, and other Chinese and English documentary evidence provided by earlier settlers in this region. There may have been additional cities and towns that also had Prairie KMT branches. Around 1913, Saskatoon's membership was ninety-five, according to a rough count of the members in Figure 4. The Fort William branch (Huiwei lin 伙偉林) included members from Kenora, White River, Schreiber, Nipigon, Longlac, and Hornepayne.

18 This branch was led by Mr. Lam Lee. Saskatchewan Genealogical Society Obituary Collection, Lee Lam.

19 Frank Quo adds, "In 1916 military units were set up in Edmonton, Lethbridge, and Saskatoon for recruitment and 'training' of volunteers. The 210 volunteers from Canada sailed for China in March, 1917 ... The troops were officially dissolved in September, 1918 ... The volunteers from Canada were paid $300 each and advised to return to North America." F. Quei Quo, "Chinese Immigrants in the Prairies," Preliminary Report Submitted to the Minister of the Secretary of State (Simon Fraser University, November 1977), Chapter 3, 3. Between 1919 and 1923, Saskatoon was also the site of a training base for the KMT. Numerous local newspapers documented the activities of the base. See, for instance, "Chinese Will Have a Plan in City Soon: Contract Let Yesterday for Erection of Hangar. Douglas Fraser to Be Instructor," *Daily Star,* June 4, 1919; and "Chinese General Was Student in Saskatoon: General Wu Hon Yen Studied Aviation at the Keng Wah School; Now Returning to China on Empress of Russia," *Daily Star,* December 21, 1921; and Ray Crone, "The Unknown Air Force," *Saskatchewan History* 30 (Winter 1977): 1, 2, 4-5, 7, 8, 10, 15, and 16.

20 Fictive kinship (not related by blood) helped develop solidarity within the Chinese community.

21 Lisa Rose Mar, *Brokering Belonging: Chinese in Canada's Exclusion Era, 1885-1945* (New York: Oxford University Press, 2010), 4.

22 The power brokers discussed here were in some ways similar to the organizing elites described in Shain and Barth's study of diaspora kinship structures. Power brokers transcended the boundaries of state and national belonging to China and Canada. But in other ways, Prairie brokers lived more ambiguous lives, sometimes as elites and at other times, non-elites. Shain and Barth's three-point analysis of the way that power is mobilized in the diaspora is too stable to be used to understand the complicated processes that governed Prairie affective regimes. See Yossi Shain and Aharon Barth, "Diasporas and International Relations Theory," *International Organization* 57, 3 (Summer 2003): 452.

23 Joan Judge writes, "In the context of early twentieth-century nationalism, the public uses of feminine talent continued to be a source of contention. While female talent and virtue were now both understood in relation to the nation, it was the publicness or privateness of this relation that generated the most controversy. At the two poles of the debate were proponents of nationalist patriarchy and radical nationalists. The former indirectly linked women to the nation through their private virtue. Privileging the domestic sphere as the crucial context for feminine self-definition, they represented the woman's national role in terms of the production of morally upright and biologically fit male offspring." See Joan Judge, "Talent, Virtue, and the Nation: Chinese Nationalisms and Female Subjectivities in the Early Twentieth Century," *American Historical Review* 106, 2 (June 2001): 766.

24 "Baohuang Nuhui Zhi Li Zhen Xiang" [Save the Emperor Women's Association Photograph], in YSP, box 104, file I, cited in Tim Stanley, *Contesting White Supremacy* (Vancouver: UBC Press, 2011), 185-86.

25 By the late 1930s and early 1940s, there is evidence that women could attend nationalist events, using their husband's KMT membership. A celebration of the Manitoba KMT held September 1, 1935, in the auditorium at 209 Pacific Avenue noted the attendance of women at the event: "There were a few female members in attendance as well, such as Mr. Huang Jiesheng's 黃傑生 wife, his daughter Yin Zhu 銀珠, and Mr. Ma Douchen's 馬竇臣 daughters Ma Lianxiang 馬蓮香 and Ma Lianxiu 馬蓮秀." (Chinese newspaper clipping, 1935, Frank Chan's scrapbook, unpublished). They, along with non-Chinese wives, made up KMT fundraising women's committees and used their needlework skills to raise

money or make clothes for the needy in China: "Chinese women of Winnipeg will not stand idly by as the people of war-torn China seek to drag themselves out of the horrors in which the war has enfolded them. This was the unanimous decision of a group of Chinese women at their first meeting held Wednesday at the home of Mrs. Annie Jones, president." The group asked Winnipeg women to donate materials or to knit or sew something and donate it for the children and women of "war-torn" China. Mrs. Charlie Foo was the secretary, along with the wives of others who were active in the KMT and Chinese Patriotic League (Mrs. W.T. Weng and Mrs. Roy Mark). "Chinese Women of Winnipeg Organize to Aid Homeland," *Winnipeg Free Press*, March 26, 1946, 9. Winnipeg's Chinese Patriotic League (Jianada Wen[nipei] Diqun Huaqiao Kangri Jiuguo Hui Yong Jian 加拿大溫地群華僑抗日救國會用箋) (CPL) branch formed in 1937. Though women could participate in limited nationalist social events and take increasingly active roles in 1930s and 1940s Chinese nationalist and patriotic organizations, it was made clear to them that their work was peripheral to the main goals of the organization and to the contribution of their husbands.

26 Charlie Foo's personal archive and Frank Chan's personal scrapbook contain many photographs and Chinese newspaper clippings of nationalist visits to Winnipeg, Regina, and northern Ontario on behalf of the CPL.

27 Chinese immigrants in Manitoba, where First Nations and Metis people were subject to intense racism, appear to have "reproduced the racial lines of closure." See Andreas Wimmer, "Herder's Heritage and the Boundary-Making Approach: Studying Ethnicity in Immigrant Societies," *Sociological Theory* 27, 3 (2009): 256.

28 Floya Anthias, "Belongings in a Globalising and Unequal World: Rethinking Trans-locations," in *The Situated Politics of Belonging*, ed. Nira Yuval-Davis, Kalpanna Kanna-biran, and Ulrike M. Vieten (London: Sage, 2006), 24.

29 Chinese and indigenous people's interactions reflect not only common physical and/or cultural segregation from British and other "white" majority populations, but also religious, economic, and social exclusion through racist legislation and specific practices such as the residential school system. Chinese and indigenous people shared values and practices including respect for ancestors, hospitality tea customs, and ritual food offerings. Even on the Prairies today, it is very difficult to find early Chinese who are willing to talk about indigenous wives, mothers, children, and adoptions within this particular mixed-race context. My suspicion is that there were comparatively fewer Chinese-indigenous relationships on the Canadian Prairies than in British Columbia, though it seems unlikely that not one of the hundreds of Chinese Canadians with whom I have spoken had a parent of First Nations or Metis descent. This leads me to suspect that Chinese-indigenous marriages were discouraged by the KMT and thus, like Daoist or Buddhist practice, were obscured. Omissions of these relationships in oral history interviews may also have resulted from a desire to downplay links to indigenous peoples and exclusion once the Chinese Immigration Act was repealed in 1947. For a discussion of Chinese-indigenous intermarriage in British Columbia, see Jean Barman, "Beyond Chinatown: Chinese Men and Indigenous Women in Early British Columbia," *BC Studies*, 177 (2013): 39-64.

30 Interviews with research participants who lived during the exclusion era (and private collections of archival material) confirm that Prairie Chinese provided free meals and lodging to soldiers and helped with fundraising during the First World War. Discrimination by Methodist, Presbyterian, and Anglican missionaries also decreased in this period, presumably because many Chinese had lived in Manitoba for almost a decade by 1918. Community interactions reduced discrimination.

31 For a discussion of the origin of the term "overseas Chinese," or *huaqiao*, see Wang Gungwu, "A Note on the Origins of Hua-ch'iao" (seminar paper of the Far Eastern History Department, Australian National University, 1976).

32 In 1923, Yee Clun made headlines as Regina's KMT leader. The *Regina Leader* also reported that though the Chinese YMCA had "a reading room and quarters in the same clubroom of the Nationalist Party, they [were] in no way connected." *Regina Leader*, December 1923, Sam Gee Papers, unpublished.

33 Quo, "Chinese Immigrants in the Prairies," Chapter 3, 3.

34 "Canadian (KMT) Members' Party Affairs Review of the Last Two Years and Future Prospects (Liang nianlai jiashu dangwu zhi hui gu yu jinhou zhi zhanwang 兩年來家屬黨務之迴顧與今後之展望)," *New Republic (Xinminguo bao* 新民國報), January 1, 1935, Frank Chan's scrapbook, unpublished.

35 Ka-che Yip, *Religion, Nationalism and Chinese Students: The Anti-Christian Movement of 1922-1927* (Bellingham, WA: Center for EAS, Western Washington University, 1980), 2. See also Jessie Gregory Lutz, *Chinese Politics and Christian Missions: The Anti-Christian Movements of 1920-1928* (Notre Dame: Cross Cultural, 1988).

36 The Chinese Dramatic Society (CDS) used the railway to smuggle boxes of rifles across the American border into Canada and over to China to convince Prairie nationalist leaders that it was strongly anti-communist. In doing so, it also demonstrated its support for the nationalists in the fight against "treasonous rebels." In 1924, clubhouses in Winnipeg and Edmonton were awarded first-class silver medals as evidence of their superior contribution. The Winnipeg certificate is still proudly displayed on the CDS clubhouse wall. Participant-observation fieldwork, Winnipeg.

37 One early missionary report about Manitoba Chinese conversions notes: "Lenny Hap Chung ... They are deep sorry their sins and was repent confess Jesus Christ is their Lord and Saviours. They said we believe the gospel is perfectly more than Confucius work. One of them will receive the Baptism." All People's Mission Papers, 1908-1941, box A, October Report, United Church of Canada Archives, Winnipeg.

38 By 1951, when the KMT had already fled to Taiwan and more women and children were coming to Canada, the number of self-identifying Confucians was a mere 5,791. This number foreshadowed the decline of Confucianism, the rise of not just a nominal Christian identity, and also the acceptance of baptism. See "Religions of the People by Provinces for 1911 and totals for 1901 and 1911," *Census of Canada,* 1911, Vol. 2 (Ottawa: C.H. Parmelee, 1913), 2-3; Table 34, "Total Population Classified According to Religious Denominations by Provinces, 1921," *Census of Canada,* 1921, Vol. 1 (Ottawa: F.A. Acland, 1924), 572-73; "Population by Religious Denomination and Sex, for Provinces and Territories, Total and Rural, 1941," *Census of Canada,* 1941, Vol. 2 (Ottawa: Edmond Cloutier, 1944), 519; and Table 38, "Population by Religious Denominations and Sex, for Provinces and Territories, 1951," *Census of Canada,* 1951, Vol. 1 (Ottawa: Edmond Cloutier, 1953), 38-41.

39 Diaspora Confucianism occasionally inflamed racist stereotypes of effeminate heathen men and submissive women with bound feet. See Arif Dirlik, "Confucius in the Borderlands: Global Capitalism and the Reinvention of Confucianism," *boundary* 2, 22-23 (1995): 229-73. But more often, its reinvention helped Chinese fit in.

40 As Ambassador Shuxi Xu remarked on a visit to Winnipeg on November 12, 1965, "Sun Yat-sen was born into a Confucian-Christian tradition just as much as into an anti-Manchu atmosphere ... Indeed he often quoted from the *[Classic] of Records* ... [one of the six Chinese Classics] the political maxim: 'The people are the basis of the state; secure the basis and the State will enjoy peace.' Again, no less often, [Sun Yat-sen] referred to the teaching of Mencius: 'The people are the most important element in a State; the spirits of the land and grain are the next; the sovereign is the lightest.'" Ambassador Xu's speech continued to refer to past Chinese wisdom and the importance of Confucian benevolence from the *Classic of Records* and Zhou dynasty history. The Chinese ambassador's speech ended by noting that "Dr. Sun was a blessing to China and mankind." Over the years I have heard other similar statements comparing Sun's love of the people and their nation to ideas in Confucian texts and practices. Shuxi Xu, "Sun Yat-sen, His Leadership and

His Political Thought" (address to the Chinese community in Canada on the centenary of the birth of Dr. Sun, November 12, 1965), 4. Manitoba KMT Archives.

41 See *Chinese Times,* September 26, 1916, 3.

42 As noted in a 1925 United Church missionary report by Anna M. Finch, assistant secretary, "Miss Annie Thuton gave an address on the work the Methodist Church was doing in China. Speaking on conditions in China she told of the Chinese religion, the teaching of Confucius, in its best and worst aspects. The Chinese she said, had a splendid code of ethics, but had not yet attained the unselfishness and universal love, which only the teachings of Christ can inspire." Anna M. Finch Report, excerpt from 1925 meeting, 153, United Church of Canada Archives.

43 Some men also worked in Winnipeg's slaughterhouses. During the 1910s, they were paid well, between forty and fifty dollars a week. Interview Transcripts: Lai Man Cheng, 1984, 16, Edgar Wickberg Fonds, Chinese in Canada Series, 8-28, 2. UBC Archives.

44 United Church file notes. "Social Centre for Chinese in Vancouver." September 30, 1921. Chinese Canadian Research Collection, box 10-6. Miscellaneous Material. 65 pages; Document 857-box 4, page 1. United Church Archives of Canada. UBC Archives.

45 Sun Yat-sen had written two wills. The first one, which I mention throughout this book, was addressed to his nationalist colleagues and gained near scriptural status. The second one was directed to his family. The political will explained the social significance of the three principles of livelihood, nationalism, and democracy, and encouraged comrades to work toward the creation of a free and democratic China.

46 Guanyin was the enshrined deity at Lytton, British Columbia's, temple in the 1880s. *Daily Colonist,* September 4, 1883, 3. Early offerings and deity veneration took place before images brought to Canada by Chinese, as well as in front of household, society, clan, and voluntary association altars. Narrative accounts suggest that altars and temple spaces were constructed in the 1870s, with the Yen Wo Society altar to Tam Gong being the first. Victoria's CCBA and CKT buildings housed Canadian altar rooms that featured major gods of the early Chinese diaspora, such as Confucius, Mazu, and Guangong. Chinese Canadian Research Collection, box 20, Interviews with Leaders, UBC Archives.

47 The men who frequented temples were mostly labourers, though until the early 1920s some temples and altars dedicated to Guanyin or to other gods received financial support from the CBA, and some merchants and power brokers would have frequented them as well. A man simply referred to as "Roy Fong's father" was one of the earliest Daoist priests offering services to Chinese in Victoria. Chinese Canadian Research Collection, box 20, Interviews with Leaders, UBC Archives. It makes sense that some of the Chinese men who immigrated to Canada would have been religious specialists who could preside over services in the temples found in more populous Chinese settlements in Victoria, Lytton, Yale, and Vancouver. Ah Chueh was reportedly Lytton's Joss House keeper in 1883, though it is difficult to determine details about his specific religious expertise. I am grateful to Koten Benson, who shared with me his research on the Lytton Joss House and its history of healing. Some of this research has been previously published in the Lions Gate Buddhist Priory newsletter. For the reference to Ah Chueh, see *Daily Colonist,* September 4, 1883, 3.

48 Winnipeg Chinese United Church Clergy Records, unpublished.

49 As the *Tribune* explained, "Winnipeg Chinese know their Confucius but they gave a reporter quite a run-around when he tried to glean something on the ancient sage whose philosophies are on everyone's tongue these days. Traditionally modest, all the Chinese interviewed politely suggested the reporter interview someone else – usually one Lee Hip ... The old philosopher urged respect, Mr. Mark [owner of the Exchange Cafe] emphasized. There were five relations of respect: father and son; brother and sister; husband and wife; junior and elder; King or prime minister. 'Maybe' he added, 'you see Lee Hip and he can tell you more about Confucius ...' Peter Owen [owner of the New China Chop

Suey] has read the *Four Books* of Confucius. He is secretary of the Chinese Nationalist
League. He first read Confucius at the age of six ... Phil Yee [added] 'We think a great deal
of Confucius ... We do not worship him as a god, but revere him, perhaps as the English
do Shakespeare or the Americans Abraham Lincoln.' Peter and Phil listed the virtues
recorded by the sage as: kindness [benevolence or *ren*], sincerity *[yi]*, knowledge [wisdom
zhi], ceremony *[yi]*." *Winnipeg Evening Tribune*, March 9, 1940, 4.

50 Winnipeg's Chinese consul, General W.T. Weng, who arrived in 1944, often gave speeches
about Chinese thought, culture, and history. He referred to Confucianism and its virtues
when discussing similarities with the West and cross-cultural understanding: "China
was the melting pot of ... widely different religions, each exerting its subtle influence
upon the Chinese mind. There was no reason to imagine that the Chinese people were
less receptive to Christianity than to the other religions. The spirit of love taught by
Christianity curiously tallies with the precepts of Confucius." *Winnipeg Evening Tribune*,
September 12, 1944, 9.

51 KMT propaganda in the 1940s continually emphasized the "cultural approach" of nationalists. In press releases and media interviews, Prairie Chinese drew on Confucianism
fashioned anew. See *Winnipeg Evening Tribune*, June 8, 1943. As Gregor and Chang note,
"It is true that Sun was convinced that his thought represented an expression of the
political philosophy of ancient China. He spoke of his political ideology as a development
and a continuation of the ancient doctrines of Confucius." James Gregor and Maria Hsia
Chang, "Wang Yang-ming and the Ideology of Sun Yat-sen," *Review of Politics* 42, 3 (July
1980): 390. The generalissimo Chiang Kai-shek enjoyed a Neo-Confucian youth and
had an "ascetic Neo-Confucian outlook." He was fond of Zeng Guofan and Wang
Yangming's Neo-Confucian ideas linking thought and practice, and he too was guided
by nationalist and modern thinking related to Confucian classics and learning: "I believe
that the book, *Great Learning,* is not only China's orthodox philosophy but also the
forbearer of scientific thought, undoubtedly the source of Chinese science. If we bind
together the *Great Learning* and the *Doctrine of the Mean*, we shall have the most complete text on the harmony of philosophy and science and the unity of spirit and matter."
Here, Chiang was referring to two classical texts written by Confucius and later chosen
to form half of Zhu Xi's *Four Books*. See Prasenjit Duara, "Knowledge and Power in the
Discourse of Modernity: The Campaigns against Popular Religion in Early Twentieth
Century China," *Journal of Asian Studies* 50, 1 (February 1991): 93. See also Jeremy Taylor,
The Generalissimo: Chiang Kai-Shek and the Struggle for Modern China (Cambridge,
MA: Harvard University Press, 2009), Chapter 1 and page 91.

52 A new form of simplified Chinese characters was introduced in 1956, and by 1957, Feng
Youlan had initiated a campaign to reinvigorate certain ideas in traditional Chinese
culture. The Land Reform movement of the 1950s placed restrictions on temple activities
and practices, but it wasn't until 1963 and the Socialist Education Campaign, also known
as the Four Cleanups, that more uniform banning of temple festivals, as well as the
manufacture and sale of incense and spirit money, took place all over China. In 1966,
universities were closed (some reopened by 1969), signalling the beginning of the prole-
tarian revolution and a backlash against intellectuals and other vestiges of a traditional
China. The famous "Criticize Li Biao and Confucius" campaign began in 1974, signalling
the authority of anti-traditionalism. But just two years later, Mao (as well as Zhou Enlai
and Zhu Dedie) died. And two years after that, in 1978, the Deng Xiaoping era began,
in which the government began to reassess past CCP public policies and former restrictions on religious freedom. In 1982, the CCP issued Document 19, which protected
certain rights related to religious freedom in Buddhism, Catholicism, Daoism, Islam,
and Protestantism. Five years later, in 1987, Taiwan's almost four decades (1948-87) of
martial law and restrictions on religious practice ended. After many years of economic,
social, cultural, and political reform, China experienced a massive movement toward

democracy, unfortunately represented by the shocking Tiananmen Incident on June 4, 1989, televised throughout the world. During the military crackdown on this widespread democracy movement in Tiananmen Square, many were killed. See Alison R. Marshall, "Confucianism/Daoism" in *World Religions: Canadian Perspectives – Eastern Traditions*, ed. Doris Jakobsh (Toronto: Nelson Canada, 2012), Chapter 6.

53 Daniel A. Bell, *China's New Confucianism: Politics and Everyday Life in a Changing Society* (Princeton, NJ: Princeton University Press, 2008).

54 In the 1980s, Winnipeg's Chinese leaders were Hung Yuen Lee, Philip Lee, Joseph Du, and Philip Chang. The group listed eight Confucian and Christian virtues that had inspired the revitalization of Winnipeg's Chinatown. See Joseph Du, ed., "Speech of Thanks," *Mr. Hung Lee and Winnipeg Chinatown* (Winnipeg: WCCCC, 2003), 38.

55 *You peng zi yuanfang lai, bu yi le hu* 有朋自遠方來,不亦樂乎?

Chapter 2: Reverend Ma Seung

1 Also known as "Ma Xiang."

2 The material in this chapter is based on English and Chinese documentary evidence (including letters and autobiographical notes, as well as missionary and church reports) and photographs shared with me by Jacque Mar (1912-2012) and his wife Pamela. Many of the materials were collected by Jacque's brothers Peter (b. 1902), Andrew (b. 1905), and George (b. 1910), and his mother and father, and were passed on to him when they died. I refer to these sources as the Ma Seung Fonds, most of which are unpublished. I additionally conducted multiple interviews by telephone, email, and in person between April 2011 and May 2013.

3 His natal village was described as "Naam Long, Baak Sa (White Sands) Moon Tien Leng (Front Edge)." Untitled typed notes on the Ma Clan, Ma Seung Fonds, unpublished.

4 Notes titled Rev. Ma Seung, ca. 1928, Ma Seung Fonds. In another note (dated 1962) among the fonds, eldest son Peter explains, "I have just picked up Father's short outline of some spotty notes on his early life ... Soon after Father returned to Canada in 1928 ... we discuss[ed] the need of some record of the early days and efforts of our early missionaries, both in South China and in Canada." Ma Seung Fonds, unpublished.

5 Rough typewritten notes on Ma Seung, 6, Ma Seung Fonds, unpublished.

6 Typed notes with heading "1962." This section also includes notes about Ma Seung's need to document his life: "As a result of this he began jotting down a few notes on Rev. Ng Mon Hing, pioneer missionary to the Chinese in Canada, and father of Dr. Peter Hing, one of the first Chinese to graduate in law from a Canadian university. This outline I still have, but it is very sketchy. At about the same time, the thought occurred to me that Father should be started on writing his autobiography in order to give us some idea of his early struggles. I still remember that when we were at Cumberland, in the cubby hole of his writing desk, where he prepared his sermons, there was a pile of manuscript, written in a neat hand with a Chinese brush, and on the old flimsy Chinese bamboo paper, some of the correspondence which flowed back and forth between him and Rev. Ng, and which resulted in Dad's conversion and [decision] to return to Canton for further training. While still at Canton I asked that these should be kept, and elaborated on, but since our many moves I have lost track of these manuscripts, and they have not been found in the papers which Dad left behind." Ma Seung Fonds, unpublished.

7 Interview with Pamela and Jacque Mar, April 2011.

8 Undated life story of Ma Seung. Notes regarding his life prior to 1900. Old handwritten Chinese notes documenting Ma Seung's early life in Canada typed in 1962 by Peter Mar from those presumably found in his father's mission office desk. Ma Seung Fonds, unpublished.

9 Autobiography, 1, ca. 1930s, Ma Seung Fonds, unpublished.

10 Ibid.

11 See Karrie M. Sebryk, "A History of Chinese Theatre in Victoria" (Master's thesis, University of Victoria, 1995); Wing Chung Ng, "Chinatown Theatre as Transnational Business: New Evidence from Vancouver during the Exclusion Era," *BC Studies* 148 (2005-6): 25-33.

12 Autobiography, 1, ca. 1930s, Ma Seung Fonds, unpublished.

13 Undated life story of Ma Seung. Notes regarding his life prior to 1900. Old handwritten Chinese notes documenting Ma Seung's early life in Canada typed in 1962 by Peter Mar from those presumably found in his father's mission office desk. Ma Seung Fonds, unpublished.

14 Gambling is a dominant subject in church documentary evidence that suggests deeply held views among the church hierarchy about inborn Chinese traits and weaknesses. The lure of gambling is a constant theme in Ma's early confessions:

> After my conversion I was subject to a great deal of temptation. Prior to this I was acquainted with a gambler whom I frequently patronized for tickets on the words lottery. After my conversion I rarely met him. Once he came to the Mission to sell me a ticket. I refused him saying that even if I could win nine out of ten times I was not willing to enjoy such ill-gotten sinful gains, much less would I participate when the odds against the purchaser was [sic] so great and hopeless. In a surprised tone he said why in a few months time, [sic] you seem to have changed into an entirely different person. Formerly you were an avid gambler. Had you taken some kind of the drug of the foreign devils or are you afraid that people will know about this, and if so, I will go with you to a secluded spot so that no one will know. To this I replied that though we may be secreted in a secret room, so that only you and I know what we are doing, how do you know that there is not still another presence in the room. Who else, he asked[.] "God will be there, He will not be seen by either you or me, but He will see us, I am not afraid of being seen by human eyes, but I am afraid of being seen by God." Hearing this he sadly turned away. In my earlier days, whenever I had lost heavily in my gambling ventures I was sorely hurt (in my heart) and often wanted to stop but was unsuccessful. One of my clan elders, the one who first invited me to go to the Gospel meetings[,] was also addicted to gambling. We both felt the need [to cut] off this evil, and so we made a pact that if any one of us were caught gambling he would be fined five dollars. However this never occurred because I was converted soon after, by which I was able to banish the devil of gambling to eternity. Trust in the power of [the] Saviour is great, why should we not praise it.

Undated life story of Ma Seung, Ma Seung Fonds, unpublished.

15 *Dictionary of Canadian Biography Online,* reference to Ng Mon Hing, http://www.biographi.ca/.

16 Undated life story of Ma Seung, 3, Ma Seung Fonds, unpublished.

17 Autobiography, 1, ca. 1930s, Ma Seung Fonds, unpublished.

18 Undated life story of Ma Seung, 3, Ma Seung Fonds, unpublished.

19 Reverend Samuel Choo (1916-96), Winnipeg's Chinese United Church minister from 1968 to 1977, noted that he likewise distinguished Christianity from Daoism. See "'Wanderer' to a Man of God," *Winnipeg Tribune,* April 26, 1975.

20 Ma Seung notes re. 1891-1900s, Ma Seung Fonds, unpublished.

21 Ibid.

22 Conversation with Pamela Mar, June 2011.

23 Autobiography, 1, ca. 1930s, Ma Seung Fonds, unpublished.

24 Archival sources hint at the possibility that, though Ma Seung saw nothing wrong with being a Christian, his parents may have regarded Christianity as a foreign superstitious belief system to be spurned.

25 Undated life story of Ma Seung, Ma Seung Fonds, unpublished.

26 Letter to Reverend MacKay from Ma Seung, September 19, 1918, Ma Seung Fonds, unpublished.

27 There is no reference to the distance between the two schools in the notes, except for the comment that while at the Christian college in Pui Ying, Ma Seung was able to visit his parents. This suggests that his former middle school and the Christian college were close enough for a visit.

28 Autobiography, n.d., n.p., Ma Seung Fonds, unpublished.

29 Peter Mar typed notes, 1960, Ma Seung Fonds, unpublished.

30 By referring to himself as a "disciple of the sages," Ma is citing his Chinese ancestral lineage and Confucian sagacity, as well as his Christian faith.

31 Interview with Pamela Mar, April 2011.

32 Traditionally, parents hired a matchmaker when their children were young to help them find a suitable spouse. Matchmakers determined the suitability of a pair based on Chinese astrological wisdom. They judged the compatibility of the animal signs associated with the birth year and hour, as well as the element of the birth year – metal, wind, water, fire, or earth. Chinese at home and abroad continue this custom today.

33 Undated life story of Ma Seung, n.p., Ma Seung Fonds, unpublished.

34 Interview with Jacque Mar, July 2011.

35 Undated life story of Ma Seung, n.p., Ma Seung Fonds, unpublished.

36 "A Brief History of the Chinese Presbyterian Church," *To God Be the Glory: The Chinese Presbyterian Church, Victoria, BC 1892-1983*, Chinese Presbyterian Church 90th Anniversary Celebration Committee, Victoria, scrapbook, n.p., Ma Seung Fonds, unpublished.

37 Ma provides details about Miss Gunn:

> 1900. Miss Carrie A. Gunn our first woman worker began a long and difficult service in Victoria in 1900. She learned her Cantonese locally, and found communications with the women and children difficult. The women were shy and most of them wouldn't even allow her inside the door. In time, she managed to get one woman to the church services, and finally eighteen were attending.

Chinese Presbyterian Church, "A Brief History of the Chinese Presbyterian Church," 1983. Some untitled notes in the Ma Seung Fonds contain material that is also found in Osterhout's *Orientals in Canada*, leading me to wonder if Ma Seung compiled and submitted entries to Osterhout's book for Carrie Gunn, himself, and others, or whether his children copied the notes from Osterhout's and other sources when they were researching his work in western Canada. See also S.S. Osterhout, *Orientals in Canada: The Story of the Work of the United Church of Canada with Asiatics in Canada* (Toronto: United Church of Canada, 1929).

38 Conversion was sometimes referred to by Methodist ministers as the "winning of souls." Ministers established their own yearly quotas for conversions. See Phyllis D. Airhart, "Condensation and Heart Religion: Canadian Methodists as Evangelicals, 1884-1925," in *Aspects of the Canadian Evangelical Experience*, ed. G.A. Rawlyk (Montreal and Kingston: McGill-Queen's University Press, 1997), 98.

39 Presbyterian and later United Church hierarchies were populated by Reverends Winchester, Armstrong, MacKay, and Noyes – all "white" men of British ancestry. By the 1920s, most of the Presbyterian leadership was based in Toronto and central Canada and had specifically British ideas about belonging in a unified national church: "The founders [of the United Church] had in mind ... white, Protestant descendant of immigrants of the British Isles. The victims of these imaginings were Aboriginal peoples,

French Canadians, non-Protestants, non-Christians, and recent immigrants." See Greer Anne Wenh-In Ng, "The United Church of Canada: A Church Fittingly National," in *Christianity and Ethnicity in Canada*, ed., Paul Bramadat and David Seljak (Toronto: University of Toronto Press, 2008), 204. They were impressed by Ng Mon Hing and Ma Seung's erudition and accomplishments, yet they never fully accepted or funded their work. Reports of Chinese ministers and mission work remained under the special heading "Oriental Work." One might see a further sign of this lack of acceptance and integration into Canadian society in the fact that some early Chinese ministers to Victoria (Ma Seung), and to Vancouver and New Westminster (Ng Mon Hing), retired and returned to China. When Ma Seung left Canada in 1934, he was still not a Canadian citizen. See also Barry Mack, "From Preaching to Propaganda to Marginalization," in Rawlyk, *Aspects of the Canadian Evangelical Experience*, 143.

40 What made Chinese missionaries such as Ma Seung virtually invisible and others such as Ng Mon Hing so noteworthy? During two visits to the Mar's home, I pored over the hundreds of letters, notes, and photographs that had been loaned to me for scanning. There was very little about Ma Seung's work in Canada. Osterhout's *Orientals in Canada* makes passing references to Ma Seung's contributions. Many of these references are inaccurate and/or only partially recognize the extent of Ma's missionary work. See Osterhout, *Orientals in Canada*, 101, 107, 110, and 128. By contrast, and notably, the same text refers to Mrs. Ma's contributions in more detail on page 183. As I came to learn, Reverend Ng Mon Hing seemed to be the Presbyterian, and later United Church, missionary favourite. A simple Google Internet search reveals instant references to Ng Mon Hing in the *Dictionary of Canadian Biography Online* and to materials about him in the United Church Archives. Most sources that might mention Ma Seung do so only in passing and in combination with the more remarkable work of Ng Mon Hing. There are liberal references to Ng Mon Hing in many academic tomes on Chinese Canadian history and religion. For instance, see Jiwu Wang, *"His Dominion" and the "Yellow Peril": Protestant Mission to Chinese Immigrants in Canada, 1859-1967* (Waterloo, ON: Wilfrid Laurier University Press, 2006), 60-63; and David Lai, *Chinatown: Towns within Cities in Canada* (Vancouver: UBC Press, 1988), 209-10. Having information with which I could compare the merits of Ma and Ng's work, I saw that, though younger, Ma was an equally successful and energetic missionary worker who was willing to take on similar difficult and remote postings. Ma had volunteered to work in the Cumberland and Winnipeg missions, and Ng had volunteered to work in Nelson. Like Ng, Ma was a decades-long missionary and Christian minister. Whereas Ng Mon Hing resided in Canada for roughly twenty-five years, from 1895 until 1919, Ma Seung lived in Canada (with the exception of four years when studying and a furlough in China for one year) for forty-three years, from 1891 to 1934.

41 See All People's Mission Papers, 1908-1941, boxes A and B, Winnipeg United Church Archives.

42 See Myra Rutherdale, *Women and the White Man's God: Gender and Race in the Canadian Mission Field* (Vancouver: UBC Press, 2002), 4-7.

43 By the turn of the last century, there were very few slaves or prostitutes entering Canada, and significantly fewer by 1910. See Lucie Change Hirata, "Free, Indentured, Enslaved: Chinese Prostitutes in Nineteenth-Century America," *Signs* 5, 1 (1979): 6.

44 According to Ma Seung's autobiography, British Columbia Chinese missionary work began four years before his 1891 arrival in the province: "The first official move by the Church in BC to share responsibility for the care of the 6,800 Chinese then in the province was made in 1887, at which time the Synod of Columbia (later to become the Synod of BC) petitioned the General Assembly to open up missionary work in Vancouver and Victoria as soon as possible." Ma Seung Fonds, unpublished.

45 Ma Seung's innovations drew on the popularity and success of Salvation Army street preaching and YMCAs in both Canada and China.

46 Here I draw on the ideas and research of Matthew Engelke, who notes the strengths and value of public forms of everyday religion and practice outside of churches and Sunday services. See Matthew Engelke, "Angels in Swindon: Public Religion and Ambient Faith in England," *American Ethnologist* 39, 1 (February 2012): 155-70.

47 Lynne Marks points out the stark differences between conversion rates and religiosity in British Columbia and elsewhere in Canada. See Lynne Marks, "A Godless Province? Religion and Irreligion in British Columbia, 1880-1914," book manuscript, Chapter 4.

48 Chinese Presbyterian Church, "A Brief History of the Chinese Presbyterian Church," 1983, scrapbook, n.p., Ma Seung Fonds, unpublished.

49 Nationalist merchants enjoyed greater cultural, social, and legal freedoms, as discussed in the Introduction to this book. For instance, travel documents were easier to obtain from nationalist-controlled Chinese consul offices until 1949.

50 Reverend C.C. Shiu was sent to Winnipeg (from Montreal) between 1924 and 1927, when Ma Seung was in charge of missions in Edmonton, Calgary, and Cranbrook, British Columbia, as well as parts of the Kootenays. Shiu left Winnipeg in 1927. Notes, Ma Seung Fonds, unpublished.

51 The split between nationalists and communist supporters resulted in three fatalities in a 1927 Vancouver shooting. See "Three Chinese Dead in Nationalist Feud Shooting at Coast," *Lethbridge Herald*, August 8, 1927, front page.

52 Surveillance of Chinese Canadians was undertaken, as I have discussed here, by both Chinese nationalist leaders and the Canadian government. For documentation of the latter practice, see Allan Rowe, "'The Mysterious Oriental Mind': Ethnic Surveillance and the Chinese in Canada during the Great War," *Canadian Ethnic Studies* 36, 1 (2004): 48-70.

53 Activities of Chinese Nationalist League [aka KMT] in Canada, RG 25, External Affairs, 1490, file 1927-246C, Library and Archives Canada (LAC). Six months after this letter was written about KMT branches communicating in code, an editor of the Chinese left-leaning newspaper *Canada Morning News* (Vancouver) was murdered.

54 David Lai's case study of the Victoria CCBA shows parallel developments in that organization and similar challenges by the KMT that continued after 1927 when the nationalist government was set up in Nanjing. See David Chuenyan Lai, *Chinese Community Leadership: Case Study of Victoria in Canada* (Singapore: World Scientific, 2010), 147-53.

55 Peter Mar report to the Foreign Mission Board, 1931, 1, Ma Seung Fonds, unpublished.

56 Mah Joe, who had come to Winnipeg in 1905 to work as the head chef of the Winnipeg General Hospital, was part of the out-migration of Chinese men of advanced age who retired to China in the mid-1930s. See *Healing and Hope, 1872-1972: A History of the Health Sciences Centre* (Winnipeg: Winnipeg General Hospital, 2009), 39. See also Winnipeg General Hospital Collection, Reports and Accounts, incomplete bound yearly statements, 1919-38; Winnipeg General Hospital Collection, Children's Hospital, Financial Records, Salary Register, 1943-52; Winnipeg General Hospital Collection, General Ledger Book, 1913-28; and Winnipeg General Hospital Collection, General Ledger Book, 1914-23. See also Winnipeg General Hospital, Dietary Department, History of Main Kitchen, as related by Miss Judy Bennett, July 1972. During 2011 and 2012, these materials, uncovered through my previous SSHRC-funded research, were digitized and submitted to the Canadian Historical Recognition Program, Chinese Canadian Stories Project at UBC.

57 Report of the Presbyterian Mission to the Chinese of Victoria, BC, 142, 1915-16. Ma Seung Fonds, unpublished.

58 Ibid., 179.

59 Letter to Reverend R.P. MacKay from Ma Seung, March 2, 1905, Ma Seung Fonds, unpublished.

60 Letter to Reverend A.E. Armstrong from Ma Seung, November 7, 1906, Ma Seung Fonds, unpublished.
61 Interview with Jacque Mar, July 2011.
62 Ibid.
63 Ibid.
64 Osterhout, *Orientals in Canada*. Wang, *"His Dominion" and the "Yellow Peril"*; Lai, "Immigration Building, 1908-1977," notes shared with me.
65 Jacque Mar, interview, January 2012. As I reflected on frequent references to the superiority of Western "science" in both my interviews with Jacque and Pamela and the hundreds of documents I had scanned in the Ma Seung Fonds, I began to see that Ma Seung's nationalism was not inspired only by Sun Yat-sen. And it certainly wasn't political or related to Generalissimo Chiang Kai-shek. Rather, it was born out of a love of China as a nation that lacked the science that made the West seem more civilized. See Mary Brown Bullock, "American Science and Chinese Nationalism: Reflections on the Career of Zhou Peiyun," in *Remapping China: Fissures in Historical Terrain*, ed. Gail Hershatter (Stanford, CA: Stanford University Press, 1996), 210-23. See also Danny B. Kwok, *Scientism in Chinese Thought, 1900-1950* (New Haven: Yale University Press, 1965).
66 Susan Yipsang was accepted at UBC in 1914. Three of the Mar boys went to the University of Manitoba and graduated in the 1920s and 1930s. After graduating from the University of Manitoba, Jacque practised medicine in Winnipeg for a period, though he would not have been able to practise in British Columbia or Saskatchewan, where licensing was tied to a right to vote. See Victor Lee, "The Laws of Gold Mountain: A Sampling of Early Canadian Laws and Cases That Affected People of Asian Ancestry," *Manitoba Law Journal* 21 (1992): 301-24. Reg Bing-wo (b. 1921) went to the University of Saskatchewan in 1943, where there were three or four other Chinese students. Interview May 2011. See also his published interview by Victor Huard, June 5, 1990, Saskatchewan History and Folklore Society R-14941, Saskatchewan Archives Board.
67 Interview with Jacque Mar, July 2011.
68 Letter from Ma Seung to Dr. J. Campbell, August 14, 1913, Ma Seung Fonds, unpublished.
69 Undated typed notes by Peter Mar comparing life in Winnipeg and Cumberland, Ma Seung Fonds, unpublished
70 Interview with Pamela Mar, June 2011.
71 While Ma Seung and Hong Lin lived in Cumberland, they had noticed a Japanese Canadian operating a photography studio there. When they arrived in Winnipeg, they saw that there was a need for a studio and opened one in the back of their home. As Ma Seung was seldom home, the studio was left to Hong Lin and the boys to operate, especially after 1923, when there was higher demand because the Chinese Immigration Act required Chinese to register and maintain up-to-date photographs for registration with the Canadian government.
72 In doing this, Ma Seung and other Canadian missionaries who opened branches in other Canadian cities initially worked alongside and later competed with the YMCA, which operated throughout Canada and China. Early Chinese Presbyterian and nationalist Ernest Mark opened Toronto's Young Men's Chinese Christian Association in 1910. A Tribute to Ernest C. Mark, MG 30, series D219, Q4-4331-A, pages 1-4, LAC.
73 Handwritten notes titled "Re Work amongst Winnipeg Chinese," 1, ca. 1918, Ma Seung Fonds, unpublished.
74 The first Chinese Boy Scout troop was in 1912 Montreal. *Globe*, April 29, 1912, 11. The Chinese Boy Scout troop started in Winnipeg by Ma Seung and celebrated by Manitoba nationalists was no doubt encouraged by "white" Christian missionaries who saw the rough frontier practices of Boy Scouts as good for cultivating an ideal "habitus" of young Chinese boys. See R.W. Connell, *Masculinities*, 2nd ed. (Berkeley: University of California Press, 2005), 195.

75 Interview with Jacque Mar, July 2011.

76 Letter to Dorothy Choy from Jacque Mar, 1986, Ma Seung Fonds, unpublished

77 Interviews with Pamela Mar, April, May, and June 2011.

78 The couple were not Chinese, but they were affectionately referred to as Jones Buck and Jones Mu (Uncle Buck and Auntie Mu). Saturday, April 11, 1970, Victoria, Notes, 1, Ma Seung Fonds, unpublished.

79 Ibid., 2.

80 The Ross girls all taught Sunday school. Lily Chan became the Presbyterian Chinese mission kindergarten teacher on February 14, 1926. Summary of the Presbyterian mission work in Victoria notes by Ma Seung, Ma Seung Fonds, unpublished.

81 "Unique Ordination of Ma Seung. Charge Delivered in Chinese by Rev. Duncan McRae," *Hong Kong Journal*, 1921, Ma Seung Fonds, unpublished.

82 George Emory, *The Methodist Church on the Prairies, 1896-1914* (Montreal and Kingston: McGill-Queen's University Press, 2001).

83 From this sum, five dollars was paid in rent. The remainder funded Ng's living expenses and those of an aunt in China who cared for his three children. After he resigned from the church in 1916, he continued to receive an annual salary of $684 until he left Canada in 1919 and retired to China. See Mona Margaret Pon, "Ng Mon Hing," *Dictionary of Canadian Biography Online, 1921-1930*, Vol. 15 (Toronto: University of Toronto/ Université Laval, 2000).

84 Peter Mar's notes on his father's baptisms and life contain these names of Chinese men who were baptized by Ma Seung: "Among his old converts are Wong Hung, Lee Woo, and the late Wong Wah, Chiu Yook who was at Comox has still living at Vancouver [sic] when we last returned, but has suffered senile degeneration and probably passed on. Ho Lem who was at Calgary during his days at Alberta has since passed on." Peter Mar, notes, Ma Seung Fonds, unpublished.

85 Global mission work of the era, influenced by the YMCA Student Volunteer Movement, commonly drew on unpaid young student labour to spread the Gospel. See "Student Volunteer Movement Handwritten Reports and Correspondence 1895-1897," China records, 1887-1937, Henry Burton Sharman material, 13, MG 30-C224, R5361-9-0-E, files 8 and 9, LAC.

86 Henry was adopted by Mrs. Ma for Ma Seung's brother, Jim, who at the time lived in southern China. He and his wife could not have children. Henry returned to China with the Mas, and Jim and his wife later returned to Regina with Henry.

87 Board of Home Missionaries Minutes, 1926, 68, Ma Seung Fonds, unpublished.

88 Letter is part of a Seung's unpublished archive shared with the author. April 12, 1924, Letter from Ma Seung to Reverend MacKay, Ma Seung Fonds.

89 See Dennis L. Butcher et al., eds., *Prairie Spirit: Perspectives on the Heritage of the United Church of Canada in the West* (Winnipeg: University of Manitoba Press, 1985).

90 Letter to Reverend MacKay from Ma Seung, March 2, 1905, Ma Seung Fonds, unpublished.

91 Quoted in Peter Bush, "The Rev. R.P. (Robert Peter) MacKay: Pietist as Denominational Executive" (paper presented to the Canadian Society of Presbyterian History, 2010, 8). http://www.csph.ca/.

92 Winnipeg mission report, 3, ca. 1918, Ma Seung Fonds, unpublished.

93 Report of the Chinese Work in Villages and Towns of Manitoba, July/August, 1921, Peter Mar, Ma Seung Fonds.

94 Ma Seung Fonds, unpublished.

95 Interviews with Pamela Mar, April, May, June, and October 2011.

96 In a letter dated January 7, 1923, to Dr. MacKay, Ma Seung noted, "Mrs. Ma has been wishing to go home ever since we moved into this city and found the cold weather here

hard for her. She had thought that the place for her is in China where she hopes to return soon and open some kind of girls work." Ma Seung Fonds, unpublished.

97 Rev. Robert Yeung, Dr. Yeung Shiu Chuen 楊少泉 Papers (private collection), page 83, Hong Kong University Library. Pamela recalls, "[He] was an Anglican crusader against the 'Mui-tsai System' of maidservant enslavement." Jacque Mar, letter to the Honourable David Lam, Lieutenant Governor of British Columbia, 1993, 2, Ma Seung Fonds, unpublished.

98 Board of Home Missionary Minutes, 1934, United Church of Canada, 20, Ma Seung Fonds, unpublished.

99 "Brilliant Chinese Family, Here Since 1916, Are Going Back to Help Native Land," *Winnipeg Tribune*, 1934, Ma Seung Fonds, unpublished.

Chapter 3: Bachelor Uncles

1 Excerpt from Chinese Canadian newspaper, titled "Canada Overseas Leader Chan Huan Zhang 1950," Frank Chan's scrapbook, unpublished. The General Register of Chinese Immigration listed him as Chan Tok Wah, who came to Canada as a ten-year-old merchant's son from Canton City in 1911. Chan Tok Wah, Serial Number 62908, General Register of Chinese Immigration.

2 Although I was able to discover many details about Frank's Prairie life, there were some things I never learned. Unlike those of many Chinese men, Frank's KMT membership register (along with those of the similarly powerful local KMT leaders) showed a blank entry for education.

3 Frank Chan obituary, *Winnipeg Free Press*, December 12, 1952, 18. According to a *Winnipeg Free Press* article, Frank visited with his wife and children in 1937 for twenty-two months, and his visit coincided with the bombing of Canton by the Japanese. Although he was able to make his way safely from China to Hong Kong, his wife and children were forced to leave their home with only the clothes they were wearing. *Winnipeg Free Press*, October 4, 1937. For many wives and children, immigration to Canada came years after the repeal of the act. I was repeatedly told by research participants that this was due to a backlog of immigration applications. I do not know why Frank's wife did not emigrate with her children in 1949.

4 The Railroad Young Men's Christian Association publication *Main Lines in the Bible* was used by railway men who studied and memorized passages that would guide them in their work. China records, 1887-1937, Henry Burton Sharman material, MG 30-C224, R5361-9-0-E, vol. 13, Library and Archives Canada (LAC).

5 Chan Shan, Line 26, Census of Manitoba and Saskatchewan, 1916, District 7, Nelson. Research participants volunteered that Frank had probably first lived in a Manitoban town whose name began with the letter "s," such as Somerset or Swan River. This census entry fits the description of Frank given to me by research participants. I was able to locate only one Chinese man, Norman Lee (d. 1996), who moved to Somerset from China in 1922 through the sponsorship of his father Lee Wing Bun. Norman attended school there for a year. Winnipeg United Church, Clergy Records, unpublished.

6 In the 1940s, Lee Foke, Lim Dick Lup, H.L. Wong, and Tony Quon continued to be active members of what was now referred to simply as the Chinese Christian Association. See *Winnipeg Chinese United Church: Celebrating 75 Years: 1917-1992* (Winnipeg, 1992), 6.

7 Chinese Canadian beach and canoe excursions sometimes ended badly. Watson Chan of Winnipeg and Susie Mah of Nanaimo presumably were unable to swim and drowned one Sunday afternoon at Grand Beach after their canoe capsized. *Winnipeg Free Press*, June 18, 1945.

8   Frank Chan travelled to Montreal to take part in a celebration to commemorate the Chinese Christian church there. *Shing Wah Daily News (Xinghua ribao* 醒華日報) June 16, 1950, Frank Chan's scrapbook, unpublished. This nationalist newspaper began in Toronto in 1922. For a list and description of Chinese newspapers to 1975, see Karl Lo and H.M. Lai, comp., *Chinese Newspapers Published in North America, 1854-1975* (Washington, DC: Center for Chinese Research Materials, Association of Research Libraries, 1977).

9   The club's aims were "to promote education and instruction in art, music, literature and science among Chinese youth. To provide for classes, conferences, discussions, lectures and public meetings calculated directly or indirectly to advance the cause of education and intellectual development among Chinese youth. To provide means of social intercourse and recreation and to cultivate good fellowship among Chinese youth. To purchase, lease or otherwise acquire, for the purposes of the society[,] any meal or personal property, and in particular buildings, furniture, fittings, club accommodation, apparatus and conveniences, books, newspapers, periodicals and musical instruments. And generally to carry on without pecuniary gain objects of a national, patriotic, charitable, philanthropic, artistic, scientific, social or sporting character." *Sanmin Zhuyi* Youth Association notes, ca. 1943, Mss. 188, PC 180, A 96-94, folder 17, University of Manitoba, Stubbs Fonds.

10 Frank worked with David Farn and his brother Isaac, who had come from Saskatchewan, to raise $5,500 by 1945. Within five years, Frank was the Chinese secretary of the organization. *Winnipeg Free Press*, October 13, 1945, front page; *Winnipeg Free Press*, February 2, 1950. The story of David and Isaac's mother is told in Chapter 7 of this book. In 1952, Frank sat as vice-chairman of the church board, which was led by David and Isaac Farn's father, Gin. *Winnipeg Free Press*, February 5, 1952, 28.

11 None of my research participants who grew up knowing Frank remembered his involvement in the Chinese Dramatic Society (CDS), though most KMT leaders did dress up, sing, and perform periodically with Winnipeg's amateur opera group. I presume that Frank's association with the Vancouver chapter of the society had been formed either when he was a boy in Vancouver or when he travelled to Vancouver on nationalist business. His grandchildren, Brant Mark and Lily Lau, were also unaware of his involvement in the opera troupe.

12 See Wing Chung Ng, "Chinatown Theatre as Transnational Business: New Evidence from Vancouver during the Exclusion Era," *BC Studies* 148 (2005-6): 39.

13 I am grateful to Tom Mitchell, who discovered this photograph, which had been miscatalogued and placed in a collection documenting indigenous peoples in the region.

14 Charlie Foo directed an opera with Toronto performers at the Winnipeg clubhouse in 1947. *Winnipeg Free Press*, January 13, 1947.

15 Among the documented members were five Lees, four Wongs, four Wus, three Chans, and several men from other clans not ordinarily seen in Manitoba Chinese organizations, such as Yip and Sha.

16 During a May 2011 fieldwork trip to the Winnipeg Chinese Dramatic Society clubhouse, I found an untitled group photograph that was hidden beneath the altar image of the first teacher of opera. The clubhouse members had told me about it when I asked if they had any old photographs that had been hidden. They said there was one old photograph but that nobody knew much about it. The photograph, dated 1917, includes in the background a portrait of Sun Yat-sen and the two flags of the new republic – a blue one with a white star and one with five bars. There are 110 mostly young men dressed in formal attire, with buttons on their lapels. But the photograph is not labelled. It could show members of an early Chinese Canadian political group, possibly the KMT, or members of the CDS throughout Canada. Confirming the identity of the group is beyond the scope of this

chapter. The more I reflect on the photograph and the fact that it was hidden beneath a photograph of the enshrined deity, accessible only by removing the picture from its frame, the more I think that the group was a political one. From Nanaimo to Montreal (and in China and the Philippines) I heard accounts of document hiding or burning after 1950. People feared a communist backlash. Nevertheless, despite these accounts of document burning, I have been able to recover a significant cache of nationalist and other materials through ethnographic research methods.

17 Anonymous research participant.

18 Tong Soon Lee, *Chinese Street Opera in Singapore* (Chicago: University of Illinois Press, 2009), 12-13.

19 Participant observation fieldwork, Winnipeg CDS. CDS culture varies from region to region. Winnipeg's amateur group formed in 1921 under specific provincial, cultural, and clan influences. Toronto's oldest amateur group, Toronto Chinese United Dramatic Society (Lanqiao jushe 聯僑劇社), formed in 1933 and was dominated by Lims (not Wongs and Lees) and men who were KMT members. The Toronto group was also different because it was larger and had more women. Toronto Chinese United Dramatic Society (Lanqiao jushe 聯僑劇社), fieldwork 2008-12.

20 Watson Chan, the Chinese schoolteacher, drowned the following summer on a community outing. See endnote 7 above.

21 *Shing Wah News (Xinghua bao* 醒華報), February 15, 1944, Frank Chan's scrapbook, unpublished.

22 Frank was a devout KMT member, active locally and nationally. He vocally opposed communism, as this 1950 *Winnipeg Free Press* article shows: "We must keep it free from Communism! ... Winnipeg's Chinese are 100 percent opposed to Communism and the Red aggression, said Frank Chan, insurance man, and also a recent visitor to China. He figures there are about 700 Chinese citizens in Winnipeg and declared that not one of them, so far as he knows, is in favour of the Red Chinese invasion. 'We are Canadians and proud of it. We are not Communists,' he declared." "Chinese Colony Here Assails Red Onslaught," *Winnipeg Free Press,* December 2, 1950, 1. His patriotism is confirmed by many Chinese newspaper clippings in his personal scrapbook as well as membership rosters and photographs of Sun Yat-sen and Chiang Kai-shek. The scrapbook also contains photographs of Wang Jingwei and Zhang Fakui, leaders of the Wuhan government. Frank Chan 陳煥章, KMT Membership number 37170, Manitoba KMT Archives, unpublished; Frank Chan scrapbook, unpublished.

23 Frank Chan, along with Sam Dong, Charlie Foo, and many others active in the KMT, would routinely fundraise for donations in the Winnipeg Chinese community, at the University of Manitoba and beyond Winnipeg in small towns and cities in Manitoba, Saskatchewan, and northern Ontario.

24 He had held many executive positions in the local and national branches of the Canadian KMT. His obituary noted: "Rites Saturday for Frank Chan, Chinese Leader. A prominent member of the Winnipeg Chinese fraternity will be buried Saturday. He is Frank Chan, 51, who was a member of the executive of the central committee of the Chinese Nationalist league; vice-president of the Chinese United Church, and chairman of the Chan Wu Yuen Benevolent society. Mr. Chan died Dec. 2 in Winnipeg General Hospital at the age of fifty-one. His funeral was delayed so that officials of Chinese National league branches throughout the dominion might be notified. Mr. Chan, who resided at 336 Elgin Avenue, was born Aug. 18, 1901, in Canton, China. He came to Canada as a young man, and for the past twenty years was associated with the Sun Life Insurance company and the Wawanesa Insurance company." *Winnipeg Free Press,* December 12, 1952, 18. Frank had been part of the KMT central branch (in Vancouver) as a member of the standing committee and a permanent committee. The details of his political involvements

come from a number of sources including English and Chinese newspaper articles, interviews, and Frank Chan's scrapbook, the Manitoba KMT, and the Ma Seung and Foo families' private collections of papers.

25 Diaspora Chinese men most often shared affective ties mediated by patriotism. Bo Ya and Zhongzi Qi of the Spring and Autumn Period during the Zhou dynasty (ca. 1050-256 BCE) were united in friendship by a love of music *(zhiyin)*. Ruan Ji (210-63), a famous Weijin period poet and member of the Seven Sages of the Bamboo Grove, likewise sought good friends, but these relationships were mediated by an appreciation of the landscape *(shangxin)*, not music or patriotism. See Alison R. Marshall, "Xie Lingyun's Reflections on the 'Appreciative Heart,'" *Journal of Indian Philosophy and Religion* 7 (2002): 131-45.

26 This is a literary allusion to the forest and spring from Tao Qian's/Tao Yuanming's (365-427) famous piece of prose, written during the Period of Disunity (220-589), entitled "Peach Blossom Spring."

27 Poem translated by Alison Marshall. I am very grateful to Terry Russell, who looked over this translation and made several helpful suggestions, which I incorporated. Chinese newspaper clipping, Frank Chan's scrapbook, unpublished.

28 Martin Wachs has observed that transportation technology played a large part in the social construction of gender roles and spheres. Wachs's comments address the social shifts introduced by rail and automobile technology and the new ways that people cultivated connections. Access to automobiles and rail passes or communicating in code empowered some groups. Martin Wachs, "The Automobile and Gender: An Historical Perspective," in *Women's Travel Issues: Proceedings from the Second National Conference* (Washington, DC: US Department of Transportation 1996), 100.

29 Frank was honoured multiple times and for several years for his prodigious sales as a Sun Life Assurance agent. Sun Life Assurance, certificate showing Frank Chan was on the company honour roll in 1942, *Agency Review,* October 1943, 12, Frank Chan's scrapbook, unpublished. Frank was also among the highest sellers (both Chinese and non-Chinese) in 1943, 1944, and 1946. Interviews suggest that Chinese Canadian men were broadly convinced of the merits of life insurance and thus bought it from Frank, making him a comparatively wealthy man. What Frank did with the money is unclear, as he lived in the KMT dormitory. He enjoyed weekly baths at the Foo family home, sent money home but didn't have a family in Canada until 1949, and though he donated funds to the local nationalists and to the United Church, his financial contributions were not outstanding.

30 Frank Chan, advertisement for Sun Life Assurance, ca. 1943 and 1944, Frank Chan's scrapbook, unpublished.

31 A newspaper article states, "There were three passengers ... bonded Chinese from Hong Kong, who passed through Winnipeg Wednesday night, en route to New York and the British West Indies over Canadian Pacific lines. Frank Chan acted as interpreter." *Winnipeg Free Press,* May 9, 1940, 2.

32 Railways had varying impacts on the private lives of men and a few women from different parts of Chinese society. Cantonese dramatic performers, coal miners, loggers, and laundry workers had no choice but to rely on the branch and main lines to move from one job or performance to the next. Low-paid Chinese missionary workers and ministers travelled by train to visit cafes and laundries. Wealthier and more powerful Chinese men were interpreters, ticket agents, activists, politicians, and community leaders. They gained economic, social, political, and cultural capital due in part to train technology. For a related discussion on the impact of technology on labour in Canadian history, see John Lutz, "Technology in Canada through the Lens of Labour History," *Scientia Canadensis: Canadian Journal of Science, Technology and Medicine* 15, 1 (1991): 5-19. Mobility, rail technology, and travel dislodged fixed impressions of difference, enabling the more

powerful Chinese leaders to make use of railways and to build intercultural bridges to non-Chinese society. Railway experiences additionally enabled the creation of multiple overlapping identities. Chinese community leaders used railway networks to break down cultural stereotypes and fixed ideas linking race, class, and appearance (but not gender) and to reinvent cultural spaces for their own use. Chinese railway representatives were often shipping agents for other railways, too, such as American President Lines. File: Ernest Mark scrapbook 1 51-100, MG 30, series D219, LAC.

33 1916 Census. Confidential interviews with exclusion-era research participants.

34 A newspaper article reports, "Chan Yen took an expensive lesson in English before Justice Flook on Thursday last. It appears that on October 27 about 7:30 p.m. Chan Yen used foul and abusive language in the dining room of the Central Hotel in spite of the warning of Constable Blake, R.N.W.M.P. who laid on information against him under clause s. Sec. 238, C.C. The case was heard on Thursday morning and the evidence of Const. Blake, corroborated by V.S. Ferguson, was explicit and convicting. Dong Sam acted as interpreter and [the] defendant pleaded guilty. As the maximum fine was fifty dollars or six months imprisonment a fine of ten dollars and costs or thirty days in default was imposed as a warning." "Chink's Bad English." *Esterhazy Observer,* November 4, 1915, 5.

35 *Esterhazy Observer,* August 28, 1913.

36 *Esterhazy Observer,* January 1, 1914, 3. "Celestial" was common slang used in North America and Australia in the nineteenth and early twentieth centuries to refer to Chinese immigrants. It was derived from assumptions about the religious and political importance of the celestial realm in Chinese civilization.

37 *Esterhazy Observer,* June 11, 1914, 3.

38 *Esterhazy Observer,* December 28, 1922.

39 He also used Sam Wong's telephone number on his business cards.

40 This is where Harry Chan, Barry Chan, Sam Dong, and Moon Dong lived for a time.

41 Vaughan recalls that when Douglas Jung came to Winnipeg and held a fundraising reception during his successful campaign to become Member of Parliament for Vancouver Centre in 1957, Sam attended. Interview and follow-up emails with Vaughan Baird, 2011.

42 "Save the Nation Association," Jiuguohui 救國會, December 11, 1939, newspaper article, Frank Chan's scrapbook, unpublished.

43 *Winnipeg Free Press,* December 19, 1960, 23; research participant interviews.

44 In an interview, Vaughan Baird told me:

Sam wanted his will done, which I did. He wanted his ashes to go back to China. His ashes had to go back with somebody. And so I was named the person to take the ashes. You had to go back with someone living. I put his ashes on the windowsill for most of the trip. I talked to Sam as we landed in Hawaii. I said to him, "Sam, we are going to rest for a few days in Hawaii." Neither of us had ever been to Hawaii. I put him in the hotel and on the windowsill there so that he could see the beach. I went swimming in the ocean and Sam could see me from the window of the hotel. Harry Chan told me what I had to do. He had told me what hotel to stay at when I arrived. Sam and I took a taxi to the hotel. I met Sam's wife and gave her the ashes. She was so nervous she almost dropped them.

45 "My Story: 'Wes Goes West'" by Westley Wong, May 4, 1942, Wong Papers (private collection).

Chapter 4: Affect through Sports

1 See Joan Chandler, *Television and National Sport* (Chicago: University of Illinois Press, 1988); Martin Crotty, "The Making of the Man: Australian Public Schoolboy Sporting Violence 1850-1914," *International Journal of the History of Sport* 20, 3 (September 2003): 1-16; Benjamin Lowe and Mark H. Payne, "To Be a Red-Blooded American Boy,"

Journal of Popular Culture 8, 2 (1974): 383-91; and D. Raey, "Psychosocial Aspects of White Middle-Class Identities: Desiring and Defending against the Class and Ethnic 'Other' in Urban Multi-Ethnic Schooling," *Sociology* 42 (2008): 1072-88.

2 Patrick F. McDevitt, *May the Best Man Win: Sport, Masculinity, and Nationalism in Great Britain and the Empire, 1880-1935* (Basingstoke: Palgrave Macmillan, 2004). Eric Dunning examines the emotional dynamics and folk customs inherent in football, or European soccer, writing, "The basic game-pattern – the character of these folk games as struggles between groups, the open enjoyment in them of excitement akin to that generated in battle, the riotousness, and the relatively high level of socially tolerated physical violence – was always and everywhere the same. In short, these games were cast in a common mould which transcended differences of names and locally specific traditions of playing." Eric Dunning, *Sport Matters: Sociological Studies of Sport, Violence, and Civilization* (London: Routledge, 1999), 89.

3 As Eric Dunning reports, "Sport can: (1) provide a source of meaning in life; (2) act as a focus of social identification; and (3) offer experiences which are analogous to the excitement and emotional arousal generated in war and other 'serious' situations like 'being in love.' Indeed, many sports fans develop love-like attachments to the teams they support, sometimes even to the detriment of their 'real' love relations." Dunning, *Sport Matters*, 221.

4 Varda Burstyn, *The Rites of Men: Manhood, Politics, and the Culture of Sport* (Toronto: University of Toronto Press, 1999), 49.

5 See, for instance, Susan Brownwell, *Training the Body for China: Sports in the Moral Order of the People's Republic* (Chicago: University of Chicago Press, 1995); and Richard Gruneau and David Whitson, *Hockey Night in Canada: Sport, Identities and Cultural Politics*, Culture and Communication Series (Toronto: Garamond Press, 1993).

6 Alameda and District Historical Society, *From Dream to Reality* (Altona, MB: Friesens, 1982), 411.

7 History Book Committee, *Windthorst Memories: A History of Windthorst and District, Saskatchewan, Canada, 1806-1981* (Windthorst, 1985), 109.

8 Two interview transcripts: Lai Man Cheng, 1984, 14, Edgar Wickberg Fonds, Chinese in Canada Series, 8-28, UBC Archives.

9 In 1897, the YMCA had 752 associations in North America. Members were classed as regular, coloured, and "Indian." "YMCA Movement by John Mott, 1899, Four Years of Progress in the Student YMCA Movement," China records, 1887-1937, Henry Burton Sharman material, 13, MG 30-C224, R5361-9-0-E, file 20, LAC.

10 Notes, Ma Seung Fonds; discussions with research participants who lived during the exclusion era.

11 Doug Ward, *Vancouver Sun*, September 12, 2011, http://www.vancouversun.com/.

12 The team was made up of members of the Chinese Young Men's Christian Association as well as those who were KMT and CKT members. In 1918, the Winnipeg team included Chong Kan, Wesley Suey, Sid Chard, Harry Mah, Young Ki, P.F. Mon, Lee Ting, Frank Fun, Gordon Lim, Y.P. Lim, and Victor Lee. *Globe*, October 19, 1918, 18.

13 *Manitoba Free Press*, July 22, 1918, 7.

14 YMCA efforts to introduce football (soccer) as a civilizing practice are evident as early as late nineteenth-century China. Shirley Garrett, *Social Reformers in Urban China: The Chinese YMCA, 1895-1926* (Cambridge, MA: Harvard University Press, 1970), 100.

15 An article highlighting Chinese Yick Wong's remarkable public speaking in a YMCA debating contest also mentioned F.W. Hobson's "eulogy of soccer football," which Hobson gave "fresh from the football field." *Manitoba Free Press*, April 11, 1924, 13.

16 Winnipeg mission report, ca. 1920s, Ma Seung Fonds, unpublished.

17 S.S. Osterhout, "Our Chinese Missions in British Columbia," *Missionary Bulletin* 13, 3 (July-September 1917): 499-500; Wang Jiwu, "Organised Protestant Missions to Chinese

Immigrants in Canada, 1885-1923," *Journal of Ecclesiastical History* 54, 4 (October 2003): 691-713; Susan Brownwell and Jeffrey Wasserstrom, *Chinese Femininities/Chinese Masculinities: A Reader* (Berkeley: University of California Press, 2001); David Howell and Peter Lindsay, "Social Gospel and the Young Boy Problem, 1895-1925," *Canadian Journal of History of Sport* 17, 1 (1986): 75-87.

18 Talal Asad, "On Discipline and Humility in Medieval Christian Monasticism," in *Genealogies of Religion: Discipline and Reasons of Power in Christianity and Islam* (Baltimore: Johns Hopkins University Press, 1993), 27-54.

19 Brian Pronger, *Body Fascism: Salvation and the Technology of Physical Fitness* (Toronto: University of Toronto Press, 2002); Daniel Boyarin, *Unheroic Conduct: The Rise of Heterosexuality and Jewish Masculinity* (Berkeley: University of California Press, 1997); Michael L. Satlow, "'Try to Be a Man': The Rabbinic Construction of Masculinity," *Harvard Theological Review* 8, 1 (1996): 19-40.

20 Stuart Hall, *Encoding and Decoding in the Television Discourse,* Vol. 7 of Media Series (Birmingham, UK: Centre for Cultural Studies, University of Birmingham, 1973). See also Stuart Hall, "Encoding and Decoding the TV Message," in *Culture, Media, Language,* ed. S. Hall et al. (London: Hutchinson, 1980), 128-38.

21 Through sport participation, Chinese men added to their cultural fields and interacted with mainstream society. See P. Bourdieu, *Outline of a Theory of Practice,* trans. R. Nice (Cambridge: Cambridge University Press, 1972).

22 Michel de Certeau, *The Practice of Everyday Life* (Berkeley: University of California Press, 1984). Clifford Putney, *Muscular Christianity: Manhood and Sports in Protestant America, 1880-1920* (Cambridge, MA: Harvard University Press, 2001).

23 Each curler "had his own style of dress as he had his own style of delivery ... Charlie Yee, operator of the cafe, greeting with 'Belly cold, belly cold,' left one wondering if he was referring to the weather or to his lack of warm clothes." Avonlea Historical Committee, *Arrowheads to Wheatfields: Avonlea, Hearne and Districts (1983 and 2009)* (Avonlea, SK, 1983), 86-87.

24 "Local Items," *Esterhazy Observer,* February 24, 1921.

25 "Curling Notes," *Morden Times,* February 16, 1922, 1.

26 Brian Pronger, *The Arena of Masculinity: Sports, Homosexuality, and the Meaning of Sex* (New York: St. Martin's Press, 1990), 3.

27 Meanwhile, in 1919, Chinese republicans in Guangdong, China, were themselves encouraging boxing training for Chinese troops. See *Globe,* April 23, 1919, 18.

28 According to Chinese tradition, at the age of twenty a boy underwent the capping ceremony, when a cap was placed on his head to mark his transition to manhood and readiness for marriage.

29 Maryfield's Farn boys were always dressed formally, even when they played. See Chapter 7 of this book in which their mother, Jung Farn, is discussed.

30 Marcel Mauss, "Les techniques du corps," *Journal de Psychologie* 32, 3-4 (1934), repr. in Mauss, *Sociologie et anthropologie* (Paris: Presses Universitaires de France, 1936); Michel Foucault, "Technologies of the Self," in *Technologies of the Self: A Seminar with Michel Foucault,* ed. L.H. Martin (London: Tavistock, 1988), 16-49; P. Bourdieu, "How Can One Be a Sports Fan?" in *The Cultural Studies Reader,* ed. Simon During (London: Routledge, 1993), 339-58; J.J. MacAloon, "Olympic Games and the Theory of the Spectacle in Modern Societies," in *Rite, Drama, Festival, Spectacle: Rehearsals Toward a Theory of Cultural Performance,* ed. J. MacAloon (Philadelphia: Institute for the Study of Human Issues, 1984), 241–80.

31 Summarizing a brief treatise of Erasmus of Rotterdam on civility, Norbert Elias emphasizes that physical behaviours are signs of collective ideas that are unique to each civilization: "Bodily carriage, gestures, dress, facial expressions – this outward behaviour with which the treatise concerns itself is the expression of the inner, the whole person." Norbert

Elias, *The Civilizing Process, Sociogenetic and Psychogenetic Investigations*, trans. Edmund Jephcott, with notes and corrections by the author, rev. ed. (Malden, MA: Blackwell, 2000), 49.

32 Bruce Kidd, *The Struggle for Canadian Sport* (Toronto: University of Toronto Press, 1996), 26.

33 Dunning, *Sport Matters*, 197-202. See also Eric Dunning, "Industrialization and the Incipient Modernization of Football," *Stadion* 1, 1 (1975): 103-39, and "Sport as a Male Preserve: Notes on the Social Sources of Masculine Identity and Its Transformations," *Theory, Culture and Society* 3, 1 (1986): 79-90.

34 Burstyn, *The Rites of Men*, 4.

35 Dominant Chinese society recognized that the railway station was the key entry point into Chinese markets and worked hard to control access to it. Until the 1950s, major clans posted representatives at the larger train stations to ensure that only those from their family could settle and open businesses there. This was common knowledge among the older generation of Chinese Canadians whom I interviewed.

36 *Morden Times*, October 5, 1922. The names of Mark Ki's wife, son, and daughter were found through a search of Winnipeg Chinese United Church Clergy Records, unpublished.

37 Morden Centennial Committee, *Morden: Mort Cheval, Pinancewaywinning, Lake Agassi* (Altona, MB: Friesens, 1981), 265. See also Morden, Manitoba Reunion Organization, *Re-union of Old Timers and Ex-Students, Morden, Manitoba, Thursday, Friday and Saturday, July 9-11, 1931: Souvenir Program* (Morden: Maple Leaf School, 1931), 24, Peel's Prairie Provinces 5570.

38 In 1922, Wing Dong, who ran the town laundry, was part of a curling team discussed earlier in this chapter. By the mid-1920s, Wing Dong had left Morden and moved to Winnipeg. Other Dongs arrived through chain migration to run the laundry.

39 "December 22, 1919," *Souvenir Booklet Committee, Morden Centennial Souvenir Booklet and Program, July 5-11* (Steinbach, MB: Derksen, 1982), 40.

40 Preliminary archival and ethnographic research suggests that Mennonite communities tended to have Chinese rather than Jewish tailors. In Winnipeg and other Prairie communities, Chinese men (who were the cafe and laundry shop owners) often lived and worked in close proximity to Jewish men who were the town or city merchant or tailor, and their families. Today, Winnipeg's Chinese and Jewish communities continue to have strong ties. The Dong clan operated the washing and cafe shops in Morden. In 1924, they ran the New York Cafe, as suggested by a photograph in the local history. See Morden Centennial Committee, *Morden*, 266.

41 Ibid., 308.

42 Ibid., 265.

43 *Morden Times*, May 27, 1940.

44 See Engin Isin, *Citizens without Frontiers* (London: Continuum, 2012).

45 Becoming a naturalized citizen on the Prairies was possible, though very difficult. A small number of Chinese men became naturalized citizens before 1950. This is covered in Alison R. Marshall, *The Way of the Bachelor: Early Chinese Settlement in Manitoba* (Vancouver: UBC Press, 2012), 54.

46 The local paper wrote:

> Mark Ki, winner of the Citizenship Trophy, 'in recognition of meritorious community service,' is seen receiving the plaque from James Baillie, president of Morden Kinsmen Club ... The quiet, unostentatious doing of good deeds, interest in the work of the Freemasons' Hospital and acts of benevolence in the nearly thirty years he has been in business in Morden, were quoted as reasons for the awarding of the third annual Citizenship Trophy to Mark Ki, retiring grocer of long standing in town ... The award

is made annually by the Kinsmen, previous recipients being George E. Cox and Dr. A.F. Menzies. Charles Walkof, past president of the club, gave the address on Wednesday night in the absence of Judge J.M. George, originator of the award as adopted by the club and donor of the handsome shield ... Mr. Walkof stressed the number of kind acts by Mark Ki that has been uncovered by the club committee during the allocation of the award. He mentioned, as an example, the case of one of Mark Ki's debtors who was suffering from tuberculosis; the bill owing had not only been written off, but the hospital bill had been paid, by Mark Ki.

"Mark Ki Receives Citizenship Award," *Morden Times,* May 12, 1948, 1 and 6.

47 My two SSHRC-funded research programs on this subject since 2008 have shown that before 1950 not a single Chinese man from Alberta to Manitoba belonged to these fraternal orders.

48 Obituary, *Winnipeg Free Press,* March 4, 1957, 32; *Winnipeg Free Press,* March 4, 1957, 23.

49 Aka Jaw Chung Hing/Jaw Chun Hing/Jang Chuen Hing and Zeng Chuanheng/Zeng Chuankeng; Happy Young passport, issued May 17, 1946, Winnipeg, Moon Dong Fonds, Chinese Canadian Stories, UBC Archives. Multiple searches for Happy Young's entry in the General Register of Chinese Immigration have not been successful, and family members indicated that his head tax certificate had been lost. Many Chinese Canadians came to Canada with purchased birth certificates. They used these names until they were no longer necessary. On June 9, 1960, the government provided amnesty to Chinese men and women who came to Canada with false immigration papers and names under the "Chinese Adjustment Statement Program."

50 By the late 1910s, Sam was spending more time in Brandon, Manitoba, as part owner of businesses there and as a travelling salesman. Esterhazy's business community took an immediate liking to Happy, who had been fortunate to settle in a town already favourably disposed to Chinese settlers.

51 Among the materials in Moon Dong's possession were investment documents. See letter dated October 11, 1951, from an investment firm to Happy, Moon Dong Fonds, Chinese Canadian Stories, UBC Archives.

52 Letter of Reference from the Codville Company Limited regarding Happy Young, May 21, 1946, Moon Dong Fonds, Chinese Canadian Stories, UBC Archives.

53 Claudio E. Benzecry aptly notes that "fans get hooked when they are still outsiders, before having an active apparatus developed to interpret the experience, or before being thoroughly socialized in what constitutes the enjoyment and how they should decode it. While there are intense instances of sociability and socialization, the temporality structure is different here than in the original model. Learning through interaction happens, not at the beginning as expected, but as the logical continuation that helps shape the initial attraction." Claudio E. Benzecry, *The Opera Fanatic: Ethnography of an Obsession* (Chicago: University of Chicago Press, 2011), 82.

54 This information was taken from interviews with research participants. As mentioned earlier and as is consistent with ethnographic methods, participants sometimes opt for their contributions to remain confidential.

55 "Local Items," *Esterhazy Observer,* January 26, 1922. Thirteen years later, the newspaper also reported that Happy had attended a sporting event in Rocanville. The local happenings section mentioned that "Happy Young put in a couple of days at Rocanville Bonspiel last week." *Esterhazy Observer,* March 7, 1935, 4.

56 On one occasion he sponsored a banquet and displayed his positive affective ties by giving a speech too: "The banquet under the supervision of Mr. Happy [Young] consisted of a table across the top of the theatre and one long table down the centre of the auditorium barely giving accommodation to the numerous members and guests. The Jazz Band

opened proceedings. In calling on Mr. Happy [Young] for a speech (which was uproariously received) the president took occasion to thank Happy for supplying the banquet at cost." "Curlers' Banquet," *Esterhazy Observer,* April 5, 1923.

57 A letter from J.G. Violet Gardiner, wife of James Garfield Gardiner (1883-1962), the fourth premier of Saskatchewan, displayed Happy's close relationships with influential people. Letter January 16, 1944, Moon Dong Fonds, Chinese Canadian Stories, UBC Archives.

58 The writers of Esterhazy's local history reflected on suggestions that there might have been ethnic divisions in the town, but seemed to counter these suggestions by adding that some of the early settlers were not Hungarian and Czechoslovakian. The local history showed Happy Young as an example: "Some studies have suggested that there was ethnic division between farmers who had their roots in Central Europe and the 'English' townspeople. In fact, there were many rural people who were not Hungarian or Czechoslovakian, and many non-English businessmen." James W. Millham and Esterhazy Book Committee, *Esterhazy and Area: From Past to Present 95 Years of History, 1903-1998* (Esterhazy: Esterhazy Book Committee, 1999), 37.

59 *Esterhazy Observer,* February 23, 1933, 3. The follow-up story on the Real Chinese Supper fundraiser read: "The Chinese Supper and Concert held by Ladies Aid on Friday was a great success, tickling the palates and musical susceptibilities of the large number attending. Happy Young is hoping for another chance. Why not, ladies?" *Esterhazy Observer,* March 9, 1933, 3.

60 Ibid., March 29, 1934, 4.

61 Quoted in Millham and Esterhazy Book Committee, *Esterhazy and Area,* 37.

Chapter 5: Married Nationalists

1 This chapter is based on extensive archival research and the examination of hundreds of unpublished KMT and other documents in both English and Chinese, as well as interviews and participant observation fieldwork. As discussed in the Introduction, my approach to researching Chinese Canadian stories has been an ethnohistorical one by necessity. In order to uncover stories of Chinese who settled beyond coastal British Columbia and Chinatowns, I spent years conducting participant observation fieldwork and building relationships. I never intended to use these relationships to obtain materials or stories. This was something that happened naturally as I spent time with people. As my involvement in the Chinese community grew and my ties became stronger, research contacts generously introduced me to others who shared photographs, material culture, written documents, and oral histories. Without this ethnographic history approach or government and university funding, I would never have gathered such a large data set or been able to piece together the global fabric of Chinese networks and everyday life.

2 Although the Manitoba register documenting membership up to the 1950s contained enough pages for 425 members, several of these were blank, reflecting the fact that many men had returned to China, died, or no longer paid their membership dues. Manitoba KMT Archives, unpublished.

3 Regina's branch was led in the early 1950s by Mr. Mah (Ma Shuzheng 馬述政). That same year, Medicine Hat's branch included just over forty members led by a Wong, with the Yees being the largest represented clan among members from an assortment of Chow, Wu, Chan, Tse/Der (Xie), and other clans. North Battleford's group, led by Mr. Chan (Chen Baishan 陳栢山), had eighteen members. Saskatoon's group, led by a Lee, also had Mas, Wongs, Chans, Mack/Mark/Mas, and others. Manitoba KMT Archives, unpublished; Ma Seung Fonds, unpublished; Foo Papers (private collection); Wong Papers (private collection); Sam Gee Papers (private collection).

4 According to the General Register of Chinese Immigration, Charles Yee (aka Yee Kee) came to Canada from the Toisan district, China, in 1901 at the age of fourteen. I presume that Charles was born in 1887 as indicated by his later 1911 census entry for Moose Jaw,

Saskatchewan (line 10). See General Register of Chinese Immigration, Serial Number 38224.

5 Paul Yee, *Saltwater City: An Illustrated History of the Chinese in Vancouver* (Vancouver: Douglas and McIntyre, 2006), 31.

6 1911 Canadian Census Survey showing Charles Yee on line 10.

7 *Davidson Leader,* May 30, 1918.

8 Davidson also had a laundry operated by Lees. "Lew Kee's Laundry," ibid., January 8, 1905.

9 Ibid., January 21, 1926, 4; December 9, 1926, 1.

10 *Davidson Leader,* May 28, 1925, 5.

11 Ibid., August 20, 1925, 1.

12 In 1911, when Charles was registered on the census, he was listed as a bachelor, and so he technically wasn't married. 1911 Canadian Census Survey showing Charles Yee on line 10.

13 Around 1950, Charles Yee helped Dennis Yee immigrate to Canada. Dennis was Charles's grandson, and although he claimed to be fourteen years old when he arrived in Canada (and the same age as Charles when he arrived), he was probably closer to twenty years old. Dennis worked for several years in Winnipeg's Chinese restaurants and then lost touch with the family.

14 The Moon Cafe was a popular hangout for Winnipeg's 1930s lesbian, gay, bisexual, and transgendered community, as Bert Sigurdson remarked in 1991:

> Chinese fellows were not bad about protecting. They didn't want anything bad to happen and they would shoo everybody out but somehow you felt more of a trust with the Chinese fellows who ran the restaurant. They never said anything negative about gays. We went to the Moon Cafe. It was run by a Chinese fellow and the three of us would go in there [in drag]. We were sitting in the booth and Pauline who was married to the Chinese fellow who owned it – she was laughing and the waitress was laughing with us. So here are the women protecting us ... The Moon Cafe was another place we would go to hang out. Pauline was very good to us.

Bert Sigurdson, Gay and Lesbian Oral History Project, 1991, University of Winnipeg.

15 *Winnipeg Free Press,* January 12, 1934, 3.

16 Ibid., April 15, 1945, 4.

17 Ibid., May 31, 1935, 22; November 5, 1936, 1; April 15, 1945, 4.

18 Winnipeg's famous Shanghai Restaurant at 236-40 King Street (aka the Coronation Block) was founded in 1940 by Lee Hoo (1886-1963) (father of Hung Yuen Lee, former head of Winnipeg's CBA), who had operated cafes in Prince Albert and Hartford, Saskatchewan, before he arrived. Obituary, *Winnipeg Free Press,* August 3, 1963, 26. For seventy years, the Shanghai Restaurant provided work and upper-floor apartments for Lees who came to Winnipeg through chain migration. It also provided popular Chinese Canadian food. Winnipeg's Coronation Block was sold in 2011 and demolished a year later.

19 Today, his generosity and place in pre-1950s society are memorialized on a donor's plaque in the Winnipeg KMT building.

20 *Winnipeg Free Press,* August 16, 1954, 12.

21 When I was writing this chapter and gathering materials, Charles Yee's children were surprised by his age when he died. His obituary had mistakenly listed his age as fifty-six and had also noted that he had lived in Canada for more than fifty years. This would have meant that Charles came to Canada when he was less than six years old, and as an unaccompanied minor.

22 For more details on Charles Yee, see Alison R. Marshall, "Interview with William Yee," in *Winnipeg Chinatown; Celebrating 100 Years: A Remarkable Achievement,* ed. Patrick Choy (Winnipeg: Winnipeg Chinese Cultural and community Centre, 2011), 46-55.

23 Foo was also known as Au Fu, Foo/Koa Hong/Koa Hong Foo.
24 Charlie Foo is listed under Serial Number 89150 as twenty-one-year-old Koa Hong on the bottom of his corresponding page in the General Register of Chinese Immigration.
25 Charlie became a naturalized citizen in 1928 and obtained a Canadian passport in 1952. See Foo Papers (private collection); Wong Papers (private collection); Manitoba KMT Archives, unpublished; and Frank Chan's scrapbook, unpublished.
26 This tradition continues today. For example, Dr. Joseph Du is addressed by nearly everyone as Dr. Du. Only very close associates (such as Manitoba's current lieutenant governor, Philip Lee) are permitted to refer to Du as "Joe" in public. In this book, I do not consider leadership from 1950 to the present, when nationalist affective regimes lost their vitality. See Alison Marshall, "A Conversation with Winnipeg's Chinese Canadian Duet," *Manitoba History* 62 (2009): 35-39, and "Early Chinese Settlers in Western Manitoba," pictorial essay of archival documents and photographs of early settlers to Western Manitoba since 1884, *Manitoba History* 62 (2009): 2-8.
27 Foo Papers (private collection).
28 When Ying sold his restaurant, he gave the Foos the equivalent of twenty dollars a month for each of the months that they had cared for the child, and then he left the city. One time he brought a box of Grandma's Marshmallows for the children. It was a memorable gift for them.
29 At the first KMT Chinese community picnic held in 1918, the group asked the Winnipeg Parks Board if the picnics could be held on Sundays. It made this request presumably because Chinese men playing in the scheduled football matches between the KMT and the YMCA had that day off. Unfortunately, the parks board disallowed the group's request because the "sporting programme arranged by the Chinese is contrary to the Lord's Day Alliance Act and the board cannot recognize public picnics on Sunday." *Manitoba Free Press*, July 4, 1918. Presumably, after that the KMT held its picnics on Saturdays. There was food, as well as the games and races that attracted young Chinese and non-Chinese bachelors. The annual picnics attracted a crowd of more than a thousand every year from all over Winnipeg and beyond, in rural regions. Only a third of the crowd was Chinese. The picnics were held at Winnipeg's Assiniboine Park, St. Vital Fair Grounds, Crescent Drive Park, and Fort Garry Park from 1918 to the 1940s, and were put on by the Chinese community. Pictures from the picnic always showed the leaders in front, along with other Chinese and non-Chinese dignitaries. A framed picture of Sun Yat-sen was in the centre of the group. He held the most revered place, and through association ranked the places of others radiating out from the centre. The group was festooned by two flags: the Union Jack and the nationalists' Twelve Pointed Star. The national anthem of the Republic of China was sung at every picnic, and after 1925 the political will of Sun Yat-sen was read.
30 On the outskirts of Winnipeg, there was a property owned by a deaf and mute non-Chinese family, which always made the Foos feel welcome. They were happy to grant permission for the Foos to walk through their property in order to access the riverbank for their picnics. Somehow they all made themselves understood, and soon the two families became quite familiar to each other.
31 *Manitoba Free Press*, May 15, 1930. 4
32 Gambling dens were sometimes referred to as the "lotteries." Lottery tickets were sold there.
33 Undated Chinese article, ca. 1930s, Frank Chan's scrapbook, unpublished.
34 The Chinese Patriotic League of Toronto, Ontario, Canada, "Japanese Aggression in China," MG 30, series D219, 1937, Library and Archives Canada (LAC). See also Renqiu Yu, *To Save China, to Save Ourselves* (Philadelphia: Temple University Press, 1992), 92.
35 The *Winnipeg Evening Tribune* reported that Toronto's nationalist Chinese community fined a member one hundred dollars and forced him to walk through Chinatown wearing

a placard indicating he was a "traitor to China." This man had publicly insulted Chiang
Kai-shek. *Winnipeg Evening Tribune,* March 24, 1939.

36 "Aid for Countrymen; Winnipeg's Chinese Population Unites to Give Homeland Help,"
Winnipeg Free Press, August 24, 1937, 1.

37 Royal Canadian Mounted Police Headquarters, Ottawa, Report 879, Weekly Summary
Report on Revolutionary Organizations and Agitation in Canada, December 22, 1937.

38 Part of Charlie's legacy is that the current lieutenant governor of Manitoba, Philip Lee,
was encouraged by him more than forty years ago to become active in the Chinese community. Charlie would be very proud if he knew that his protégé had attained such a
position.

39 Also called the Double Tenth Festival, Nationalist Day falls on October 10 each year,
marking the anniversary of the Wuchang Uprising on October 10, 1911.

40 *Winnipeg Tribune,* August 11, 1943.

41 Ibid., August 14, 1943.

42 See "Army of Canvassers to Launch Community Chest's Fund Drive," *Winnipeg Free
Press,* October 13, 1951, 1; "Chinese Hold Annual Picnic," *Winnipeg Free Press,* July 31,
1939, 11; "Restaurant to Aid Chinese Relief Fund," *Winnipeg Free Press,* July 13, 1940, 13;
and "Community Chest Returns Less than Half of Objectives," *Winnipeg Free Press,*
October 21, 1946, 1.

43 "Chinese Give Show to Aid Navy League," *Winnipeg Free Press,* September 18, 1944, 18;
"Chinese Fund in Manitoba Reaches a Total of $124,000," *Winnipeg Free Press,* December
7, 1943, 1. See also *Winnipeg Free Press,* January 13, 1947.

44 Ibid., March 25, 1944, 7; and March 27, 1944, 1.

45 Stubbs Fonds, Mss 188 PC 180, A, folder 17, University of Manitoba.

46 *Winnipeg Free Press,* December 7, 1943, 1.

47 The details of Charlie's political involvements come from a number of sources, including
English and Chinese newspaper articles from the *Winnipeg Free Press,* Frank Chan's unpublished scrapbook, and the Ma Seung and Foo families' private collections of unpublished papers.

48 Frank Quo adds, "Local officers of KMT are often awarded government positions such
as membership in the National Assembly, Overseas Chinese Commission, and sometimes
even the Central Committee of KMT itself. There is more prestige than financial benefit
to gain in these positions. The junket trips to Taipei and red-carpet treatment, usually
an audience with the old Generalissimo, reinforce these old patriots' commitment to
KMT. Junket trips were valuable ways to reward loyal community members for their
service and loyalty." F. Quei Quo, "Chinese Immigrants in the Prairies," Preliminary
Report Submitted to the Minister of the Secretary of State (Simon Fraser University,
November 1977), Chapter 3, page 4.

49 In the late 1930s, Charlie also began to travel to Taiwan and to attend secret KMT meetings there (interview, exclusion-era research participant). Photographs show Charlie with
Frank Chan and other members of the Canadian KMT. Preliminary research suggests
that these were nationalist meetings with a view to setting up operations in Taiwan.

50 In the 1930s, Charlie left his job as a meat and seafood salesman to sell refrigerators
at Ashdown's Hardware close to city hall on Winnipeg's Main Street, which he did
until he became a partner at Chan's Cafe. For years, he had driven to Chan's Cafe after
he had finished his regular job and his children had gone to bed. He would help out in
front "running the till." He had an office in the back of Chan's, and as the cafe manager,
he hired the staff. Later, when Chan's opened a nightclub, he booked the entertainment.
He had been to Hong Kong and learned from what he saw there. When he came back, he
thought he could do the same in Winnipeg, and this is how it was that he opened
the nightclub. He became connected with an agency in Chicago that sent various
entertainers.

51 *Winnipeg Free Press,* November 19, 1957, 4. Chan's two upper floors opened in November 1957 and were the result of a $200,000 renovation. The second floor, which was decorated with eight "Chinese fairies" painted by Walter Lee, was the Lotus Lounge. On the third floor was the nightclub, which was eventually known as the Moon Room. The first floor continued to be for dining. Chinese community weddings and political banquets, once Charlie became a partner of Chan's, were held mostly on the second floor. He had a vision that the Moon Room should be available to everyone. Chan's Cafe was the site of many Chinese banquets that brought Chinese and non-Chinese communities together.

52 "Chinese Community Leader Talks of His Past," *Winnipeg Free Press,* November 23, 1974, 6.

53 By the 1960s, Manitoba was led by the CBA, now lacking ties to nationalism. This group quietly worked to "protest the possible admission of Communist China to the United Nations" by writing letters to Manitoba's Members of Parliament, including J.N. Mandziuk, Ed Schreyer, and Bud Sherman. Letter from L.R. (Bud) Sherman, M.P., to Mr. Harry Chan, the CBA of Manitoba, November 30, 1966, private collection. In 2014, Ed Schreyer is the honorary president of the WCCCC.

Chapter 6: Women beyond the Frame

1 See Jan Vansina, *Oral Tradition as History* (Madison, Wisconsin: University of Wisconsin Press, 1985).

2 Although there is no single perfect method for researching social history, I try to openly resist systems that have traditionally marginalized women and Chinese in Prairie Canada. Therefore, I employ interdisciplinary methods and theories to understand and expose gendered structural and related political, cultural, and religious inequalities. See Sumi Cho, Kimberlé Williams Crenshaw, and Leslie McCall, "Toward a Field of Intersectionality Studies: Theory, Applications and Praxis," *Signs* 38, 4 (2013): 797; and Daiva Stasiulis, "Feminist Intersectional Theorizing," in *Race and Ethnic Relations in Canada,* 2nd ed., ed. Peter Li (Toronto: Oxford University Press, 1999), 347-97.

3 See, for instance, Carolyn Brewer and Anne-Marie Medcalf, eds., *Researching the Fragments: Histories of Women in the Asian Context* (Quezon City, Philippines: New Day, 2000). See also Evelyn Huang with Lawrence Jeffery, *Chinese Canadians: Voices from a Community* (Toronto: Douglas and McIntyre, 1992); and Momoye Sugiman, ed., *Jin Guo: Voices of Chinese Canadian Women* (Toronto: Canadian Scholars' Press, 1992). One of the best sources on Chinese Canadian women's experiences can be found in the film *Under the Willow Tree: Pioneer Chinese Women in Canada,* dir. Dora Nipp, prod. Margaret Wong (Montreal: National Film Board of Canada, 1997), 51 minutes. See also Woon Yuen-Fong, *The Excluded Wife* (Montreal and Kingston: McGill-Queen's University Press, 1999). There are a number of biographical and fictionalized accounts of Chinese women's lives in North America, including Lily Hoy Price, *I Am Full Moon: Stories of a Ninth Daughter* (Victoria, BC: Brindle and Glass, 2009); Wayson Choy, *Paper Shadows: A Chinatown Childhood* (Toronto: Penguin, 1999); and Maxine Hong Kingston, *The Woman Warrior: Memoirs of a Girlhood among Ghosts* (New York: Vintage, 1989).

4 Canadian immigration officials used a special column in the General Register of Chinese Immigration to note particular moles, scars, and other distinguishing features. See Ellen Scheinberg, "Evidence of 'Past Injustices': Records Relating to the Chinese Head Tax," *Archivist* 20, 2 (1994): 29. The Canadian policy to photograph Chinese immigrants who entered after 1910 follows American legislation passed in 1893 and again in 1909. See Anna Pegler-Gordon, "Chinese Exclusion, Photography, and the Development of US Immigration Policy," *American Quarterly* 58, 1 (March 2006): 51-77.

5 Quongying, a Chinese Canadian wife whose story is the subject of Chapter 8, was detained in the immigration hall for five weeks. For a discussion of Victoria's hall, see David Chuenyan Lai, *A Brief Chronology of Chinese Canadian History: From Segregation to*

Integration (Vancouver: Simon Fraser University, David See-Chai Lam Centre for International Communication, 2011).

6 Letter to the Supervisor of the Women's Branch, Immigration Inspector-in-Charge, Montreal, June 9, 1932. RG 76, 140, 309, file 33175, 3, 1927-1933, Library and Archives Canada (LAC).

7 Train conductress reports stressed the privileging of Victorian food customs on board. Passengers and conductresses complained about the lack of access to "fire," tea kettles, dishes, and utensils to make tea: "You know the old country people love their cup of tea, and they can drink many, many cups of it journeying from Quebec to Vancouver." Letter from Margaret Lewis, October 3, 1930, RG 76, 140, file 33175, 3, 1927-1933, 463, LAC.

8 Train conductress reports contain correspondence from passengers (presumably only the "white" ones) who were shocked by a train's unsanitary conditions and lack of water and food. They described the problems that people encountered when they wanted to buy fruit, milk, or meals for the journey. And they reported complaints when passengers were patronizing the better and cheaper Chinese-run station restaurants, rather than the officially sanctioned British-run lunch rooms and dining cars. The reports also emphasized the need for racial segregation: "white" British passengers, and especially young British girls, risked racial and social contamination during train travel. British passengers did not like sharing cars with "Russians, Czechs, the scum of Europe and Chinese." Conductress Report: Miss Burnham, August 20, 1928, RG 76, 140, file 33175, 3, 1927-1933, LAC. Chinese passengers were to be contained in special cars, or Immigrant Specials. At the very least, conductresses asked that when British girls shared cars with Chinese, the compartments be curtained off. Letter to Lady-in-Charge, Queen Mary's Coronation Hostel, October 6, 1928, RG 76, 140, file 33175, 3, 1927-1933, LAC.

9 As Sucheng Chan and others have explained, Chinese wives customarily observed filial duties that privileged the care of parents-in-law in China, not overseas husbands. See Sucheng Chan, "The Exclusion of Chinese Women, 1870-1943," in *Entry Denied: Exclusion and the Chinese Community in America, 1882-1943*, ed., Sucheng Chan (Philadelphia: Temple University Press, 1991), Chapter 4."

10 Ottawa had equally few Chinese women. See "The Chinese Sweethearts," *Regina Leader,* March 23, 1911, 12. The estimate for Winnipeg and Regina's number of Chinese women in 1911 comes from conversations with Chinese research participants and descendants of settlers in those cities. This evidence is confirmed by the General Register of Chinese Immigration database that lists destinations.

11 Lucie Change Hirata, "Free, Indentured, Enslaved: Chinese Prostitutes in Nineteenth-Century America," *Signs* 5, 1 (1979): 6; Peter Ward, *White Canada Forever* (Montreal and Kingston: McGill-Queen's University Press, 1978), 8. See also Liam O'Reilly, "Missionaries and Women in Victoria's Chinatown: The Establishment and Evolution of the Chinese Rescue Home, 1886-1900" (Master's research paper, Department of History, University of Victoria, 2011).

12 Peter Li notes that there were seventy prostitutes in 1885 British Columbia. Peter Li, *The Chinese in Canada*, 2nd ed. (Toronto: Oxford University Press, 1998), 63. See Canada, *Report of the Royal Commission on Chinese Immigration* (Ottawa: The Commission, 1885), 363. Aside from providing free lodging to girls, there was little practical need for rescue homes because there were so few girls who needed rescuing. See also Karen Van Dieren, "The Response of the WMS to the Immigration of Asian Women 1888-1942," in *Not Just Pin Money: Selected Essays on the History of Women's Work in British Columbia*, ed. Barbara K. Latham and Roberta J. Pazdro (Victoria: Camosun College, 1984), 79-95.

13 I asked Jacque Mar if there were ever Chinese prostitutes in this area. He was adamant that there were never prostitutes in Winnipeg. He knew this, having lived for seventeen years in Winnipeg and having talked to his three brothers and parents about Manitoba's life and culture during the period. What Jacque said was confirmed by several research

participants who lived on the Prairies during the exclusion era. A preliminary search of Winnipeg police records confirms the existence of one Chinese and Japanese jointly operated brothel in 1909 Winnipeg but no Chinese prostitutes. Police Court Record Book 1909, #16, M1219, Roll #10, page 124. There is also evidence of one Japanese woman who was "an inmate of a bawdy house." Yuka Taki, Winnipeg Police Court Record Book, 1909, #16, M1219, Roll #10, page 340. Evidence of Chinese prostitutes is scanty, with only one reference to a Grace Lee who "frequented a bawdy house" but whose name could easily be non-Chinese. Winnipeg Police Court Record Book, 1909, #16, M1219, Roll #10, page 265. If Grace was in fact a Chinese Lee, she would have belonged to one of the province's two most powerful clans. Even in 1909, Manitoba's Chinese network was relatively well established, and Lee clan members would have been aware that a Lee girl was involved in the sex trade. Given the paucity of women of marriageable age and the high demand for Chinese brides at this time, I doubt that the powerful Lee men would have allowed one of their own to be a prostitute. There were no Chinese concubines who also worked as family slaves. Chinese prostitutes, slaves, or concubines generally were part of life in larger coastal settlements. See Tamara Adilam, "A Preliminary Sketch of Chinese Women and Work in British Columbia 1858-1950," in Latham and Pazdro, *Not Just Pin Money*, 57; and Peggy Pascoe, *Relations of Rescue: The Search for Female Moral Authority in the American West, 1874-1939* (New York: Oxford University Press, 1990), 94.

14 Adilam, "A Preliminary Sketch of Chinese Women," 80.

15 Marilyn Whiteley, "'Allee Samee Melican Lady': Imperialism and Negotiation at the Chinese Rescue Home (Women Missionary Societies Set Up the Chinese Rescue Home to Save Chinese Women from Prostitution)," *Resources for Feminist Research* 22, 3-4 (Fall 1992/Winter 1993): 48.

16 R.P. MacKay, secretary of the Presbyterian Church of Canada, and W.D. Noyes, executive secretary of the Eastern Canada Mission of the Presbyterian Church of Canada, were vocal opponents of the Chinese Immigration Act passed in 1923. See Wang Jiwu, *"His Dominion" and the "Yellow Peril": Protestant Missions to the Chinese Immigrants in Canada, 1859-1967* (Waterloo, ON: Wilfrid Laurier University Press, 2006), 69-71.

17 The General Register of Chinese Immigration shows eleven women (three of them daughters) residing with mothers in pre-1920 Manitoba and eight women (two daughters) residing with mothers in pre-1920 Saskatchewan. Most of the Manitoba Chinese wives were married to Lees, Wongs, and Mas. Most of the Saskatchewan Chinese wives were married to Gees, Yees, and Mas. Sixteen more women arrived in Manitoba between 1920 and 1924, and fourteen more between 1920 and 1924 in Saskatchewan. Census data for Saskatchewan and Manitoba Chinese women are roughly consistent with this dataset. The 1921 census shows much higher numbers of Chinese women in Saskatchewan (seventy-four) and Manitoba (fifty-two). It reflects the number of Chinese daughters and wives who migrated to Canada from China, and Canadian-born Chinese girls who moved to the Prairies to marry Chinese husbands.

18 Catherine A. Lutz and Lila Abu-Lughod, eds., *Language and the Politics of Emotion* (Cambridge: Cambridge University Press, 1990), 9.

19 In my research, the General Register of Chinese Immigration was a better source to gauge the number of women living in Saskatchewan, though it too was not as accurate as first-hand accounts related to me by research participants. Seven more women arrived in 1922 and 1923, and no more came to Saskatchewan until 1948 and 1949.

20 These women were Miss Au Wong (in 1920), who was Sam Wong's first wife; Daniel Lim/Wong's birth mother, who was Ukrainian (in 1928 or 1929); and Mah Joe's first wife (1913).

21 According to the General Register of Chinese Immigration, which has data on the destination of Chinese immigrants beginning in 1910, only eight wives came to Winnipeg

before 1920. Among them was Mah Joe's second wife, who replaced the one who had died in childbirth in 1913.

22　The first woman, Miss Au Wong, arrived in 1918 and died in childbirth in 1920.

23　The General Register of Chinese Immigration notes the names of the Moose Jaw women as Mrs. Wong and Mrs. Wong Louie. These women were known to research participants, who indicated that they eventually left Moose Jaw.

24　Total number of party members starting from 1943 (*Dangyuan zong mingce, Zhonghua Mingguo sanshier nian yuanyue li* 黨員總名冊,中華民國三十二年元月立), Manitoba KMT register, unpublished.

25　I interviewed dozens of children born in the 1910s, 1920s, and 1930s to Chinese Canadian fathers, so my observations are limited to this child-to-parent perspective, undoubtedly skewed by the strong Chinese cultural requirement of loyalty to and respect for one's parents.

26　One such event was the annual grave custom, which saw the community's Chinese elders drive in a procession from Chinatown to the cemetery where the region's earliest Chinese settlers were buried.

27　By 1920, a National Council of Chinese Women had been established by Mrs. Chau Hsin in Canton, China, with the aim to "unite the women of China to promote the freedom of women in political, academic, industrial, and other activities." The group was reportedly petitioning the National Assembly to grant women the right to vote. *Globe,* February 23, 1920, 10.

28　According to the Naturalization Act (1914), Chinese wives arriving in Canada took on the legal status of their husbands, most of whom were not citizens. See Sandra Ka Hon Chu, "Reparation as Narrative Resistance: Displacing Orientalism and Recoding Harm for Chinese Women of the Exclusion Era," *Canadian Journal of Women and the Law* 18, 2 (2006): 404.

29　Nationalists and Chinese communists attempted to reconfigure and redirect traditional affections and bonds away from the family and toward the state. Local household religious practice from a modernist perspective was deemed superstitious. See David Strand, "Community, Society and History in Sun Yat-sen's Sanmin Zhuyi," in *Culture and State in Chinese History: Conventions, Accommodations, and Critiques,* ed. Theodore Huters et al. (Berkeley: Stanford University Press, 1997), 327-31; and Harriett Evans, "The Gender of Communication: Changing Expectations of Mothers and Daughters in Urban China," *China Quarterly* 204 (2010): 980-1000. See also Rebecca Nedostup, "Ritual Competition and the Modernizing Nation-State," in *Chinese Religiosities: Afflictions of Modernity and State Formation,* ed. Mayfair Mei-hui Yang (Berkeley: University of California Press, 2008), 91.

30　Ethnographic research suggests that they had been introduced to their husbands through Methodist and Presbyterian maiden homes, which suggests that they were Christians.

31　Karen Dubinsky, *Babies without Borders: Adoption and Migration across the Americas* (Toronto: University of Toronto Press, 2010), 12.

32　As Hill Gates observes, "Women were sometimes valuable in the PCMP [petty capitalist mode of production] for their work and their persons, but they were essential for their ability to bear children ... A woman's failure to bear sons could be compensated through purchase or adoption. But lineage rules restricted such transactions, the price of boys was high, and adopted sons were often stereotyped as unfilial." Hill Gates, "The Commoditization of Chinese Women," *Signs* 14, 4, Special Issue: Common Grounds and Crossroads: Race, Ethnicity, and Class in Women's Lives (Summer 1989): 817. See also Ann Beth Waltner, "The Adoption of Children in Ming and Early Ch'ing China" (PhD diss., University of California, Berkeley, 1981).

33　Erving Goffman, *The Presentation of Self in Everyday Life* (New York: Doubleday, 1956).

34 See Leela Gandhi, *Affective Communities: Anti-Colonial Thought, Fin-de-siècle Radicalism and the Politics of Friendship* (Durham, NC: Duke University Press, 2006), 6-7.

35 In 2007, I discovered Howard's (Hou Minyi 侯民一) dance-lesson card among his belongings in an abandoned steamer trunk in Winnipeg's Chinatown. These lessons probably helped him to learn social graces with women, as well as dance skills. I am not, however, suggesting that "dance lessons" were a euphemism for lap-dancing and prostitution.

36 From the materials I found in Howard's steamer trunk, I learned that he had been a high-ranking nationalist comrade who became ill during the late 1930s and some time later moved to Winnipeg, where he became branch secretary of the KMT. At a 2009 Winnipeg Chinatown street festival, one elderly woman recognized him in a photograph as one of Winnipeg's 1940s Chinese teachers. Apparently, he had also been active in the CDS. Winnipeg Chinese Dramatic Society Papers (private collection); Manitoba KMT Archives, unpublished. See also *Winnipeg Evening Tribune*, June 15, 1942, 13.

37 Stuart Hall encourages us to complicate and look beyond these conjunctures to understand the forces and situations that fix hegemonic structures. See Stuart Hall, "Notes on Deconstructing the Popular," in *People's History and Socialist Theory*, ed. Ralph Samuel (Boston: Routledge and Kegan Paul, 1981), 227-39.

Chapter 7: Early Chinese Prairie Wives

1 Mah Joe's wife, Mrs. Mah Joe, gave birth to Winnie (Ma) Paktong (1912-2013), and then to a son the following year. Both mother and son died in childbirth. Current Winnipeg leadership often refers to Winnie Ma as the first Chinese child born in Manitoba, whereas research participants stated that she was the second. I doubt that she was either. Hundreds of Chinese lived in Manitoba for thirty-five years before Winnie was born, with the first documented three settlers (including one woman) arriving in 1877. Early Prairie Chinese Canadians preferred home births, and as a result many early births went undocumented. Chinese also moved frequently until 1909 when settlements stabilized. This does not detract from Winnie's remarkable life. She was born in 1912 in Winnipeg and lived in wartime China. In July 2012, she celebrated her 100th birthday at the WCCCC. This party was attended by Chinese Canadian lieutenant governor Philip Lee, as well as local Members of Parliament and most Winnipeg city councillors. See also C. Millien, E. Woo, and P. Yeh, *Winnipeg Chinese* (Ottawa: Department of the Secretary of State, 1971), 27.

2 The 1916 census lists Jessie as thirteen years old when she arrived in Canada in 1910 (b. 1897), though it incorrectly lists her birth year as 1903.

3 Letter from May Lee to Jacque and Pamela Mar enclosing the obituary of Gilbert Lee. February 2, 1997, Ma Seung Fonds, unpublished.

4 In 1916, the KMT was located at 263 King Street in the heart of Chinatown. *Winnipeg Free Press*, January 3, 1916, 5.

5 Unfortunately, the Chinese community records that I have been able to access, most of them from the 1930s, do not include references to Lee Mon, who may already have died or returned to China by this time. I have also been unable to find Lee Mon in either the 1916 or 1917 Winnipeg KMT membership roster. However, Lee Mon, like his son Gilbert, was a KMT member. Additionally, he was a founding member of the 1917 Chinese Young Men's Christian Association (see Ma Seung Fonds, unpublished). According to the 1911 census, forty-year-old Lee Mon immigrated to Winnipeg in 1903. At the time, he resided with eight other Chinese men in Chinatown.

6 Confidential interview with exclusion-era research participant.

7 Three attempts over five years were made to interview Winnie (Ma) Paktong (daughter of Mah Joe).

8 Chinese repeatedly referred to Mah Joe as a wealthy merchant who wore a silk hat and walked with a gold-tipped cane. They also remembered his generosity to other Ma clan members and the families of nationalist leaders.

9 Interview with Jacque Mar, January 2012.

10 Obituary. Jessie Lee Tsutin. Winnipeg Chinese United Church, Clergy Records. 1992. Unpublished.

11 Aka Yeung Hong Lin, Ma Seung's wife, and Ma Yeung Kut Tong.

12 In my research, I repeatedly heard that Chinese men competed to court and marry Canadian-born Chinese girls, from the 1920s to the 1960s. News about eligible girls spread quickly throughout Chinese communities. Madeline Y. Hsu writes that American-born Chinese girls were deemed less virtuous wives than those born in China; I never heard that Canadian-born Chinese girls were too. See Madeline Y. Hsu, *Dreaming of Gold, Dreaming of Home: Transnationalism and Migration between the United States and South China, 1882-1943* (Stanford: Stanford University Press, 2000), 102.

13 Interview with Jacque Mar, April 2011.

14 See Sunera Thobani, *Exalted Subjects: Studies in the Making of Race and Nation in Canada* (Toronto: University of Toronto Press, 2007), Chapter 3.

15 Kenneth McDonald, "The Presbyterian Church and the Social Gospel in California, 1890-1910," *American Presbyterians* 72, 4 (1994): 249.

16 Interviews with Pamela Mar, June and July 2011.

17 Hong Lin used her bean sprout business to pay for her first son's university education. In turn, Peter was expected to pay for Andrew's education, Andrew was expected to pay for George's education, George was expected to pay for Jacque's education, and Jacque was expected to reimburse his mother for the cost of his education.

18 Eng Shee Yee (aka Dang Woon Gok, Ung Shu, Mrs. Yee Quon Theen) Regina 1919-32 and 1941-47. I am grateful to Yee Clun and Eng Shee Yee's children, Kate, Mamie, Dan Hin, and grandson Clarence, who contributed materials, edited, and commented on this section.

19 Jee Clein appears in the 1911 census data for Rouleau. The handwriting is not very legible.

20 Rouleau and District History Book Committee, *1995 Rouleau and District History, 1894-1994: The Buckle of the Grain Belt* (Altona, MB: D.W. Friesen and Sons, 1995), 9.

21 Yee Clun formed a partnership with Jow Tai (Chow) to open the Exchange Grill/cafe. There may have been other shareholders, as well. Jow Tai's wife (Dai Jow/Mrs. Jew Noey Ai) arrived in Regina in 1920. The BC Vital Statistics Index lists Mr. and Mrs. Tai as Dai Jow and Leon Yee. Mrs. Tai is listed in the General Register of Chinese Immigration under C.I. 5 certificate number 91595. The Tai family became close friends with the Yee family and remain so to this day.

22 Email correspondence, Mamie Yee, April 24, 2013.

23 Aka Jean Farn, Jung Shee, Mrs. Jin Gim Foon.

24 Information about Mrs. Tom Jung Jean Farn was gathered from the General Register of Chinese Immigration, as well as from interviews with her son Isaac Farn and other research participants in this study who grew up in Saskatchewan and Manitoba and visited with the Farns. I have also examined the Winnipeg Chinese United Church Marriage Register, articles in the *Winnipeg Free Press,* and *Across the Border and Valley,* by the Maryfield and District Historical Society.

25 *An Act to Prevent the Employment of Female Labour in Certain Capacities,* 1912, 2 Geo. V, c. 17 required that Chinese and Japanese men must obtain a licence if they wished to hire "white" waitresses: "30(1) No Chinese person shall employ in any capacity or have under his direction or control any female white persons in any factory, restaurant or laundry." In Saskatchewan, the act was struck down in 1969. There was also support for the ban in Vancouver and Toronto. See Toronto newspaper article: "White Girls Cannot Work for Orientals: Mayor McBride Will Move to Halt Illegal Practice-Law Section Covers," MG 30, series D219, August 22, 1928, 151; MG 30, series D219, Ernest Mark scrapbook 1, 157, LAC.

26 Maryfield and District Historical Society, *Across the Border and Valley: The Story of Maryfield and Fairlight and Surrounding Districts,* 2 vols. (Maryfield, SK: Maryfield and District Historical Society), vol. 1, 389-90.

27 Interviews with research participants suggested that families returned to the villages of their mother or father during the wartime era of the 1930s and 1940s. Living in a mother's village went against tradition. Owing to the fact that fathers had children late in life, their parents were often dead by the time the family returned to China.

28 Winnipeg Chinese United Church Marriage Register, unpublished.

29 The information in this section on Mary Wong was gathered through multiple interviews with Lil Chow, as well as non-Chinese and Chinese who knew Mary during the exclusion era in Saskatchewan. Information was also gleaned from newspaper articles and local histories.

30 Jake had two cousins who lived in Moose Jaw, both of whom were Wongs. They brought their wives to Canada in 1922. Lil Chow recalls that one of the wives returned to China.

31 Lil adds that he also worked in Ontario.

32 Lil Chow, their daughter, has always wondered about the matchmaker who introduced her parents and thinks that it could have been a matchmaker who ran a maiden house. Hong Lin, the wife of Reverend Ma Seung, ran a maiden house in 1920s Winnipeg, where Saskatchewan men met their future wives.

33 Timothy J. Stanley, *Contesting White Supremacy: School Segregation, Anti-Racism and the Making of Chinese Canadians* (Vancouver: UBC Press, 2011), Chapter 1.

34 By this time, King Wong's wife had already returned to China.

35 Wong Tong, 1911 Indexed Census, Nanaimo: Mountain District.

36 Rootsweb, an ancestry.com community. See http://www.rootsweb.ancestry.com/.

37 Cantonese: Yue Chock, Yee Chuck.

38 General Register of Chinese Immigration, Yue Chock, November 15, 1903, C.I. certificate 00798 issued July 29, 1912, for Yee Chuck of Lethbridge, Alberta.

39 See the Lethbridge section in Wong Kin, comp. *International Chinese Business Directory of the World for the Year 1913,* (San Francisco: International Chinese Business Directory, February 10, 1913).

40 Stamped certificate of naturalization, Bing-wo Yee, family's personal collection.

41 Aka Esther Lew Bing-wo Yee.

42 Chinese Canadian Women: 1923-1967, April 10, 2014. http://www.mhso.ca/chinese canadianwomen/.

43 I interviewed Reg Bing-wo in Regina, Saskatchewan, in May 2011.

44 Church-agency-forced adoptions are well documented in Canada, Australia, and Korea. In the course of my research, I heard of at least seven Chinese boys and girls who either came to Canada with Christian missionaries and church-affiliated individuals or were raised by them there. In all cases, the details of stories told to me about adoptive mothers, fathers, and guardians were vague. For example, Wesley Lee (aka Lee Quok-Ho, b. 1901) was brought over to Canada in 1913 when he was twelve years old by an Anglican minister to be educated by the family in Canada. Once he arrived in Winnipeg, Lee lived with that family and presumably went to school. Then, defying his upbringing, he became a very successful professional gambler and interpreter. He did not become a Christian; instead, he opened one of the many gambling houses on Pacific Avenue. Despite a detailed search of the General Register of Chinese Immigration and the *Winnipeg Free Press,* I was unable to locate Wesley Lee. He may have used a number of different names, or he may have been able to keep his name out of the paper. I did find references to Wesley Lee in Ma Seung's papers. I also found photographs of him at early Winnipeg community picnics and later in Hong Kong. Confidential interviews with research participants who lived during the exclusion era in Winnipeg; Ma Seung Fonds, unpublished. See also Kathryn Blaze Carlson, "Your Baby Is Dead," *National Post,* March 23, 2012, and "Australia Urged

to Apologise for Forced Adoptions," *Telegraph*, February 29, 2012. See also Tobias Hübinette, "From Orphan Trains to Babylifts: Colonial Trafficking, Empire Building, and Social Engineering," in *Outsiders Within: Writing on Transracial Adoption*, ed. Jane Jeong Trenka, et al. (New York: South End Press, 2006), 139-50. See Laura Briggs, "Mother, Child, Race, Nation: The Visual Iconography of Rescue and the Politics of Transnational and Transracial Adoption," *Gender and History* 15, 2 (2003): 179-200.

45 See Liam O'Reilly, "Missionaries and Women in Victoria's Chinatown: The Establishment and Evolution of the Chinese Rescue Home, 1886-1900" (master's research paper, Department of History, University of Victoria, 2011), 32.

Chapter 8: Quongying's Coins and Sword

1 I did not find any evidence that Prairie Chinese wives were naturalized citizens and voted before the 1950s. I did, however, find evidence that Manitoba Chinese male citizens and non-Chinese wives voted. After 1912, networks expanded and became sharply gendered as thousands of young Chinese, mostly between the ages of eight and twenty-two, emigrated and, once in Canada, moved beyond Chinatown. Forty years after the first Chinese settled on the Prairies, there were still very few families, or women.

2 Gary Seaman, "The Sexual Politics of Karmic Retribution," in *The Anthropology of Taiwanese Society*, ed. Emily M. Ahern and Hill Gates (Stanford, CA: Stanford University Press, 1981), 382.

3 See Tam Wai Lun, ed., *Folk Buddhist Research* (*Minjian Fojiao Yanjiu* 民間佛教研究) (Beijing: Zhonghua shuju, 2007).

4 See Kenneth Dean with Zheng Zhenman, *Epigraphical Materials on the History of Religion in Fujian: Nanan, Hui'an, Yongchun, Dehua, and Anxi Counties, with Zheng Zhenman, Fuzhou* (Fuzhou, Fujian Renmin Chubanshe, 2003).

5 Men and second-generation children overcame stereotypes that Chinese were so different from European migrants that they were unable to fit in. Early Chinese wives continued to be discriminated against. This racism was culturally based and also the result of traditional rules that kept women inside the family home and unable to have social interactions (and thus create intercultural bridges) of their own. For a discussion of this aspect of racism, see Verena Stolcke, "Talking Culture: New Boundaries, New Rhetorics of Exclusion in Europe," *Current Anthropology* 36, 1, Special Issue: Ethnographic Authority and Cultural Explanation (February 1995): 1-24.

6 Louise Edwards examines women's suffrage campaigns during Republican period China, and shows that although women no longer had bound feet, they were still bound by Confucian patriarchy and inferior social roles: "Eventually China's women suffrage activists would have to attack the premise that Confucian gender hierarchies were essential to Chinese nationalism for their cause to be successful." Louise Edwards, "Chinese Women's Campaigns for Suffrage: Nationalism, Confucianism and Political Agency," in *Women's Suffrage in Asia: Gender, Nationalism and Democracy*, ed. Louise Edwards and Mina Roces (London: Routledge, 2004), 70. Women were not even allowed to be Lee or Ma clan association members until after 1950. Fieldwork. Vancouver, August and February 2014.

7 See also Judy Yung, *Unbound Feet: A Social History of Chinese Women in San Francisco* (Berkeley: University of California Press, 1995), 55.

8 Women began to get involved in nationalist fundraising in the 1940s. In Winnipeg in 1946, the Chinese Women of Winnipeg Group formed to help with fundraising in aid of China. See *Winnipeg Free Press*, March 26, 1946, 9. The women belonging to the group were not all racially "Chinese." The group included Mrs. Charlie Foo, Miss Daisy Ross, and Mrs. Annie Jones (president), who were all non-Chinese and of British ancestry.

9 Also known as *yin-yang* masters, *feng shui* experts, or *fashi* (masters of the law, or ritual masters), they are highly sought after for their services and are usually quite wealthy as

a result. However, in the Chinese hierarchy of religious functionaries, geomancers have low social status in comparison to Daoist priests, who perform the liturgy. Usually, these lesser-ranked religious functionaries are associated with practices that, in China after 1900, became commonly referred to as superstition.

10 Chinese male labourers who chose involvement in Winnipeg's Chinese Dramatic Opera (CDS) over nationalism were branded as communists in the same period. They were encouraged in increasingly aggressive ways to align themselves with the nationalists and to distance themselves from unorthodox religious practices that weakened the acceptance of Chinese Canadian community members. Understanding their role in the nationalist project, as related elsewhere in this book, Prairie CDS members purchased and delivered guns to China on behalf of the overseas nationalist branch. This information was gleaned through my research with dozens of participants who lived during the exclusion era as well as from participant observation fieldwork.

11 General Register of Chinese Immigration, Serial Number 87866, Ow Shee.

12 It should be noted that there are a number of categories and names for children, though mostly for girls, who were bought and sold in republican China. Parents and sometimes kidnappers (including Western missionaries) engaged in differently motivated trafficking of young children. As mentioned, parents typically bought a daughter as an infant to marry one of their sons when she was an adolescent. With this kind of marriage, the family could avoid paying for a matchmaker and the higher price of a bride. The family would also not have to incur the expenses of wedding parties and other lavish celebrations; this kind of "minor marriage" (as opposed to "major marriage," where a girl married out of a family) was thus more attractive to poorer families. Research on marriage and adoption in China in the early republican period is complicated by the fact that surviving documentation is dominated by official accounts and non-Chinese missionary accounts, both of which are skewed for different reasons. Whereas non-Chinese missionaries viewed Chinese culture and practices as exotic, Manchurian and early republican accounts reflected a bias for orthodox customs and disdain for so-called uncivilized southerly traditions. See Margery Wolf, Roxane Witke, and Emily Martin, *Women in Chinese Society* (Stanford, CA: Stanford University Press, 1975), 92. See also James L. Watson, "Transactions in People: The Chinese Market in Slaves, Servants, and Heirs," in *Asian and African Systems of Slavery* (Berkeley: University of California Press, 1980), 223-50. Arthur Wolf and Chieh-Shan Huang report that the adoption of a young girl intended for a minor marriage in pre-1925 China was more widespread than previously thought and was found in both northern and southern China, but was most common in the south. Arthur P. Wolf and Chieh-Shan Huang, *Marriage and Adoption in China, 1845-1945* (Stanford, CA: Stanford University Press, 1980), 5. Precise numbers during this period are difficult to determine, given the bias in reporting. Girls purchased for marriage to sons at a young age are in a different class than the *mui-tsai* (*mui-tsai* became famous in Hong Kong), who were bought when they were older and by wealthy families for use as slaves, servants, and prostitutes, or married out of the family as secondary wives. By the 1910s, the sale of young girls intended as wives, concubines, maids, slaves, or prostitutes had become so prevalent in Hong Kong that it had attracted the attention of local Chinese Christians. They banded together and pressured the Hong Kong government to enact *mui-tsai* legislation, prohibiting the practice. Hong Lin Ma is the sister of Yeung Shiu Chuen, a prominent Hong Kong dentist and Anglican who lobbied the government to enact this bill. I interviewed his son Robert in April 2012.

13 Miss Wong's brother by adoption, Charlie Foo, arrived in Canada the following year and came to Winnipeg. It is likely that he visited Sam Wong and his sister when he arrived in Manitoba, thus explaining how Sam Wong and Charlie Foo knew each other. Whereas Sam Wong had been an active member of the KMT since at least 1916 in Montreal, Foo appears to have gotten involved in nationalism only after he arrived in Winnipeg.

14 *Brandon Daily Sun,* February 23, 1920.

15 According to Chinese astrological wisdom and a twelve-year cycle of animals, 1920 was the year of the Monkey. Each animal sign within the system is also assigned a colour and one of the five elements (wood, fire, water, earth, metal).

16 A tombstone in the Brandon cemetery marks the grave of Miss Au Wong, and beside it is a cross without a name, presumably in memory of her son. Since 2006, I have spoken with and interviewed more than a dozen people who are related to her husband, and none of them remembers hearing anything about the death other than that it was terrible.

17 Ghost month is traditionally regarded in Chinese culture as an ill-advised time for travel. Family members doubt that photographs were exchanged during the matchmaking process, in which someone was hired to check the compatibility of the couple's birth signs, eight characters *(bazi),* and horoscopes. Within two years, Lim's daughter came as a new wife. Quongying embarked on the voyage from Hong Kong to Victoria in the late summer of 1921.

18 Chineseness and dirt are often conflated in communities where early overseas Chinese resided. See Nayan Shah, *Contagious Divides: Epidemic and Race in San Francisco's Chinatown* (Berkeley: University of California Press, 2001).

19 David Lai describes the conditions of the facilities where newly migrated women and men were housed. Westerners called the rooms "halls and sheds," but, as noted, Chinese used more negative language, calling them "piggy huts": "During this time, the Chinese immigrants were confined to rooms where all openings were covered with iron screens and bars to prevent their escape." See David Chuenyan Lai, *A Brief Chronology of Chinese Canadian History: From Segregation to Integration* (Vancouver: Simon Fraser University, David See-Chai Lam Centre for International Communication, 2011).

20 Among the poems recovered by Lai were those written in both pentasyllabic verse (with five characters per line), and seven-character poems, styles that became common during the Han dynasty. "Ku-shih shi-chiu shou" (Nineteen Old Poems), in William H. Nienhauser Jr., ed. and comp., *The Indiana Companion to Traditional Chinese Literature* (Bloomington: Indiana University Press, 1986), 212 and 489-90. David Lai, "A 'Prison' for Chinese Immigrants," *Asianadian* 2, 4 (Spring 1980): 16-19, "Rescuing the Artless Art of Early Chinese Immigrants," *Discovery* 28, 5 (January 2001): 4-5, and "Piglet's Hut: 'Prison' for Chinese New Immigrants in the Old Days," *Chinese Canadian Post,* August 5, 2006, 4. For a discussion of Chinese poetry written on the walls of the immigration prison, see Him Mark Lai, Genny Lim, and Judy Yung, *Island: Poetry and History of Chinese Immigrants on Angel Island, 1910-1940"* (Seattle: University of Washington Press, 1993).

21 A classical Chinese saying that poetry expresses what is intent upon the mind *(shiyan zhi* 詩言志) is first found in the *Classic of Documents (Shangshu),* which dates from the Spring and Autumn Period (c. 771-453 BCE) of Chinese history. For an expert discussion of the meaning, history, and use of this phrase, see Stephen Owen, *Readings in Literary Thought* (Cambridge, MA: Harvard University Asia Center, 1992), 28-30.

22 The poems also associate the filth and insufficient food for detainees with the "unprincipled character of the black devils [foreigners]" *(heigui wu daoli* 黑鬼無道理*).* This is an excerpt from a poem written on the piggy hut wall by a Lee on September 4, 1911. The black devils are the captors.

23 Sam Wong was a merchant, and his two wives came to Canada as merchant wives. However, unlike other merchant wives, they were not exempted from paying five hundred dollars in head tax. In this and in other cases where some Chinese had not been required to register with the government after 1923, I noticed the inconsistent application of law.

24 Residents of women's rescue homes received instruction in "white" Victorian Christian customs such as drinking tea, singing from Methodist hymnals, and, of course, the domestic arts, assumed to be essential to future labour or spousal work in the home. As

Mariana Valverde reports about Methodist rescue homes, "The work of the rescue home, widely publicized through the reports of the Women's Missionary Society of the Methodist Church, probably helped to shape the attitudes of many ordinary Canadians, including many feminists, to[ward] both Chinese men and Chinese women." Mariana Valverde, *The Age of Light, Soap, and Water: Moral Reform in English Canada, 1885-1925* (Toronto: McClelland and Stewart, 1991), 88. See also Vijay Agnew, "Canadian Feminism and Women of Color," *Women's Studies International Forum* 16, 3 (1993): 217-27; and Marilyn F. Whiteley, "'Allee Samee Melican Lady': Imperialisms and Negotiation at the Chinese Rescue Home (Women Missionary Societies Set Up the Chinese Rescue Home to Save Chinese Women from Prostitution)," *Resources for Feminist Research* 22, 3-4 (Fall 1992/Winter 1993): 1-9. See also Myra Rutherdale, *Women and the White Man's God: Gender and Race in the Canadian Mission Field* (Vancouver: UBC Press, 2002).

25 As discussed on page 218, note 13, a preliminary search of Winnipeg police records revealed no Chinese prostitutes.

26 I know that the outfits were unworn because each of the tunic necks was still sewn together.

27 In the 1930s, Quongying's father was discovered to have been involved in the opium trade and was deported. Walker Wong recalls meeting his grandfather for the first and last time in southwestern Manitoba:

> I remember going on a train when I was very young. I didn't know at first why we went on a train with Mother. We travelled as far as Virden, Manitoba. I later learned that we went on the train so that we could meet my mother's father. He was travelling from Ottawa back to China, via Vancouver. The reason why he was going back was because he was expelled from Canada for selling opium. He was deported. My mom wanted us to meet our *gonggong* (grandfather). I didn't know who he was until I was an adult. I thought he was a foreign person because he took no interest in his grand kids [sic]. I remember that he seemed to only want to talk to my mother. I remember that when we got on the train in Brandon we were the only ones in that coach. We were treated okay. We dressed up to go on the train.

Within the next decade, Quongying's parents had one more child, a boy. Then during the war they died, and presumably the brother was raised by Quongying's elder sister in their village. Quongying never met her younger brother but corresponded with him regularly until the end of her life. For the majority of women in this study, the closest male relationship beyond their husband was with a brother. When Quongying died, that younger brother's photograph was the only family photograph from China on her bedroom dresser. Most Chinese mothers in Canada didn't talk about their families in China, and children seldom knew any of the details about what had happened to family members during the second Sino-Japanese War and the civil war, when the nationalists were defeated. Most mothers talked only generally about the hardships they had experienced while living in China. See, for instance, Linda Gee-Hamilton, *A Full Bowl of Rice: Memories of Morly and Sam Gee* (San Francisco: Blurb, 2012).

28 Brigitte Baptandier, *The Lady of Linshui: A Chinese Female Cult* (Stanford, CA: Stanford University Press, 2008), 70, 82, and 86.

29 See Bernard Faure, *Buddhism, Purity and Gender* (Princeton, NJ: Princeton University Press, 2003); Kristin De Troyer, *Wholly Woman, Holy Blood: A Feminist Critique of Purity and Impurity, Studies in Antiquity and Christianity* (Harrisburg, PA: Trinity Press International, 2003); and Jen-der Lee, "Gender and Medicine in Tang China," *Asia Major* 16, 2 (2003): 1-29.

30 For a discussion of feminine taboos in Asian culture and religion, see Lisa Kuly, "Religion, Commerce, and Commodity in Japan's Maternity Industry" (PhD diss., Cornell University,

2009), 26. I am grateful to Lisa, who read and commented on an early version of this chapter.

31 See Mary Douglas, *Purity and Danger: An Analysis of Concepts of Pollution and Taboo* (London: Routledge, 1996); Bernard Faure, *The Red Thread: Buddhist Approaches to Sexuality* (Princeton, NJ: Princeton University Press, 1998); Thomas Buckley and Alma Gottlieb, *Blood Magic: The Anthropology of Menstruation* (Berkeley: University of California Press, 1988); and Cordia Ming-Yeuk Chu, "Menstrual Beliefs of Chinese Women," *Journal of the Folklore Institute* 17, 1 (1980): 38-55.

32 It is fairly common even today in southern China for a ritual master *(fashi)* or geomancers to give people coins that have been sewn together with auspiciously coloured red thread.

33 I am very grateful to Brigitte Baptandier for her insightful comments incorporated here on the meaning of the coins and their religious usage.

34 See Hill Gates, "Money for the Gods," *Modern China* 13, 3, Special Issue: Symposium on Hegemony and Chinese Folk Ideologies, Part II (July 1987): 266-68; and Hou Ching-lang, *Monnaies d'offrande et la notion de trésorerie dans la religion chinoise*, Mémoires de l'Institut des hautes études chinoises, vol. 1 (Paris: Collège de France, 1975), 35 and 48.

35 See Hou, *Monnaies d'offrande*, 105-6 and 220-21.

36 This figurine is white and shows a seated scholar with a heart-shaped object resting on his shoulder.

37 Throughout the research, people told me about many mothers who privately and secretly burned incense, chanted, and used beads in their daily prayers to Guanyin.

38 I am grateful to Elizabeth Johnson, who provided insights on the embroidered items and the significance of their colours, provenance, and uses.

39 Email dated February 18, 2012.

40 Pinyin: *maomu neng kan qianli ming* 眊目能看千里明.

41 Pinyin: *baojing guanghui* 寶鏡光煇.

42 Pinyin: *neng ke tongqing dai* 能客通情待.

43 Interview with Irene Lea, July 2011.

44 Margery Wolf adds, "Beyond the expense and danger of a hospital and the ritual impropriety of bearing a child in someone else's home, it is simply considered proper for a son, and all unborn children who are presumed to be sons, to be born in the home of his ancestors." Wolf, *Women and the Family*, 54.

Chapter 9: Chinese Prairie Daughters

1 See Constance Backhouse, "White Female Help and Chinese-Canadian Employers: Race, Class, Gender and Law in the Case of Yee Clun, 1924," *Canadian Ethnic Studies* 26, 3 (1994): 34-40, and *Colour-Coded: A Legal History of Racism in Canada, 1900-1950* (Toronto: University of Toronto Press, 1999), 164. Mamie, Katie, and Dan Yee were interviewed in Vancouver on 13 July 2011. Follow-up interviews were conducted via email in 2012 and 2013. Helen Wong was interviewed multiple times in person, by telephone, and via email from 2006 to 2014.

2 Yee Clun's lawsuit became quite famous in Canada through Constance Backhouse's research, but his children knew nothing about the suit until grandson Clarence did an Internet search a few years ago. Yee was also part owner of lesser-known chop suey houses and a general merchandise store.

3 Their children are not sure if Eng Shee had political views, but they know that she attended KMT functions with Yee Clun in the 1920s, 1930s, and 1940s.

4 Regina Chinese organized to open a Chinese school in 1957, but only after the repeal of the Chinese Immigration Act, when more families and children had come to the area. This school, however, was not strongly affiliated with the KMT. "Chinese School Planned," *Leader Post*, October 12, 1957, 3.

5 Another Chinese girl named Anna Lee (daughter of Lee Foon from Baldur, Manitoba) was also a student during the time that Mamie was at the university.

6 Yee Clun didn't drive but he had friends who did. He had always been interested in taking trips with his family to various Prairie cities, towns, and villages. Through these trips, the family developed connections and alliances with Chinese in Maple Creek, Shaunavon, Cabri, Glenside, and many other places.

7 Trans Nation Emporium, 89 East Pender Street, aka Kuo Seun Importers.

8 Some of the youths whom Helen would have known included Thomas Ma, Mah Leng King, Der Tong, Mamie Wong, Pearl Wong, Frank and Wesley Chan, Gordon Lim, Frank Wong, Walter Lee, Goo Wong, May and Lily Ma (daughters of Joe Mah), Fay Lee, Annie Lee, Rosy Lee, Margaret Yee (daughter of Charles Yee), Don Tong, and Gilbert Lee. This list has been compiled from information found in the Ma Seung notes on the Jones family, as well as from interviews with research participants.

9 While they lived in Winnipeg, Tao Wong Weng, consul general for the Republic of China, and his family resided at 76 Yale Street. A Winnipeg property registry search shows the home was transferred to Charlie Foo and other members of the Chinese community in 1949, when Tao Weng and his family left Winnipeg. After 1949, when the nationalists fled to Taiwan, and China became ruled by Mao Zedong and the Communist Party, there were no more consul generals for the Republic of China. The Chinese community retained the house until 1956, when it was sold. In 1972, Charlie Foo visited with Tao Weng and his wife in Taiwan. The owners and purchase dates of 76 Yale from 1938 to 1956 include: the Imperial Life Assurance Company of Canada (July 14, 1938); Tao Weng of the city of Winnipeg in Manitoba, consul at Winnipeg for the Republic of China (December 3, 1945); the Toronto General Trusts Corporation (March 7, 1946); Gin Gain Roy, restaurateur, Charlie San Wong, CNR, ticket agent, both of the city of Winnipeg in Manitoba; Charlie Foo, restaurateur, of the city of St. Boniface, in Manitoba (October 19, 1949); Harry Chan, restaurateur (June 8, 1950); and Iva Marie Walker (November 30, 1956).

10 The couple returned to Brandon, Manitoba, where Westley headed the Physics Department of Brandon College. He was a distinguished professor, eventually holding positions as vice-president and dean of Science. Following his retirement, Brandon University bestowed a doctor of laws degree on Westley in recognition of his many contributions to Brandon College and later Brandon University. See also "My Life and Times," by Westley G. Wong, Foo/Wong Fonds, UBC Archives.

11 Helen recalls visiting Happy Young in Esterhazy with Frank Chan.

12 I am struck by the similarities between Marcelle Gibson's adoption and that of Canadian author Wayson Choy, who shares Marcelle's maiden name and whose father (an unknown) had also been part of a travelling opera troupe. See Wing Chung Ng, "Chinatown Theatre as Transnational Business: New Evidence from Vancouver during the Exclusion Era," *BC Studies* 148 (2005-6): 25.

13 Marcelle Gibson was interviewed by telephone and via email from July, 2011 to December, 2012.

Conclusion

1 Newly arrived men could go for meals at 10 a.m., later at 5 p.m., and then at 10 p.m., presumably when there were few customers in the restaurant. Interview transcripts: Lai Man Cheng, 1984, 8-9, Edgar Wickberg Fonds, Chinese in Canada Series, 8-28, 2, UBC Archives. The interview describes Chinese Prairie life fifty years prior to the interview.

2 Patrick A. Duane, "Geographies of Sexual Commerce and the Production of Prostitutional Space: Victoria, British Columbia, 1860-1914," *Journal of the Canadian Historical Association* 19, 1 (2008): 115-42.

3 An example of one such marriage alliance that united KMT Manitobans and Ontarians was the union between Helen Foy from Elm Creek, Manitoba, and Jacky Jung from Fort William, Ontario. Fittingly, the wedding took place in the Manitoba KMT hall. *Winnipeg Free Press,* October 23, 1941, 11.

4 "Seed Capital: How Immigrants Are Reshaping Saskatchewan's Farmland," *Globe and Mail,* October 12, 2012. I have also heard through research participants of Chinese increasingly bidding on several farms for sale south of Winnipeg.

5 Network building and elder connections are specific to each community and are determined by that community's cultural, political, and religious past and present. Chinese settlers discussed in this book came to Canada for the most part before 1950 and from a nation with divided political, not religious, alliances. Settlers who remained on the Prairies were usually right-leaning nationalists and nominal (unbaptized) Christians. They were not usually communist supporters.

Glossary

Chinese Character Glossary: Cantonese (CAN), Mandarin (Pinyin), or Canadianized, as noted

Au 區 (Pinyin) clan

Au Fu (Pinyin) 區富 (1894-1980)

Au Xiansheng (Pinyin) 區先生 (1894-1980) Mr. Au/Charlie Foo

Bak Yeung (CAN) 上閣北洋 village in the District of Toisan, China

Baojing guanghui (Pinyin) 寶鏡光輝 the precious mirror of radiance

Bazi (Pinyin) 八字 eight characters (fate)

Bing-wo Yee (CAN) 炳和余 (b. 1882-?) aka Yue Chock, Yee Chuck

Binghe guaye (Pinyin) 炳和瓜業 Bing Wo and Company, Vegetables, Lethbridge, Alberta

Bo Ya (Pinyin) 伯牙 friend of Zhongzi Qi during the Spring and Autumn Period, Zhou dynasty (ca. 1050-256 BCE), who shared affective ties through music (zhiyin)

Canton City 廣州 Guangzhou

Chan, Frank 陳煥章 (1901-52) aka Chan Shan

Chan, Mr. Watson (CAN) 陳榮光 (d. 1945)

Chan (CAN) 陳 clan

Chan Tok Wah (CAN) 陳煥章 (1901-1952) aka Frank Chan

Chee Kung Tong (CAN) 致公堂 Chinese Freemasons

Chen Baishan (Pinyin) 陳栢山 North Battleford KMT branch leader in the early 1950s

Chin (CAN) 甄 clan

Choi (CAN) 蔡 clan

Chong (CAN) 張 clan

Chow (CAN) 周 clan

Choy (CAN) 蔡 clan

Chu (CAN) 朱 clan

Dao (Pinyin) 道 the way, or the *dao*

Dare (CAN) 謝 clan

Deer (CAN) 謝 clan

Deng (CAN) 鄧 clan

Der (CAN) 謝 clan

Dong (CAN) 曾 clan

Dong, Sam (CAN) 曾森 (1891-1960)

Dong Huli (Pinyin) 東湖里 Au clan hamlet called East Lake in Hoiping, China

Dong On (CAN) 曾森 (1891-1960)

Dong Sum (CAN) 曾森 (1891-1960)

Du (Pinyin) 杜 clan

Eng Shee Yee (CAN) 鄧隱菊 (1897-1954) Dang Woon Gok, Ung Shu, Mrs. Yee Quon Theen

Farn, Isaac (CAN) 甄培森 (b. 1925)

Farn, Mrs. Zhen (CAN) 甄 aka Mrs. Gin Fon

Fashi (Pinyin) 法師 masters of the law, or ritual masters

feng shui (Pinyin) 風水 literally: wind and water, geomancy

Fong (CAN) 馮 clan

Foo, Charlie 區富 (1894-1980)

Gean (CAN) 甄 clan

Gee (CAN) 朱 clan

Gen (CAN) 甄 clan

Gene (CAN) 甄 clan

Gin (CAN) 甄 clan

Gonggong (Pinyin) 公公 grandfather

Guan (CAN) 關 clan

Guan Dongxian (Pinyin) 關動賢 Chinese Canadian who wrote poem for Frank Chan

Guangdong province (Pinyin) 廣東 also known as Canton

Guangzhou (Pinyin) 廣州 also known as Canton City

Guanxi (Pinyin) 關係 relationships, connections

Guanyin (Pinyin) 觀音 goddess of compassion

Guo (CAN) 郭 clan

Guomindang (Pinyin) 國民黨 KMT, Chinese Nationalist League

Gwok (CAN) 郭 clan

Heigui wu daoli (Pinyin) 黑鬼無道理 unprincipled black devils

Hoiping (CAN) 開平 aka Kaiping

Hong (CAN) 馮 clan

Hou Minyi (Pinyin) 侯民一

How Min Yet (CAN) 侯民一

Howard (Mr.) 侯民一

Huang Daxian (Pinyin) 黃大仙 Chinese deity

Huang Rongsheng (Pinyin) 黃容生

Huiwei lin (Pinyin) 伙偉林 Fort William branch of KMT

Jang Chuen Hing (CAN) 曾傳亨/曾傳鏗 (1890-1956) aka Happy Young

Jaw Chun Hing (CAN) 曾傳亨/曾傳鏗 (1890-1956) aka Happy Young

Jaw Chung Hing (CAN) 曾傳亨/曾傳鏗 (1890-1956) aka Happy Young

Jen (CAN) 任 clan

Jianada Wen(nipei) Diqun Huaqiao Kangri Jiuguo Hui Yong Jian (Pinyin) 加拿大溫地群華僑抗日救國會用箋 Chinese Patriotic League

Jiaren (Pinyin) 佳人 traditional beauties

Jidu jiao Xiehehui (Pinyin) 基督教協和會 Chinese United Church

Jinghun jushe (Pinyin) 警魂劇社 Wake Up the Soul Opera Troupe (Chinese Dramatic Society)

Jiuguohui (Pinyin) 救國會 Save the Nation Association

Junzi (Pinyin) 君子 gentleman

Kaiping (Pinyin) 開平 aka Hoiping

Koa Hong (CAN) 區富 (1894-1980)

Koa Hong Foo (CAN) 區富 (1894-1980)

Kwan (CAN) 關 clan

Kwok (CAN) 郭 clan

Lam (CAN) 林 clan

Lanqiao jushe (Pinyin) 聯僑劇社 Toronto Chinese United Dramatic Society

Lau (CAN) 劉 clan

Lee (CAN) 李 clan

Lee, Gilbert (CAN) 李瑞麟 (1911-97)

Lee Hip (CAN) 李協 (d. 1977)

Lee Mon, Jessie (CAN) (1897-1992) 李鳳愛

Lee Mon, Wong (Mrs.) (CAN) 李黃民氏 (b. 1875)

Lee Tong Duey (CAN) (1897-1992) 李鳳愛

Leung (CAN) 梁 clan

Li Biaoyi (Pinyin) 李標宜

Liang (CAN) 梁 clan

Lim (CAN) 林 clan

Lim Quongying (CAN) 林羣英 (1900-93) aka Lim Koon Ying

Liu (CAN) 劉 clan

Lo Cheung (CAN) 盧章

Low/Lowe (CAN) 劉 clan

Lü Dongbin (Pinyin) 呂洞賓 Chinese deity

Lum (CAN) 林 clan

Ma (Pinyin) 馬 clan

Ma Douchen (Pinyin) 馬寶臣 ca. 1930s Manitoba Chinese merchant

Ma Lianxiang (Pinyin) 馬蓮香 daughter of Manitoba Chinese merchant Ma Douchen 馬寶臣

Ma Lianxiu (Pinyin) 馬蓮秀 daughter of Manitoba Chinese merchant Ma Douchen 馬竇臣

Ma Seung (CAN) 馬相 (1872-1951) Reverend Ma Seung

Ma Shuzheng (Pinyin) 馬述政 Regina KMT branch leader in the early 1950s

Ma Xiang (Pinyin) 馬相 (1872-1951) Reverend Ma Seung

Mack (CAN) 麥 clan

Mah (CAN) 馬 clan

Maomu neng kan qianli ming (Pinyin) 眊目能看千里明 the bewildered eye may see a thousand miles clearly

Mar, Arthur (CAN) 馬寬平 aka Mah Ping Chong

Mar, Jacque G. 馬基澤 fourth son of Reverend Ma Seung

Mark (CAN) 麥 clan

Mazu (Pinyin) 媽祖 Chinese deity

Mui-tsai (CAN) 妹仔 literally: little sister (Chinese girls purchased as slaves, wives, servants, and prostitutes)

Muwu (Pinyin) 木屋 piggy hut (literally: a log cabin, the name used by the Chinese community for the accommodations at Victoria's old detention hall); also referred to as immigration sheds and cells by non-Chinese

Neng ke tongqing dai (Pinyin) 能客通情待 the host understands feelings and behaves [accordingly]

Ng Mon Hing (CAN) 伍文興 (1858-1921)

Ning (CAN) 任 clan

Pang (CAN) 彭 clan

Peng (CAN) 彭 clan

Phang (CAN) 彭 clan

Qi nuzi (Pinyin) 奇女子 extraordinary women

Quan (CAN) 闕 clan

Ren (CAN) 任 clan

Ren (Pinyin) 仁 benevolence

Renqing (Pinyin) 人情 human sentiment or favour

San Wui (CAN) 新會 aka Xinhui

Sanmin zhuyi (Pinyin) 三民主義 Three Principles

Sanmin zhuyi qingnian tuan (Pinyin) 三民主義青年團 Three Principles Youth Group

Seto (CAN) 司徒 clan

Sha (CAN) 沙 clan

Shacheng Guomindang Tongren (Pinyin) 沙城國民黨同人 Saskatoon City Nationalist Comrades

Shangxin (Pinyin) 賞心 appreciative heart

Shiyan zhi (Pinyin) 詩言志 poetry expresses what is intent upon the mind

Soong (CAN) 宋 clan

Taishan (Pinyin) 台山 Toisan

Toisan (CAN) 台山 Taishan

Tongmeng Hui (Pinyin) 同盟會 Chinese United League

Tongs (CAN) 堂 or hall, also known as "gangs"

Tsai (CAN) 蔡 clan

Tsang (CAN) 曾 clan

Tseng (CAN) 曾 clan

Tzeng (CAN) 曾clan

Wang Chuting (Pinyin) 王楚亭

Wong (CAN) 黃 clan

Wong, Helen (CAN) 黃區蓮好 (b. 1924)

Wong Tai Sin (CAN) 黃大仙 Chinese deity

Woo (CAN) 吳 clan

Xiansheng (Pinyin) 仙生 Immortal Born

Xiao (Pinyin) 孝 filiality

Xinhui (Pinyin) 新會 aka San Wui

Yam (CAN) 任 clan

Yan (CAN) 甄 clan

Yang Xianglian (Pinyin) 楊香蓮 (1880-1962) aka Ma Seung's wife, Ma Yeung Kut Tong

Yee, Charles (CAN) 余精一 (1887-1954) Yee Kee

Yee, Clun (CAN) 余毓傑 (1881-1967)

Yee, Kee (CAN) 余精一 (1887-1954) Charles Yee

Yen (CAN) 甄 clan

Yen Wo (CAN) 人和 dialect society altar dedicated to deity named Tam Gong 譚公

Yeung Hong Lin (CAN) 楊香蓮 (1880-1962) Yang Xianglian, aka Ma Seung's wife, Ma Yeung Kut Tong

Yi (Pinyin) 義 righteousness

Yin Zhu (Pinyin) 銀珠

Yin-yang (Pinyin) 陰陽

Ying (CAN) 甄 clan

Yip (CAN) 葉 clan

Young (CAN) 曾 clan

Young, Happy (CAN) 曾傳亨 (1890-1956)

Yuan (CAN) 袁 clan

Yuen (CAN) 袁 clan

Yum (CAN) 任 clan

Zeng (CAN) 曾 clan

Zhang (CAN) 張 clan

Zhen Huayue (Pinyin) 振華閱 Inspiring Chinese Experiences

Zhengming (Pinyin) 正名 rectification of names

Zhi Gongtang (Pinyin) 致公堂 Chinese Freemasons

Zhiyin (Pinyin) 知音 knowledge of music, friendship formed through a love of music (Bo Ya and Zhongzi Qi)

Zhong (Pinyin) 忠 loyalty

Zhongguo Guomindang (Pinyin) 中國國民黨 KMT, Chinese Nationalist Party

Zhongshan (Pinyin) 中山 Sun Yat-sen's native county

Zhongzi Qi (Pinyin) 鍾子期 during the Spring and Autumn Period, Zhou dynasty (ca. 1050-256 BCE), shared affective ties with Bo Ya through music (Zhiyin)

Zhou (Pinyin) 周 clan

Zhu (Pinyin) 朱 clan

Bibliography

Archival Sources
BC Vital Statistics Index
Dr. Yeung Shiu Chuen 楊少泉 Papers (private collection)
Edgar Wickberg Fonds, UBC Archives
Foo Papers (private collection)
Foo Wong Fonds, Chinese Canadian Stories, UBC Archives
Frank Chan's scrapbook
Gay and Lesbian Oral History Project, 1991, University of Winnipeg
General Register of Chinese Immigration
Glenbow Archives
Library and Archives Canada (LAC)
List of Electors of the City of Brandon, 1895 to 1925. Daly House Museum, Brandon, Manitoba.
List of Electors of the City of Winnipeg, 1911 to 1947. City of Winnipeg Archives, Manitoba.
Ma Seung Fonds, Chinese Canadian Stories, UBC Archives
Ma Seung Fonds (private collection)
Manitoba Archives
Manitoba KMT Archives (private collection)
Manitoba Vital Statistics Index
Moon Dong Fonds, Chinese Canadian Stories, UBC Archives
Peel's Prairie Provinces
Royal Canadian Mounted Police Reports
Sam Gee Papers (private collection)
Saskatchewan Archives Board
Saskatchewan Genealogical Society Obituary Collection
Saskatchewan History and Folklore Society
St. Thomas-Wesley United Church Archives
Stubbs Fonds, University of Manitoba
United Church of Canada Archives, Winnipeg
Winnipeg Chinese Dramatic Society Papers (private collection)
Winnipeg Chinese United Church Burial Register (private collection)
Winnipeg Chinese United Church Clergy Records (private collection)
Winnipeg Chinese United Church Marriage Registers (private collection)
Winnipeg General Hospital – Dietary Department, History of Main Kitchen as related by Miss Judy Bennett, July 1972
Winnipeg General Hospital Collection, Children's Hospital – *Financial Records* – Salary Register, 1943-52
Winnipeg General Hospital Collection, *General Ledger Book*, 1913-28

Winnipeg General Hospital Collection, *General Ledger Book,* 1914-23
Winnipeg General Hospital Collection, *Reports and Accounts* – incomplete bound yearly
statements, 1919-38
Winnipeg Land Titles
Winnipeg Police Records
Wong Papers (private collection)

Newspapers
Brandon Daily Sun
Brandon Sun
Chinese Canadian Post
Chinese Times
Daily Colonist
Daily Star
Davidson Leader
Esterhazy Observer
Globe
Globe and Mail
Hong Kong Journal
Leader Post
Lethbridge Herald
Manitoba Free Press
Morden Times
Morning Leader
National Post
Regina Leader
Telegraph
Vancouver Sun
Winnipeg Evening Tribune
Winnipeg Free Press
Winnipeg Tribune
Xinminguo bao (New Republic)

Directories
Henderson Directories. *Henderson's City of Regina Directory.* Winnipeg: Henderson
Directories, 1911-57.
–. *Henderson's Manitoba and Northwest Territories Gazetteer and Directory.* Winnipeg:
Henderson Directories, 1894.
"Lovell's Classified Business Directory." *Manitoba Northwest Gazetteer,* 1901. Legislative
Library, Winnipeg, Manitoba.
Wong Kin, comp. *International Chinese Business Directory of the World for the Year 1913:*
A Comprehensive List of Prominent Chinese Firms and Individuals (Wangguo Jixin
Bianlan). San Francisco: International Chinese Business Directory, February 10, 1913.

Census Data
Census of Canada, 1891. Vol. 1. Ottawa: S.E. Dawson, 1893.
Census of Canada, 1901. Vol. 1. Ottawa: S.E. Dawson, 1902.
Census of Canada, 1911. Vol. 2. Ottawa: C.H. Parmalee, 1913.
Census of Canada, 1921. Vol. 1. Ottawa: F.A. Acland, 1925.
Census of the Northwest Provinces, 1906. Ottawa: S.E. Dawson, 1907.
Census of Prairie Provinces, 1916. Ottawa: J. de Labroquerie Taché, 1918.

Dominion Bureau of Statistics. Census of Canada, 1931. Vol. 2. Ottawa: J.O. Patenaude, 1933.

–. *Census of Canada*, 1941. Vol. 2. Ottawa: Edmond Cloutier, 1944.

–. *Census of Canada*, 1951. Vol. 1. Ottawa: Edmond Cloutier, 1953.

Selected Local Histories

Alameda and District Historical Society. *From Dream to Reality, 1882-1982*. Altona, MB: Friesens, 1982.

Arcola Kisbey History Book Committee. *Arcola-Kisbey Golden Heritage: Mountain Hills to Prairie Flats*. Arcola, SK: 1987.

Avonlea Historical Committee. *Arrowheads to Wheatfields: Avonlea, Hearne and Districts*. Avonlea, SK: 1983.

Boissevain History Committee. *Beckoning Hills: Ours Is a Goodly Heritage: Morton-Boissevain, 1881-1981*. Altona, MB: Friesens, 1981.

Cartwright and District History Committee. *Memories along the Badger Revisited: Cartwright, Manitoba, 1885-1985*. Altona, MB: D.W. Friesen and Sons, 1985.

Clark, Floyd, and Driver and District History Book Committee. *Along the Buffalo Coulee: History of Driver, Victory, Teo Lake*. Altona, MB: Friesens, 1978.

Coteau History Committee. *Echoes of Coteau: A History of the Area and Residents, Past and Present, within the Boundaries of the Rural Municipality of Coteau, No. 255*. Altona, MB: Friesens, 1981.

Cypress River Community Club. *Pioneers, Perseverance and Progress: Cypress River, 1885-1995*. Cypress River, MB: The Club, 1986.

Edenwold Anniversary Committee. *Where Aspens Whisper: Edenwold*. Altona, MB: Friesens, 1981.

Enns, Garry. *Window on the Northwest*. Gretna, MB: Village of Gretna History Committee, 1987.

Epp-Tiessen, Esther. *Altona: The Story of a Prairie Town*. Altona, MB: Friesens, 1982.

Fosston Flashbacks: The History of Fosston and District. Fosston, SK: Fosston and District Reunion, 1980.

Hamm, H.H. *Sixty Years of Progress, Diamond Jubilee, 1884-1944: The Rural Municipality of Rhineland*. Altona, MB: D.W. Friesen and Sons, 1944.

Healing and Hope, 1872-1972: A History of the Health Sciences Centre. Winnipeg General Hospital. Winnipeg, MB: 2009.

History Book Committee. *Windthorst Memories: A History of Windthorst and District, Saskatchewan, Canada, 1806-1981*. Windthorst, SK: 1985.

History Committee of R.M. of the Gap 39. *Builders of a Great Land: History of the R.M. of the Gap No. 39, Ceylon and Hardy*. Altona, MB: Friesens, 1980.

Lightbody, Irene. *Times Past to Present*. Allan, SK: Allan and District History Book Committee, 1981.

Lightbody, Irene, ed., and Bateman Homemakers' Club, comp. *Journey to Yesteryear: Reminiscences of Bateman District Pioneers: 1907-1967*. Bateman, SK: 1967.

Maryfield and District Historical Society. *Across the Border and Valley: The Story of Maryfield and Fairlight and Surrounding Districts*. 2 vols. Maryfield, SK: Maryfield and District Historical Society, 1984.

Memories Forever: Elstow and District: 1900-1983. Altona, MB: Friesens, 1983.

Millham, James W., and Esterhazy Book Committee. *Esterhazy and Area: From Past to Present 95 Years of History, 1903-1998*. Esterhazy, SK: Esterhazy Book Committee, 1999.

Moorhouse, Myrtle G. *Buffalo Horn Valley, Recollections of Myrtle G. Moorhouse*. Regina, SK: Banting, 1973.

Morden, Manitoba Reunion Organization. *Reunion of Old Timers and Ex-Students, Morden, Manitoba, Thursday, Friday and Saturday, July 9-11, 1931: Souvenir Program.* Morden, MB: Maple Leaf School, 1931. Peel's Prairie Provinces 5570.

Morden Centennial Committee. *Morden: Mort Cheval, Pinancewaywinning, Lake Agassi.* Altona, MB: Friesens, 1981.

Radville Laurier Historical Society. *Radville-Laurier, the Yesteryears.* Radville, SK: 1983.

Somerset History Booklet Committee. *Reflections-Reflets: Somerset and Area.* Altona, MB: Friesens, 2000.

Souris and District Heritage Club. *The People of Souris and Glenwood: From Earliest Beginnings to the Present.* Brandon, MB: Leech Printing, 2006.

Souvenir Booklet Committee. *Morden Centennial Souvenir Booklet and Program, July 5-11.* Steinbach, MB: Derksen, 1982.

Thompson Rural Municipality History Committee. *The Hills of Home: A History of the Municipality of Thompson.* Miami, MB: The Committee, 1967.

Town of Plum Coulee. *Plum Coulee: A Century-Plus, 1901-2001.* Altona, MB: Friesens, 2001.

Waddell, James McKercher, and Shannon Waddell Friesen, eds. *Dominion City: Facts, Fiction and Hyperbole.* Dominion City, MB: D.W. Friesen and Sons, 1970.

Zado, Phyllis, ed., and Lake Johnston-Sutton Historical Society. *Furrows and Faith: A History of Lake Johnston and Sutton R.M.'s Expanse, Dunkirk, Bishopric, Mitchellton, Ardill, Mossbank, Vantage, Ettington, Mazenod, Palmer.* Altona, MB: Friesens, 1980.

Other Sources

Adilam, Tamara. "A Preliminary Sketch of Chinese Women and Work in British Columbia 1858-1950." In *Not Just Pin Money,* ed. Barbara K. Latham and Roberta J. Pazdro, 53-78. Victoria: Camosun College, 1984.

Agnew, Vijay. "Canadian Feminism and Women of Color." *Women's Studies International Forum* 16, 3 (1993): 217-27.

Airhart, Phyllis D. "Condensation and Heart Religion: Canadian Methodists as Evangelicals, 1884-1925." In *Aspects of the Canadian Evangelical Experience,* ed. G.A. Rawlyk, 90-105. Montreal and Kingston: McGill-Queen's University Press, 1997.

Anderson, Kay J. *Vancouver's Chinatown: Racial Discourses in Canada, 1875-1980.* Montreal and Kingston: McGill-Queen's University Press, 1991.

Andrews, Gail. "'The Picturesqueness of His Accent and Speech': Methodist Missionary Narratives and William Henry Pierce's Autobiography." In *Canadian Missionaries, Indigenous Peoples: Representing Religion at Home and Abroad,* ed. Alvyn Austin and Jamie S. Scott, 69-70. Toronto: University of Toronto Press, 2005.

Anthias, Floya. "Belongings in Globalising and Unequal World: Rethinking Translocations." In *The Situated Politics of Belonging,* ed. Nira Yuval-Davis, Kalpanna Kannabiran and Ulrike M. Vieten, Chapter 1. London: Sage, 2006.

Archer, John H. *Saskatchewan: A History.* Saskatoon: Fifth House, 1980.

Arendt, Hannah. *Imperialism: Part Two of the Origins of Totalitarianism.* New York: Harvest, 1968.

Asad, Talal. "On Discipline and Humility in Medieval Christian Monasticism." In *Genealogies of Religion: Discipline and Reasons of Power in Christianity and Islam,* 27-54. Baltimore: Johns Hopkins University Press, 1993.

Asselin, Mark Laurent. "The Lu-School Reading of 'Guanju' as Preserved in an Eastern Han Fu." *Journal of the American Oriental Society* 117, 3 (1997): 427-43.

Austin, Alvyn J. *Saving China: Canadian Missionaries in the Middle Kingdom, 1888-1959.* Toronto: University of Toronto Press, 1986.

Backhouse, Constance. *Colour-Coded: A Legal History of Racism in Canada, 1900-1950.* Toronto: University of Toronto Press, 1999.

–. "White Female Help and Chinese Canadian Employers: Race, Class, Gender and Law in the Case of Yee Clun, 1924." *Canadian Ethnic Studies* 26 (1994): 34-52.

Bakhtin, Mikhail. *Rabelais and His World.* Bloomington: Indiana University Press, 1984.

Bannerji, Himani. *The Dark Side of Nation: Essays on Multiculturalism and Gender.* Toronto: Canadian Scholars' Press, 2000.

Baptandier, Brigitte. *The Lady of Linshui: A Chinese Female Cult.* Stanford, CA: Stanford University Press, 2008.

Barman, Jean. "Beyond Chinatown: Chinese Men and Indigenous Women in Early British Columbia." *BC Studies* 177 (2013): 39-64.

Bashi, Vilna. *Survival of the Knitted: Immigrant Social Networks in a Stratified World.* Stanford, CA: Stanford University Press, 2007.

Beaman, Lori G., ed. *Religion and Canadian Society: Traditions, Transitions and Innovations.* Toronto: Canadian Scholars' Press, 2006.

Behar, Ruth, and Deborah A. Gordon, eds. *Women Writing Culture.* Berkeley: University of California Press, 1995.

Belenky, Mary Field, Blythe McVicker Clinchy, Nancy Rule Goldberger, and Jill Mattuck Tarule, eds. *Women's Ways of Knowing: The Development of Self, Voice, and Mind.* New York: Basic Books, 1997.

Belisle, Donica. *Retail Nation.* Vancouver: UBC Press, 2011.

Bell, Daniel A. *China's New Confucianism: Politics and Everyday Life in a Changing Society.* Princeton, NJ: Princeton University Press, 2008.

Benzecry, Claudio E. *The Opera Fanatic: Ethnography of an Obsession.* Chicago: University of Chicago Press, 2011.

Biographies of Virtuous Women and Supplementary Notes (Lienü zhuan buzhu 列女傳補註). Ed. Liang Duan. SBBY edition. Shanghai: Zhonghua shuju, 1933.

Birdwhistell, Joanne D. *Mencius and Masculinities: Dynamics of Power, Morality, and Maternal Thinking.* Albany: State University of New York Press, 2007.

Bourdieu, P. "How Can One Be a Sports Fan?" In *The Cultural Studies Reader,* ed. Simon During, 339-58. London: Routledge, 1993.

–. *Outline of a Theory of Practice.* Trans. R. Nice. Vol. 16. Cambridge: Cambridge University Press, 1972.

Bourdieu, Pierre, and Loïc J.D. Wacquant. *An Invitation to Reflexive Sociology.* Chicago: University of Chicago Press, 1992.

Boyarin, Daniel. *Unheroic Conduct: The Rise of Heterosexuality and Jewish Masculinity.* Berkeley: University of California Press, 1997.

Boyd, M. "Family and Personal Networks. In International Migration: Recent Developments and New Agendas." *International Migration Review* 23 (1989): 638-70.

Brewer, Carolyn, and Anne-Marie Medcalf, eds. *Researching the Fragments: Histories of Women in the Asian Context.* Quezon City, Philippines: New Day, 2000.

Briggs, Laura. "Mother, Child, Race, Nation: The Visual Iconography of Rescue and the Politics of Transnational and Transracial Adoption." *Gender and History* 15, 2 (2003): 179-200.

Brouwer, Ruth Compton. *New Women for God: Canadian Presbyterian Women and India Missions, 1876-1914.* Toronto: University of Toronto Press, 1990.

Brownell, Susan. *Training the Body for China: Sports in the Moral Order of the People's Republic.* Chicago: University of Chicago Press, 1995.

Brownell, Susan, and Jeffrey Wasserstrom. *Chinese Femininities/Chinese Masculinities: A Reader.* Berkeley: University of California Press, 2001.

Buckley, Thomas, and Alma Gottlieb, eds. *Blood Magic: The Anthropology of Menstruation.* Berkeley: University of California Press, 1988.

Bullock, Mary Brown. "American Science and Chinese Nationalism: Reflections on the Career of Zhou Peiyun." In *Remapping China: Fissures in Historical Terrain,* ed. Gail Hershatter, 210-23. Stanford, CA: Stanford University Press, 1996.

Burstyn, Varda. *The Rites of Men: Manhood, Politics, and the Culture of Sport.* Toronto: University of Toronto Press, 1999.

Bush, Peter. "The Rev. R.P. (Robert Peter) MacKay: Pietist as Denominational Executive." Paper presented to the Canadian Society of Presbyterian History, 2010.

Butcher, Dennis L., Catherine Macdonald, Margaret E. McPherson, Raymond R. Smith, and A. McKibbin Watts, eds. *Prairie Spirit: Perspectives on the Heritage of the United Church of Canada in the West.* Winnipeg: University of Manitoba Press, 1985.

Canada. *Report of the Royal Commission on Chinese Immigration.* Ottawa: The Commission, 1885.

Cassel, Susie Lan. "Footbinding and First-World Feminism in Chinese American Literature." *Journal of Asian American Studies* 10, 1 (February 2007): 31-58.

Chan, Anthony. *Gold Mountain: The Chinese in the New World.* Vancouver: New Star, 1982.

Chan, Jachison. *Chinese American Masculinities: From Fu Manchu to Bruce Lee.* New York: Routledge, 2001.

Chan, Kwok Bun. *Smoke and Fire: The Chinese in Montreal.* With a Foreword by Wang Gungwu. Hong Kong: Chinese University Press, 1991.

Chan, Sucheng. "The Exclusion of Chinese Women, 1870-1943." In *Entry Denied: Exclusion and the Chinese Community in America, 1882-1943,* Chapter 4. Philadelphia: Temple University Press, 1991.

Chandler, Joan. *Television and National Sport.* Chicago: University of Illinois Press, 1988.

Chang, Kornel. "Enforcing Transnational White Solidarity: Asian Migration and the Formation of the US-Canadian Boundary." *American Quarterly* 60, 3 (September 2008): 671-96.

Chau, Adam. "Efficacy, Not Confessionality: On Ritual Polytropy in China." In *Sharing the Sacra: The Politics and Pragmatics of Inter-communal Relations around Holy Places,* ed. Glenn Bowman, Chapter 5. Oxford: Berghahn, 2012.

–. "Household Sovereignty and Religious Subjectification: China and the Christian West Compared." In *Religion and Household Studies in Church History,* No. 50, ed. John Doran, Charlotte Methuen, and Alexandra Walsham, Chapter 33. Suffolk: Boydell and Brewer, 2014.

–. "Modalities of Doing Religion (Zuo Zongjiao de Moshi)." *Journal of Wenzhou University (Wenzhou Daxue Xuebao) Social Sciences (Shehui Xue)* 22, 5 (2009): 18-27.

–. *Religion in Contemporary China: Revitalization and Innovation.* London: Routledge, 2010.

Chinese Canadian Women, 1923-1967. "Esther Lew." http://www.mhso.ca/.

Cho, Sumi, Kimberlé Williams Crenshaw, and Leslie McCall. "Toward a Field of Intersectionality Studies: Theory, Applications and Praxis." *Signs* 38, 4 (2013): 785-810.

Choy, Wayson. *Paper Shadows: A Chinatown Childhood.* Toronto: Penguin, 1999.

Christophers, Brett. *Positioning the Missionaries: John Booth Good and the Confluence of Cultures in Nineteenth-Century British Columbia.* Vancouver: UBC Press, 1998.

Chu, Cordia Ming-Yeuk. "Menstrual Beliefs of Chinese Women." *Journal of the Folklore Institute* 17, 1 (1980): 38-55.

Chu, Sandra Ka Hon. "Reparation as Narrative Resistance: Displacing Orientalism and Recoding Harm for Chinese Women of the Exclusion Era." *Canadian Journal of Women and the Law* 18, 2 (2006): 387-437.

Chun, Allen. "The Changing Times of a Village Temple Alliance System in the Northern New Territories of Hong Kong: An Analysis of a Tianhou Cult." In *Development and Change in Mazu Cult Worship (Mazu Xinyang de fazhan yu bianqian* 媽祖信仰的發展與變遷),

ed. Lin Meirong 林美容主編, 57-78. Taipei: Taiwan Association for Religious Studies, 2003.

–. "From Culture to Power and Back: The Many 'Faces' of *Mianzi* (Face), *Guanxi* (Connection), and *Renqing* (Rapport)." *Suomen Anthropologi* 274 (2002): 19-37.

Chun, Allen, John Clammer, Patricia Ebrey, David Faure, Stephan Feuchtwang, Ying-Kuei Huang, P. Steven Sangren, and Mayfair Yang. "The Lineage-Village Complex in Southeastern China: A Long Footnote in the Anthropology of Kinship [and Comments and Reply]." *Current Anthropology* 37, 3 (June 1996): 429-50.

Clifford, James. *The Predicament of Culture: Twentieth-Century Ethnography, Literature, and Art.* Cambridge, MA: Harvard University Press, 1988.

Clifford, James, and George E. Marcus. *Writing Culture: The Poetics and Politics of Ethnography.* Berkeley: University of California Press, 1986.

Collier, John Jr. *Visual Anthropology: Photography as a Research Method.* New York: Holt, Rinehart and Winston, 1967.

Con, Harry, Ronald J. Con, Graham Johnson, Edgar Wickberg, and William E. Willmott. *From China to Canada: A History of the Chinese Communities in Canada.* Toronto: McClelland and Stewart in association with the Multiculturalism Directorate, Department of the Secretary of State and the Canadian Government Publishing Centre, Supply and Services Canada, 1982.

Connell, R.W. *Masculinities.* 2nd ed. Berkeley: University of California Press, 2005.

Crotty, Martin. "The Making of the Man: Australian Public Schoolboy Sporting Violence 1850-1914." *International Journal of the History of Sport* 20, 3 (September 2003): 1-16.

Cruikshank, Julie. *The Social Life of Stories: Narrative and Knowledge in the Yukon Territory.* Vancouver: UBC Press, 1998.

Csikszentmihalyi, Mihaly, and Eugene Rochberg-Halton. *The Meaning of Things: Domestic Symbols and the Self.* Cambridge: Cambridge University Press, 1981.

de Certeau, Michel. *The Practice of Everyday Life.* Trans. Steven Rendall. Berkeley: University of California Press, 1984.

de Troyer, Kristin. *Wholly Woman, Holy Blood: A Feminist Critique of Purity and Impurity, Studies in Antiquity and Christianity.* Harrisburg, PA: Trinity Press International, 2003.

Dean, Kenneth, with Zheng Zhenman. *Epigraphical Materials on the History of Religion in Fujian: Nanan, Hui'an, Yongchun, Dehua, and Anxi Counties.* Fuzhou/Fujian: Fujian Renmin Chubanshe, 2003.

Delgado, Grace. *Making the Chinese Mexican: Global Migration, Localism, and Exclusion in the US-Mexico Borderlands.* Stanford, CA: Stanford University Press, 2011.

Despeux, Catherine, and Livia Kohn, eds. *Women in Daoism.* Cambridge, MA: Three Pines Press, 2003.

Dhamoon, Rita. *Identity/Difference Politics: How Difference Is Produced and Why It Matters.* Vancouver: UBC Press, 2009.

Dirlik, Arif. "Asians on the Rim: Transnational Capital and Local Community in the Making of Contemporary Asian America." In *Across the Pacific: Asian Americans and Globalization,* ed. E. Hu-DeHart, Chapter 2. Philadelphia: Temple University Press, 1999.

–. "Confucius in the Borderlands: Global Capitalism and the Reinvention of Confucianism." *boundary* 2, 22-23 (1995): 229-73.

Douglas, Mary. *Purity and Danger: An Analysis of Concepts of Pollution and Taboo.* London: Routledge, 2002.

Duane, Patrick A. "Geographies of Sexual Commerce and the Production of Prostitutional Space: Victoria, British Columbia, 1860-1914." *Journal of the Canadian Historical Association* 19, 1 (2008): 115-42.

Duara, Prasenjit. "Knowledge and Power in the Discourse of Modernity: The Campaigns against Popular Religion in Early Twentieth Century China." *Journal of Asian Studies* 50, 1 (February 1991): 67-83.

Dubinsky, Karen. *Babies without Borders: Adoption and Migration across the Americas.* Toronto: University of Toronto Press, 2010.

Dunaway, David D., and Willa K. Baum. *Oral History: An Interdisciplinary Anthology.* Walnut Creek, CA: Altamira Press, 1996.

Dunning, Eric. "Industrialization and the Incipient Modernization of Football." *Stadion* 1, 1 (1975): 103-39.

–. "Sport as a Male Preserve: Notes on the Social Sources of Masculine Identity and Its Transformations." *Theory, Culture and Society* 3, 1 (1986): 79-90.

–. *Sport Matters: Sociological Studies of Sport, Violence, and Civilization.* London: Routledge, 1999.

Ebrey, Patricia Buckley. *Confucianism and Family Rituals in Imperial China: A Social History of Writing about Rites.* Princeton, NJ: Princeton University Press, 1991.

Ebrey, Patricia Buckley, and James L. Watson, eds. *Kinship Organisation in Late Imperial China, 1000-1940.* Berkeley: University of California Press, 1986.

Edwards, Louise. "Chinese Women's Campaigns for Suffrage: Nationalism, Confucianism and Political Agency." In *Women's Suffrage in Asia: Gender, Nationalism and Democracy,* ed. Louise Edwards and Mina Roces, Chapter 3. London: Routledge, 2004.

Eidheim, Harald. "When Ethnic Identity Is a Social Stigma." In *Ethnic Groups and Boundaries,* ed. Frederick Barth, 39-57. Boston: Little Brown, 1969.

Elias, Norbert. *The Civilizing Process, Sociogenetic and Psychogenetic Investigations.* Trans. Edmund Jephcott. Rev. ed. Malden, MA: Blackwell, 2000.

Emory, George. *The Methodist Church on the Prairies, 1896-1914.* Montreal and Kingston: McGill-Queen's University Press, 2001.

Eng, David L. *Racial Castration: Managing Masculinity in Asian America.* Durham, NC: Duke University Press, 2001.

Engelke, Matthew. "Angels in Swindon: Public Religion and Ambient Faith in England." *American Ethnologist* 39, 1 (February 2012): 155-70.

Evans, Harriett. "The Gender of Communication: Changing Expectations of Mothers and Daughters in Urban China." *China Quarterly* 204 (2010): 980-1000.

Faure, Bernard. *Buddhism, Purity and Gender.* Princeton, NJ: Princeton University Press, 2003.

–. *The Red Thread: Buddhist Approaches to Sexuality.* Princeton, NJ: Princeton University Press, 1998.

Fawcett, James T. "Networks, Linkages and Migration Systems." *International Migration Review* 23, 3 (1989): 671-80.

Feld, Steven, and Keith H. Basso, eds. *Senses of Place.* Santa Fe: School of American Research Press, 1997.

Feuchtwang, S. *Popular Religion in China: The Imperial Metaphor.* London: Routledge, 1991.

Fonow, Mary Margaret, and Judith A. Cook, eds. *Beyond Methodology: Feminist Scholarship as Lived Research.* Bloomington: Indiana University Press, 1991.

Foucault, Michel. "Technologies of the Self." In *Technologies of the Self: A Seminar with Michel Foucault,* ed. L.H. Martin et al., 16-49. London: Tavistock, 1988.

Friesen, Gerald. *The Canadian Prairies: A History.* Toronto: University of Toronto Press, 1987.

Gandhi, Leela. *Affective Communities: Anti-Colonial Thought, Fin-de-siècle Radicalism and the Politics of Friendship.* Durham, NC: Duke University Press, 2006.

Garrett, Shirley. *Social Reformers in Urban China: The Chinese YMCA, 1895-1926.* Cambridge, MA: Harvard University Press, 1970.

Gates, Hill. "The Commoditization of Chinese Women." *Signs* 14, 4, Special Issue: Common Grounds and Crossroads: Race, Ethnicity, and Class in Women's Lives (Summer 1989): 799-832.

—. "Money for the Gods." *Modern China* 13, 3, Symposium on Hegemony and Chinese Folk Ideologies, Part 2 (July 1987): 259-77.

Gee-Hamilton, Linda. *A Full Bowl of Rice: Memories of Morly and Sam Gee.* San Francisco: Blurb, 2012.

Ginsburg, Fay, and Anna Lowenhaupt Tsing, eds. *Uncertain Terms: Negotiating Gender in American Culture.* Boston: Beacon, 1990.

Gluck, Sherna Berger, and Daphne Patai. *Women's Words: The Feminist Practice of Oral History.* New York: Routledge, 1991.

Goffman, Erving. *The Presentation of Self in Everyday Life.* New York: Doubleday, 1959.

Grant, Beata. "Women, Gender and Religion in Premodern China: A Brief Introduction." *Nan-nu-Men, Women and Gender in Early and Imperial China* 10 (2008): 2-21.

Greenhill, Pauline. *Make the Night Hideous: Four English-Canadian Charivaris, 1881-1940.* Toronto: University of Toronto Press, 2010.

Gregg, Melissa, and Gregory J. Seigworth, eds. *The Affect Theory Reader.* Durham, NC: Duke University Press, 2010.

Gregor, James, and Maria Hsia Chang. "Wang Yang-ming and the Ideology of Sun Yat-sen." *Review of Politics* 42, 3 (July 1980): 388-404.

Gruneau, Richard, and David Whitson. *Hockey Night in Canada: Sport, Identities and Cultural Politics.* Culture and Communication Series. Toronto: Garamond Press, 1993.

Hall, Stuart. *Encoding and Decoding in the Television Discourse.* Vol. 7 of Media Series. Birmingham, UK: Centre for Cultural Studies, University of Birmingham, 1973.

—. "Encoding and Decoding the TV Message." In *Culture, Media, Language,* ed. S. Hall et al., 128-38. London: Hutchinson, 1980.

—. "Notes on Deconstructing the Popular." In *People's History and Socialist Theory,* ed. Ralph Samuel, 227-39. Boston: Routledge and Kegan Paul, 1981.

Haraway, Donna. "Race: Universal Donors in a Vampire Culture. It's All in the Family: Biological Kinship Categories in the Twentieth Century United States." In *The Haraway Reader,* 251-56. New York: Routledge, 2006.

Harris, R.C. "Regionalism and the Canadian Archipelago." In *Heartland and Hinterland: A Geography of Canada,* ed. L.D. McCann, 533-59. Scarborough: Prentice-Hall, 1984.

Hirata, Lucie. "Free, Indentured, Enslaved: Chinese Prostitutes in Nineteenth-Century America." *Signs* 5, 1 (1979): 3-29.

Ho, Clara Wing-chung. "Male Expression of Emotions: Observations from Collections of Birthday Greetings and Bereavement Messages for Women in Late Imperial and Republican China." Paper presented at Association of Asian Studies annual meeting, San Diego, March 22, 2013.

Ho, Wan-Li. "Daoist Nuns in Taiwan: A Case Study of the Gaoxiong Daode yuan." *Journal of Daoist Studies* 2 (2009): 137-64.

Hoe Ban Seng. "Adaptive Change and Overseas Chinese Settlements, with Special Reference to a Chinese Community in the Canadian Prairies." Master's thesis, Department of Sociology, University of Alberta, 1971.

—. *Enduring Hardship: The Chinese Laundry in Canada.* Gatineau, PQ: Canadian Museum of Civilization, 2003.

Hofmeyer, Isabel. *The Portable Bunyan: A Transnational History of "The Pilgrim's Progress."* Princeton, NJ: Princeton University Press, 2004.

Hou Ching-lang. *Monnaies d'offrande et la notion de trésorerie dans la religion chinoise, Mémoires de l'Institut des hautes études chinoises.* 1. Paris: Collège de France, 1975.

Howell, Colin D. *Blood, Sweat, and Cheers: Sport and the Making of Modern Canada*. Toronto: University of Toronto Press, 2001.

Howell, David, and Peter Lindsay. "Social Gospel and the Young Boy Problem, 1895-1925." *Canadian Journal of History of Sport* 17, 1 (1986): 75-87.

Hsieh, Tehyi. *Confucius Said It First*. N.p.: Chinese Service Bureau, 1936.

Hsu, Immanuel. *The Rise of Modern China*. 6th ed. New York: Oxford University Press, 2000.

Hsu, Madeline Y. *Dreaming of Gold, Dreaming of Home: Transnationalism and Migration between the United States and South China, 1882-1943*. Stanford, CA: Stanford University Press, 2000.

Huang, Evelyn, with Lawrence Jeffery. *Chinese Canadians: Voices from a Community*. Toronto: Douglas and McIntyre, 1992.

Huang Rongxi. Xinning Xianzhi 新寧縣志 *Gazetteer of Xinning [Toisan/Sunning/Taishan] Province*, Guangdong.26 卷 何福海 光緒 17, 1893.

Hübinette, Tobias. "From Orphan Trains to Babylifts: Colonial Trafficking, Empire Building, and Social Engineering." In *Outsiders Within: Writing on Transracial Adoption*, ed. Jane Jeong Trenka, Julia Sudbury, Julia Chinyere Oparah, and Sun Yung Shin, 139-49. New York: South End Press, 2006.

Huehls, Mitchum. "Structures of Feeling: Or, How to Do Things or Not with Books." *Contemporary Literature* 51, 2 (2010): 419-28.

Huffman, Ivy, and Julia Kwong. *The Dream of Gold Mountain*. Winnipeg: Hyperion, 1991.

Isin, Engin. *Citizens without Frontiers*. London: Continuum, 2012.

Jaschok, Maria, and Suzanne Miers, eds. *Women and Chinese Patriarchy: Submission, Servitude and Escape*. Hong Kong: Hong Kong University Press, 1994.

Johnson, Allan G. *The Gender Knot: Unraveling Our Patriarchal Legacy*. Philadelphia: Temple University Press, 1997.

Judge, Joan. "Talent, Virtue, and the Nation: Chinese Nationalisms and Female Subjectivities in the Early Twentieth Century." *American Historical Review* 106, 2 (June 2001): 765-803.

Kaiping Gazetteer (*Kaiping Xianzhi* 開平縣志). Beijing: Zhonghua shuju, 2007.

Keddie, Philip. "Changes in Rural Manitoba's 'Ethnic Mosaic,' 1921 to 1961." *Manitoba Historical Society Transactions* 3, 31 (1974-75). http://www.mhs.mb.ca/.

Keevak, Michael. *Becoming Yellow: A Short History of Racial Thinking*. Princeton, NJ: Princeton University Press, 2011.

Kidd, Bruce. *The Struggle for Canadian Sport*. Toronto: University of Toronto Press, 1996.

Kingston, Maxine Hong. *The Woman Warrior: Memoirs of a Girlhood among Ghosts*. New York: Vintage, 1989.

Kuly, Lisa. "Religion, Commerce, and Commodity in Japan's Maternity Industry." PhD diss., Cornell University, 2009.

Kwok, Danny B. *Scientism in Chinese Thought, 1900-1950*. New Haven, CN: Yale University Press, 1965.

Kymlicka, Will. "Ethnocultural Diversity in a Liberal State: Making Sense of the Canadian Model(s)." In *Belonging? Diversity, Recognition and Shared Citizenship in Canada*, vol. 3, ed. Keith Banting et al., 39-86. Montreal: Institute of Research on Public Policy, 2007.

Lai, David Chuenyan. *A Brief Chronology of Chinese Canadian History: From Segregation to Integration*. Vancouver: Simon Fraser University, David See-Chai Lam Centre for International Communication, 2011.

–. *Chinatown: Towns within Cities in Canada*. Vancouver: UBC Press, 1988.

–. *Chinese Community Leadership: Case Study of Victoria in Canada*. Singapore: World Scientific, 2010.

–. *The Forbidden City within Victoria*. Victoria: Orca Book Publishers, 1991.

–. "Immigration Building, 1908-1977." Notes.

–. "Piglet's Hut: 'Prison' for Chinese New Immigrants in the Old Days." *Chinese Canadian Post,* August 5, 2006, 4.

–. "A 'Prison' for Chinese Immigrants." *Asianadian* 2, 4 (Spring 1980): 16-19.

–. "Rescuing the Artless Art of Early Chinese Immigrants." *Discovery* 28, 5 (January 2001): 4-5.

Lai, Him Mark, Genny Lim, and Judy Yung, eds. *Island: Poetry and History of Chinese Immigrants on Angel Island, 1910-1940.* Seattle: University of Washington Press, 1993.

Laycock, David. *Populism and Democratic Thought in the Canadian Prairies, 1910-1945.* Toronto: University of Toronto Press, 1990.

Lee, Erika. "Enforcing the Borders: Chinese Exclusion along the US Borders with Canada and Mexico 1882-1924." *Journal of American History* 89, 1 (2002): 54-86.

Lee, Jen-der. "Gender and Medicine in Tang China." *Asia Major* 16, 2 (2003): 1-32.

Lee, Josephine. *The Japan of Pure Invention: Gilbert and Sullivan's "The Mikado."* Minneapolis: University of Michigan Press, 2010.

Lee, Victor. "The Laws of Gold Mountain: A Sampling of Early Canadian Laws and Cases That Affected People of Asian Ancestry." *Manitoba Law Journal* 21 (1992): 301-24.

Lee Tong Soon. *Chinese Street Opera in Singapore.* Chicago: University of Illinois Press, 2009.

Letherby, Gayle. *Feminist Research in Theory and Practice.* Buckingham: Open University Press, 2003.

Li, Peter S. "Chinese Immigrants on the Canadian Prairie, 1910-1947." *Canadian Review of Sociology and Anthropology* 19, 4 (1982): 527-40.

–. "The Use of Oral History in Studying Elderly Chinese-Canadians." *Canadian Ethics Studies* 17, 1 (1985): 67-77.

Li, Siu Leung. *Cross-Dressing in Chinese Opera.* Hong Kong: Hong Kong University Press, 2006.

Li, Zeng. "Chinese Community." *The Encyclopedia of Saskatchewan.* Regina: Canadian Plains Research Center, 2005, 170.

Lim, Andrea Rae. "Kingston's Chinese: The Formation of an Enclave, 1891-1980." Master's thesis, Department of History, Queen's University, 2005.

Lo, Karl, and H.M. Lai, comp. *Chinese Newspapers Published in North America, 1854-1975.* Washington, DC: Center for Chinese Research Materials, Association of Research Libraries, 1977.

Loewen, Royden, and Gerald Friesen, eds. *Immigrants in Prairie Cities: Ethnic Diversity in Twentieth-Century Canada.* Toronto: University of Toronto Press, 2009.

Louie, Kam. "Defining Modern Chinese Culture." In *The Cambridge Companion to Modern Chinese Culture,* ed. Kam Louie, 1-19. Cambridge: Cambridge University Press, 2008.

–. *Theorising Chinese Masculinity: Society and Gender in China.* Cambridge: Cambridge University Press, 2002.

Louie, Kam, and Louise Edwards. "Chinese Masculinity: Theorising Wen and Wu." *East Asian History* 8 (1994): 135-48.

Lowe, Benjamin, and Mark H. Payne. "To Be a Red-Blooded American Boy: Sports, A Social Scoreboard." *Journal of Popular Culture* 8, 2 (1974): 383-91.

Lowe, Lisa. "Heterogeneity, Hybridity, Multiplicity: Marking Asian American Differences." In *Theorizing Diaspora: A Reader,* ed. Jana Evans Braziel and Anita Mannur, 132-55. Malden, MA: Blackwell, 2003.

Lutz, Catherine A., and Lila Abu-Lughod, eds. *Language and the Politics of Emotion.* Cambridge: Cambridge University Press, 1990.

Lutz, John. "Riding the Horseless Carriage to the Computer Revolution: Teaching History in the Twenty-First Century." *Histoire Sociale/Social History* 34, 68 (November 2001): 427-35.

–. "Technology in Canada through the Lens of Labour History." *Scientia Canadensis: Canadian Journal of Science, Technology and Medicine* 15, 1 (1991): 5-19.

MacAloon, J.J. "Olympic Games and the Theory of the Spectacle in Modern Societies." In *Rite, Drama, Festival, Spectacle: Rehearsals toward a Theory of Cultural Performance*, ed. J. MacAloon, 241-80. Philadelphia: Institute for the Study of Human Issues, 1984.

MacIntyre, D.E. *Prairie Storekeeper.* Toronto: Peter Martin, 1970.

Mack, Barry. "From Preaching to Propaganda to Marginalization." In *Aspects of the Canadian Evangelical Experience*, ed. G.A. Rawlyk, 137-53. Montreal and Kingston: McGill-Queen's University Press, 1997.

MacKay, Ian. *The Quest of the Folk: Antimodernism and Cultural Selection in Twentieth-Century Nova Scotia.* Montreal and Kingston: McGill-Queen's University Press, 1994.

Mann, Susan, ed. "Gender and Manhood in Chinese History." Forum of Five Contributions. *American Historical Review* 105, 5 (2000): 1559-1667.

Mann, Susan, and Cheng Yu-Yin, eds. *Under Confucian Eyes: Writings on Gender in Chinese History.* Berkeley: University of California Press, 2001.

Mar, Lisa Rose. *Brokering Belonging: Chinese in Canada's Exclusion Era, 1885-1945.* New York: Oxford University Press, 2010.

Marks, Lynne. "A Godless Province? Religion and Irreligion in British Columbia, 1880-1914." Chapter 4. Book manuscript.

Marshall, Alison R. "Chinese Immigration to Western Manitoba since 1884: Wah Hep, George Chong, the KMT and Protestant Christianity." *Journal of Canadian Studies* 42, 3 (Fall 2008): 28-54.

–. "Confucianism/Daoism." In *World Religions: Canadian Perspectives – Eastern Traditions*, ed. Doris Jakobsh, Chapter 6. Toronto: Nelson Canada, 2012.

–. "A Conversation with Winnipeg's Chinese Canadian Duet: The Honourable Philip Lee and Joseph Du." *Manitoba History* 62 (2009): 35-40.

–. "Early Chinese Settlers in Western Manitoba." Pictorial essay of archival documents and photographs of early settlers to western Manitoba since 1884. *Manitoba History* 62 (2009): 2-8.

–. "Everyday Religion and Identity in a Western Manitoban Chinese Community: Christianity, the KMT, Foodways and Related Events." *Journal of the American Academy of Religion* 77, 3 (2009): 573-608.

–. "Four Pillars of Winnipeg Chinatown: Philip Lee, Joseph Du, Hung Yuen Lee and Charlie Foo." In *Winnipeg Chinatown: Celebrating 100 Years, a Remarkable Achievement*, ed. Patrick Choy, 37-42. Winnipeg: Winnipeg Chinese Cultural and Community Centre, 2011.

–. "The History of Winnipeg Chinese Community Organizations." In *Winnipeg Chinatown: Celebrating 100 Years, a Remarkable Achievement*, ed. Patrick Choy, 29-32. Winnipeg: Winnipeg Chinese Cultural and Community Centre, 2011.

–. "Homosociality, Ambiguity and Efficacy in the Everyday Practices of Early Chinese Manitoban Settlers." In *Everyday Religion*, ed. Liza Debevec and Samuli Schielke, Chapter 3. EASA Series. Oxford: Berghahn Books, 2012.

–. "Interview with Inky Mark." In *Winnipeg Chinatown: Celebrating 100 Years, a Remarkable Achievement*, ed. Patrick Choy, 56-65. Winnipeg: Winnipeg Chinese Cultural and Community Centre, 2011.

–. "Interview with William Yee." In *Winnipeg Chinatown: Celebrating 100 Years, a Remarkable Achievement*, ed. Patrick Choy, 46-55. Winnipeg: Winnipeg Chinese Cultural and Community Centre, 2011.

–. "Manitoba Chinese Immigration Registers and Head Tax Payments and Destinations." In *Winnipeg Chinatown: Celebrating 100 Years, a Remarkable Achievement*, ed. Patrick Choy, 156-58. Winnipeg: Winnipeg Chinese Cultural and Community Centre, 2011.

–. "Railways, Racism and Chineseness." In *Place and Replace,* ed. Leah Morton, Esyllt Jones, and Adele Perry, Chapter 6. Winnipeg: University of Manitoba Press, 2013.

–. "Through the Lens of the Grave Custom: The Public and Private Face of the Western Manitoban Restaurant." *Western Folklore* 70, 1 (2011): 99-126.

–. *The Way of the Bachelor: Early Chinese Settlement in Manitoba.* Vancouver: UBC Press, 2012.

–. "Winnipeg's Chinatown: A Century in the Making." *Manitoba History* 62 (2009): 37-39.

–. "Xie Lingyun's Reflections on the 'Appreciative Heart.'" *Journal of Indian Philosophy and Religion* 7 (2002): 131-45.

Massumi, Brian. *Movement, Affect, Sensation: Parables for the Virtual.* Durham, NC: Duke University Press, 2002.

Mauss, Marcel. "Les techniques du corps," *Journal de Psychologie* 32, 3-4 (1934). Repr. in Mauss, *Sociologie et anthropologie,* Paris: PUF, 1936.

McCardle, Bennett. "The Records of Chinese Immigration at the National Archives of Canada." *Canadian Ethnic Studies* 19, 3 (1987): 163-71.

McDevitt, Patrick F. *May the Best Man Win: Sport, Masculinity, and Nationalism in Great Britain and the Empire, 1880-1935.* Basingstoke: Palgrave Macmillan, 2004.

McGuire, Meredith B. *Lived Religion: Faith and Practice in Everyday Life.* New York: Oxford University Press, 2008.

McIntire, C.T. "Unity among Many: The Formation of the United Church of Canada, 1899-1930." In *A History of the United Church of Canada,* ed. Don Schweitzer, Chapter 1. Waterloo, ON: Wilfrid Laurier University Press, 2012.

McKeown, Adam. "Conceptualizing Chinese Diasporas, 1842 to 1949." *Journal of Asian Studies* 58, 2 (May 1999): 306-37.

McManus, Sheila. *The Line Which Separates: Race, Gender, and the Making of the Alberta-Montana Borderlands.* Edmonton: University of Alberta Press, 2005.

Messer-Kruse, Timothy. "Memories of the Ku Klux Klan Honorary Society at the University of Wisconsin." *Journal of Blacks in Higher Education* 23 (Spring 1999): 83-93.

Miller, Stuart Creighton. *The Unwelcome Immigrant: The American Image of the Chinese, 1785-1882.* Berkeley: University of California Press, 1969.

Millien, C., E. Woo, and P. Yeh. *Winnipeg Chinese.* Ottawa: Department of the Secretary of State, 1971.

The Modern Girl around the World Research Group, Alys Eve Weinbaum, Lynn M. Thomas, Priti Ramamurthy, Uta G. Poiger, Madeleine Yue Dong, Tani E. Barlow, eds. *The Modern Girl around the World: Consumption, Modernity, and Globalization.* Durham, NC: Duke University Press, 2008.

Moore, Henrietta L. *A Passion for Difference.* Bloomington: Indiana University Press, 1994.

Moss, Mark. *Toward the Visualization of History: The Past as Image.* Lanham, MD: Lexington Books, 2008.

Mou, Sherry J. *Gentlemen's Prescriptions for Women's Lives: A Thousand Years of Biographies of Chinese Women.* Armonk, NY: M.E. Sharpe, 2004.

Moy, James S. *Marginal Sights: Staging the Chinese in America.* Iowa City: University of Iowa Press, 1993.

Nedostup, Rebecca. "Ritual Competition and the Modernizing Nation-State." In *Chinese Religiosities: Afflictions of Modernity and State Formation,* ed. Mayfair Mei-hui Yang, 87-112. Berkeley: University of California Press, 2008.

Nee, Victor G., and Brett de Bary Nee. *Longtime Californ': A Documentary Study of an American Chinatown.* Stanford, CA: Stanford University Press, 1986.

Ng, Greer Anne Wenh-In. "The United Church of Canada: A Church Fittingly National." In *Christianity and Ethnicity in Canada*, ed. Paul Bramadat and David Seljak, 204-46. Toronto: University of Toronto Press, 2008.

Ng, Wing Chung. "Chinatown Theatre as Transnational Business: New Evidence from Vancouver during the Exclusion Era." *BC Studies* 148 (2005-6): 25-54.

Nienhauser, William H. Jr., ed. and comp. *The Indiana Companion to Traditional Chinese Literature*. Bloomington: Indiana University Press, 1986.

Nipp, Dora, and Margaret Wong, dir. and prod. *Under the Willow Tree: Pioneer Chinese Women in Canada*. Montreal: National Film Board of Canada, 1997, 51 minutes.

Nurse, Andrew. "Regionalism, Citizenship, Identity." *Canadian Diversity* 2, 1 (2003): 43-44.

–. *Rethinking the Canadian Archipelago: Research Trajectories in Region, Identity, and Diversity in Canada*. 2003. http://canada.metropolis.net/.

Nyitray, Vivian-Lee. "Treacherous Terrain: Mapping Feminine Spirituality in Confucian Worlds." In *Confucian Spirituality*, ed. Wei-ming Tu and Mary Evelyn Tucker, 463-79. New York: Crossroad, 2004.

O'Reilly, Liam. "Missionaries and Women in Victoria's Chinatown: The Establishment and Evolution of the Chinese Rescue Home, 1886-1900." Master's research paper, Department of History, University of Victoria, 2011.

Osterhout, S.S. *Orientals in Canada: The Story of the Work of the United Church of Canada with Asiatics in Canada*. Toronto: United Church of Canada, 1929.

–. "Our Chinese Missions in British Columbia." *Missionary Bulletin* 13, 3 (July-September 1917): 499-500.

Owen, Stephen. *Readings in Literary Thought*. Cambridge, MA: Harvard University Asia Center, 1992.

Pan, Lynn. *The Encyclopedia of the Chinese Overseas*. With Preface and Introduction by Wang Gungwu. 2nd ed. Singapore: Nanyang Technological University Press, 2006.

Pappas, Nick T., Patrick C. McKenry, and Beth Skilken Catlett, eds. "Athlete Aggression on the Rink and off the Ice: Athlete Violence and Aggression in Hockey and Interpersonal Relationships." *Men and Masculinities* 6, 3 (January 2004): 291-312.

Pascoe, Peggy. *Relations of Rescue: The Search for Female Moral Authority in the American West, 1874-1939*. New York: Oxford University Press, 1990.

Pegler-Gordon, Anna. "Chinese Exclusion, Photography, and the Development of US Immigration Policy." *American Quarterly* 58, 1 (March 2006): 51-77.

Perry, Adele. "Hardy Backwoodsmen, Wholesome Women, and Steady Families: Immigration and the Construction of a White Society in British Columbia, 1849-1871." *Histoire Sociale/Social History* 33, 66 (2000): 343-60.

–. *On the Edge of Empire: Gender, Race and the Making of British Columbia, 1849-1871*. Toronto: University of Toronto Press, 2001.

Peterson, Glen. "House Divided: Transnational Families in the Early Years of the People's Republic of China." *Asian Studies Review* 31, 1 (2007): 25-40.

Pinterics, Natasha. "Riding the Feminist Waves: In With the Third?" *Canadian Woman Studies* 21, 4 (2001): 15-21.

Pon, Mona Margaret "Ng Mon Hing." *Dictionary of Canadian Biography Online. 1921-1930*. Vol. 15. Toronto: University of Toronto/Université Laval, 2000. http://www.biographi.ca/.

Price, Lily Hoy. *I Am Full Moon: Stories of a Ninth Daughter*. Victoria: Brindle and Glass, 2009.

Pronger, Brian. *The Arena of Masculinity: Sports, Homosexuality, and the Meaning of Sex*. New York: St. Martin's Press, 1990.

–. *Body Fascism: Salvation and the Technology of Physical Fitness.* Toronto: University of Toronto Press, 2002.

Putney, Clifford. *Muscular Christianity: Manhood and Sports in Protestant America, 1880-1920.* Cambridge, MA: Harvard University Press, 2001.

Quo, F. Quei. "Chinese Immigrants in the Prairies." Preliminary Report Submitted to the Minister of the Secretary of State. Simon Fraser University, BC, November 1977.

Raey, D. "Psychosocial Aspects of White Middle-Class Identities: Desiring and Defending against the Class and Ethnic 'Other' in Urban Multi-Ethnic Schooling." *Sociology* 42 (2008): 1072-88.

Ramirez, Bruno, with Yves Otis. *Crossing the 49th Parallel: Migration from Canada to the United States, 1900-1930.* Ithaca: Cornell University Press, 2001.

Raphals, Lisa. *Sharing the Light: Representations of Women and Virtue in Early China.* Albany: State University of New York Press, 1998.

Razack, Sherene. "Making Canada White: Law and the Policing of Bodies of Colour in the 1990s." *Canadian Journal of Law and Society* 14, 1 (1999): 159-84.

Reinharz, Shulamit. *Feminist Methods in Social Research.* New York: Oxford University Press, 1992.

Riddle, Ronald. *Flying Dragons, Flowing Streams: Music In the Life of San Francisco's Chinese.* Westport: Greenwood Press, 1983.

Ristock, Janice, and Joan Pennell. *Community Research as Empowerment: Feminist Links, Postmodern Interruptions.* Toronto: Oxford University Press, 1992.

Robin, Martin. *Shades of Right: Nativist and Fascist Politics in Canada, 1920-1940.* Toronto: University of Toronto Press, 1992.

Rowe, Allan. "'The Mysterious Oriental Mind': Ethnic Surveillance and the Chinese in Canada during the Great War." *Canadian Ethnic Studies* 36, 1 (2004): 48-70.

Roy, Patricia. "British Columbia's Fear of Asians." *Histoire Sociale/Social History* 13, 25 (1980): 161-72.

–. *The Oriental Question: Consolidating a White Man's Province.* Vancouver: UBC Press, 2003.

–. *A White Man's Province: British Columbia Politicians and Chinese and Japanese Immigrants, 1858-1914.* Vancouver: UBC Press, 1989.

Rutherdale, Myra. *Women and the White Man's God: Gender and Race in the Canadian Mission Field.* Vancouver: UBC Press, 2002.

Sangren, P. "Female Gender in Chinese Religious Symbols: Kuan Yin, Ma Tsu, and the 'Eternal Mother.'" *Signs* 9 (1983): 4-25.

Sanneh, Lamin. *Disciples of All Nations: Pillars of World Christianity.* Oxford Studies in World Christianity. London: Oxford University Press, 2007.

Saskatchewan Cemeteries Project. Laurier Cemetery, Radville. An ancestry.com Community. http://www.rootsweb.ancestry.com/.

Satlow, Michael. L. "'Try to Be a Man': The Rabbinic Construction of Masculinity." *Harvard Theological Review* 8, 1 (1996): 19-40.

Sawin, Patricia E. *Listening for a Life: Bessie Eldreth, a Dialogic Ethnography.* Logan: Utah State University Press, 2004.

Scheinberg, Ellen. "Evidence of 'Past Injustices': Records Relating to the Chinese Head Tax." *Archivist* 20, 2 (1994): 26-30.

Schneider, Dorothee. *Crossing Borders: Migration and Citizenship in the Twentieth-Century.* Cambridge, MA: Harvard University Press, 2011.

Seaman, Gary. "The Sexual Politics of Karmic Retribution." In *The Anthropology of Taiwanese Society,* ed. Emily M. Ahern and Hill Gates, 381-96. Stanford, CA: Stanford University Press, 1981.

Sebryk, Karrie M. "A History of Chinese Theatre in Victoria." Master's thesis, University of Victoria, 1995.

Shah, Nayan. *Contagious Divides: Epidemic and Race in San Francisco's Chinatown.* Berkeley: University of California Press, 2001.

–. *Intimate Strangers: Contesting Race, Sexuality and the Law in the North American West.* Berkeley: University of California Press, 2011.

Shain, Yossi, and Aharon Barth. "Diasporas and International Relations Theory." *International Organization* 57, 3 (Summer 2003): 449-79.

Sher, Julian. *White Hoods: The Ku Klux Klan in Canada.* Vancouver: New Star, 1983.

Shiga, Ichiko. "The Manifestation of Lüzu in Modern Guangdong and Hong Kong: The Rise and Growth of Spirit-Writing Cults." In *Daoist Identity: History, Lineage, and Ritual,* ed. Livia Kohn, and Harold David Roth, Chapter 9. Honolulu: University of Hawai'i Press, 2002.

Sieg, Katrin. "Ethnic Drag and National Identity: Multicultural Crises, Crossings, and Interventions." In *The Imperialist Imagination: German Colonialism and Its Legacy,* ed. Sara Friedrichsmeyer, Sara Lennox, and Susanne Zantop, 295-319. Ann Arbor: University of Michigan Press, 1998.

–. *Ethnic Drag: Performing Race, Nation, Sexuality in West Germany.* Ann Arbor: University of Michigan Press, 2002.

Siu, Paul C.P. *The Chinese Laundryman: A Study of Social Isolation.* Ed. John Kuo Wei Tchen. New York: New York University Press, 1987.

–. "The Sojourner." *American Journal of Sociology* 58 (July 1952): 34-44.

Smith, David E., ed. *Building a Province: A History of Saskatchewan in Documents.* Saskatoon: Fifth House, 1992.

Smith, Raymond R. "The Chinese United Church of Winnipeg." In *Prairie Spirit: Perspectives on the Heritage of United Church of Canada in the West,* ed. Dennis L. Butcher, 296-301. Winnipeg: University of Manitoba Press, 1985.

Spinoza, Baruch. "Ethics." In *Complete Works,* ed. Edwin Curley, part 3. Princeton, NJ: Princeton University Press, 1985.

Stanford University's Spatial History Project. "The Chinese Canadian Immigration Pipeline, 1912-1923." http://www.stanford.edu/.

Stanley, Timothy J. "'Chinamen, Wherever We Go': Chinese Nationalism and Guangdong Merchants in British Columbia, 1871-1911." *Canadian Historical Review* 77, 4 (1996): 475-503.

–. *Contesting White Supremacy: School Segregation, Anti-Racism, and the Making of Chinese Canadians.* Vancouver: UBC Press, 2011.

Stasiulis, Daiva. "Feminist Intersectional Theorizing." In *Race and Ethnic Relations in Canada,* ed. Peter Li, 347-97. 2nd ed. Toronto: Oxford University Press, 1999.

Stevens, Sarah E. "The New Woman and the Modern Girl in Republican China." *NWSA Journal* 15 (Autumn 2003): 82-103.

Stolcke, Verena. "Talking Culture: New Boundaries, New Rhetorics of Exclusion in Europe." *Current Anthropology* 36, 1, Special Issue: Ethnographic Authority and Cultural Explanation (February 1995): 1-24.

Strand, David. "Community, Society and History in Sun Yat-sen's Sanmin Zhuyi." In *Culture and State in Chinese History: Conventions, Accommodations, and Critiques,* ed. Theodore Huters, Roy Bin Wong, and Pauline Yu, 326-45. Stanford, CA: Stanford University Press, 1997.

Tam Wai Lun, ed. *Folk Buddhist Research (Minjian Fojiao Yanjiu* 民間佛教研究*).* Beijing: Zhonghua shuju, 2007.

Tan, Sor-Hoon. "Modernizing Confucianism and 'New Confucianism.'" In *The Cambridge Companion to Modern Chinese Culture,* ed. Kam Louie, 135-54. Cambridge: Cambridge University Press, 2008.

Taylor, Jeremy. *The Generalissimo: Chiang Kai-Shek and the Struggle for Modern China.* Cambridge, MA: Harvard University Press, 2009.

Teng, Jinhua Emma. "The Construction of the 'Traditional Chinese Woman' in the Western Academy: A Critical Review." *Signs* 22, 1 (1996): 115-51.

Ticineto Clough, Patricia. "Introduction." In *The Affective Turn: Theorizing the Social,* ed. Patricia Ticineto Clough and Jean Halley, 1-33. Durham, NC: Duke University Press, 2007.

Valverde, Mariana. *The Age of Light, Soap, and Water: Moral Reform in English Canada, 1885-1925.* Toronto: McClelland and Stewart, 1991.

van der Does, Patricia, Sonja Edelaar, Imke Gooskens, Margreet Lieftin, and Marijie van Mierlo. "Reading Images: A Study of a Dutch Neighborhood." *Visual Sociology* 7, 1 (1992): 4-68.

Van Dieren, Karen. "The Response of the WMS to the Immigration of Asian Women 1888-1942." In *Not Just Pin Money: Selected Essays on the History of Women's Work in British Columbia,* ed. Barbara Latham and Roberta J. Pazdro, 79-95. Victoria: Camosun College, 1984.

Van Maanen, John. *Tales of the Field: On Writing Ethnography.* Chicago: University of Chicago Press, 1988.

Vansina, Jan. *Oral Tradition as History.* Wisconsin: University of Wisconsin Press, 1985.

Vickers, Jill. "Methodologies for Scholarship About Women." In *Gender, Race, and Nation: A Global Perspective,* ed. Vanaja Dhruvarajan and Jill Vickers, 64-92. Toronto: University of Toronto Press, 2002.

Volpp, Leti. "Divesting Citizenship: On Asian American History and the Loss of Citizenship through Marriage." *UCLA Law Review* 53, 2 (2005): 405. http://scholarship.law.berkeley.edu/.

Wachs, Martin. "The Automobile and Gender: An Historical Perspective." In *Women's Travel Issues: Proceedings from the Second National Conference.* Washington, DC: US Department of Transportation, 1996.

Waiser, Bill. *Saskatchewan: A New History.* Saskatoon: Fifth House, 2005.

Walker, Barrington, ed. *The History of Immigration and Racism in Canada.* Toronto: Canadian Scholars' Press, 2008.

Waltner, Ann Beth. "The Adoption of Children in Ming and Early Ch'ing China." PhD diss., University of California, Berkeley, 1981.

Wang, Gungwu. "A Note on the Origins of Hua-Ch'iao." Seminar paper of the Far Eastern History Department, Australian National University, 1976.

Wang, Jiwu. *"His Dominion" and the "Yellow Peril": Protestant Missions to Chinese Immigrants in Canada, 1859-1967.* Waterloo, ON: Wilfrid Laurier University Press, 2006.

–. "Organised Protestant Missions to Chinese Immigrants in Canada, 1885-1923." *Journal of Ecclesiastical History* 54, 4 (October 2003): 691-713.

Wang, Robin, ed. *Images of Women in Chinese Thought and Culture: Writings from the Pre-Qin Period through the Song Dynasty.* Indianapolis: Hackett, 2006.

Ward, Peter. "Class and Race in the Social Structure of British Columbia, 1870-1939." *BC Studies* 45 (1980): 17-35.

–. "The Oriental Immigrant and Canada's Protestant Clergy, 1858-1925." *BC Studies* 22 (Summer 1974): 40-55.

–. *White Canada Forever: Popular Attitudes and Public Policy toward Orientals in British Columbia.* Montreal and Kingston: McGill-Queen's University Press, 1974.

Watson, James L. "Transactions in People: The Chinese Market in Slaves, Servants, and Heirs." In *Asian and African Systems of Slavery,* ed. James L. Watson, 223-50. Berkeley: University of California Press, 1980.

Wesley, Jared J. *Code Politics: Campaigns and Cultures on the Canadian Prairies.* Vancouver: UBC Press, 2011.

White, Richard. *Railroaded: The Transcontinentals and the Making of Modern America.* New York: W.W. Norton, 2011.

Whiteley, Marilyn F. "'Allee Samee Melican Lady': Imperialism and Negotiation at the Chinese Rescue Home (Women Missionary Societies Set Up the Chinese Rescue Home to Save Chinese Women from Prostitution)." *Resources for Feminist Research* 22, 3-4 (Fall 1992/Winter 1993): 45-50.

Wickberg, Edgar. "Chinese Associations in Canada 1923-1947." In *Visible Minorities and Multiculturalism: Asians in Canada,* ed. Victor Ujimoto and Gordon Hirabayashi, 23-31. Toronto: Butterworths, 1980.

—. "Overseas Chinese: The State of the Field." *Chinese America: History and Perspectives* (2002): 1-8.

—. "Vancouver Chinatown: The First Hundred Years." Paper presented at the workshop "The Vancouver Chinatown: Past, Present, and Future," Institute of Asian Research, UBC, April 21, 2001.

Williams, Raymond. *Marxism and Literature.* London: Oxford University Press, 1977.

Willmott, W.E. "Some Aspects of Chinese Communities in British Columbia Towns." *BC Studies* 1 (Winter 1968-69): 27-36.

Wimmer, Andreas. "Herder's Heritage and the Boundary-Making Approach: Studying Ethnicity in Immigrant Societies." *Sociological Theory* 27, 3 (2009): 244-70.

Winnipeg Chinese United Church: Celebrating 75 Years, 1917-1992. Winnipeg, 1992.

Wolf, Arthur P., and Chieh-Shan Huang. *Marriage and Adoption in China, 1845-1945.* Stanford, CA: Stanford University Press, 1980.

Wolf, Margery. *Women and the Family in Rural Taiwan.* Stanford, CA: Stanford University Press, 1972.

Wolf, Margery, Roxane Witke, and Emily Martin. *Women in Chinese Society.* Stanford, CA: Stanford University Press, 1975.

Women's Book Committee, Chinese Canadian National Council. *Jin Guo: Voices of Chinese Canadian Women.* Toronto: Canadian Scholars' Press, 1993.

Woon Yuen-Fong. *The Excluded Wife.* Montreal and Kingston: McGill-Queen's University Press, 1999.

Wright, Robert A. *A World Mission: Canadian Protestantism and the Quest for a New International Order, 1918-1939.* Montreal and Kingston: McGill-Queen's University Press, 1991.

Xu, Wenying. "Masculinity, Food, and Appetite in Frank Chin's *Donald Duk* and 'The Eat and Run Midnight People.'" *Cultural Critique* 66 (Spring 2007): 78-103.

Yang, Martin C. *A Chinese Village: Taitou, Shantung Province.* New York: Columbia University Press, 1945.

Yang, Mayfair Mei-hui. "The Gift Economy and State Power in China." *Comparative Studies in Society and History* 31, 1 (January 1989): 25-54.

—. *Gifts, Favors and Banquets: The Art of Social Relationships in China.* Ithaca, NY: Cornell University Press, 1994.

Yee, Paul. *Chinatown: An Illustrated History of the Chinese Communities of Victoria, Vancouver, Calgary, Winnipeg, Toronto, Ottawa, Montréal, and Halifax.* Toronto: James Lorimer, 2005.

—. *I Am Canada: Building the Railway, Lee Heen-gwong, British Columbia, 1882.* Toronto: Scholastic, 2010.

Yen, Hsiao-pei. "Body Politics, Modernity and National Salvation: The Modern Girl and the New Life Movement." *Asian Studies Review* 29, 2 (June 2005): 165-86.

Yen, Ling Shek. "Asian American Masculinity: A Review of the Literature." *Journal of Men's Studies* 14, 3 (2006): 379-91.

Yip, Ka-che. *Religion, Nationalism and Chinese Students: The Anti-Chinese Movement of 1922-1927*. Bellingham, WA: Center for East Asian Studies, Western Washington University, 1980.

Yu, Henry. *Thinking Orientals: Migration, Contact and Exoticism in Modern America*. New York: Oxford University Press, 2001.

Yu, Renqiu. *To Save China, to Save Ourselves: The Chinese Hand Laundry Alliance of New York*. Philadelphia: Temple University Press, 1992.

Yuan, Ryan, comp. "Commentary and Subcommentary to the *Book of Rites* (*Liji Zhushu* 禮記注疏)." In *Commentary and Subcommentary on the Thirteen Classics* (*Shisan jing zhushu* 十三經注疏). Beijing: Zhonghua shuju, 1957.

Yung, Judy. *Unbound Feet: A Social History of Chinese Women in San Francisco*. Berkeley: University of California Press, 1995.

Zhou, Zuyan. *Androgyny in Late Ming and Early Qing Literature*. Honolulu: University of Hawai'i Press, 2003.

Index

Note: "(f)" followed by a number indicates a figure

Chinese Patriotic League (CPL): Charlie Foo and, 104, 105-7; Frank Chan and, 73; and fundraising for China in Sino-Japanese War, 105-6; KMT as, 104
Chinese schools, 39, 156-57, 158(f), 227n4
Chinese United Church (*Jidujiao Xiehehui;* Winnipeg), 69-70, 133
Chinese United League (Tongmeng Hui), 11
Chinese War Relief Fund, 106
Chinese Women of Winnipeg Group, 223n8
Chinese Young Men's Christian Association: Frank Chan and, 69; gender in rosters of, 60; and sports, 84-85; YMCA vs., 201n72
Chow, Lil (née Wong), 133, 134
Chow Yucho, 58
Choy, Wayson, 228n12
Christian Fellowship Associations, 84
Christianity: and athletics, 83-84; bachelors and, 34; communism and, 34, 35-36; and Confucianism, 36, 45-46, 50-51, 123, 195n50; conversion to, 44, 45, 47, 50-51, 52-53, 65, 112; of European wives, 115-16; and head tax, 49; Lee Mon family and, 122; Ma Seung's conversion to, 44; and modernity, 35; nationalism and, 34, 53, 65, 118; nominal, 46, 53, 88, 90, 115, 118, 138, 164, 168; and racism, 22-23, 34; religious practices unrelated to, 146; sports and, 85; women and, 20, 115, 126, 130
Chu Cut-lay, 41
Chun, Allen, 172n3
churches: and adoptions, 222n44; and Chinese Sunday schools, 157; and gambling, 103; and immigrants, 112; as social networks for women, 126; Yee Clun/Eng Shee's children and, 152
citizenship: church affiliation and, 49; Happy Young and, 93; of Mark Ki, 89-90; naturalized, 210n45, 223n1; sports and, 88; US Exclusion Act and, 7
CKT. *See* Chinese Freemasons (Chee Kung Tong; CKT)
clubhouses: CDS, 193n36; Chinese United League, 11; drama, 71-72, 74; KMT, 77, 107, 157, 168; nationalist, 6, 151, 152, 167; visiting with friends at, 12
coin sword, 145-46, 168-69

coins, 144-45
Colman, C.A., 50, 60
communism: and Christianity, 35-36; and Confucianism, 39; Frank Chan and, 73; and labourers, 224n10; in Manitoba, 94; nationalism and, 53-54, 105, 108-9, 114; in power in China, 108-9; and redirection of familial affections to state, 219n29. *See also* Chinese Communist Party (CCP)
concubines, 112, 142, 217-18n13
Confucianism: and 2008 Beijing Olympics, 39; about, 188n127; bachelors and, 123; and children, 39; Christianity and, 36, 45-46, 50-51, 123, 195n50; communism and, 39; diaspora, 190n8; and education, 36-38; Ma Seung and, 42, 47-48; nationalism and, 36, 38-39, 115, 118; Neo-, 195n51; practice on Prairies, 36; in Saskatchewan in 1901, 31; self-identification as, 36; study of classical texts, 37; WCCCC and, 40; and women, 223n6
Confucius: birthday of, 36; and CBA offering halls, 175n20. *See also Analects Confucius 2010,* 39
cross-border travel: nationalism and, 33
Cumberland (BC), 11, 44-46, 55-57, 60
curling, 85, 86, 91, 96

Daoism, 45-46, 47, 138, 139, 144
Davidson (SK): Charles Yee in, 95-97; Chinese–non-Chinese relationship in, 95; masquerades in, 21-22; Owl Cafe, 95-96; Union Hotel and Cafe, 95, 96-97
de facto Chinese nationalist state: and membership registers, 30; networks and, 28
Depression: Charles Yee and Moon Cafe and, 98; and donations, 35; and fundraising, 77; and nationalist membership, 54; and return to China, 130, 131, 153
Dhamoon, Rita, 14
discrimination: in Manitoba, 14-15; in religion, 15; in Saskatchewan, 14-15; winning at sports as, 81; and Yee sisters, 156
domestic arts: Eng Shee and, 129-30; Esther Lew and, 135-36; Jung Farn and, 132; Ma Hong Lin and classes in, 126; Mary Wong and, 134; women and, 25-26

merchant exemptions from, 5, 114, 122, 128, 225n23; payment in Vancouver, 111; photographs attached to certificates, 122
Home Restaurant (Morden), 124
Hong Kong: Mas' retirement in, 66-67; Yeung Shiu-Chuen and women of, 66
Hood, James and Mrs., 60
hotels: Charlie and Bill Dong and, 89; fires, 97; Maryfield, 131
Howard, Mr. (How Min Yet; Hou Minyi), 119
Hsu, Madeline Y., 221n12
Huang Xing, 38

immigrants: arrival of, 111, 141; Canadian destinations, 8(f); Chinese origins of, 175n19; churches and, 112; illegal, 9; infectious diseases and, 9-10; as labourers, 167; US Exclusion Act and, 7
immigration: and borderlands, 7, 9; chain, 121; racism in, 30; from US, 7, 9; by young males alone, 28
Immigration Hall, 111
infectious diseases, 10
Inspiring Chinese Experiences (Zhen Huayue), 69
Isin, Engin, 89

Ken Richa cafe (Kenora), 69
Kenora (ON), Ken Richa cafe, 69
Kep (Lee Choy family friend), 163, 165
Kidd, Bruce, 87
kites, 83
KMT branches: Brandon, 31; Fort William, 31; Moose Jaw, 32; North Battleford, 32, 35; Regina, 31; Saskatoon, 32; Swift Current, 32; Winnipeg, 35; Yorkton, 32
Knox United Church (Regina), 152
Ku Klux Klan (KKK), 14
Kuomintang (KMT): and affective regimes, 174-75n15; Bing-wo Yee as leader, 135; centre in Winnipeg, 31-32; Charles Yee and, 95, 96, 99; Charlie Foo and, 104; Chinese schools, 156-57; Chinese United League (Tongmeng Hui) and, 11; CKT vs., 103; clubhouses, 168; on cultural approach of nationalism, 195n51; Depression and, 35; destruction of membership evidence, 109; education by, 37-38; Frank Chan and, 69,

72-73, 104; fundraising by, 32; as illegal, 175-76n21; leaders as rulers, 29-30; Lee Mon and, 122; local officers in government positions, 215n48; Medicine Hat branch, 212n3; membership in, 53; and networking, 168; Regina branch, 94; in Taiwan, 107; universal affiliation/membership in, 7, 168; in Winnipeg, 94, 102-3; Winnipeg picnic, 7(f); women and, 94, 114. *See also* nationalism
Kwan, Bing, 124

labourers: in CDS, 224n10; Chinese immigrants as, 167; communism and, 224n10; Lee Choy as, 162; merchants compared to, 5, 118-19; nationalism and, 53-54, 224n10; railways and, 7; and traditional religion, 38; wages, 61, 65; wives of, 137
Lac du Bonnet (MB), Goodway Cafe, 5
Lai, David, 141
Lai Man Cheng, 83
laundries: about, 5-6; boys/sons working in, 37; first Chinese settlers in Winnipeg and, 173n9; Lee Choy and, 162-63; in Maryfield, 132; in Saskatchewan, 31
leaders: children of, 156; patriotism and, 4; of WCCCC, 40
Lee, Erika, 176n23
Lee, Gilbert, 121, 123, 124
Lee, Jessie: arrival in Canada, 122; and CDS, 124; as convert, 60; education, 123; English language skills, 123; in Hong Lin's needlework class, 126; marriage to Bing Qwan, 124; marriage to Tsutin, 124; as Methodist, 123; photo, 122(f), 123(f); and Presbyterian activities, 123; and United Church, 124; in Winnipeg, 122-24
Lee, Liliane, 161, 163, 164(f)
Lee, Mary, 121, 122
Lee, Mr. (Li Biaoyi), 72
Lee, Philip, 215n38
Lee, Wesley, 222n44
Lee Choy: about, 164-65; adoption of Marcelle, 161, 162; as CDS performer, 162; death, 165; early life, 161-62; and gambling houses, 163; labour of, 162; and nationalism, 162; personality, 164-65; photo, 164(f); and religion, 164
Lee Hip (Li Xie), 38

Contemporary Chinese Studies

Glen Peterson, *The Power of Words: Literacy and Revolution in South China, 1949-95*

Wing Chung Ng, *The Chinese in Vancouver, 1945-80: The Pursuit of Identity and Power*

Yijiang Ding, *Chinese Democracy after Tiananmen*

Diana Lary and Stephen MacKinnon, eds., *Scars of War: The Impact of Warfare on Modern China*

Eliza W.Y. Lee, ed., *Gender and Change in Hong Kong: Globalization, Postcolonialism, and Chinese Patriarchy*

Christopher A. Reed, *Gutenberg in Shanghai: Chinese Print Capitalism, 1876-1937*

James A. Flath, *The Cult of Happiness: Nianhua, Art, and History in Rural North China*

Erika E.S. Evasdottir, *Obedient Autonomy: Chinese Intellectuals and the Achievement of Orderly Life*

Hsiao-ting Lin, *Tibet and Nationalist China's Frontier: Intrigues and Ethnopolitics, 1928-49*

Xiaoping Cong, *Teachers' Schools and the Making of the Modern Chinese Nation-State, 1897-1937*

Diana Lary, ed., *The Chinese State at the Borders*

Norman Smith, *Resisting Manchukuo: Chinese Women Writers and the Japanese Occupation*

Hasan H. Karrar, *The New Silk Road Diplomacy: China's Central Asian Foreign Policy since the Cold War*

Richard King, ed., *Art in Turmoil: The Chinese Cultural Revolution, 1966-76*

Blaine R. Chiasson, *Administering the Colonizer: Manchuria's Russians under Chinese Rule, 1918-29*

Emily M. Hill, *Smokeless Sugar: The Death of a Provincial Bureaucrat and the Construction of China's National Economy*

Kimberley Ens Manning and Felix Wemheuer, eds., *Eating Bitterness: New Perspectives on China's Great Leap Forward and Famine*

Helen M. Schneider, *Keeping the Nation's House: Domestic Management and the Making of Modern China*

James A. Flath and Norman Smith, eds., *Beyond Suffering: Recounting War in Modern China*

Elizabeth R. VanderVen, *A School in Every Village: Educational Reform in a Northeast China County, 1904-31*

Norman Smith, *Intoxicating Manchuria: Alcohol, Opium, and Culture in China's Northeast*

Juan Wang, *Merry Laughter and Angry Curses: The Shanghai Tabloid Press, 1897-1911*

Richard King, *Milestones on a Golden Road: Writing for Chinese Socialism, 1945-80*

David Faure and Ho Ts'ui-P'ing, eds., *Chieftains into Ancestors: Imperial Expansion and Indigenous Society in Southwest China*

Yunxiang Gao, *Sporting Gender: Women Athletes and Celebrity-Making during China's National Crisis, 1931-45*

Peipei Qiu with Su Zhiliang and Chen Lifei, *Chinese Comfort Women: Testimonies from Imperial Japan's Sex Slaves*

Julia Kuehn, Kam Louie, and David M. Pomfret, eds., *Diasporic Chineseness after the Rise of China: Communities and Cultural Production*

Bridie Andrews, *The Making of Modern Chinese Medicine, 1850-1960*

Kelvin E.Y. Low, *Remembering the Samsui Women: Migration and Social Memory in Singapore and China*

Jiayan Zhang, *Coping with Calamity: Environmental Change and Peasant Response in Central China, 1736-1949*